The Sexual Metaphor

The Sexual Metaphor

Helen Haste

Harvard University Press
Cambridge, Massachusetts
1994

This book is printed on acid-free paper, and its binding materials
have been chosen for strength and durability.

Library of Congress Cataloging-in-Publication Data

Weinreich-Haste, Helen.
    The sexual metaphor / Helen Haste.
        p.   cm.
    Includes bibliographical references and index.
    ISBN 0-674-80282-9
    1. Feminist theory.   2. Culture.   3. Sex role.   4. Metaphor.
    I. Title.
HQ1190.W456   1994
305.42'01—dc20   93-50568
                                                            CIP

For Beverly (13 June 1933 – 30 April 1991)
who made all things possible, especially the
invention of masculinity and femininity

Contents

Preface

Straddling the Atlantic—even for a short period—makes one acutely aware that, though there are common themes and common ideals in discussions about gender worldwide, they take subtly different forms in different cultures. North Americans and Britons share an Anglophone literature, so we are lulled into a false sense of unity, common history, and culture. The history of feminism—indeed, the history of women's social and cultural position—in the United States and Britain is somewhat different. I will spell this out more formally later, but it is made vividly clear in personal experiences. Many years ago I met a woman from Minnesota whose mother had borne eight children, without medical attention, in the remote homestead she and her husband had built when they arrived from Scandinavia. Such a story is part of a folk heritage of North American life. I do not have that pioneering history, or its metaphors, to inform my personal concepts of "endurance" or "independence." My training in those virtues was fuelled by very different folk memories. This woman could, if necessary, do what her mother had done; nothing in my background equips me for such rigours.

This book is about language and culture; the *way* that language and culture are interwoven is a universal process even though the *manifestations* of language and culture, and what is seen as important or taken for granted, are culture-specific. I write as an Englishwoman, but most of this book is about things that are central to any discussions of the origins of gender roles, the potential for change, and the implications of change. My particular concern is with the role of metaphor. I have come to see metaphor as critical for understanding gender. I am not original in arguing that metaphors are crucial to thinking as well as

communicating; sociolinguists and even cognitive scientists have said
this for some time. Metaphors are not just peripheral linguistic frills.
They provide analogies, models for explanation, and therefore facilitate
innovative thought. New scientific ideas, for example, frequently arise
through a shift to a new metaphor. Metaphors are a bridge in communication; because speaker and audience share a common culture, a metaphor from one domain can enlarge meaning in another. And by using a
familiar metaphor, we can communicate novel concepts. Furthermore,
when a specialist field brings in new metaphors, these metaphors can
rapidly become available for lay use in a wide range of fields: the idea
of evolution in the nineteenth century came to be the core metaphor
for change, and computers in the late twentieth century dominate our
concepts of mind and brain.

Metaphor is a rhetorical process, and an important insight from rhetoric is that in every communication there are things that are taken for
granted and things that are problematic. If something is taken for
granted, it lends itself to shorthand expression and needs neither elaboration nor advocacy. What is problematic, however, must be explained
and justified. Changing social values or deep-seated beliefs requires
challenging what is taken for granted to make it problematic in new
ways. I argue in this book that feminism is concerned with making
problematic about gender what has hitherto been taken for granted,
holding up to question some of our most commonsensical assumptions
and beliefs.

The common themes of feminism are about overcoming inequalities
and discrimination, about getting rid of the stereotypes and misconceptions that interfere with the fulfilment of individual potential. Within
these common themes I explore in detail the major distinction between
the *pursuit of rational justice* and the *search for authenticity*. This distinction
cuts across national boundaries but is manifested in different ways in
different cultures. The pursuit of rational justice starts from the position
that women have been excluded from power, denied opportunities,
and kept in a position of dependence and subservience through both
economic and legal constraints, and especially through the perpetuation of myths about essential sex differences. This situation is unjust
and must be countered by laws to constrain discriminatory practices,
by undermining the myths of difference, and by restructuring the socialisation of girls' and boys' sex-role identities. This is the position
expressed in both "liberal" and "socialist" feminism. It is also a position
sustained by sociological and psychological work that emphasises the
environmental (and therefore, by implication, malleable) origins of gender roles.

The search for authenticity has different premises. It rests upon the
argument originally put particularly strongly by Simone de Beauvoir

that mainstream culture has been defined by male culture and that women are not only excluded from this culture, they in fact define a *negation* of it. Woman is "Other." Not only is she different from man, the male, the masculine (and therefore by implication unequal), she is *that which man is not: the definition of the masculine is sustained by the negation of the feminine.* The task of feminist theory, therefore, is to find an authentic feminine selfhood that is not merely the negation of, the reflection of, or the absence of the masculine. This requires not just undermining stereotypes, asserting that the picture is incorrect, but discovering—indeed reinventing—something that has been hidden. Nor does it necessarily *deny* difference. Rather, it argues that the picture is distorted—and inauthentic. The task is to analyse how language constructs and reproduces ideas and meaning. It goes beyond a concern with law and even education to the roots of the meaning system of the culture. This position is expressed—in very different ways—by the forms of feminism I have defined as "radical" and "cultural."

In the Prologue I describe my own personal intellectual journey from rationalist socialist-feminism to cultural feminism. I explore the role of metaphor in the cultural construction of gender. I describe the rhetorical processes that have sustained gender roles and beliefs about sex differences, and what is required to bring about change. The major argument of this book is that the "Otherness" of women is one manifestation of a deep-seated metaphor permeating the category systems of the Western mind. This is the metaphor of duality or polarity. We think in terms of either-or, we define things in terms of their negation or antithesis, which makes it difficult to hold two contrasting concepts in mind simultaneously. So we define good as not evil, we define active as the antithesis of passive, and we are drawn to define masculine by its negation of the feminine. We then map masculinity and femininity onto the other deep polarities of the culture. We cast as conceptual contrasts things that could logically coexist. But there is a further anxiety: the negative pole becomes a potential threat to the positive. By a sort of "leakage" the negative may contaminate the positive. Passivity may undermine the active, sapping its force. Rationality is continually threatened by chaos and must defend against it; indeed, that which is perceived not to be rational is *therefore* defined as potentially chaotic. And most powerfully, the masculine is challenged by leakage or incursion from the feminine. So the power of the duality of masculine-feminine is not only a product of the anxiety arising from rigid sex-role socialisation; it stems from the mapping of masculine and feminine onto our much more extensive and deeply embedded tendency to think in terms of polarity, antithesis, and negation.

Most of this book is devoted to exploring how these metaphors work in ways that are common to Western culture. But there are differences within the Anglophone world about what is taken for granted, and therefore in how the roots of sex roles and sexual inequality are analysed, and about strategies for change. These differences can be seen in ordinary language and in common sense, and in the social theories that inform the public debate. These differences arise from history; different things have been salient, different assumptions made about the causes and cures of social issues. But what is perhaps most important and least appreciated is that common metaphors and ideas have different meanings. Two examples will make the point. In Chapter 12, where I talk about changing masculinity, I discuss the metaphor of the "frontier." This metaphor is very important in American culture. The "frontier" is the boundary between the safe and the unsafe, the tame and the wild, the mundane and the exciting. It implies that civilisation is challenged by the wilderness beyond, which may encroach if the borders are not maintained, but it also means a place where the intrepid may go to prove their strength, to extend their personal limits. For Europeans, however, a frontier is a boundary between two adjacent, long-established states. Crossing the frontier means entering novel and possibly alien territory, unfamiliar *culture* and, on occasion, defending oneself from the encroachment of that culture but not from the encroachment of wilderness.

Another example is "democracy." This apparently shared concept divides Anglophone cultures in rather subtle ways. For Europeans, commonsense concepts of democracy are about consultation and involvement in decision-making, but this is, in effect, about a group with a common identity and common interests having the power to be heard in society. The individual's access is via an elected representative. It is the political party, the trade union, and the pressure group that are seen to exercise democratic power; the individual is only effective as part of the collective. While this is equally true in practice in the United States, there is still a folk memory of democracy as the "town meeting," the face-to-face involvement of all free persons in decision-making. "Increasing democracy" means giving more *free persons* access to power sources; the collective, the party, is strategically useful, rather than a source of strong identification. An American First World War recruiting poster said "Save the world for democracy" (which still resonates in America's international relations). This would have cut little ice in Europe, where the battles, and the rhetoric, were about the threat of invasion.

So, though the language is the same, the concepts differ and their invocation has a different meaning. In the case of feminism, there are similar debates on both sides of the Atlantic between those who pursue rational justice and those who seek more authenticity, but they resonate differently because the roots of feminism are different. The roots of

American feminism are in the antisegregationist politics of the nine-teenth century, with some elements of moral crusades like the temper-ance movement. The recent revival of feminism in the United States drew initially on two very different strands, one tapping into individu-alism, self-fulfilment, and the question of equal opportunity—the main-stream American cultural messages—and the other into the moral and political radicalism of the civil rights issues of the sixties. Both empha-sised a rhetoric of rights, and both could claim that American culture and the U.S. Constitution accorded these rights in principle. But in practice they were denied, although laws did not need to be changed, only fully implemented.

The roots of British feminism are closely entwined with the develop-ment of socialism, even though many suffragists around the turn of the century did not identify with the nascent Labour Party and, indeed, the first woman MP was a Conservative. But British feminists did not emerge from a culture that took equality for granted, and the battle for their credibility was compounded by deep-rooted fears, tied as much to social class as to gender, that universal suffrage was destabilising. Recent British feminism has been more tied to socialism not only by party identification but in terms of the social theory sustaining its analy-sis. The equation of gender with class or caste has been much more explicit in Britain than in the United States and meshes with the strongly neo-Marxist basis of much British social theory.

There are many strands of neo-Marxist analysis in American feminist thought also, but the equation of class, ethnicity, and gender sits much more uneasily in American social theory. In parallel, the emphasis on individualism and individual development and liberation, though pres-ent in British feminism, sits uneasily in a theoretical framework that prefers to identify the origins of oppression in historical and economic factors and is suspicious of "psychologistic" explanations. An interest-ing manifestation of these differences is in the rhetoric of "rights." The United States political system is rooted in Enlightenment ideas of "natural rights," which are very salient and very explicit in discussions of inequality and of the ideals to which change is directed. Debates in the United States—particularly at the grassroots level—are much more likely to invoke the language of rights than they are in Britain. While both nations have debated abortion in terms of "woman's right to choose," on the whole the American prolife lobby has countered with "fetal rights" whereas the British prolife lobby has countered with "murder." On a different plane, objections to smoking in the United States use concepts like "right to clean air" even in ordinary conversa-tion, whereas in Britain appeals emphasise health and consideration for others. The salient themes of American culture, embedded in a history that presumes the rights of all free and equal citizens, inform the rhetoric of feminism; women have been *deprived* of their natural rights. In British culture there is less certainty—the idea is less deeply embedded—that women have been deprived of something *already* rightfully theirs. More pervasive is the rhetoric of "unfairness" and of "powerlessness." The battle is over gaining power to establish the right.

These national differences are important in understanding what is explicit and what is implicit. In this book I have described "socialist feminism" and contrasted it especially with "cultural feminism." There is an explicit, self-conscious coherence in the British socialist feminist position because it is firmly embedded within a social theory deriving from socialism and neo-Marxism. The analysis of women's position is couched in the debates within this social theory, and feminism itself contributes to the wider social theory. The strategy for change is one of overcoming the existing stereotypes, especially about the extent and origin of difference, and so removing any justification for inequality. The debate about why beliefs in sex differences persist—and, indeed, why they were constructed in the first place—takes place within an analysis of economic and social forces, and in terms of power and class relations.

The position that underpins explicit socialist feminism in Britain, that we should challenge culture and science to overcome mistaken (and pernicious) beliefs about sex difference, can be found widely in the United States, especially in early feminist writings. This position has extensively informed both the development of American feminist theory and the associated work in social science (especially psychology) that undermines traditional views of sex difference. The difference between the United States and Britain lies in the extent to which it is tied to mainstream social theory and particularly, mainstream politics. But the assumptions underlying socialist feminism, the conceptual framework within which political and social theory has progressed, are common to certain strands of feminism in both Britain and the United States. The difference is that in Britain this conceptual framework is more explicitly part of a highly articulated version of Left-wing thought, which has a considerable power base in mainstream politics.

The diversity of ethnicity is another factor that to some extent divides the two cultures. It may also explain why what I have termed "cultural feminism" developed earlier in the United States than in Britain and why the idea of *reevaluating* rather than *denying* difference has been more acceptable in the United States than in Britain. This is partly historical; depending on its origins, ethnic diversity has very different political—and psychological—meaning. In the United States it has two primary sources: the immigration of people who found a common identity as Americans after fleeing from economic hardship or political and religious persecution, and the importation of cheap labour whose descendants have continued to suffer social and economic oppression. For the first group, the tensions are between retaining a cultural identity and ensuring a proper representation in the dominant cultural and social institutions. This had been easier for some immigrant groups than for others. For groups who have been economically and socially oppressed, the dominant social group's denial of their culture is an important part of social control and the maintenance of oppression. The affirmation of an authentic worldview is as important as gaining access to the dominant culture's institutions, and indeed may be an important motivation in the struggle to do so. In Britain there are many immigrants who have fled—over six hundred years—from persecution and economic deprivation, but much modern ethnic diversity has its roots in colonialism and the use of colonial resources for cheap labour. Although ex-colonial groups experience disregard for their culture in Britain (or have, at least, until recently), they suffered this even more forcefully under colonial rule. In fact, I have chosen not to deal with either ethnicity or class in this book, but I am conscious that some of the developments of cultural feminism and the search for authenticity in the United States have been fostered by the successful determination among women who are not part of a white middle-class culture to generate a new, authentic self-definition and a worldview that truly challenges the Otherness imposed by white male culture. While this is also beginning to happen in Britain, it has not yet impinged in the same way or to the same extent.

I have also chosen not to get into the debates surrounding lesbian identity and its role in feminist theory. I made this choice because I feel that as a heterosexual woman, I am not equipped to deal with its complexities and subtleties. But some of the same arguments that apply to ethnic groups apply here. Challenging the mainstream picture of one's world by redefining one's self through the affirmation of a true, authentic alternative takes a rather different form than a redefinition that is designed to justify one's admission through the previously excluding portals.

In this book I have mainly chosen to take on issues that are, if not universal, at least meaningfully transferable. I have drawn upon examples from both American and British sources (and indeed, from French, Canadian, and Australian sources as well). One chapter that makes extensive use of British material is Chapter 13, "Backlash." Here, especially in the second part, I have portrayed the raw emotions of British reaction by using recent journalistic writings. Although these examples are parochial, their defensive message reaches out across cultures. This book, then, is about the processes of culture and language. An awareness of diversity between the cultures to which it is addressed is an enhancement, not an obfuscation, of that message.

Acknowledgements

This book evolved over a number of years, and many people have directly and indirectly contributed to my thinking about gender and metaphor during that time. Particularly I want to acknowledge the people who have helped me collect and analyse the various sets of data that I report: Lindy Wingfield, Barrie Lipscombe, Jane Baddeley, Ian Graham, Linda Jackson, Fay Sharpley, Clive Stephens, Bekki Love and Simon Coulton. I also want to thank the women who appear as 'Fiona', 'Laura', 'Melanie' and 'Sandra' in Chapter 6. I am also grateful to Judy Harbutt and Jenny Gilling, who typed versions of the manuscript.

I have had many very illuminating, stimulating and confrontational discussions about gender, feminism and metaphor, all of which have valuably contributed to the evolution of my thinking. When one becomes obsessional about a subject, no one is free from being drawn into one's preoccupations. None of the following can be blamed for the effects that their tolerance (or intolerance) of my ideas had on the final outcome, but I want to thank them for their constructive and supportive involvement: John Archer, Halla Beloff, Michael Billig, John Broughton, Jerome Bruner, Anne Colby, Carol Feldman, Howard Gardner, Carol Gilligan, William Gosling, Richard Gregory, Howard Gruber, Rom Harré, Cate Haste, Frances Haste, Lynne Jones, Ellen Langer, Mal Leicester, Peggy Newton, Jonathan Potter, Peter Reason, Ellie Scrivens, Suzanne Skevington, Peggy Judith Torney-Purta, Doris Wallace, Jo Weinreich, Ellen Winner, Tom Wren – and the many people who engaged in discussions in seminars, in several universities, including my own students over the years at the University of Bath.

Farrell Burnett of Harvester Wheatsheaf has been a constant support and critic, and has made most valuable suggestions for revisions, excisions and clarifications. I also want to thank the University of Bath for allowing me a period of time in which I could complete the manuscript, and the Henry Murray Center, Radcliffe College, for hosting me as a Visiting Scholar while I did so.

But the main acknowledgement goes to Beverly Halstead. He was the book's midwife, its major critic and in many ways its inspiration. At a very early stage, in the summer of 1986, he became impatient with my tentative preliminary steps. He set up our dining-room as a 'radio studio'. Every four hours I came down and presented a chapter from my notes, as a 'live radio broadcast'. In this way we recorded a complete draft manuscript in three days. The book went through many changes thereafter, and Beverly was at all stages an engaged commentator, especially of my style and accessibility to a wider audience – he was a palaeontologist, and a brilliant communicator.

He died in a road accident on 30 April 1991. This book is my memorial to him.

Helen Haste
Bath, England and Cambridge, MA, March 1993

Prologue

Meta-foresight

In the Bristol Exploratory, the hands-on science centre, there is a two-way mirror. I sit with a companion, one on each side of the mirror. By adjusting the controls, I can change the lighting; one moment I see only myself, another moment I see only my companion. There is one moment, however, when I can hold the image of both of us: myself in reflection, my companion in vision. But when I see only myself, in reflection, I know that the other person can see me also; it is only an illusion that I alone see myself. When I see only my companion, I know that they cannot see me; it is their own eyes into which they are gazing, not mine.

Just for a moment, in that little cubicle in the Exploratory, it is possible to know the whole story, to have insight into what my 'reflection' really means in that situation. Most of the time we don't have such insight. The companion's image is hidden behind our own reflection. Mostly – indeed, nearly always – we are not aware that it is even possible to shift the lighting, to know that the mirror can do more than one thing. In fact it can be very disturbing even to think such a thing possible. We want our glass *either* to reflect, *or* to be a window.

This book is inevitably the outcome of a personal journey. No one can write about sex, sexuality and gender at this point in time without reflecting one's participation in the major upheaval of thought of the last twenty-five years. Scholarship has burgeoned – about substantive issues of gender, and also about the effect of the onslaught on our traditional conceptions of masculinity and femininity, on the pursuits of social science, philosophy, history and literature. My personal journey has been through changing conceptions of what it is to be a woman – and what it might be possible for the culture to recognise as 'being a woman'. It has also been a journey through theoretical perspectives on human development. This book is about the interweaving of these changes – how exploring a personally satisfactory theory of gender has fed into critiques of developmental and social psychology. The book is not aimed only at a scholarly audience; I hope it will be accessible to a wide readership. Those who are familiar with the debates in psychology and related fields will pick up the more esoteric aspects from cues in the text and the notes. This book is about men and women, and the problems of finding a valid gender identity in a distorted world. It is also about how those distortions permeate large areas of our lives, and our thinking – including our conceptions of rationality. I argue that we can best understand changing gender roles if we recognise the role gender plays in how we make sense of the world. In particular, I look at the role of *metaphor*.

My journey has shifted from 'socialist feminism' to what I term 'cultural feminism'. As a well-educated and highly motivated woman I have striven for achievement in the mainstream world. I am a competent practitioner of the ethos and frameworks of that world, yet I have always felt that an aspect of my selfhood has had to be denied. I have always felt that I am an honorary member of a club which, to a great extent, defines itself by denial of things which are an essential part, if not of me specifically, at least of the world which I inhabit. In the end it became untenable to continue to say 'Yes, but *I'm* not like that, even if other women are'.

The voice of socialist feminism said: *These things are stereotypes. They are not real. The differences which men ascribe to us women are merely illusions. In reality we should all strive for androgyny.* And yet, and yet. This is not how it felt. There was something about my feelings of femaleness, which was not to be denied or devoured by androgyny. I delighted in the easy movement between my own masculinity and femininity – and the equally fluid movement between the masculinity and femininity of my partner; yet for this I needed to affirm the separate existence, the exquisite quality of difference, out of which such unity and entwining could come – not only in the context of sexuality, but also in the context of the most sophisticated intellectual communication. That is the personal dimension: not scientific, not objective, but a perpetual irritant to analyses or political positions that strove for rational androgyny and the denial of difference; a gritty objection that came from deep within. I realised I had no valid language, no valid framework, no cultural history, to accommodate these feelings.

Socialist feminism argues that conceptions of sex roles, sex differences and their origins, can be explained primarily as an outcome of capitalism and the patriarchy which serves it. I now consider that the problem lies far deeper. It lies in the primacy of a *metaphor of dualism* in our culture.

We have a deep predilection for making sense of the world in terms of either/or, in terms of polarities. But most significantly, we map the polarity of masculine versus feminine on to other polarities. The polarity of masculine and feminine is an extremely powerful idea. It has such clear boundaries and such clear antitheses, in all cultures – though cultures differ in exactly what those boundaries and antitheses are. But in addition, masculinity and femininity are laden with a very great deal of emotional baggage. We inherit our culture's anxieties, taboos and expectations; they shape our social behaviour and our personal identity.

Metaphors of dualism and Otherness

We should never, however, underestimate the power of cognitive categories, as work on intergroup relations shows. Stereotyping mini-mises the intellectual effort of dealing with the mass of information about new persons.[1] It is extremely convenient to make assumptions simply on the basis of whether a person is male or female. To have these neat assumptions challenged or questioned disturbs the cool tenor of the mind. Therefore, even if dualism were only a cognitive category, there would be problems in changing it. By mapping masculine and feminine on to so many other dimensions to which we also ascribe polarity, we deepen the problem. When I give lectures on this, I put up a list of these polarities and ask people to classify each. Everyone can do it – even though their rational selves resist stereotyping. Examples are *light–dark, public–private, arts–science, rational–intuitive (and rationality–chaos), sun–moon, active–passive, hard–soft, thinking–feeling*. I invite you to try the thought experiment.

In this book I elaborate especially *public–private, active–passive and rationality–chaos*. The public–private polarity defines the boundaries between male and female space, and prescribes the attributes that sustain those boundaries. Active–passive ascribes characteristics of masculinity and femininity, and prescribes and proscribes relations between the sexes. Rationality–chaos maps extensively on to our rela-tionship with the external world, ideas of control, mastery and harmony, and our insecure sense of survival in the face of the unknown – a sense that gave us the terrifying concept of chaos as the alternative to a rational, controlled universe in the first place. This dichotomy has given Western culture an elevated faith in rationality itself. The tendency to regard the darker aspects of sexuality as a threat to rationality has deepened the equation of a mind–body split with masculine–feminine tension – aligning the feminine with chaos.

My personal disillusion with what I see as an overrationalist socialist feminist perspective comes from a growing appreciation of the darker side of these dualistic frameworks, and their force in sustaining our world-views. Socialist feminism locates sex discrimination in an economic and social system; the problem is power relations between social groups. The stereotypes of masculinity and femininity which currently deprive women of a proper public role, and men of the full richness of a private family role, are seen as the product of a work ethic. They also fly in the face of scientific studies; sex difference is neither so extensive nor so immutable as stereotypes would have us believe. Therefore, a rational solution is in sight: change the economic system, undermine the fallacies of sex difference, and move towards a more androgynous conception of men and women. Not only would this be a rational process, it also presumes a rational world of natural rights, from which women have been excluded. The outcome of rational changes would be the emergence of a rational society without our current gender problems.

This picture takes too little account of the depth of our engagement with our own gender identity, and it certainly fails to take account of the mapping of masculinity and femininity on to so many areas of cultural life. An example is Camille Paglia's controversial description of the opposition between the Apollonian and the Dionysian.[2] The former is associated with rationality, with distance from the physical, the sensual, the sensuous – and with masculinity. The latter is associated with nature, with the life force, with the physical and sexual; it is something of which women are a part, and from which they have much greater difficulty than men in escaping. This model springs from the Apollonian – male – perspective, which fears and cannot deal with the Dionysian dimension. Paglia argues that feminism will fail because it does not take account of this fundamental dichotomy.

I find myself in agreement with Paglia's recognition of the power of this tension in our culture, though I depart from her conclusions. Socialist feminist writers have largely ignored or dismissed the psycho-dynamic tensions that erupt in any efforts to change gender roles. This is reflected in the divisions within the diversity of feminist theories. Feminists are united by the goal of improving women's position in society, and overcoming the legal, cultural and attitudinal factors which inhibit this – in particular the myths about the 'true' nature of men and women which have sustained the status quo. Feminist theory is divided quite deeply about whether the route to attaining this goal is through rational justice or the search for authenticity.

The route of rational justice takes for granted a rational world, a single, valid and commonly shared definition of rationality, from which women have been – irrationally – excluded. Beliefs about sex difference, and about masculinity and femininity, are distorted by the needs of dominant power groups. The strategy for change is to demonstrate these fallacies, and to diminish difference. Women's goal is to join the Rationality Club, to assert their rightful place and their long-denied rights. That Rationality and its Club are not questioned.

In contrast, the route of the search for authenticity does question the model of rationality profoundly. The challenge to the world-view is not that women have been excluded; it is to its premises. The argument is that the dominant world-view has been entirely from a male perspective, a perspective that has assigned to masculinity those characteristics which serve rationality, truth-seeking, logic. Woman – and the feminine – are cast in this scenario as the antithesis, the negation, and most particularly as the Other. The Other is not just different; it is *antithetical*. The metaphor of dualism which maps on to masculinity and femininity logically requires that one pole is the negation of the other.

To illustrate the difference between these two perspectives on changing gender roles, let us consider the metaphor I used at the beginning, the two-way mirror. If I look into the two-way mirror and see only my own reflection, I am unaware of the existence of my companion. Furthermore, the message I get back from the mirror is only what I present to it; it is my *own* image, the image *I own*, the image *I create*, the image *of me*. The only way my companion can enter into that image – can be seen by me – is to come out from behind the mirror and join me on my side of the screen, become part of my picture. And if she does that, there is no one behind the screen any longer, no one hidden, no other perspective.

If, however, I adjust the lighting, I become aware that my companion exists. I know that she can see me, even though I cannot see her. Furthermore, if we are really skilful with the lighting, we can simul-taneously see our own reflections and each other's face. So I now know that she has an independent reality. Even when I look only into my own reflection, I can no longer deny her existence. I know also that her perspective is different from mine. We can both know that each of these perspectives exists, even if we choose to take only one at any moment. The search for authenticity is the search for just such a multiple perspective. But the first stage of that search is to recognise that there might even be more than one person in the cubicle.

The problem of women's Otherness was first extensively presented by Simone de Beauvoir, though in the history of women's writing there is plenty of reference to a sense of being invisible to the culture, and of female experience being ignored.[3] If women are described in mainstream culture only from the male perspective, this is not only absence of a satisfactory account; it goes deeper. In a dualistic metaphor,

A is defined as being not-B; it is defined as the negation of B. Women and the feminine, therefore, exist as *that-by-which-men-define-themselves-as-not-being*. The Other, therefore, is not only hidden – in the sense of being behind the two-way mirror, or not having a voice to speak of her own self. The Other must be cast as the *antithesis*.

Yet women have always passed folklore from mother to daughter. What is missing is the expression of this in the dominant culture, its integration into mainstream thought. To overcome this problem would free women from Otherness imposed by male culture, but it would also confront that culture with an important challenge. Not only has the image of woman been wrong and distorted; also, the possibility of an alternative exists. An authentic perspective on female experience changes the status of the feminine from being simply the negation of the masculine. A parallel, alternative perspective, which coexists with and is not merely, of itself, antithetical to the dominant perspective, challenges the assumption that there is only one – or only one kind of – explanation. It is a plea for pluralism – for seeing both the images in the two-way mirror.

But what is meant by 'female experience' here? Are those who search for authentic alternative perspectives looking only for a female view of peculiarly female things – menstruation, parturition, lactation – which men can never experience? Or does it extend to areas of life for which women have primarily been responsible – nurturing, sustaining family relationships, and household organisation, areas which do not exclude men in the same way, but which men tend to interpret from the perspective of the person who is serviced rather than the point of view of the performer?

Representing even those areas of 'female experience' more authentically in mainstream culture would enrich symbol, images and metaphors. An example is the metaphor of *cyclicity*. Women's lives are experienced, in so many areas, in terms of cycles – physical and biological cycles, diurnal cycles of nurturance and preparation of food, cycles of caring, cleansing, and the annual cycles of family life. The lives of modern industrial men can be metaphorically constructed in terms of finite, achievable tasks; only in the agricultural world are cycles still pervasive for men. So taking such aspects of women's lives seriously would bring into mainstream culture metaphors and images that are lacking in a masculine world-view.

In fact, the search for authenticity goes beyond finding a language for describing experience which is absent from masculine discourse. The argument is that completely new frameworks for thinking are needed in order to escape Otherness. In Chapter 1 I consider several of these – atomistic replaced by holistic, linear logic by intuitive or even stream-of-consciousness thinking, metaphors of harmony rather than mastery. These are not confined to those areas of women's experience excluded by the dominant world-view. The search for authenticity then becomes *innovation*, creating new meaning and expression, new ways of conceptualising; enlarging the vocabulary not only for describing women's lives, but for describing everything. But there is still the question: how far are such innovations tied to the feminine? One argument is that women are more comfortable with the holistic, the cooperative, the harmonious. The claim is that a more authentic perspective would recognise these modes of thought that are common to women in their private female world. Do women have a special privileged access to such ways of thinking – and if so, why? Do the requirements of women's roles make certain world-views more functionally useful – as well as offering different metaphors? The socialist feminist position is that any alternative consciousness which women may have derives from the status of being subordinate, outsiders. It would disappear once women took their rightful place in equality with men. Cultural feminists seeking authenticity want to validate, bring into the open, something which is inherently part of women's condition, making it public so that it can become a true culturally available alternative – for everyone. But is this discovery or invention? Is it opening up an existing, hidden world, or is it actually creating a new vocabulary, a new perspective, in order to provide a language for making sense of that which could not be properly expressed before?

Carol Gilligan has argued that men think about moral issues in terms of justice, resolving conflicts by applying rules, codes and contracts, whereas women think about morality in terms of responsibility and caring, preferring to resolve conflicts by negotiation and by considering needs rather than rights. Other work suggests a tendency for women to be more holistic – to take a wider view of a situation, bearing in mind more elements at the same time – whereas men take a more atomistic view, focusing on just one aspect of the situation and ignoring the wider field.[4] I discuss this in several chapters, and consider critically just how strong is the evidence for actual gender difference. But it is interesting how differences are viewed. Is the sex that does less well deficient; is there *one kind* of ability of which each sex has more or less? Another perspective sees difference as an alternative way of doing things, rather than as a deficit. Even when a difference in style is recognised, however, its description as 'feminine' may give it lesser status. An example is intuition, perceived as a feminine quality and regarded with suspicion in comparison to its opposite pole, rationality. This evaluation makes it difficult to consider that both might be rather useful. Intuition is necessary to creative thinking by either sex, but it is denied in public accounts of thinking, especially in science.

The search for authenticity raises all these questions. In the long run, I believe that it will provide a better framework for making sense of women's experience, and will bring into mainstream culture accounts which give the growing girl more than the harsh choice between being a negating antithesis of the masculine, a supportive emotional and sexual appendage to the male ego, or an 'honorary male' role which has no place for the feminine.

Models of development: the active little scientist in a social context

I began life as a cognitive developmentalist.[5] Cognitive-developmental theory focuses on how the individual makes sense of the world. This is seen as an active process; the child is in effect a little scientist, generating explanations out of experience. Development is manifested by increasingly complex 'theories' of how the world works. These changing theories characterise *stages of development*. They are challenged through exposure to more complex, more adequate explanations – either through the individual's own reflection upon experience, or from the stimulation of others' questioning. This perspective assumes that the processes of human development are universal: children in all cultures will go through similar stages. Other people can be important catalysts in the process of reflection, but it is what goes on inside the child's own head that matters.

A markedly contrasting view places all the emphasis on language and social interaction. We are created by social forces, and we behave in ways designed only to meet social expectations. So our 'selves' are merely scripts to present ourselves as acceptable members of the social group. There is a huge gap between cognitive-developmental psychologists, who see an active individual constructing meaning relatively unaffected by the social context, and the extreme social-deterministic position, which casts the individual as essentially passive, the product of social processes. But an important difference, also, is that for the cognitive developmentalist, the growing individual is progressing along a single route of increasingly adequate rationality. For social determinists, in contrast, knowledge, meaning and concepts, and even the processes by which these are acquired, are infinitely variable, and subject to local cultural conditions. Not only *what* is known, but *how* it is known, is created by social context. Social determinists consider that the cognitive-developmental approach falls for the delusion of universals, *a priori* truths that are to be discovered. Cognitive developmentalists object to social determinists' denial of individual activity in the construction of meaning, and their failure to take account of evidence that does support increasing developmental complexity of thought – higher, more complex stages of reasoning cannot be faked or accelerated.[6]

Those are the battle lines, but there has long been a middle ground. The Russian psychologist Lev Vygotsky, who is experiencing a major revival at present, sixty years after his death, argued that the child first generates a concept in dialogue with others – peers or adults – and only later does it appear in the child's own internal construction. Thus language and interaction constitute the crucible of understanding, but not its only cause; the individual actively makes sense of the world, but language has a vital role in communication, and in the construction of the child's understanding of meaning.[7] Furthermore, all this takes place in a fluid sociohistorical context, which begs many questions about 'cultural universals'.[8]

The debate about the role of language is wider than developmental psychology; it pervades other fields of psychology, and also sociology, philosophy and anthropology. It is part of a major debate about rationality. Is language the medium for the communication of individual thought, a monologue where one person expresses ideas in logical form and another listens and receives that logic? Or is language a process of rhetoric, negotiation and persuasion, a bridge between the starting positions of each participant, mutual efforts to find common ground? In Chapter 2 I discuss the recent burgeoning of research on rhetoric which emphasises the dialogic nature of speech. The recognition of the importance of rhetoric in communication – and, indeed, in innovation – owes a great deal to the psychologist Michael Billig.[9] A key concept of rhetoric is that communication depends upon what is taken for granted, and what is regarded as problematic. If something is taken for granted, it assumes shared meaning. Things do not need to be explained, or if they are, the explanation affirms naturalness, inevitability. However, if something is problematic, we need to explain and justify it. A bridge has to be made for understanding.

Treating language as negotiation can lead to the position that everything is a social construction and the individual is no more than a voice in the discourse process, just as treating language as a formal system of meaning can lead to the extreme cognitive position that the child is merely discovering a mono-logic, one universalisable rational system. But there is room for the Vygotskian position within a rhetorical perspective, where the individual makes sense through active reflection but in constant interaction and language. The social context provides a repertoire, a resource, of concepts and ideas, and sets the terms of reference for what is acceptable, comprehensible and legitimate; the individual draws upon this repertoire for making sense, and for negotiating concepts and meaning in interaction with others.[10]

It is a measure of the polarised perspectives in the field that during 1990 I gave exactly the same talk to two different groups – one espousing a social-determinist position, the other comprising mainly classical cognitive developmentalists. The first group accused me of being an idealist, a reductionist, and wholly ignoring the social dimensions of language and thought. The second group accused me of being a sociologist and reneging on my heritage as a researcher on the development of an active, thinking individual.

The common feature of my progress in thinking about development and my thinking about gender and feminism is a shift away from the search for a rationality that has to be discovered, to a rationality that is invented. Socialist feminism looks for a solution to the problems of gender by appeals to a more rational world-view, and does not question the rational orthodoxy. But socialist feminism also assumes an environmentalist view of human development: what has been created by culture can be easily undone by culture. It ignores the darker tensions that arise from the cultural inventions of masculinity and femininity. Cultural feminism focuses on how masculine and feminine are invented through language, but recognises that they need to be *reinvented*, not just denied by rational fiat.

Vygotskian psychology overcomes the assumption that *a priori truths are discovered*, that development is an increasing approximation to one form of rationality. It also avoids the extremes of social determinism which presume that culture is external, and that what it has created can easily be changed. Language is fluid and dynamic; meaning is constructed by both individual and social processes. The individual makes sense of the world through language and in interaction with others, but is active in this process. This is the model which underpins the arguments of this book.

Metaphor and lay social theory

I argue in Chapter 1 that the individual holds 'lay social theories' about the world. A lay social theory is a scenario for explanation which contains schemas about how things work. The scenario tells a story, gives an account, provides a script. An example is crime. If one has the schema that criminals are deterred by punishment, then in the lay social theory deriving from this, severe punishment plays an important role. The 'script' in this case would be the means for establishing such a regime. A lay social theory implies certain desirable outcomes (in this example, a crime-free society). It also implies shared, socially acceptable concepts and beliefs. The presumption is that the individual can communicate his or her lay social theory because it is derived from the cultural repertoire that is available to the growing individual. The individual actively works out his or her own version of the scenario or script, but the resources for this making sense are available within the culture, and are constantly socially negotiated in ordinary interaction.

In any discussion – lay or expert – about gender, it is immediately obvious that there is an underlying theory, a scenario of what works and why, and why these things are inevitable (or inevitably have to be changed). Whether one is engaged in a search for authenticity or in the demolition – or support – of traditional concepts of gender, even the most ordinary discussion expresses theories of why the sexes are so, and what would be the consequences – desirable or otherwise – of altering things.

In Chapters 1 and 2 I argue that metaphor is central to lay social theory. Metaphor is the bridge between individual thinker and social context, between existing ideas and new ideas, between where one person is and where the interlocutor wants to take that person. We need metaphors and analogies to explain new concepts, to resolve uncertainty or misunderstanding. We need metaphors to communicate new ideas, to move between the familiar and the unfamiliar.[11] Metaphors underpin our taken-for-granted assumptions about the world. Nowadays we take for granted the metaphor of the brain as a computer, and we hold schemas of software and hardware, bytes, algorithms. We use the metaphor of mastery and control in relation to our own lives and in relation to the environment; as we change our view of the environment, we are shifting to the metaphor of harmony. Metaphors are an essential part of the rhetorical process. Because we share metaphors, we can share ideas.

Metaphors permeate gender. Our conceptions of sex difference, sex roles and sexual relations are couched in metaphors that explain and justify, and the metaphors derived from gender and sexuality invade vast other areas of life. The primary metaphor of gender is *dualism and polarity*. The metaphor of dualism automatically casts A in antithesis to B; it makes the definition of A as the negation of B. This metaphor would be sufficient to create the deep roots which, I argue, attach to the meaning of gender in our lives and in our culture, roots that are mightily resistant to our tampering. But the extra power of the metaphor comes from mapping other dualities on to gender, entwining masculinity and femininity with such dualities as active–passive, public–private, rational–intuitive. These enrich the meaning of masculinity and femininity, but they also become contaminated with the associations of masculine and feminine. The whole operates as a continual feedback loop, reinforcing and reproducing itself.

Metaphors operate as analogies; they offer models for how things work. The analogy, the similarity perceived between two things, becomes a working model, an explanation, a theory. In seeking to understand the unfamiliar, we look for analogies. In common-sense ideas, such as those associated with gender, the analogies are deeply rooted in ordinary thinking. We take them for granted; they are so embedded that we are not conscious that they are metaphors. For example, we describe male and female in terms of *soft* and *hard*; we even strive to achieve these metaphorical states through physical exercise or cosmetics, and the textures we choose for our clothes. We then extrapolate physical hardness and softness to psychological hardness and softness, in traits, in interaction styles, in body language.

The metaphor of dualism, of affirmation by antithesis and negation, also carries overtones of control. Western culture has a strong tradition of rationality overcoming the forces of chaos that is closely interwoven with masculine versus feminine, and body versus mind. One pole is not only antithetical to, it triumphs over, the other pole. Dark forces must be challenged and conquered. I explore in several chapters the anxieties that femininity will sap masculinity, contaminate it, undermine it. So maintaining masculinity requires *suppression* of the feminine. Such a metaphor of conflict is not only a cognitive polarity, but an affectively laden struggle of some intensity. It is not surprising that such metaphors are deeply rooted in our identity, and resistant to questioning.

The metaphor as an explanation becomes explicit when masculinity and femininity are justified either by their inevitability or by their functional use. Things must be so because of biology, or because they have evolved – they are functional to our evolutionary progression. The debate about biologically based sex difference continues, and indeed there has been some genuine scientific progress,[12] but this is accompanied by a great deal of metaphoric engagement. I describe in Chapters 1 and 2 how the metaphor of Man the Hunter is used in scientific and popular explanations, how it affects the interpretation of data. There was a timely challenge to Man the Hunter in October 1992, arguing that really Palaeolithic Man (*sic*) was a scavenger, not a hunter. The metaphorically romantic hunting skills were not required; our intelligence was directed to a different kind of adaptation – planning and cunning, which sound rather less heroic.[13]

Changing the picture

The major thesis of this book is that change is very difficult, given the power of metaphors of sex and gender, and the anxieties associated with them. In Chapters 6 and 7 I explore some of the changes that have occurred over the last two decades. These studies illustrate the changing lay social theories of gender, and the metaphors that have come in the wake of changing consciousness. They show women struggling with new conceptions of gender. Different prescriptions for changing metaphors come out of different feminist perspectives. Socialist feminism focuses on diminishing the metaphors of difference and confirming the metaphors of rationality, particularly extending and clarifying these in order to remove justifications for discrimination. Cultural feminism focuses on finding new and more authentic metaphors.

To illustrate what happens when we try to change metaphors, let us look at the concept of androgyny. Traditional scales of masculinity and femininity were constructed in a way that exactly reflected how psychologists thought about the concept. A single bipolar scale was used; the higher one scored on masculinity, the lower one scored on femininity. This reflected the *antithesis and negation–affirmation* of conventional metaphors of the relationship between masculinity and femininity. Furthermore, scores 'inappropriate' to one's actual sex were considered psychologically unhealthy; the measures equated masculinity with maleness, and femininity with femaleness. Sandra Bem's work challenged this by changing the way the traits were actually measured.[14] She devised scales which separately assessed masculinity and femininity: so one could score high on both measures, low on both, or high on one and low on the other. This measure broke the metaphor of dualism and polarity. People may still use relative masculinity and femininity as descriptions, but in a pluralist, not a dichotomous, sense. Moreover, Bem and others found that the person who was androgynous – scoring high on both sets of characteristics – was psychologically more competent and adaptable than the person who was sex-typed – scoring high on one scale and low on the other (irrespective of whether or not this 'matched' their actual sex).[15]

Bem's measure did have problems: it took for granted traditional descriptions of masculine and feminine traits, rather than eliciting more accurate reflections of men's and women's sexual identity. In this sense, it was closer to rationalist reconstruction than to finding new authenticity. Indeed, the paradox of Otherness is only partly met even by a model of androgyny that breaks the frame of either/or. Challenging the metaphor of Other in the search for authenticity requires understanding what that metaphor of Otherness means, and what social and psychological functions it serves. What is needed is not the *denial* of Otherness but a more authentic definition of Otherness, the development of more accurate metaphors. To go back to my mirror metaphor: it is the realisation that one can alter the lighting level to achieve a whole range of images, not just arguing that one person's reflection excludes the person behind the glass.

I spoke above of rhetoric and the distinction between what is taken for granted and what is problematic. The main aim of any search for authenticity must, in my view, be to challenge what is taken for granted about gender, and make it problematic. When social scientists began to question sex-difference research, back in the late 1960s, they were not just challenging the evidence – how accurate the data were – they were beginning to challenge assumptions behind the research questions. In publishing research one can only report significant difference; the absence of difference is not worthy of mention. If, in a hundred studies on sex differences in mathematical ability, only three showed any differences, the other ninety-seven would not be publishable. So what enters into the canon of knowledge, common sense and received wisdom is that there *are* differences. The only way to get a more accurate picture was to review research on other issues which *incidentally* included data on sex difference. Such reviews considerably modified the picture.[16] But this is only part of the issue. Questions asked about sex differences were based largely on common sense and cultural stereotypes; the research merely set out to quantify what was already part of received wisdom. The initial challenge to the taken-for-granted was confronting those very questions: were they the right ones to ask? This made sex difference problematic in a new way.

A part of the concept of rhetoric is the idea of a *logos*. This is the state of the art, the received wisdom, the accepted concept. To confront the *logos* requires not just an attack, a questioning, but creation of an *anti-logos*. The *anti-logos* is an alternative picture, a different explanation, which challenges the argument of the *logos* in terms which undermine – and ideally, replace – it. Demolishing assumptions about sex difference was the first step towards creating such an *anti-logos*, but it was really when the underlying question was asked – why were sex differences being researched in the first place? – that the *anti-logos* began. The model of androgyny made a further dent. But the resolution of Otherness needs to create an *anti-logos* that challenges the ordering of the world in terms of a metaphor of dualism. It must challenge the metaphors which operate within that duality – for example metaphors of rationality versus chaos, control and mastery versus harmony.

Furthermore, it opens up the possibility of looking at difference in a new way, taking account of differences that were ignored by the traditional framework – or, if they were acknowledged, were perceived through a distorting lens. The *anti-logos*, therefore, is more than saying 'You've got the wrong answers'; it is saying 'You're asking the wrong questions'. It's the old Irish (Polish, in the United States) joke: 'If I was going there, I wouldn't start from here.' The challenge is to the basic metaphors used in thinking about gender, and the generation of more authentic ones. But the concepts we carry for making sense of the world have so deeply entered our consciousness, our gender identities; there is a great deal of emotional investment in our world-views. To confront the problem of Otherness entails acknowledging the role that such anxieties play in sustaining the existing frameworks – and also the role that existing frameworks play in assuaging those anxieties. It is by no means clear that everyone will be comfortable playing with the lighting controls and extending the possibilities of the two-way mirror. Dwelling on the reflection of one's safe and known self is reassuring.

This book pursues these arguments. In the early chapters I explore the concepts of metaphor, lay social theory and rhetoric, and show how this exploration leads us to an understanding of the role of metaphor in thinking, and why metaphors are deep-rooted. I then explore the metaphors of gender that characterise traditional ways of thinking – and have a very long history indeed. In particular I look at the metaphors of active–passive, public–private, rationality–chaos which map on to gender, and show how they sustain the dualistic metaphor of either/or, and also how they support two major metaphors of relations between the sexes, *hierarchy* and *functional complementarity*. Hierarchy implies that a deficit in one partner is supported by the other's strengths, but this has different evaluations for men's and women's 'strengths'. Functional complementarity means the coexistence of two parallel but interwoven sets of characteristics, each necessary for effective team performance. I look at these both in ordinary life and in the development of certain scientific theories, particularly sociobiology. I take two historical examples, people whose world-view particularly reflected a deep-rooted metaphor of sex – and sexuality – that has pervaded, albeit in diluted form, our thinking over two millennia. The first is Philo of Alexandria; the second is Otto Weininger. Although they are two thousand years apart, they both express profound anxieties about masculine sexuality and the mind–body split, which are sustained by metaphors that map the feminine on to the irrational, the chaotic, the sensual.

In Chapter 5 I spell out the distinction between different strands of feminist theory. I am not concerned here to present a definitive overview of feminist theories – such overviews are widely available in other sources. Nor am I presenting a history of feminism. My concern is to demonstrate the main differences which underpin various positions, and in particular to show how assumptions about masculinity and femininity, about the nature and origins of difference, and about strategies of change, vary profoundly amongst different theories. I deal with two 'rationalist' models, socialist feminism and liberal feminism, and two 'cultural' or language-based models, radical feminism and cultural feminism.

To illustrate how change has affected lay thought, and how women have struggled to find new *anti-logoi* to the traditional views on gender, I refer in Chapters 6 and 7 to several of my own studies relating to changing ways of thinking about gender. I quote in some detail from two sets of verbal material: an early account by Micheline Wandor of a consciousness-raising group, published in 1971, and an extended group interview that I conducted in 1985 with women who had only recently become self-defined feminists. These accounts illustrate world-views in reconstruction, and the development of new metaphors for gender.

Sexuality, as I argue, is the real battleground, and in Chapter 8 I explore how the tensions and anxieties about sexuality are dealt with in our culture – through distortion, defence and romanticisation – and how certain issues, like rape, are crucial to the metaphors we hold about masculinity and femininity, and about the relations between the sexes.

Chapters 9 through 12 are concerned with change. How are metaphors changing in the creation of an *anti-logos*, a challenge to traditional ways of thinking? Chapter 9 explores how authenticity is being sought through redefining and reconstructing metaphors, and reclaiming symbols. In Chapter 10 I look in detail at the research on 'different voices'. Carol Gilligan has argued that women and men use different metaphors for describing selfhood. Women see people as connected to each other; men see people as separate from each other. Her work raises a question about reconstructing Otherness. Does the 'connected' self particularly characterise women, is it a more authentic picture of how women think, or can both sexes use both connected and separate thinking? This makes her work relevant to a wider issue – that cultural feminism is part of a larger critique of rationality. It is a challenge to a monolithic world-view; the acknowledgement that there is more than one route to truth, knowledge, discovery, undermines a unitary model of rationality.

Members of the French feminist school, whom I also discuss in this chapter, go further. Gilligan is 'discovering' an alternative voice, present but hidden from mainstream culture, and seen by both women and men as more authentically feminine. Hélène Cixous, Julia Kristeva and Luce Irigaray are trying to invent a new mode of expression, not merely new metaphors, in order to authenticate the feminine. Their argument is that all expression, logic and metaphors in mainstream culture are the product of a masculine world-view, and cannot adequately reflect the feminine, the female. They are exploring novel inventions for expressing and articulating the feminine. This work underlines the extent of the problem of overcoming Otherness. If one believes that the metaphor of Otherness is necessarily embedded in all current mainstream metaphors of relating, and all forms of language, then just disengaging the polarity – as was begun by unpacking the masculinity–femininity scale in the search for androgyny – is not enough.

In Chapter 12 I trace the deconstruction and reconstruction of the metaphors of masculinity. Some arise out of a rationalist reconstruction that diminishes difference; others acknowledge deeper forces. The controversial new 'masculinism', associated with Robert Bly and Sam Keen, attempts to come to terms with the defences that underpin male assertions of power, and denial of emotion, and to find new metaphors for masculinity.

The final chapter is on the backlash against feminism. Again, I shall not present an overview; it has been well reviewed by Susan Faludi.[17] My concern is to show how the language of backlash asserts the traditional metaphors of gender – yet with an awareness of change. The metaphors of backlash reflect anxieties about the perceived changes in the rhetoric of gender, expressed as lay social theories about the 'dire consequences' of changing gender roles, and assertions about 'natural' sex differences and relations between the sexes. Backlash is a fascinating rhetorical process; it is trying to rebuild the rhetorical boundaries, to appeal to shared assumptions about the assault on 'normality'. Backlash also reveals how far changes have been assimilated into the culture. What is problematic is defined by what is seen to have been lost, whereas for the reformer, what is problematic is defined by what is yet to be achieved.

This book does not always follow the neat and direct paths that are expected of a conventional scholarly text. I have drawn upon empirical work – my own and other people's – and engaged in discussion of many theoretical and philosophical positions. But I have done so in the course of exploring ideas, provoking argumentation and laying out what I see as unrecognised, unconfronted issues. So there is a certain amount of peregrination, of wandering off the path to explore relevant, but slightly aslant, examples and questions. I do not, I think, provide the solutions to the problems I raise; it is my intent to make problematic what has been taken for granted, rather than to provide a new orthodoxy. This is a work of persuasion, not of didactic assertion. I have sometimes imposed my own alternative metaphors as a way of challenging the existing ones. These metaphors give me insight, and enable me to take the perspective, hear the voice, which seems to be ignored in the original texts. In doing this, I take (humbly) support from Gillian Beer's account of Charles Darwin's *On the Origin of Species*:

Darwin's is not an austere Descartian style. . . . The book seeks to persuade, not by any attempt to 'force belief' but through a more and more intricate taking in of possible causes for disbelief and the elaboration of doubts. . . . The need to please his readers as well as to unsettle and disturb them is as vital to Darwin as it was to Dickens.[18]

In making this comparison I am not making any claims for my own text, but I am pointing out obliquely that eminent scientists have not always been hidebound by the constraints of linear logic and non-rhetorical style.

There are things I have not attempted in this book. Throughout I have asserted that feminism – at least cultural and radical feminism – parallels, and is part of, a critique of Enlightenment rationality and a unitary world-view. I discuss this in various places, but I have not devoted to these assertions the depth of scholarly analysis that I might have done had this been my main preoccupation. There is only so much one can do in a book that crosses disciplinary boundaries.[19]

Notes

1. H. Tajfel (ed.), *Differentiation Between Social Groups*, London: Academic Press, 1978.
2. C. Paglia, *Sexual Personae: Art and decadence from Nefertiti to Emily Dickinson*, New Haven, CT; Yale University Press, 1990.
3. S. de Beauvoir, *The Second Sex*, trans. H. M. Parshley, London: Jonathan Cape, 1953.
4. H. A. Witkin, R. B. Dyk, H. F. Faterson, D. Goodenough and S. A. Karp, *Psychological Differentiation*, New York: Wiley, 1962; H. A. Witkin, D. R. Goodenough and S. A. Karp, 'Stability of cognitive style from childhood to young adulthood', *Journal of Personality and Social Psychology*, 7, pp. 291–300, 1967.
5. I was working especially within the framework of Lawrence Kohlberg's theory of moral development. See L. Kohlberg, *The Psychology of Moral Development*, San Francisco: Harper & Row, 1984.
6. See A. Colby and L. Kohlberg, *The Measurement of Moral Judgement*, Cambridge: Cambridge University Press, 1987.
7. L. Vygotsky, *Mind and Society*, Cambridge, MA: Harvard University Press, 1978.
8. See J. W. Stigler, R. Shweder and G. Herdt (eds), *Cultural Psychology; Essays on comparative human development*, Cambridge: Cambridge University Press, 1990; H. Haste, 'Morality, self and sociohistorical context; the role of lay social theory', in G. Noam and T. Wren (eds), *The Moral Self*, Cambridge, MA: MIT Press, 1993
9. M. Billig, *Arguing and Thinking*, Cambridge: Cambridge University Press, 1987.
10. J. Bruner and H. Haste, *Making Sense: The child's construction of the world*, London: Methuen, 1987.
11. In an article entitled 'Images of creative thought', in the *Newsletter* of American Psychological Association, Division 10, Psychology and the Arts, Winter/Fall 1992, Howard Gruber uses the illustration of an Athenian removal van bearing the legend 'Metaphorai'.

12. D. Kimura, 'Sex differences in the brain', *Scientific American*, **267(3)**, pp. 118–25, September 1992.
13. R. J. Blumenschine and J. A. Cavallo, 'Scavenging and human evolution', *Scientific American*, **267(4)**, pp. 90-7, October 1992.
14. S. L. Bem, 'The measurement of psychological androgyny', *Journal of Consulting and Clinical Psychology*, **42**, pp. 155–62, 1974.
15. S. L. Bem, 'Sex-role adaptability; one consequence of psychological androgyny', *Journal of Personality and Social Psychology*, **31**, pp. 634–43, 1975.
16. E. E. Maccoby and C. N. Jacklin, *The Psychology of Sex Differences*, Oxford: Oxford University Press, 1975.
17. S. Faludi, *Backlash! The undeclared war against women*, London: Chatto & Windus, 1992.
18. G. Beer, *Darwin's Plots: Evolutionary narrative in Darwin, George Eliot and nineteenth century fiction*, London: Routledge & Kegan Paul, 1983, p. 39.
19. See, for example, M. Foucault, whose influence on this approach to language and thought is pervasive: M. Foucault, *The Order of Things: An archaeology of the human sciences*, New York: Random House, 1970; G. Gutting, *Michel Foucault's Archaeology of Scientific Reason*, Cambridge: Cambridge University Press, 1989.

Chapter 1: What are little girls made of?

When I was a little girl, I learnt certain actions and certain skills. I learnt to sew, I learnt to plait my hair, I learnt the games that little girls know: I learnt to skip, I learnt to play hopscotch, I learnt to play at house. I learnt also that certain words, certain images, are applied to girls and women: pretty, associated with flowers, sweet-smelling. These are all images of the feminine. I also learnt the behaviours symbolic of being female. These were often quite trivial things, like doing my coat up one side rather than the other, parting my hair a particular way, going into school first, before the boys. I also learnt that certain parts of the playground were boys' territory and certain parts were girls' territory; space, as well as behaviour, was symbolically associated with gender.

I also learnt about grown women, famous women who had done things regarded as important – women like Florence Nightingale, Marie Curie, Joan of Arc, Mary Kingsley and, of course, Queen Elizabeth I. Some were intrepid and enterprising. Others selflessly cared for other people; they were virtuous or saintly. Some were just extremely beautiful. So I learnt that there were women who had done very important things, and I realised that these women's qualities were regarded as important for little girls like me to acquire. Florence Nightingale was a nurse, a role symbolising many features of femininity. Joan of Arc was a soldier – hardly a feminine role, but she was religious, brave and virtuous. But Elizabeth I's statement, 'I know I have the body of a weak and feeble woman, but I have the heart and stomach of a king' was a message to little girls like me that there was a disjunction between leadership and femininity.

These images gave me certain role models for womanhood. I realised very soon that they constrained me; with the exception of Marie Curie, the women presented to me in history and story books had made a choice, or a choice had been forced upon them. If they were heroic, they were usually unmarried – in fact they were usually virgins, and part of their virtue seemed to lie in their virginity. They certainly did not combine family life and sexual love with their heroism. Later on I learnt of women who were famous because their beauty had attracted famous lovers, or husbands, whom they influenced. And I found that when a woman had made a contribution to science or culture, if she was the wife or mistress of an interesting man, her importance seemed to lie as much in her relationship to that man as in her own achievements. So the message came through to me that women choose between greatness, and a family and sexual life.

Finally, I read fairy tales and novels, and I saw films. The messages in such narratives again said a great deal about what was possible for boys and girls, men and women – what was expected. There was very clear appropriate behaviour for princesses, for example. There was a script for poor girls who found happiness by marrying the right man. Probably the first film I ever saw, at the age of five or six, was *Red Shoes*; the message of this film is that if you choose a career rather than a husband you will be unhappy and come to a tragic end.

This vast variety of information gave me a rich basis for developing my own understanding about what it was to be a woman. I was learning, first of all, to make a category distinction between men and women, and that it was very important to know what that difference meant for all one's behaviour. I learnt that to be comprehensible as a person, I must fit into the appropriate feminine roles. I was learning a cultural theory about gender; I was learning to describe sex differences, and to explain their function, nature and origin, through everyday enactment of my femaleness.

My experience as a British child growing up in the postwar era is typical of any child anywhere in the world. All that differs across cultures are the actual symbols of gender, and how important gender is as a social category. The child may learn through direct precept, being told what little boys and little girls should or shouldn't do. Learning takes place more indirectly through the experience of gender metaphors in everyday life. Much of life is permeated with metaphors linked to gender. Masculinity and femininity spill over into other categories: hard–soft, light–dark, night–day, public–private, nature–nurture, rational–intuitive, The child gets the message that there is a symbolic association between gender and other apparently unrelated fields of life.

Perhaps the most important way the child learns this is through behaviour. The child enacts, in all areas of life, gender role and gender symbolism. If parts of the playground are 'boys' ' areas; and parts are 'girls' ', a girl does not walk in the boys' area. There is no need for sanction; a child daily defines herself as female through the recognition of such territorial distinctions. Everyday actions are symbolic affirmations of one's gender. Some actions are male actions, some are female; cooking and sewing are female tasks, taking rubbish out, constructing shelves, are male tasks. Division of tasks carries the assumption that certain skills are inherently attributes of one sex or the other. So in performing the ordinary actions of everyday life, observing others performing them, and learning how to interpret this, the child acquires understanding of gender symbolism.

This has been strikingly described by the anthropologist Pierre Bourdieu,[1] who studied the Kabylia, a Moroccan people who have very gender-marked behaviour and symbols. Not only space but also time is gender-marked; parts of the village are exclusively male territory at certain times of day, and parts are exclusively female. Women will not go into the men's area and men will not go into the women's area. Many cultures have similar time and territory boundaries; in many Mediterranean cultures, women do not sit in cafés in the square during the lunchtime period, though they might at other times of the day. In Western Europe and the United States, shopping areas are gender-marked: men may feel comfortable in the supermarket, or the launderette, but they do not go into haberdasher's shops. Women often do not feel happy entering tool shops, even to buy a pair of scissors or some other domestic implement.

The meaning of gender is socially constructed. No culture limits the social definition of gender to biologically determined sex differences. There are a number of universal behaviours, and there are certain necessary functions in any society: child care, fighting, hunting, disposal of waste, care of the elderly, decision-making in the community. They are not universally allocated to particular genders – indeed, in some cultures they are gender-linked, in some they are not. But when they are assigned to gender, this is explained by some 'natural' attribute, and the masculinity or femininity of the task takes on symbolic meaning – so fighting is not just what males do, it becomes a definition of manhood to be a good fighter.

Beliefs about sex differences can enhance what appears to be there. Gender differences may be exaggerated or elaborated. If gender is symbolically important in a given society, most tasks in that society may be gender-marked. Alternatively, a culture may diminish or ignore actual biological differences, or treat them as irrelevant. Sex differences may be compensated for. A paradox of Anglophone culture is that we recognise that boys have more difficulty than girls in learning to read, and we also recognise that girls have more difficulty with mathematics than boys. But we tend to compensate boys' reading deficit by making a particular effort to provide them with remedial reading; we have tended to accept girls' lesser mathematical skills as a fact of nature, and to make less effort to compensate them.[2] Where a skill is deemed central to cultural survival, it is probable that if one sex possesses it to a greater degree than the other, the deficient sex will have special training to compensate. In contrast, where a particular skill is symbolic of a particular sex, it may even be carefully ensured that the other sex does not acquire it.

What is believed about gender tends to become real. For example, the belief that females are incapable of making decisions may become true in a society where girls are given no opportunity to develop such skills. The belief that males are unable to sew becomes true when the culture makes sure that no boy ever gets his hands on a needle. So something which is socially constructed within the culture's theory of gender may become reality. Once something becomes substantively true in this way, that socially created fact may be enhanced, it may be diminished or ignored, it may be compensated for, or it may be adjusted to.

We see here the operation of cultural theories of gender. Such a theory is more than a simple description of sex differences. A theory also provides stories and explanations about the origins, functions and necessity of sex differences. The child encounters this theory through behaviours, direct instruction and the more subtle process of discovering what is taken for granted, and what is seen as needing to be explained and justified. This is more explicit when there is a threat to the status quo, a questioning of what has been deemed normal – something that is likely to spark off predictions of dire consequences. At the end of the last century, Tennyson wrote:

Man to the field, and woman to the hearth,
Man to the sword, and to the needle she,
Man with the head, woman with the heart,
Man to command and woman to obey.
All else confusion.

Later, Rupert Brooke said: 'This mixture of the sexes is all wrong; and any intermingling of the two is calamitous. Male is male and female is female . . . manliness is the one hope of the world.'[3]

These assertions about the consequences of altering roles were written at a time when there was considerable debate about gender. In 1906, speaking in the House of Commons on the issue of women's enfranchisement, William Randolf Kramer, Member of Parliament for Shoreditch, spelt out the cultural theory that underpinned his objections:

He had always contended that if once they opened the door and enfranchised even so small a number of females, they could not possibly close it. It ultimately meant adult suffrage. The government of the country would therefore be handed over to a majority who would not be men but would be women. Women are creatures of impulse and emotion and did not decide questions on the ground of reason as men did. He was sometimes described as a 'woman hater'; he had had two wives and he thought that was the best answer he could give to those who called him a 'woman hater'. He was too fond of them to drag them into the political arena, and to ask them to undertake responsibilities, duties and obligations which they did not understand and did not care for. What did one find when one got into the company of women and talked politics? They were soon asked to stop talking silly politics. Yet that was the type of people to whom honourable members were invited to hand over the destinies of the country. It was not only because he thought women were unfitted by their physical nature to exercise political power, but because he believed the majority of them did not want it and would vote against it, that he asked the House to pause before they took the steps suggested . . . . He believed that if women were enfranchised, the end would be disastrous to all political parties.[4]

This expresses a whole variety of assumptions – not only about the physical nature of women, but also about their social nature, and about what women want. Like Tennyson and Brooke, Kramer predicted dire consequences of changing sex roles and the relationship between the sexes. The dangers are not only in giving women more rights but in changing the metaphors and symbols – changing the underlying theory of what constitutes natural sex difference. For Tennyson, an unspecified 'confusion' implied a disturbance of morality as well as a disturbance of nature. For Rupert Brooke, the loss of the masculine ethos meant a decline into the feminine. For Kramer, the outcome of female suffrage would be chaos arising from women's incompetence. These are very different fears; each has a long tradition, tied to different theories not only of gender difference but of the necessary relation and interrelation between male and female, and between 'masculine' and 'feminine'.

Over the last two decades the Women's Movement as a social movement, and feminism as a set of social theories, have consciously challenged conventional cultural wisdom, taken-for-granted beliefs about sex differences and the relations between the sexes. The whole tenor of this activity is that issues of gender are not confined to legal rights but are about underlying ordinary, lay theories about gender differences and gender relations. Feminist ideas have affected what we take for granted about gender. Change is not only about the relative number of women lawyers and men nurses in 1965 and 1995; it depends on what such different representation of the sexes means symbolically. In this book I am not addressing how many more Top People today are female than was the case thirty years ago; I am interested in the cultural changes which accompany – and facilitate – the greater incidence of female top persons.

Lay social theory, ordinary explanation and metaphor

My key argument is that what has changed are *lay social theories* of gender. We decode events and experiences in order to make sense of them. What counts as 'sense' depends upon our implicit theories of how things work, how things ought to be, and what is appropriate. We hold concepts or schemas about how things work, and we have scenarios or scripts for behaviour. In effect, we have a personal library or 'available repertoire' of options for action, for interpreting and evaluating events and our own and other people's behaviour. The schemas and scripts which constitute our lay social theory are not constructed by the individual in isolation; they are part of the culture. The growing child becomes aware of the explanations and evaluations which form the culture's repertoire. The culture also limits the range of choice in various ways. Some explanations are not available because they are unknown. Others are not deemed appropriate because they defy conventions about what counts as rational, or because they fly in the face of other beliefs – evolution theory, for example, has been considered a taboo explanation in some American States.

Lay social theory has to be understood in the context of culture. Because human beings are social creatures who use language, it follows that most human activity (some would say all) takes place within a social context. Expressing a belief, whether about fact or value, is an act of communication; one must be aware of other people's potential responses. In any social context there are shared assumptions about what constitutes 'fact' and what constitutes proper ways of going about solving problems: in some situations, for example, it is deemed necessary to cite evidence for one's statements; in others it is conviction or intuition that carries persuasive weight.

Language is not important simply because it is a means for communicating logical premises or conclusions. Through the use of language people move towards shared solutions, but they do this by starting from shared assumptions and beliefs, and by refining definitions and interpretations in such a way as to arrive at a shared conclusion. In persuasive interaction the persuader deliberately uses common assumptions and meanings, and shared values, to alter the perspective of the listener. This is the *rhetorical process*. So knowledge, understanding and belief may be held by the individual, but the mechanisms by which they are formed and communicated depend upon shared language and shared metaphors and images.

Metaphor and image have become increasingly important in our scientific understanding of language and thought. Metaphors, once regarded merely as elegant literary devices which make speech more 'poetic', are now recognised as part of our process of understanding. Metaphor and analogy are part of the common currency of ordinary language and ordinary thinking; they provide a bridge between the known and the unknown. But they are also an essential part of communication; by the use of a shared metaphor or analogy we can convey a novel idea.[5]

There is one metaphor which beautifully reveals lay social theory about gender – and illustrates how metaphor works. This particular metaphor is widely available in common-sense and lay thought – so it is relevant to everyday life – and is also rooted in scientific thought. So it demonstrates how gender is embedded in culture. Ordinary ideas about gender influence scientific ideas about gender, and scientific activity sustains and changes lay conceptions of gender.

The metaphor is Man the Hunter, an important metaphor in our culture. Undoubtedly an actual Man as Hunter is a part of our evolutionary history, but the metaphor's cultural importance lies not in whether some men were once hunters, or even in the fact that all men were once hunters; it lies in its prominent role in our interpretation of *present-day* male behaviour. We choose to explain many aspects of twentieth-century behaviour in terms of our image of Man the Hunter – and this is done both by scientists and by lay people. It is that image which is symbolically important, and how it is extended and embellished way beyond any actual evidence about our early life in the savannah.

In this image, Man is sometimes alone but more usually in a group of other men – never with women. He is engaged in an exacting task, hunting quarry. The quarry is usually an animal, but it may be another man. The task involves skill – strategy, accurate use of sophisticated weapons, understanding of the habits of the prey. It requires courage, patience and determination. The motivation of the Hunter is pursuit and conquest. His tools will be valued as fine pieces of craftsmanship. The social behaviour of the Hunter involves camaraderie, bonding, and sharing glory and achievement when the quarry is successfully caught.

This powerful image implies personal characteristics, technology, social behaviours and motivations, all of which are seen as functional to successful performance. The significance of the image becomes apparent when we see to how wide a range of human behaviour it can be applied. Man is a 'hunter' when the quarry being hunted is woman. Man is

Hunter when his prey is the country's enemy; man the soldier becomes Man the Hunter under certain conditions. The combat pilots of the First World War, the Spitfire pilots of the Second, in particular, were not soldiers; their battles are described in the iconography of war, and remain in legend and public imagination, as hunter and prey. There are quite different metaphors and images associated with mundane soldiering. The lone fighter pilot is a romantic and skilful hunter.

In popularisations of sociobiological theories about the origins of human behaviour – and even in the original scientific versions – the hunter is a romantic figure, who embodies many characteristics supposed to belong to modern males. The key argument is that because we spent a very long period in the hunter-gatherer state, there evolved psychological and social, as well as physical, characteristics of which we are now the heirs. This makes a lot of sense, except that the hard evidence for what actually went on during those millennia is scarce. To compensate for the limited information from history, scientists extrapolate from present-day parallels, including primates and current hunter-gatherer cultures.

The actual palaeontological evidence indicates that early humans probably generally lived in kin-related small bands and hunted small game, which they ate, and with whose skins they clothed themselves. Some large game was hunted, but it was probably a rare and minor source of food. There is good evidence from southern France that at certain periods, many groups came together for a short time each year to collaborate in the hunting of straight-tusked elephant. They lived in shelters and divided the spoils of the hunt amongst the groups. What they did for the rest of the year is unknown.[6]

There is a logic in the sexual division of labour, if only because small children impede rapid movement, and certain tasks do genuinely require greater physical strength. But as present-day cultures show, there is enormous variation in how child-care arrangements can free able-bodied women for necessary subsistence activities, and in what activities are deemed appropriate to the strengths and skills of each sex. So while there is an argument for sexual division of labour, there is much less of an argument for such a rigidly consistent division of labour and social life lasting long enough to create changes in the genetic code. Furthermore, it seems unlikely that the kind of male bonding that recent popularisers have seen exemplified in present-day sporting activities would be necessary to trap hare or wild pig. Even the popular view that dogs were originally trained as man's faithful hunting companion falls down: dogs were domesticated some time after many other domestic animals, presumably to act as assistants in shepherding.

Another counter-argument to Man the Hunter is that early humans actually scavenged rather than hunted. This somewhat unheroic activity at first seems to require less intelligence than hunting. However, Blumenschine and Cavallo argue that scavenging was a very effective way of getting hold of protein supplements to a mainly plant diet; humans used their intelligence to monitor other predators:

> Scavenging may have been more common than hunting two million years ago. Flaked stone toolmaking, the practice of butchering large animals and the evolution of big-brained *Homo* all make their first known appearance in the physical record at this time . . . . The earliest hominids probably scavenged and took small prey with their hands, as chimpanzees and baboons do. Only their next step was unique; they began to use tools to butcher large carcasses that non-human primates cannot exploit. The difficulty of this leap belies the charge that scavenging offers no challenge that might select for human qualities

– such as a larger brain and manual dexterity.[7]

So metaphors are not just ways of finding nice analogies in poetic language. A metaphor carries some very important explanatory baggage; what is described is seen as having the attributes of that with which it is metaphorically associated. Our symbolic hunter requires certain necessary skills and attributes. If these had to evolve over the years in the savannah, we can assume that they are 'natural'. If we think we see parallel skills and behaviours in modern man, we are constructing a theory: that these modern behaviours are really 'hunting' and, furthermore, that they are encoded in our genes. So by implication they are inevitable – be it male bonding in various forms of gang, or the submissive and patient female awaiting the hunter's return to the cave. It is tempting to cast as a modern hunter the man seeking a commercial takeover, an elusive contract, assisted by a team of fellow males and backed up by the supportive females in the office cave, and to extrapolate to other 'hunters' of the past or of other cultures in order to 'explain' him. This fanciful theory now has common-sense status; it is part of popular wisdom, but it has also informed the questions that serious science asks.

The power and symbolic significance of the Man the Hunter metaphor becomes even clearer when we look at a contrasting cultural metaphor, the female hunter. We have but one mythic huntress, who becomes the metaphor for any female who actually does hunt. When we examine the metaphoric baggage that she carries in our culture, it becomes obvious why she has not had the attentions of science.

Diana or Artemis also hunted in a single-sex group, but she and her companions were virgins; they did not return home bloodstained and weary to the supportive male. Indeed, Diana rejected men, and killed the one who approached too close – she was not only a feminist, but a radical separatist. But she had the necessary skills of the hunter, skills attributed to males: she was fleet of foot, sure of eye, strong of arm. Her team is also seen to have a special, mystical camaraderie. It is interesting that when myth or cultural beliefs endow women with camaraderie it is seen either as frivolous and trivial or as mystical and threatening to men.

The myth of Diana is a convenient metaphor for describing women who participate in actual or symbolic hunting, but she is not really analogous to Man the Hunter, who is a creature of flesh and blood, even in myth. She is mysterious, odd, deviant from conventional female roles. She may hunt animals as men do, but without the male bloodlust – somehow it is a mystical communion with nature, rather than a conquest of it. Man the Hunter does not need Diana the huntress by his side; he needs his little gatherer back in the warm cave to approve, console, heal.

Man the Hunter illustrates some key points of my argument. The image implies a scenario or script for certain aspects of male behaviour. It contains a set of rules for behaviour, motives, skills and – most importantly – relations with others. This scenario is understood by all members of the culture. It gives meaning and symbolism beyond the literal context – the commercial entrepreneur is perceived as a metaphoric hunter, and his actions are construed in terms of a hunter's performance, skilfully pursuing prey, seeking spoils and returning to the female for approval. Very different symbol and value would be attributed to such behaviour if the entrepreneur were seen as a pirate, or as a cunning fox and wily diplomat. The metaphor does not only make an analogy, it gives an explanation for other behaviours in the script, in addition to specific stalking and catching prey.

Metaphors, symbols and images play a key role in explanation, and they define what is deemed to be salient. They are important, therefore, both in the individual's own interpretation and in communication with others; shared metaphors, symbols and images are crucial for the effective negotiation of meaning. Such examples show how lay social theory is created, sustained and given importance. But lay social theories inevitably also generate inconsistencies, paradoxes and uncomfortable truths, which have to be dealt with. For example, the common stereotype was that women were incompetent at making decisions. If this were true, for either social or biological reasons, it would have inconvenient consequences. So schemas were generated which allowed women's incompetence but diminished its possible dangers. One method was to argue that men were rational but women had alternative qualities; moreover, irrationality and incompetence were endearing characteristics, and women were seen as sexually attractive if they were relatively stupid, and so more likely to marry. These elegant adjustments were given a pseudo-scientific gloss when women's irrationality was seen as an aid in rapport with children, an asset for their child-rearing role.[8]

But what happens when reality impinges, and lay social theory is inadequate to cope with it? William Kramer was confronted with women who wanted to vote, were prepared to fight quite hard to get the vote, and asserted their capacity to enter politics. He countered by invoking theories about women's biologically based incompetence and about most women's lack of interest in having the vote, so casting the desire to vote as an attribute of a deranged minority; and he concluded that if women were given the vote, disaster would ensue. His own 'love of women' was confined to his wives in their very specific domestic role; he loved 'real' women, not deviant viragos.

I identify a number of ways of dealing with unfortunate truths about men and women who disobligingly fail to fit the stereotypes of Western culture. These illustrate the adjustments of lay social theories to sustain the status quo. Unfortunately, they are as much a part of the repertoire today as they were in Kramer's time.

There is *denial* – even in the face of evidence – that one sex or the other possesses certain abilities or attributes. By *isolation*, a person who has – or claims – inappropriate characteristics is isolated and treated as a deviant; they are labelled as exceptional, mad, ill, or evil. A number of religious traditions engage in *vilification*, treating women as fundamentally unclean, or particularly prone to evil. Through *trivialisation*, demands or statements are regarded as irrelevant or frivolous. Trivialisation was a characteristic response to the early Women's Movement; reports of 'bra-burning' were an example of this. The women who marched a hundred miles in 1981 to the air base at Greenham Common to protest at the siting of Cruise missiles were enraged that journalists were more interested in their blisters, and what their husbands thought, than in the purpose of the exercise.

Another ploy is *compartmentalisation*, separating and dealing with things one at a time, rather than taking them as a whole. Structural compartmentalisation excludes women from areas of men's lives, so that they impinge on men only in the domestic sphere. But compartmentalisation can also order mental life; Byron's 'Man's love is of man's life a thing apart; 'tis woman's whole existence' reflects the expectation that men will treat love as only one part of their life, and give other parts equal importance. Compartmentalisation defuses the power of unpleasant truth by treating it as something that can be dealt with within a particular context.

In *generalisation*, a small sample of womanhood or manhood is taken to be representative of the whole. The 'normal' man or woman is the one most consistent with the accepted theory of gender. Anyone who does not fit into that category is seen as deviant. In the construction of family benefits and aspects of law and social policy in the immediate postwar period in Britain, the nuclear family was taken as the norm from which generalisations were made about womanhood, manhood, marriage and family.[9]

Finally, there is the device of *reclassification*. The behaviour, or the symbol, is reinterpreted. Female assertiveness is perceived as aggression, and aggression is seen as unsuitable for women. Compassion in men is classified in certain contexts as weakness. Because the behaviour does not fit into the theory of gender, it is reclassified symbolically to diminish its significance. Another example arises from fear of women's competence, so women's organising role is located purely in the domestic sphere. Margaret Thatcher applied the metaphor of housekeeping to the running of government, making it for the first time a positive metaphor in the public domain.

All these are ways of dealing with deviations or anomalies within the terms of reference of the lay social theory; they adjust the meaning of behaviour to make it acceptable to, and part of, that theory. So they sustain the structure and power of the theory. Efforts towards social change involve changing consciousness by confronting people with their own implicit lay social theory of gender. Such efforts attack defence mechanisms, descriptions, particular metaphors and rhetoric, in order to reconstruct the principles underlying lay social theories of gender.

Feminism and the challenge to some cherished beliefs about the nature of truth

The main themes of this book are how lay social theory of gender sustains gender roles, and how feminist theories have confronted existing lay social theories. A major argument is that changing gender roles and gender theories is a matter not only of countering factually incorrect beliefs about the sexes with alternative evidence, but of questioning the very basis of those beliefs. The challenge of feminism is not just to males' power to hog positions of authority and prestige, nor is it the threat that they may need to take an equal role in washing their socks or the baby's nappies. I argue that feminism is concurrent with, and contributes to, a substantive change in the way Western culture conceptualises rationality. Beliefs about gender roles are part of, and map on to, beliefs about the nature of rationality. The prevailing model of rationality is currently under attack from many perspectives, and feminism is consistent with, and a part of, many of the arguments which constitute that attack.

The link between gender and models of rationality starts from the dualistic perspective which is so central to Western culture. In order to define something, we have to know its opposite; we can know 'good' only if we have the antithesis of 'evil' to compare it with. 'Dark' is not a useful concept unless it is contrasted with 'light'. Very early on – at the hand of Aristotle, if not earlier – a split occurred between rationality and emotion, with emotion seen as interfering with, and being a contrast to, rationality. It was Aristotle, too, who originally mapped this on to gender: females were more emotional; they were therefore less rational.[10]

This looks like bad logic, which could in principle be countered by any evidence that removed sex differences from the equation. Unfortunately, the heritage of such dualism has been to treat emotion as a dangerous threat to rationality, not merely another aspect of experience. So it is not enough, for example, to say that women are different because they are more in touch with emotion; instead, it has followed that the feminine (emotion) becomes a threat to the masculine (reason); so sustaining 'masculinity' – and rationality – becomes a struggle that demands constant vigilance. This, with other 'mappings-on' of gender to cultural dualities, strengthens the picture of thesis and antithesis, and makes it very difficult for simple logic to counter. It is in fact necessary to undermine the very model of dualism and polarity itself.

We have inherited from the Enlightenment a monolithic model of rationality, sustained by thesis and antitheses. This model pervades our world, and in so many areas it is closely allied with masculinity. It is not just that men Do Rationality in powerful places and in large numbers, but the definition of rationality depends upon the exclusion of that which is perceived to be the Feminine. Feminist theory has tackled the mapping of rationality on to masculinity in different ways. Some feminists argue that the model of rationality itself is all right, but it is not correct to assume that the feminine is different from the masculine in the ways that matter – or, indeed, at all. Thus, they wish to undermine the logic which maps gender on to rationality, and to assert women's entitlement to join the Rationality Club.

Other feminists, in contrast, argue that the problem lies with the model of rationality itself. They see it deriving from the need to sustain a single, monolithic world-view. The argument is that women's experience differs considerably from that of men, and out of that experience comes an appreciation that there is more than one way to make sense of the world. At the very least, the dominant model of rationality is inauthentic as an expression of this different experience. If one recognises multiple forms of experience, it follows that there should be the possibility of multiple rationalities. This plea for pluralism aligns feminism with other current developments in Western thought. There have always been parallel models of how one is able to know, interact with and control (or be controlled by) the external world, and how truth is arrived at. Two traditions exemplify the contrast: the Cartesian (which came to full fruition in the Enlightenment) and the Humanistic, which came out of the rhetorical approach of Protagoras.

Characteristic of the first, the Enlightenment approach, is the belief that Truth is something to be discovered. Logic is the exercise of the individual mind through which one arrives at Truth; language is a means to communicate knowledge, rather than necessarily embedded in thought. It follows that careful, objective logic and analysis is the path to Truth. The second tradition believes that Truth is arrived at through *negotiation*, that one cannot 'know' truth independently of one's cultural and historical context, because that context makes certain things available. Context also defines certain things as problematic and needing explanation, but not others. An important element of this tradition is that one can know that which is perceived as necessary and useful only within a context, not in abstraction. One cannot know, either, simply through detachment and objectification; one must gain knowledge through *participation*. Language and communication are vitally important, because our concepts depend on the language available to us. Persuasion – the recognition of the other's point of view and the accommodation of one's arguments to that point of view – is essential for comprehension and the development of ideas, not merely in order to sway the other's emotions or values.

The critique of equating rationality with masculinity is central to feminist reconstruction. It is crucially related to the problem of 'Otherness', and how it is conceptualised. What unites all feminists is the recognition that the dominant culture fails to give authenticity to female lives, treating women as 'Other'. What divides feminists is the meaning of this 'Otherness', and how to transcend it. Simone de Beauvoir first discussed the problem of Otherness in *The Second Sex*.[11] She saw it as a necessary aspect of dualism and the categorisation of persons. One can be Self only if one has the Other as contrast. She argued that women have no Selfhood in this sense, because they are defined as Other to men – by men and by themselves. This, she argued, is because to define oneself as Self would break the necessary interrelation between men and women, and require men and women to live separately, which she considered impossible. Even dependent minority groups in thrall to colonial masters can at least identify themselves as 'different' and as potentially free; this is not, she argued, an avenue open to women.

The Otherness of woman's subjective experience is a central issue in feminist consciousness and feminist theory-building. A crucial question concerns 'epistemological privilege'. If women have a different perspective, is this the outcome of their oppressed position, or is it a particular kind of understanding which has authenticity, a valid alternative to the understanding that comes out of male experience? On this issue feminists differ. Socialist feminists tend to argue that the 'alternative' understanding that women seem to have – based on connection, empathy, holism, subjectivism – comes out of being an oppressed group. Such perceptions of the world come from being 'underneath'. Women share this perspective with other oppressed groups, and there is nothing specifically 'feminine' about it. Another version of this view is that women have been deprived of their 'own' voice, and can see things only through the lens of the patriarchy. So if women accept the idea of differences, however much these differences are re-evaluated and made positive, this must necessarily reflect the model imposed by the dominant group: so far from a different perspective being an 'epistemological privilege', it may come close to a 'happy slave' mentality. It would follow that once women attain recognised equal status with men, such a perspective would disappear. This view is entirely consistent with the belief that the prevailing concept of rationality is not problematic, and that women should be able to join the Rationality Club.[12]

Other feminists do claim epistemological privilege. Some radical feminists, for example, subscribe to essential sex difference, and to a different experience which is exclusively female. The task is not to get men to share this, nor to extend the conception of rationality. It is to recognise the validity of difference, and how doing so undermines or replaces the orthodox masculine world of rationality, at least for women. A less essentialist feminist view makes a plea for a more pluralist rationality. According to this perspective, women's Otherness comes out of different experience which leads to development of alternative perspectives. These perspectives sensitise women to the limitations and inconsistencies of the dominant viewpoint. But also, because women, in some ways, are free from the need to constrain their rationality within that narrow mould, they can explore and develop other perspectives. Ultimately, this may contribute to a pluralistic rationality which both sexes can share.

Notes

1. P. Bourdieu, *Outline of a Theory of Practice*, Cambridge: Cambridge University Press, 1977.
2. R. Walden and V. Walkerdine, *Girls and Mathematics: From primary to*

    secondary schooling, Bedford Way Papers 24, London: Heinemann, 1985; V. Walkerdine, *Counting Girls Out*, London: Virago, 1989.

3. Rupert Brooke, quoted in C. Hassall, *Rupert Brooke: A biography*, London: Faber & Faber, 1964.

4. W. R. Kramer, Hansard, 1906.

5. I. A. Richards, *The Philosophy of Rhetoric*, Oxford: Oxford University Press, 1936; G. Lakoff and M. Johnson, *Metaphors We Live By*, Chicago: University of Chicago Press, 1980.

6. L. B. Halstead, *Hunting the Past*, London: Hamish Hamilton, 1982.

7. R. J. Blumenschine and J. A. Cavallo, 'Scavenging and human evolution', *Scientific American*, **267(4)**, pp. 90–7, October 1992.

8. There are inumerable examples of this, but one of the most amusing is A. M. Ludovici, *Woman: A vindication*, London: Constable & Co., 1926.

9. E. Wilson, *Women and the Welfare State*, London: Tavistock, 1977; W. Beveridge, *Report on the Social Insurance and Allied Services*, Cmnd 6404, London: HMSO, 1943.

10. Aristotle, *De Generatione Animalium*, trans. A. Platt, Oxford: Clarendon Press, 1910; Aristotle, *Metaphysics*, in R. McKeon (ed.), *The Basic Works of Aristotle*, New York: Random House, 1971.

11. S. de Beauvoir, *The Second Sex*, trans. H. M. Parshley, London: Jonathan Cape, 1953.

12. Especially L. Segal, *Is the Future Female?*, London: Virago, 1987.

Chapter 2: Making sense of the world: Imagery, metaphor and rhetoric

I used the example of Man the Hunter as an illustration of ways we use metaphor and image to make sense of the world. In *The Blind Watchmaker*, Richard Dawkins writes:

> The human mind is an inveterate analogiser. We are compulsively drawn to see meaning in slight similarities between very different processes. I spent much of a day in Panama watching two teeming colonies of leafcutter ants fighting, and my mind irresistibly compared the limb-strewn battlefield to pictures I had seen of Passchendaele. I could almost hear the guns and see the smoke.[1]

We saw how the metaphor of Man as Hunter gives us a script, a set of rules for male behaviour, motives, skills and – most importantly – relations with others. This script is understood by all members of the culture; any male who chooses to adopt that persona will be interpreted accurately. The metaphor does not only make an analogy, it provides an explanation for the behaviour. The individual who has 'fox-like cunning' is interpreted as having other fox-like behaviours; by making the comparison we extend the range of interpretation, going beyond the surface information and drawing on material that is inherent in the metaphor.

The supposed relationship between the evolutionary past and the behaviour of the present provides a theory which explains why man is a hunter. Behaviour found today is a function of the behaviour, motivation, relationships and skills associated with our evolutionary heritage. We are no longer saying 'It's *as if* it were so'; we are saying 'It is so, but translated into the modern context'. Man is not *like* a hunter; man *is* a hunter. In the case of Man the Hunter there is the further element: scientific legitimacy. As a popular theory of man's origins it has a long cultural heritage – it was a common metaphor of nineteenth-century poets. But it has now taken on, in the twentieth century, the aura of science. The script for being a hunter, a metaphoric role, has become an explanation of the cause and function of that behaviour.

Drawing an analogy means seeing similarities between apparently unrelated things. An analogy shades into metaphor when the comparison moves from 'as if' to making equivalences, and the metaphor's characteristics start to set the agenda for asking questions. So if we say the entrepreneur is *like* a hunter, this may set us on the path to finding comparisons and similarities. If we say man *is* a hunter, we are effectively enclosing the whole concept of man in 'hunterness'. If we say the mind is *like* a computer, we seek similarities; if we say the mind *is* a computer, we become tempted to ask only those questions about its functions that would arise from asking how a computer works, and fail to notice other questions that would arise, for example, if we saw the mind metaphorically as a library.

Children become skilled in the use and understanding of metaphor very early. Ellen Winner has shown that preschool children actually create their own original metaphors as tools for making sense.[2] Indeed, the innovative preschooler can make vivid efforts to express meaning; my daughter, at the age of three, said she had 'fizzy feet' – meaning the more conventional metaphor of pins and needles. Once children reach middle childhood, they effectively use the normal metaphors of the culture – they have learnt the official models for analogy. They are able to use metaphor as a tool of both personal thought and communication.

Richard Dawkins's example shows a trained observer finding metaphor and analogy useful as tools for making sense. Analogy is as important for innovation in science as it is in the growing understanding of the four-year-old. As Dawkins says, scientific advances often 'come about because some clever person spotted an analogy between a subject that was already understood, and another still mysterious subject'.[3]

Our metaphors are embedded in our culture, and we draw upon the conventional wisdom and symbols of our time. The social roles available for metaphor change; Shakespeare had justices, murderers and whores, but we had to wait until the nineteenth century for detectives and dope fiends. Contemporary gadgets and mechanical devices have always stimulated analogy and metaphor. Descartes was fascinated by the automata that worked the fountains in the gardens of Paris, and by the mechanical toys of his time. Scientific advances themselves spawn major metaphors. When Richard Owen defined dinosaurs in 1842 he gave the world access to a whole new repertoire of monsters, and metaphors for chaos, struggle, catastrophe and extinction.[4]

Metaphor is important for change. A new idea becomes a frame for analogy and explanation in an extraordinarily wide range of fields. Dawkins argues that Darwin's theory of evolution took on the status of metaphor and was applied extensively – to 'the changing form of the universe, to developmental "stages" of human civilisations, in fashions in skirt lengths'. Many scientific developments in this century have transformed the metaphors people use to make sense of everyday life; relativity, computers, lasers, all transformed the metaphors of how things might work, in fields way beyond their original application. The French psychologist Serge Moscovici has described how the concepts of psychoanalysis have permeated French culture and ordinary beliefs about the mind.[5] The opening-up of the Americas in the sixteenth century made possible the very idea of 'new worlds'; John Donne even used the metaphor for his mistress: 'O my America! my new-found-land'.

Metaphors, therefore, are a part of ordinary explanation or lay theory. In everyday life we use metaphors as models of how things work, for how things should be valued, and how they relate to other things. The assumption behind ideas of 'ordinary explanation', 'folk model' or 'lay theory' is that the individual actively constructs meaning, but does so in a social context, interacting with others and their social worlds. We decode events and experiences in order to make sense of them. What counts as 'sense' depends upon our implicit theories of how things work, how things ought to be, and what is appropriate. An individual has a repertoire of schemas and lay theories; which one is drawn upon in a particular situation depends on the context and the individual's interpretation of cues. An individual may have a schema of Man the Hunter, but he or she may also have a schema of Man as Scientist – just as useful, but with very different implications. Which is invoked depends on context.

Why do we need to think of this process in terms of 'theory'? We can see how it works in the use of the Man the Hunter metaphor. There are basically three ways of interpreting experience: that what is happening is *entirely natural and normal*; that what we are experiencing is *an anomaly*, a deviation, from what is to be expected; and that what is happening is *quite new and outside our experience*. What we choose to explain is what we deem it necessary to explain. The normal, the natural, are taken for granted. They are part of the accepted world; any explanations we give will be designed to assert their necessity. So, when Man the Hunter's characteristics are seen as normal for males in our culture, they will be explained as functional to present-day male role requirements (defence, family support, sexual effectiveness) and will have the bonus that they also served the male role in evolutionary history. Even the negative aspects of Man the Hunter – his aggression, his promiscuity, his reluctance to take responsibility – are explained in the same functional terms: they may be inconvenient, but they are not surprising; indeed, in the long run they may even have survival value.

Mostly, however, we find it necessary to explain the anomalous, the unusual, the deviant, the surprising. We do this mainly by reference to the same theories that explain the taken-for-granted: the anomalous has occurred because something has gone awry, contingencies have created something out of the ordinary – accident, divine intervention, faulty upbringing or genes. The language used to describe the deviation itself reflects the departure from the norm, the prototype. George Lakoff points out that our very language defines something as anomalous; 'housewife' is a prototypical role, as is 'mother'. 'Working mother' is an expression which indicates that something anomalous is happening; 'mothers' do not 'work'. The prototype – the norm – transmits certain information; the additional information warns the listener, in effect, not to make the assumptions implied by the prototype.[6]

In dealing with the novel and the uncertain, familiar images and metaphors are invoked to make sense of the unfamiliar. But novel ideas may themselves be developed through applying metaphor and analogy in original ways. It is generally true that change and innovation begin when we take seriously the possibility that an anomaly might require a new explanation, that there are limitations in our normal way of thinking, rather than seeing the anomaly as a mistake, or as an isolated deviation. Persuading people to change their lay social theories means persuading them to take notice of the unusual. This is true even within science; major breakthroughs come from taking the anomaly seriously, noticing it and seeking a novel explanation.

Obviously, schemas and scripts of lay social theory are not constructed by the individual alone. The culture delineates and, indeed, limits what schemas are available; within the culture are repertoires of schemas and scripts to which the individual has access.

Illness as a case study of metaphor

Explanations of illness are an interesting example. In Western society we rarely attribute illness to divine retribution; when this was done in relation to AIDS, the ensuing outcry demonstrated that it contravened the accepted models for rational explanation. But this outcry was also about what should be legitimate *moral* boundaries – it was deemed inappropriate to regard all AIDS victims as responsible for their illness. The dominant schemas for explaining illness in Western culture are contagion and vulnerability. Contagion implies an alien biological form entering the body; it may occur in conjunction with vulnerability. Both contagion and vulnerability seem value-neutral, but in fact they may be seen as self-induced, the consequence of carelessness or over-indulgence, which brings in a moral element.

A historical example of illness metaphor comes from Nicholas Culpeper. In his seventeenth-century *Complete Herbal* he argued that health in-volved recognising the concept of balance, within the body and between the body and the forces of the planets. The functions of healing plants, therefore, included both the chemical process of restoring the body's internal balance, and also participation in a wider cosmic balance. Herbs were governed by astrological forces, and there were correct times for harvesting them.[7] We retain the idea of 'balance' in modern conceptions of health and illness, particularly with regard to the self's responsibility for avoiding vulnerability, but we also apply it to chemical processes (such as diet) or psychological states (such as the avoidance of stress).

Modern metaphors of illness have been investigated in particular by Susan Sontag, and by Claudine Herzlich, who studied French people's beliefs about the causes of illness.[8] She found that although they were fully aware of germs and contagion, the French attached greater importance to toxicity, which includes both pollution and vulnerability. Both contain an element of personal responsibility and control. One can control internal pollution by refraining from smoking and drinking alcohol, and one may control external pollution by choosing where to live. The former implies a moral dimension; the latter does not. Thus, French people have access to an official medical schema of illness, but they also share an alternative schema. Yet even though this departs from orthodoxy on certain points, it still retains an assumption of scientific explanation and rational causality. Since Herzlich's book was published in 1973, the growth of alternative medicine and, in particular, increased preoccupation with 'natural' products and eating habits, have strengthened pollution metaphors in health and illness.

Susan Sontag contrasts conceptions of illnesses where there is a metaphor of 'harmony with Nature' in relations with the physical world, and where the metaphor is of Nature as 'chaos which has to be appeased'. In writing of cancer, she says:

> The disease is often experienced as a form of demonic possession – tumours are 'malignant' or 'benign', like forces – and many terrified cancer patients are disposed to seek out faith healers, to be exorcised . . . . For the more sophisticated, cancer signifies the rebellion of the injured ecosphere; Nature taking revenge on a wicked technocratic world.[9]

So a curiously medieval view of cancer does not feel inconsistent with a modern view that cancer is caused by environmental factors and pollution; it is a disease for which we as a society are responsible.

The metaphor of loss of control extends to descriptions of the disease itself. Tuberculosis – also known as consumption – was prevalent during the development of capitalism; it was described as 'a pathology of energy, a disease of the will', at a time when rapid expansion needed boundless energy: 'Energy, like savings, can be depleted, can be run out or used up, through reckless expenditure. The body will start "consuming" itself, will "waste away".'[10] Today's image of cancer is of energy outstripping control and regulation, at a time when overproduction and lack of environmental control are causes of destruction: 'The language used to describe cancer evokes a different economic catastrophe; that of unregulated, abnormal, incoherent growth. The tumour has energy, not the patient; "it" is out of control.'[11]

These are not only lay metaphors; experts also use the metaphor of growth and restraint. Metaphors are part of a cultural context; metaphors resonate, make sense, across separate domains of experience which are not obviously related. That which is explained here by reference to other metaphors becomes itself a metaphor. Cancer (and formerly tuberculosis) are themselves metaphors for evil, for subversion, for rot in the body politic. The explanations of their growth, and means for their eradication, are the metaphors drawn from the disease model.

In the light of this, it is interesting to consider how alternative medicine uses metaphors in dealing with cancer. The Bristol Cancer Centre provides additional alternative treatment for people who are already receiving conventional medicine for cancer. A key message is that individuals take control of their own cancer, feel *in charge of their bodies*, to give their bodies the ability to fight the cancer. This model of cancer is somewhat different from the conventional medical one; external pollutants are seen as contributing to the disease, but the patient may reverse this process and prevent future vulnerability. Something may be 'out of control' – at least biochemically – but the chaos and inevitability normally associated with this are not acknowledged, and the patient's power to exercise control is emphasised. The model of individual empowerment extends to the doctor–patient relationship. The impotence and passivity normally implied for the patient with the 'doctor-as-expert' role is removed by encouraging the patient to take control. But the metaphor of taking control is not only the usual one of power assertion and military imagery; it is *ownership*. Patients are encouraged to 'own' their cancer, and to own their bodies – which have been removed from their possession both by the cancer and by the conventional medical system.[12]

In a more recent book, Susan Sontag has argued that the metaphors of AIDS have altered some basic conceptions of illness.[13] Cancer is becoming less stigmatised, less 'evil', partly because, as she says: 'It seems that societies need to have one illness which becomes identified with evil, and attaches blame to its 'victims', but it is hard to be obsessed with more than one.'[14] AIDS is rich in metaphor. A 'foreigner' agent enters the body, transforming formerly defensive cells into agents that attack the body itself – a scenario ripe for paranoid imagery. Whereas in cancer cells are overproduced, in AIDS cells die, leaving the body vulnerable to the ravages of other infection.

AIDS has other elements which cancer lacks. First, it is infectious, so it is people who 'pollute' – rather than the carcinogenic environment. Secondly, in Europe and the United States it is associated in the popular mind with morality; those who suffer from AIDS are already, as Sontag says, the 'pariahs'. 'Gay plague' tabloid catchphrases, intemperate talk about God's punishment, and pleas for the incarceration of victims express a moral panic which is enhanced rather than diminished by the existence of 'innocent victims' – haemophiliacs, or children pricked by addicts' waste needles. Their innocence is contrasted with the depravity of those AIDS victims who are deemed personally responsible for their fate. In 1989 an Australian prostitute who was HIV positive was 'sentenced' to incarceration in a hospital; she was not tried under criminal law for plying her trade without adequate protection, but detained on grounds of public health.

Sontag points out that AIDS has revived the 'plague' metaphor. An 'epidemic' is about illness, usually contagious, which is out of control, and 'epidemic' can be applied to any phenomenon which is seen to be analogous. A plague may not even be of epidemic proportions, but it has an apocalyptic quality, a presumed certainty of death and a terrible uncertainty about contagion. It is interesting that when AIDS first came to public awareness liberal opinion focused on the potential 'epidemic' element – AIDS was a dangerous disease which anyone might get if they were not careful. In contrast, more reactionary perspectives isolated the 'plague', built metaphoric boundaries around the depraved groups of subversives who undermine 'our' health and 'our' morality – and so denied their own vulnerability.

The apocalyptic metaphors of AIDS are new, but perhaps they owe a little to the approach of the second millennium. They have replaced the fear of nuclear war which showed a striking upsurge in the early 1980s.[15] An apocalypse has all the elements of chaos, an unpredictable event which comes from 'out there'; it fits a model of a world out of human control, governed by forces beyond our technology. But it also has a moral force; even if we are not punished for our sins in a modern Sodom and Gomorrah, we have let the whirlwind into our world through failure to control that always problematic 'energy' – sexuality. Even if we confine ourselves to heterosexual relations, the more 'uncontrolled' we are, the more likely that somewhere in the chain of connection there may be contagion.

It is interesting to compare the effect of Herpes and the effect of AIDS, When people began to recognise the full impact of AIDS, some sophisticates made the wry joke 'Remember Herpes?' – meaning, of course, that Herpes, the great 'scare' of the 1970s, suddenly seemed innocuous. In fact Herpes was always an epidemic, never a plague. Initially it seemed controllable through the use of barrier contraception (at a time when such methods were very unfashionable), but it then became controllable because it was – at least in males – very visible in eruption and predictable in its course; a little abstinence was all that was required of responsible people. It even became socially acceptable to admit that one had Herpes; badges saying 'I have Herpes' appeared which, perhaps, had a metaphoric parallel with the red camellia worn every month by Marguerite Gautier. So AIDS and Herpes contrast dramatically as examples of plague versus epidemic, and of sexuality as the agent of apocalypse versus sexuality as the controlled pleasure of the civilised Epicurean.

Metaphor in action: making sense of the world

These examples illustrate the role of metaphor in the way we think of illness, and how our beliefs about illness become metaphors for other things. Metaphors, in effect, provide schemas, models for explanation, and models for what things are connected and how the connections function. A metaphor transforms meaning. Common metaphors are shared; meaning is easily communicated through them, and the novel is easily made familiar. Metaphors help us to communicate familiar ideas; they help us to generate novel ideas, and facilitate their transmission. Metaphors provide frameworks within which we are able to think, and to communicate. Metaphors are components of lay social theory which set the agenda for the way we will conceptualise the issues, and for the solutions we will find. Incidentally, I shall concentrate on metaphor, and to a lesser extent on metonymy; other tropes are important for the analysis of rhetoric, but I would argue that metaphor and metonymy have specific psychological properties relating to their role in both cognition and communication.

Metaphors are frames: They serve as categories for grouping things. An example is dualistic thinking. Western children learn very early to categorise in terms of dualities. They learn to think in terms of 'either–or', and that they must choose because the existence of one implies the negation of the other. 'Negation' may mean that if you have the chocolate cake you can't have the ice cream, or it may mean that if one thing is good then its opposite is bad. Thesis and antithesis order the world such that A is defined by being not-B.

Polarity or dualism is a common principle for categorisation: light versus dark, public versus private, mind versus body, rational versus intuitive, black versus white. The effect is that once symbols, metaphors or images have been attached to one pole, by implication their negative becomes attached to the other: things of the body become other than things of the mind. Non-white people, in certain social contexts (such as Britain), become Black – whatever the diversity within that category. We have seen that masculinity and femininity, with all their associations, get mapped on to other dualities. Duality is not, of course, the only category system; there are trinities. Where there are metaphors of trinities as well as dualities, then dualism is not necessarily a limiting frame. But frames become specific. Things to which dualistic categories are appropriate do not also attract trinities, and vice versa.

Hierarchy is another example of a metaphoric frame. An instance of hierarchy as a limiting metaphor is in thinking about competition and achievement. A race is *competition between persons*, where one person wins because they are better, or brighter, or faster. But if individual achievement is conceptualised as climbing a ladder, or reaching a target, competition – and hierarchy – are not involved. If all the available metaphors for success imply a hierarchy, then competition becomes equated with achievement.

Metaphors are models for mechanisms or processes: As in Richard Dawkins's examples, analogies between different things imply that explanations of one are explanations of another. There are many examples in scientific progress. Darwin did not create the metaphor of evolution which became so pervasive, but he made it accessible to the lay mind. In his own work, it was the application of Malthus's metaphor of 'the struggle for existence' to his own ideas of adaptation which gave him the key to natural selection. He also used the model of a 'branching tree'.[16] Without such a model, conceptualising evolution would be difficult; how could one conceptualise progress and diversification within the earlier metaphor of the 'Great Chain of Being'? Even Lamarck's 'ladder', although it implied progress, could not account for diversification.[17] In cognitive science the computer metaphor has enormous importance.[18]

Metaphors carry evaluative connotations: Certain metaphors are widely used in a way that is not apparently metaphoric, yet they still carry meaning. The word 'open' for example, can be applied, with exactly the same meaning of accessibility, lack of boundaries and lack of hidden elements, to people, ideas, arguments, interactions, sources of information, organisational systems, structures both human and physical – and so forth. More problematic are examples where different evaluation applies to different topics; an example is 'hard' (as opposed to 'soft'). Hard science, hard evidence, are 'good' things. A 'hard man' has macho qualities; a 'hard person', on the other hand, is usually not fulfilling our assumptions of true personhood, which include a 'soft' heart. There is strong metaphoric association between hardness and masculinity – but what exactly is the underlying 'hardness' presumed to be? Do toughness and solidity contrast with malleability, or is there a connotation of sexual potency?

Metaphors of roles constrain and prescribe: The role of Man the Hunter defines man and limits the ways in which his behaviours should be explained. The role of mother is similar. The actual term 'woman as mother' is not often used in the same way as Man as Hunter; nevertheless, it is a metaphor that dominates models and explanations of women's behaviour. Girls' behaviour in doll-play or care of siblings is 'explained' as potential 'mothering'. Appropriate areas of work for women can be interpreted or prescribed by convention as an extension of the mother's nurturing qualities. Women's sexual motivation is sometimes even explained as really a desire for parenting. Similar overinclusion happens when the role of 'father' is equated with the role of leader; it prescribes a certain style of leadership which may, in fact, be functionally quite inappropriate in the context. The metaphor affects interpretation and explanation of behaviour, and assumption of what is expected. Metaphors of role are culturally significant; they both limit and prescribe the options for interpreting behaviour.

Metaphors explain relationship: In a dualistic metaphor the implied relationship between the two aspects or poles is negation. The relations between things are key elements of explanation; knowing how something 'works' means understanding the functional interrelatedness of its components. If dualism implies negation and antithesis, then it is difficult to conceptualise a duality in harmony or in synthesis. Within a clockwork or mechanical model, for example, there can be only a certain kind of relationship of physical events. One part must 'act' and, in doing so, trigger activation or cessation in another part. Parts may operate independently of each other, but still according to similar principles of causality. Where mechanical parts are 'in harmony' or 'in tune', it is because they are in fact 'in synchrony' – activated to the same time sequence, or 'in gear' – literally linked, so that the action of one part affects the action of the other.

The musical metaphor reflects another kind of relationship, one much closer to organic metaphors. 'Harmony' implies that two systems or parts of systems have autonomous existence and autonomous energy, but operate together. Organic models, therefore, are different from clockwork models; there is a wider range of options for relating, and which parts may relate. Furthermore, there is potential for adaptation or growth, which is not implied in the clockwork model. Yet another model of relationship is chemical; here the interaction of two elements leads to their transformation into something altogether new.

The operation of relationships is clearer in physical examples, but we can extend the examples to the social world. Relations between men and women depend very much on whether the metaphor is derived from the model of dualism and polarity, or from an organic model of separate systems which have a potential for adaptive cooperation. If, like Tennyson, we conceptualise men and women as two separate parts of a dualistic system, then necessarily whatever man is, woman must be its antithesis.

Metaphors of the relationship of the human being and the physical world hang upon ideas of control and rights of possession. The rise of Green consciousness has brought changing metaphors of the human being's relationship to the environment and the physical world. There have been, historically, three main models of this relationship. One model is that the external world is a dangerous place with unpredictable forces at work, outside human control. Another model is that benign and organic Mother Nature will provide for humankind, so long as we remain in harmony with her. A third model, evolved in the seventeenth century, formed the basis of the scientific revolution, and has pervaded Western scientific thinking ever since: the metaphor that the earth is made of mechanical rather than organic forces, which can be controlled by human reason and technology.

These models and metaphors are not confined to concerns about laying waste or dumping waste; like other frames and models, they are translated across domain boundaries. Metaphors of 'mastery' of the environment and 'mastery of one's fate' both assume control and manipulation. People who see the environment as organic and holistic tend also to use similar metaphors in human relationships, in medicine and in problem-solving.

Metaphors of mind and thought processes are not confined to psychology and philosophy. Every person – consciously or not – reflects upon and tries to make sense of the elusive process of thought. Everyday metaphors of thinking are rich – drawing, for example, on eating (assimilating, digesting, swallowing), on fighting (struggling, conquering, battling), on the sorting of physical materials (teasing out, unravelling, weaving, separating strands). The mind itself may be a container (holding everything), a machine or computer (which mechanically processes ideas), an organic thing (which uses eating or growth metaphors), a conduit or hydraulic system (things run through, flow through or well up) or a dark or wild physical place (haunted by thoughts, which spring out of nowhere).[19]

Models of mind also overlap with metaphors of mechanism, and metaphors of relationships with the physical world. They echo the contrast between organic models of human beings in harmony with living nature, and mechanical models of humans controlling nature through technology. These are reflected in the question of objectivism versus subjectivism. 'I know because I am part of, and tuned into, something' presupposes some form of organic model, and knowing as *participative experience*; the knower must in some sense be in a relationship with that which is known. This is subjectivism. Objectivism, on the other hand, requires a more mechanical model of mind: 'I know because I am detached from and can observe without being part.' This is more in tune with a machine-like analysis.

These categories of metaphor show how metaphors operate as models and frames, and also how metaphors in one domain of interpretation spill over into others. In these ordinary metaphors and the ordinary explanations they imply, there is a very rich repertoire of lay social theories, schemas and scenarios. Furthermore, these examples also illustrate not only how metaphors are involved in innovation, but how they become part of common-sense, ordinary language and taken-for-granted ideas; today's metaphor is tomorrow's received wisdom.

Metaphors and science

I explored the workings of metaphor in lay social theories of illness. Another rich domain of metaphor is scientific thought and, indeed, lay understanding of science. A major revolution of thought, and a dramatic change of metaphor, occurred in the seventeenth century. The old model of an organic nature, a cosmos in balance with which humankind was in harmony, was replaced by a new model which took the metaphor of the machine, especially clockwork, and applied it not only to the cosmos but eventually to the whole domain of human thought. In fact, although the machine model became highly influential, the old organic model stayed around as part of the cultural repertoire of metaphors, and continued to underlie much lay – if not scientific – theory. There has recently been a resurgence of a 'living' metaphor of nature. As the historian Carolyn Merchant says, ecological or Green movements have 'emphasised the need to live within the cycles of nature, as opposed to the exploitative, linear mentality of forward progress'.[20] This very sentence expresses some key metaphors. 'Living within' nature – as opposed to controlling or operating upon it. 'Cycles' – which are natural and predictable, though not controllable. Mechanical cycles are controllable by the operator – one does not 'live within' such a cycle, and one changes it if it is inconvenient. A 'linear model' implies the absence of cycles; it implies a starting point with a goal, and the trajectory to that goal. 'Forward progress' – a tautology – is an accepted 'good thing' in our culture, but our present-day conception of progress itself depends upon active human control and self-improvement.

In the seventeenth century, the idea of Earth as 'nurturing mother' coexisted with the idea of wild and uncontrollable forces in the cosmos. Both models applied equally to the relationship of people with nature, and relations between people in society. Merchant describes it thus:

> A designed hierarchical order existed in the cosmos and society corresponding to the organic integration of the parts of the body – a projection of the human being on to the cosmos . . . . A second image was based on nature as an active unity of opposites in dialectical tension. A third was the Arcadian image of nature as benevolent, peaceful, rustic.[21]

These models could variously imply the maintenance of existing social and natural order, change towards a new ideal, or retreat from the problems of urban life. But the point was that nature, and the metaphors of nature, assumed a living being or living models, and the metaphors of society equally drew upon organic metaphors. Harmony – and order – depended upon 'living within' the rhythms of the organic. Destroying the balance and harmony led to disorder. Knowledge, and the power given by knowledge, came from communion with God and nature. Although such a model was generally used to justify the status quo, it was also possible to change nature, and society, by organic cooperation with it.

The development of mechanistic metaphors had far-reaching implications. Mechanical clocks were developed in the fourteenth century, and came to form an important part of the iconography. As early as 1370 Nicole Oresme, Bishop of Lisieux compared God to a divine clockmaker. In 1605, Johan Kepler argued that the 'celestial machine is to be likened not to a divine organism but to a clockwork'.[22] A few decades later, René Descartes wrote:

> And as a clock, composed of wheels and counterweights, observes not the laws of nature when it is ill-made, and points out the hours

incorrectly, than when it satisfies the desire of the maker in every respect; so likewise if the body of man be considered as a kind of machine, so made up and composed of bones, nerves, muscles, veins, blood and skin that although there were in it no mind, it would still exhibit the same motions which it at present manifests involuntarily.[23]

He also argued that we should 'render ourselves the masters and possessors of method'. A mechanical model can both be controlled and control; the observer who is detached from that which is observed, rather than a part of it, can operate upon that which is observed. If that which is observed is seen not as a living thing but as a mechanical thing governed by laws, then the constraints on what one can do to it are practical constraints of power, not the constraints of ethics. The Romans, for example, were ambivalent about mining, seeing it as an attack on earth, a living thing.

The metaphor of the machine became a model for human organisation also. Technological intervention, rather than cooperation with the organism, became the mechanism for change and cure. A metaphor of potential control, intervention, and the concept of 'laws' facilitated ideas of control which were not possible earlier. The idea of an ordered, essentially benevolent nature coexisted with a view of nature as wild and untameable forces. Scientific advances undermined traditional secure beliefs, and contributed to this sense of uncertainty. There was therefore a need for control; humankind had lost dominion over nature with the Fall, and needed, according to Francis Bacon, to regain that control through the enslavement of nature to human needs.[24] Through artifice and technology, humankind could control the 'perverseness, violence and forwardness' of nature. Later, Thomas Hobbes applied a mechanical model of economy to counter the disorderly, competitive and hostile nature of society.[25]

These are *metaphors of mechanism and process metaphors* – metaphors of how things work, and of the relationship between the human being and the physical and social world. By the middle of the seventeenth century nature become conceived of as modular, made up of discrete parts, and motion was transferred from part to part, an atomistic process which contrasted with the holism model implied in an organic metaphor. But this was not confined to the physical world; conceptions of mind changed:

The rise of mechanism laid the foundation for a new synthesis of the cosmos, society and the human being, construed as ordered systems of mechanical parts subject to governance by law and to predictability through deductive reasoning. A new concept of the self as a rational master of the passions housed in a machine-like body began to replace the concept of the self as an integral part of a closeknit harmony of organic parts united to the cosmos and society.[26]

I have dwelt on changing metaphors in the seventeenth century because there was at that time such a revolution in thought, lay and scientific theory, and in metaphor, in so many aspects of life. But other periods have shown equally dramatic metaphoric change. In the nineteenth century, for example, new metaphors of the relationship between humans and the natural world drew upon geology and evolution; these issues were under public discussion long before Charles Darwin and Alfred Russel Wallace identified the mechanisms of evolution. People were preoccupied by questions about the human being's relationship with the Creator, and the implications for free will and responsibility of a continuity between humans and animals. The emerging fossil evidence – and, indeed, developments in physiology which directly touched upon the mind–body relationship – challenged both conventional theology and lay theories which had conventional theological assumptions. But the effect was not to undermine theology; instead, it was to extend the notion of a 'Grand Design' to a greater complexity; to enhance, rather than diminish, the role of the Creator.[27]

The seventeenth-century upheavals did not occur without challenge and reaction. The idea of a fundamental organic unity, even of life permeating all things (vitalism), continued to influence not only the layperson but also the scientist. Lively debates between atomism and holism continued; the latter did not die out. Since the emergence of social sciences, especially psychology, this debate has continued and generated different strands of explanation. But one figure who countered the Cartesian model at the time, and has subsequently proved very important, was the Italian Humanist Giambattista Vico (1668–1744).[28]

Vico sustained a prolonged attack on the influence of Descartes and the sort of rationalism that was emerging from the new mechanistic tradition. In his view, the emphasis on method which accompanied this rationalism meant that no distinction was made between 'topic' and 'critique' – terms which go back to Aristotle, and were developed by Cicero. The important difference is between that which is 'discovered' or 'found' – an 'original vision' which cannot be reduced to rational deduction – and that which is analysed, divided and judged. Cartesian rationality, argued Vico, conflated the two by concentrating only on the latter and ignoring or subsuming the former in the latter. The implication of this is that we must grasp something before we can draw conclusions or make deductions from it.

This model of mind echoes current debates in cognitive psychology (and also earlier debates on pragmatism), but Vico's importance to our present argument extends beyond this for two reasons. First, Vico makes what we would call 'insight' an integral part of the rational process, not something which is tangential to it. This is a crucial difference from the Cartesian tradition. But Vico's particular importance to our understanding of lay social theory is that he saw human beings as sociable creatures, communicating and, therefore, making effective sense only if ideas could be shared. He saw pure logic merely as a monologue. The wider implication is that one can understand things only in terms of one's current historical position, or in terms of their practical usefulness. Things acquire meaning out of people's concrete relationship to them, and their efforts to cope with them. So Vico argued that we can understand other cultures and other historical periods only by a supreme effort of divesting ourselves of the assumptions of our own period and entering into an understanding of other times.[29] This position has re-emerged in social science by a variety of routes – through anthropology and cross-cultural research, and in particular through the Hegelian tradition reflected in psychology in the work of Lev Vygotsky.

Metaphor, social context and rhetoric

How does the individual develop lay social theory? We have seen how metaphors and images constitute a repertoire of schemas, scripts and scenarios which have common currency in a culture, and frame culturally shared meaning. The individual does 'make sense of the world', but not in isolation from the social world. In interaction with peers, parents and other significant persons, the individual negotiates a shared intepretation of events. The adult or older child 'scaffolds' the thought of the youngster by negotiating the space between where the child is currently at and where the more experienced person is helping them to get to.

Both individual cognition and social interaction take place within the wider social, cultural and historical context. I have used the example of illness; a child learns early the social as well as the subjective meaning of 'being ill'. It is a change in her own state which needs explanation, and it is an event which affects her social life. In the ordinary process of explaining her own illnesses and those of her acquaintances, the child will have access to some schemas but not others, or she may have access to several schemas but become aware that some are legitimate and some are not.

Even by making some things legitimate and others not, the message is conveyed that 'legitimacy' is important. Telling a child that 'sensible' people don't go out in the rain and get wet conveys several things: a model of the causes of illness, the idea that one has personal responsibility for one's vulnerability – and the importance of being 'sensible'. The child will encounter many examples which reinforce her understanding that good order and effective living are sustained by sensible people, in contrast to the chaos and failure that 'silly' or 'irresponsible' people create. If she lives in the right place or at the right historical moment, however, she may come into contact with alternative ideas – for example, that 'sensibleness' is the hallmark of the repressed and unfulfilled, and that 'living for the present' and risk-taking are the pathway to personal growth and understanding. 'Personal growth and understanding' may be desirable goals that she previously thought were attained by the route of 'being sensible'. So here is an example where the child may be exposed to conflicting theories about the achievement of a commonly valued goal.

In order fully to understand the role of metaphor and the operation of lay social theory, we must deal with rhetoric. So far, I have argued that the individual's schemas and scenarios for making sense of the world are drawn from the repertoire of cultural resources, and shown how metaphors provide not only analogies, but frameworks for inter-pretation. Being part of a social world means being able to communicate one's ideas to others. This communication is more effective if it makes an appeal to shared concepts and beliefs. Because mutual under-standing is possible only through shared metaphors and values, one's own thinking can come only – or mainly – from that which is available in the culture, the frames and models which are taken for granted and commonly understood.

Let us start with an example of rhetoric in action. There was a rather obnoxious popular song in the 1950s, sung – supposedly – by a child in that nasal lisp which combines winsome innocence with precocity:

Tell me a story, tell me a story, tell me a story,
Remember what you said.
You promised me, you said you would.
You've gotta give in so I'll be good.[30]

This song contains two very different appeals; one is morally acceptable to the average parent, the other is not, though it is a reasonable prediction about the behaviour of nauseating children who don't say 'please'. The rhetorical process in the first statement is that the child shares with the parent the value of promise-keeping; the second statement implies that both child and parent appreciate the sanctions that the child can invoke if he fails to get his own way. Alternatively, there is an implied contract between parent and child that the child will be 'good' in anticipation of rewards for being good – but enhanced by threat ('You've gotta give in'). This song uses rhetoric as a persuasive appeal (which will probably fail, because the moral validity of the first argument is outweighed by the moral invalidity of the second).

We have come to regard rhetoric with suspicion. The phrase 'empty rhetoric' (itself, of course, a rhetorical phrase) implies distrust of elegant language or emotive appeals designed to override logic. This distrust implies exactly the same distinction between rational and non-rational, objective and subjective, which is the heritage of Cartesian rationality. Truth is arrived at through logic; therefore attempts to reach truth through other means cannot meet the criteria. The act of communicating one's conclusions should, therefore, present the logic of one's reasoning, so that others may see their justification. The most extreme form of this type of communication, of course, is the scientific paper. The conviction that there is but one way to arrive at 'truth' (through individual deductive reasoning) and one acceptable way of presenting that truth persists both in popular and scientific view, despite the fact that there is an equally long and honourable tradition of arriving at truth through adversarial argumentation – the legal system, at least in Britain and the United States, reflects this. Ostensibly, scientific activity also includes this – the idea of proof and counter-proof is, in principle, adversarial, leading to competing interpretations of data.

However, the tradition that is reflected in the ideas of the philosopher Karl Popper takes a different view. According to Popper, scientific progress depends upon hypotheses being falsified.[31] Hence a crucial experiment should establish the truth or otherwise of a theory. As an ideal, this is consistent with the Cartesian rationalist tradition. In practice, very few experiments serve this clinching function; indeed, experimenters tend to adjust and modify their models rather than throw them out when their experiments fail. The – vital – distinction comes down to whether one is discovering a truth or generating a better argument.

The art of persuasion is the art of tuning into appropriate images and shared assumptions, manipulating the conceptual and evaluative responses of the listener so that they come to the conclusions intended by the persuader; Mark Antony's funeral speech in Shakespeare's *Julius Caesar* is a classic rhetorical piece in this sense. In this view, rhetoric is a linguistic activity which facilitates and manipulates concepts. Any act of communication must involve some use of analogy, metaphor or imagery to convey meaning. It follows that it is impossible to convey meaning without going outside the substantive subject, without drawing upon shared images. The logic of this is that thought itself must depend on culturally shared assumptions. It is here that we see the integration of metaphors and rhetoric. The pursuit of truth is a social process. A basic principle of rhetorical analysis is that intellectual progress depends on argumentation.

Rhetoric is not just beautiful, emotive language bearing no relationship to 'fact' or 'logic', designed to persuade, and depending for its effect upon the shared assumptions of speaker and audience. Its classical meaning is increasingly being recognised as a fundamental attribute of thought. According to Platonic tradition, it was assumed that there were absolute truths and absolute values, which could be arrived at by thought – the search for 'essences'. While there could be differences of opinion, there could not be differences of fact or truth. Truth was 'discovered', not 'discussed'.

Michael Billig has traced the history of rhetoric and demonstrated why we need to take it seriously. Billig returns to the rhetoric of the Humanists and their ancestors, Cicero, Quintilian and, ultimately, Aristotle.[32] The battle between logic and rhetoric long predates Descartes; Zeno used the metaphor of a closed fist (logic) and an open palm (rhetoric). Billig cites Protagoras, who attacked the Platonic tradition. Protagoras propounded the view that there were two sides to every question – which upset the notion of absolute fact. It follows that truth can be arrived at only by argumentation, the presentation of alternative perspectives – necessarily requiring rhetoric and social communication.

Analysis of rhetoric, therefore, requires substantially more than the analysis of the persuasive communication. Recognising the existence of two perspectives implies that for every position – *logos* – there is an opposing one, an *anti-logos*. This conception does more than present an alternative viewpoint; it places upon the holder of the *logos* the obligation to defend it against the *anti-logos* position. Therefore an idea is not formulated in isolation, but in response to, or reaction against, another idea. As Billig says, any communication can be decoded in terms of what it is an argument *against*, as well as what it is explicitly an argument *in favour of*. The disputational nature of rhetoric becomes apparent when there is a need for justification – when something must be justified because it cannot be taken for granted. What is not being taken for granted, and what is being justified, give clues to what is being defended against: 'To understand an individual philosopher's argument, one must understand the social argument, or debate, in which it is situated . . . 'one should ask oneself, not "what is this about?" but "what is this attacking?"'[33]

In ordinary conversation – for example, in political or other interest-group discourse – people are skilled at decoding a situation which they perceive as 'rhetorical'. But the very scepticism about rhetoric in such a context is a consequence of a general belief that there is a path to absolute truth and solid evidence which cannot be gainsaid – and that persuaders are somehow dodging this and trying to pull the wool over the audience's eyes. Such sophistication is not so apparent where the *anti-logos* is not self-evident; we tend not to challenge experts.

Billig's examination of the way rhetoric actually works in ordinary discourse illustrates how extensively the process of communication depends. on shared cultural assumptions, schemas, categories and explanations. He argues that any statement presupposes shared know- ledge of premises and a tacit assumption of what is, and what is not, taken for granted – both facts and values. If something is being *justified*, this indicates that it is perceived as problematic. If something is being *explained*, this indicates that it is not assumed to be shared knowledge. If an example is used in justification or explanation, it is presumed that this example is common ground between speaker and listener. What is left out indicates what is taken for granted. So analysing rhetorical language gives some of the most comprehensive clues to underlying lay social theories.

An example of this process is the shortened syllogism, the 'enthymeme' of Aristotle, in which the full syllogism is omitted because the culture shares the knowledge, so statements are seen as logically correct even if they are only partial. Much ordinary discourse takes place through enthymemes; we either know that fellow members of the culture share our premises, or we make the assumption that they do, even though in fact they may share only our conclusions. When the situation makes it clear that the premiss or the conclusion is not in fact shared, disputation and justification follow. Let us consider a common situation in which a great deal is implied. Here are three hypothetical exchanges between a person in authority and an underling:

1. A   It's ten thirty
    B   I went to the dentist
    A   OK

2. A   It's ten thirty
    B   I went to the dentist
    A   Oh yeah?

3. A   It's ten thirty
    B   I went to the dentist
    A   Was it an emergency?

In the first example, 'I went to the dentist' is without elaboration, read as an explanation for lateness at work, based upon the assumption that such lateness is justified and accepted in the context; this is clearly shared. In the second example, the first part of this premiss is questioned, and A is either accusing the speaker of lying or, possibly, suggesting that the socially acceptable excuse is really a euphemism for something less acceptable, such as a hangover. In the third example what is in question is the legitimacy of attending to one's health during working hours.

Understanding the rhetorical nature of thought, as well as communication, is central to the analysis of lay social theory, but it is also necessary to the analysis of social change. My argument is that changes in gender roles are about changes in the metaphors and explanations for sex difference and, indeed, of the very nature of masculinity and femininity. Such changes have taken place by confronting an existing *logos* with an *anti-logos*, and by unpacking the enthymemes which reflect – and sustain – the status quo. Partly this has been deliberate; feminist theories have challenged most basic assumptions that formed the traditional *logoi* of gender. Partly it has been contingent upon social change; for example, the sheer statistical force of the divorce rate has undermined the nuclear family norm. Even the backlash against change, and against the new rhetorics of feminism, draws upon new rhetoric; the old *logoi* are no longer either legitimate or comprehensible.

Our picture of lay social theory now includes the analysis of metaphor and rhetoric. I have illustrated how, in ordinary speech and ordinary thinking, the culturally shared metaphors, schemas and models are invoked to explain the familiar and taken-for-granted, and to communicate both shared and controversial ideas. But what happens when things change? Innovative ideas – whether in the domain of ordinary life or in the domain of scientific and intellectual advance – need to be made comprehensible. As we have seen, new ideas and explanations of newly discovered phenomena frequently rely upon an existing metaphor. But changing ideas also require changing metaphors; it is necessary to shed the old models and assumptions. Part of innovation includes realising the limitations of the old models and metaphors.

The task of change is to undermine taken-for-granted assumptions: asking questions which had hitherto not been asked, revealing through such questions that things are now problematic which hitherto were not. But it is also a matter of restocking the repertoire of metaphor and category. New models are needed in order that we can understand and justify. Billig distinguishes usefully between *changing essences* and *changing boundaries*. Changing essences means altering what is – or what, at least, is seen to be. Changing boundaries retains the conception of the essence, but alters what is included in it. Billig gives the example of changing usury laws in the sixteenth century. These did not alter the concept or evaluation of usury, but did redefine what counted as usury; only certain types of usury (no longer called usury) were permitted by law. A similar thing has happened with some sexual crimes in this century, only here the boundaries have been extended rather than reduced – as with the criminalisation of sexual harassment, and the extension of rape into marriage.

Asking the 'right' questions begins the process of redefinition by setting up an *anti-logos* against the *logos*, and by making problematic what had been shared assumptions. Setting up a new frame of reference may ultimately have such different underlying assumptions from that which it originally attacked that it is no longer in dialogue with it. In the early nineteenth century, for example, sophisticated arguments about evolution were mostly not – *pace* the Huxley–Wilberforce debate – about whether evolution theory undermined belief in God, but about what were the actual boundaries of religion and science, and how evolution theory could be seen as evidence of the greater, rather than the lesser, glory of the Creator. Another historical example concerns the legitimacy of regicide. Alan How has pointed out that before 1789, the legitimate grounds for killing a king included removing a tyrant or a madman. The revolutionaries recognised the need to have legal justification for removing Louis XVI, because the long-term reconstruction of the state depended upon an acceptable redefinition of the legal relationship between citizen and government. This turned out to be an exercise of some difficulty.[34]

Notes

1. R. Dawkins, *The Blind Watchmaker*, Essex: Longman, 1986, p. 195.
2. E. Winner, *The Point of Words*, Cambridge, MA: Harvard University Press, 1988.
3. Dawkins, *The Blind Watchmaker*, p. 195.
4. H. Torrens, 'When did the dinosaur get its name?', *New Scientist*, **134(1815)**, pp. 40–4, 4 April 1992; H. Haste, 'Dinosaur as metaphor', *Modern Geology*, **18**, pp. 347–68, 1993; R. Owen, 'On British fossil reptiles', *Report of the Eleventh Meeting of the British Association for the Advancement of Science*, London: John Murray, pp. 60–204, 1842.
5. S. Moscovici, *La Psychanalyse, son image et son public*, 2nd edn, Paris: Presses Universitaires de France, 1976.
6. G. Lakoff, *Women, Fire and Dangerous Things*, Chicago: University of Chicago Press, 1987, ch. 4.
7. N. Culpeper, *Complete Herbal*, London: Foulsham, n.d.
8. C. Herzlich, *Health and Illness: A social psychological analysis*, London: Academic Press, 1973.
9. S. Sontag, *Illness as Metaphor*, New York: Farrar, Straus & Giroux, 1977, p. 69.
10. *ibid.*, p. 62.

11. *ibid.*, pp. 62–3.

12. B. Halstead, 'The biology and philosophy of cancer', *New Humanist*, **103(2)**, pp. 17–19, 1988.

13. S. Sontag, *AIDS and Its Metaphors*, London: Allen Lane, 1988.

14. *ibid.*, p. 16.

15. H. Haste, 'Everybody's scared but life goes on: coping, defence and action in the face of nuclear threat', *Journal of Adolescence*, **12**, pp. 11–26, 1989; *International Journal of Mental Health*, **15** [whole], 1986, ed. M. Schwebel.

16. R. M. Young, *Darwin's Metaphor: Nature's place in Victorian culture*, Cambridge: Cambridge University Press, 1985; H. E. Gruber, *Darwin on Man: A psychological study of scientific creativity, together with Darwin's early and unpublished notebooks transcribed and annotated by Paul H. Barrett*, London: Wildwood Press, 1974; A. O. Lovejoy, *The Great Chain of Being: A study of the history of an idea*, Cambridge, MA: Harvard University Press, 1936 and 1964.

17. J. B. de Lamarck, *Zoological Philosophy: An exposition with regard to the natural history of animals (1809)*, trans. H. Elliott, London: Macmillan, 1914. Reprint New York: Hafner, 1963.

18. H. Gardner, *The Mind's New Science: A history of the cognitive revolution*, New York: Basic Books, 1987; D. Dennett, *Consciousness Explained*, London: Allen Lane, 1991.

19. D. E. Leary (ed.), *Metaphors in the History of Psychology*, Cambridge: Cambridge University Press, 1990; R. J. Sternberg, *Metaphors of Mind*, Cambridge: Cambridge University Press, 1990.

20. C. Merchant, *The Death of Nature: Women, ecology and the scientific revolution*, San Francisco: Harper & Row, 1980, p. xvii.

21. *ibid.*, p. 6.

22. *ibid.*, p. 129.

23. R. Descartes, 'The meditations', *in Meditations and Selections from the Principles of Philosophy*, La Salle, IL: Open Court, 1952, p. 98.

24. F. Bacon, *Works*, ed. J. Spedding, R. L. Ellis and D. D. Heath, London: Longman, 1870; 'De Augmentis', vol 4.

25. T. Hobbes, *Leviathan*, London: Andrew Crooke, 1651.

26. Merchant, *The Death of Nature*, p. 214.

27. *The Bridgewater Treatises*, especially T. Chalmers, *On the power, wisdom and goodness of God as manifested in the adaptation of external nature to the moral and intellectual constitution of Man*, London: Henry G. Bohn, 1853 (Chalmers's Dedication is dated 1833).

28. L. Pompa (ed.), *Vico: Selected writings*, Cambridge: Cambridge University Press, 1982; E. Grassi, *Rhetoric as Philosophy: The Humanist tradition*, University Park, PA: Pennsylvania State University Press, 1980.

29. Pompa (ed.), *Vico: selected writings*.

30. The author has made every effort to trace the copyright holder of this song, but with no success. She would be glad to receive information in this respect.

31. K. Popper, *Conjectures and Refutations: The growth of scientific knowledge*, London: Routledge & Kegan Paul, 1963.

32. M. Billig, *Arguing and Thinking*, Cambridge: Cambridge University Press, 1987.
33. *ibid.*, p. 92.
34. A. R. How, 'Habermas' theory of social evolution: the case of Louis XVI', Paper presented to the MOSAIC Annual Meeting, Brighton, July 1987.

Chapter 3: Describing difference

We inhabit an en-gendered world. Gender is the primary category of our social relationships. It is the first thing ascertained about us when we enter the world, and children become aware of it early in the second year of life. It is a crucial part of everyone's identity. In language, symbol and metaphor, we reflect and reproduce this primary categorisation. It is so much a part of us that we take it for granted. Indeed, it is so much a part of our world-view that we construct many folk models and lay social theories to explain and justify our conception of gender and sex difference. And we are overinclusive; because gender is a primary category for differentiation, other dualities map on to metaphors of masculinity versus femininity.

There are endless gender-marked models, symbols and metaphors, part of the cultural heritage, enshrined in folk wisdom. But our science comes out of the same heritage, and scientific data, wittingly or not, often reinforce the folk models and lay social theories. This is not surprising; we ask different kinds of questions when we wish to justify the status quo from those we ask when we wish to explain the anomalous. If folk wisdom does not query gender, why should science? It is only when ideas are changing that the anomalous is taken seriously as new data; normally it is treated as error, or a deviation from the expected, so it is explicable in terms of the expected. Most of the time, the exception, as they say, proves the rule.

In this chapter I shall look at lay social theories of gender in action, particularly how they apply to *essences* – beliefs about the nature of masculinity and femininity, and the difference between them; how the relationship between the sexes is conceptualised; and how metaphors and images of gender map on to other domains. Such mapping reflects and reinforces lay social theories of gender, and assumptions about the essence of masculinity and femininity.

Difference and the essence of gender

There is an enormous and contradictory literature on the nature, functions and origins of sex differences. It would be easy to oversimplify, and to suggest that there was a consistent *logos*, a single perspective over hundreds of years. This is especially untrue of beliefs about sexuality. In the last three hundred years, there have been dramatic changes: women have variously been seen as insatiably lustful, passive and asexual, and as having similar sexual motivation to men.

At any historical period, or in any place, the division of labour and power according to sex is taken for granted as self-evident and 'natural'. This division is supported by an appeal to 'essence', the fundamental quality of maleness and femaleness – an appeal to innate physical or psychological abilities deemed functional to the sex-appropriate task. So certain work demands physical strength, certain power roles require aggression or detachment, certain caring roles require nurturing skills. Such essential sex-related characteristics, and such necessary task requirements, mean that the sexes would not be equipped to cross role boundaries. Prototypes of masculinity and femininity are established.

Much of this is sustained by 'common sense', and by cultural narratives such as folk tales and myths. But expert opinion and supportive data can be invoked. Early research on the brain appeared to find a sex difference in the size of specific areas associated with functions deemed more appropriate for males – but when it was found that these were in fact relatively larger in females, there was a convenient change in the interpretation of their function.[1] This may be an extreme case, but there is a chequered history of research on physiological and neurophysiological sex differences.

Appeals to 'naturalness' are justifications of the status quo. Anomalous examples (single male parents, women working in the mines, women who inherit power and exercise it) are dealt with in ways that do not upset the 'natural' arguments. Sometimes the boundaries are shifted to deny the threat to essence – it is a particular kind of 'rough' lower-class woman (or woman from another culture) who is able to work in the pits. The male single parent may compensate through the help of female relatives, or the lack of too much of a feminine perspective may even be seen as valuable for a boy. The woman in power may 'really' be relying on her husband or advisers (as with several queens, including Victoria), or training and genetics give her special talents (as with Elizabeth I). Another boundary shift argues that the qualities of strength and power possessed by women working in the fields or running committees, or nurturance possessed by men in professions like social work or the Church, are not really 'the same kind' of strength or power or nurturance as those possessed by men and women in their traditional roles.

When, however, the status quo is apparently under threat, when the boundaries can no longer be shifted to defuse the exceptional case, the rhetoric of 'dire consequences' comes into play. This strengthens the prototype, the categories harden, and the standard explanations are affirmed. The dire consequences may be for social order, or the health of the next generation, but sometimes the victim is just the deviant individual. The arguments against women's suffrage were partly in essentialist terms – women were too stupid, ill-informed, or unmotivated to use their vote properly, and enfranchising them would lead to the dire consequences of political chaos. When British women first gained the vote, it was limited to presumably less 'essentially' ill-equipped women, those who had 'masculine' property responsibilities; the boundaries were not wholly relaxed. Other early 'dire consequences' arguments against equality held that it would put too great a strain on women's frail health, but even objections to girls' education – that it would overheat their brains or stunt their growth – were really a concern about social consequences, damage to future generations; women with brains should be passing their genes on by breeding, not teaching.[2]

In a letter to Martha Bernays, then his fiancée, Sigmund Freud expressed most of the rhetorical points about female essence and its functions:

> It is really a stillborn thought to send women into the struggle for existence exactly as men . . . . It is possible that changes in upbringing may suppress all a woman's tender attributes, needful of protection and yet so victorious, and that she can then earn a livelihood like men. It is also possible that in such an event one would not be justified in mourning the passing away of the most delightful thing the world can offer us – our ideal of womanhood. I believe that all reforming action in law and education would break down in front of the fact that, long before the age at which a man can earn a position in society, Nature has determined a woman's destiny through charm, beauty and sweetness. Law and custom may have much to give women that has been withheld from them, but the position of women will surely be what it is: in youth an adored darling and in mature years a loved wife.[3]

This letter was written in response to some mildly feminist murmurings. It affirms a natural difference of essence; it considers the dangerous consequences for femininity of boundary changes. It also endorses the inevitability and irresistibility of the force of Nature. Finally, the 'inevitability' of such an essence is that he loves her. She hadn't a chance; such rhetoric does indeed make the forces of Nature irresistible.

The most explicit models of gender as essence appeal to physical and psychological attributes that are perceived to aid survival. Some emphasise *hierarchy*. Essentially male qualities are more conducive to legitimate power, more appropriate to the public domain. Much of the rhetoric concerning essentially female qualities either compares them unfavourably with male qualities or permits their expression only in a context of male protection, and for the benefit of the male's performance of his role. There is another strand of argument which focuses on the *function* of natural difference, rather than on the inferiority of one sex *vis-à-vis* the other. The premiss is that the division of roles – and therefore distribution of tasks – benefits society and promotes individual beneficence. Functional difference assumes a *complementary* set of skills and behaviours which make for effective family life and effective reproduction. Biological functionalists are concerned with species reproduction, sociological and social-psychological functionalists with societal reproduction. The emphasis is on how natural sex differences equip each sex for its role in the reproductive process, rather than how they limit performance.

So, woman's 'natural' nurturance and her sensitivity to others' needs equip her particularly for an expressive, rather than an instrumental, role in the social group of the family, and indeed in social groups generally. While hierarchical arguments are used to limit women's participation in the public world, the functionalist position is, rather, that they should participate in public and private fields most suited to their natural talents. Men's 'natural' instrumentality, their greater drive for achievement and lesser sensitivity to the weak and dependent, equip them for leadership in the home and in the external world. In functionalist models man and woman are a team, and the performance of both tasks is necessary for effective living. Logically, no dire consequences follow if males and females step outside their natural roles – provided that the roles *per se* are performed by someone.

One functionalist model has generated considerable ire amongst feminist critics, but also amongst people who are reluctant to make overgeneralised comparisons between human beings and other species. Sociobiology is currently the main biological functionalist model. The major criticisms of sociobiology are that some exponents, and many popularisers, have extrapolated from animal to human natural essence. But a further charge is that the interpretation even of animal behaviour makes assumptions about what is natural and necessary for survival which are, in fact, highly dubious extrapolations from the social conditions of post-industrial human society.[4]

Sociobiology sets out to account for functional effectiveness in species reproduction. The perspective goes beyond traditional biological explanations in suggesting that, first, it is the reproduction of an individual's genes which is the driving force, rather than the individual's own survival; and secondly, that successful rearing of offspring is as important to species survival as successful conception. Certain behavioural and motivational consequences follow from these two premises. Behaviour – such as altruism or even self-sacrifice – which ensures the survival of close kin will be biologically useful, and will therefore become adapted over evolutionary time. The mating process, especially mate selection, is not indiscriminate but is designed to ensure from the male point of view (as it were) that his sperm has led to the offspring in which he invests care, and from the female's point of view (as it were) that any male who impregnates her has attributes which will guarantee survival and eventual reproduction of her offspring. What this means in practice is that in species where males are involved with infant care, the female will select those males who show manifestations of the attributes useful to parenting, as well as appearing to have the right characteristics for siring healthy offspring.

Stated thus, the model applied to animal behaviour is fairly unexceptional; indeed, it is a major theoretical advance. However, when sociobiology is used to support explanations of essential differences in human behaviour, its metaphoric and rhetorical qualities become more obvious – and more problematic. First, natural or innate characteristics are assumed to have evolved over the long period of time during which human beings led relatively stable lives with unchanging behaviour – the period covered by Man the Hunter. For example, Edward O. Wilson, the main theorist of human sociobiology, concedes the importance of cultural developments, but as these have lasted for only ten thousand years they could not, he argues, have had much genetic effect.[5] Secondly, a major source of information about the history of human behaviour comes from analogies with primates, our nearest evolutionary relatives. The evidence for the fine details of past hunter-gatherer societies is limited, as I have indicated, and what has tended to happen is that an evolutionary explanation is generated for behaviours which are currently seen as 'normal' and taken for granted. Primates at least are available for observation, and indeed, it is legitimate to draw analogies – provided that the right primate group is selected for the comparison, and the right behaviour is selected for explanation. There is, after all, a very wide range of sexual and social arrangements amongst primate groups, including harems, monogamy and promiscuity.

The main domains of behaviour covered by the theory of sociobiology are reproduction and the rearing of offspring, but there is also a substantial amount written about social organisation and power. The metaphors and explanations invoked depend greatly on what behaviour is deemed necessary to be explained, and – even more important – how the behaviour is actually interpreted. A crucial issue is sexual selection. A fundamental premiss of sociobiology, whether it applies to the fruit fly *Drosophila* or to *Homo sapiens*, is that the male pursues and the female is selectively responsive to her suitors. In other words, it is taken for granted that females do not have autonomous sexual feeling, only a desire for procreation. One has only to think what a difference it would make to both rhetoric and metaphor if the phrase commonly used by sociobiological writers about women was 'the human female is continuously sexually demanding' rather than, as is the case in their literature, 'the human female is continuously sexually receptive'.

Here is an example of the different rhetorical analysis of what is taken for granted and what is problematic. If women are merely 'receptive', it would mean that strong sexual desire in some women would be something that has to be explained; indeed, we find that in the past this has been the case – there is no male parallel of 'nymphomaniac', and the very word suggests a pathology. Female sexuality has a history of causing great distress and confusion in conceptualisating prototypes of femininity.

But even within the terms of sociobiology, the question is still begged: what does motivate women (or fruit flies, or starlings, or mice) to be 'receptive' to male advances? If the satisfaction of sexual desire is not enough, we must find desirable attributes which serve reproduction or survival; this turns out to be tricky with regard to some obviously non-functional male characteristics, like pretty tails or hairy chins.[6]

The selection for female and male pairings is only part of the story told by sociobiology. It is then necessary for the male to make sure that it is his sperm which are successful; this means excluding other males from the inamorata's body. In species that mate for life, of course, this works, and another advantage is guaranteed offspring care by two adults, but it does rather restrict the number of mating opportunities. Another strategy is a male hierarchy in which only certain males have access to females. But in this situation, two things have to operate: the males must be effective in signalling their superiority (and inferiority) to one another in such a way as to inhibit inappropriate mating behaviour, and – even more important – the females must be aware of the status symbols to which they are supposed to respond.

Amongst humans it is rare for high-status males actually to prevent other males having access to 'their' females; maintaining an exclusive harem is possible only if it is backed up by institutional power (and vast wealth). Even in the animal world, the maintenance of power is a precarious process. Male and female, deer, for example, occupy separate herds (each with their own hierarchy) for most of the year. Although the males fight for dominance during the rut, and achieve harems when successful, they are obliged to defend them against other males, and are quite quickly replaced by other males as they become exhausted or injured, so the situation is very unstable even during the four-week rutting season.[7] Although other animals may be a little more successful, it does appear that the model of the harem owes not a little to extrapolation from a type of sexual organisation that appeals to the fantasies of some male scientists.

An alternative argument is that females are sexually attracted to males who are successful competitors in the male hierarchy. Males compete for their position with other males, and females respond to signs of high status in the male hierarchy. This makes competition central to male behaviour, and also assumes that females have, and need, less competitive motivation. Undoubtedly certain species do behave in some of the ways described, but using this metaphor – and, by extrapolation, the same explanation – for human behaviour defines male competition as the behaviour which is taken for granted, and therefore which needs to be explained by an appeal to function and essence. And of course, arguing that a female (of any species) chooses a suitable mate to help her rear offspring makes sense only where there is shared parenting by opposite-sex beings. The logic of selecting the male at the top of a hierarchy for this purpose is not, in itself, obvious; it becomes interesting only if it is assumed that there must be some adaptive link between male competition and female partner-seeking. The popular sociobiological literature abounds with rather loose and unconvincing speculation that high-status males are 'good providers'.

Relationships between the sexes

Functionalist explanations of natural and essential sex differences make assumptions about what is necessary in relationships, particularly with regard to division of labour and sexuality. Both sociological functionalism and sociobiology assume that *role reciprocity* is necessary for the successful performance of tasks. The task is the focus of the explanation, though who actually performs it may be explained by an appeal to essential skills or strengths. Hierarchical models, in contrast, assume two things: that the hierarchical relationship is natural and conducive to order, and that role reversal would be disastrous. This is because the *hierarchy itself* is tied to concepts of essence; neither sex is equipped to perform the role of the other, and attempting role reversal would mean loss of essence and – especially for males – loss of status.

In the hierarchical model, male superiority requires female inferiority and followership. It is expressed in innumerable common metaphors and songs: wearing the trousers, too many chiefs and not enough Indians, henpecked, hag-ridden, and the equation of a deviant lack of masculinity with homosexuality. These are justified by appeal to natural differences, rooted in biology. As a generalisation, male characteristics are deemed of greater worth. The exceptions are caring, nurturance and patience. To accommodate these exceptions the boundaries shift so that female superiority is acceptable, rhetorically, within domains where such characteristics are required, notably home and social relationships. But there is more to hierarchy than relative power and prestige. Two areas illustrate this particularly: relationships of caring and serving, and of activity and passivity.

Mutual caring between the sexes is not, of course, inconsistent with a hierarchical model; indeed, it would be a gross exaggeration to suggest that the males who believed passionately in the superiority of their sex either failed to care for their wives or failed to value caring *per se*. There is a problem that some critical literature looks only at difference and its evaluation, and ignores the relational aspects of the hierarchical model. This oversimplifies how the different attributes are valued. In fact, within a hierarchical model, service and caring maintain the efficient functioning of the lead figure. The nature of the serving and caring is defined in terms of what is needed to maintain that efficiency. The hierarchy arises from the assumption of *deficit*, where one partner's lack is met by the other partner.

Taking the female first: her superiority lies (in the traditional sex-role model) in child care, and also in virtues which can be sustained only by distance from corrupting or roughening influences – gentleness, purity, innocence. The caring and serving function of the male is to provide financial support and protection (both physical and psychological) which she could not provide for herself but needs in order to perform her particular domestic functions. Male superiority, in contrast, rests in instrumentality, leadership, work, rationality and competition. Women's servicing and serving of men provide the physical and psychological support to sustain those attributes; this means physical care, stress-reduction and boosting morale. (The psychologist Richard Gregory has wittily suggested, within the terms of this model, that women are 'perpetual emotion machines' and men are 'esteem engines'.[8])

The lack of equity in the situation comes not from the roles *per se* but from the evaluation of the various functions, and how this evaluation is built into the concept of the servicing role. Seeing the Other's difference in terms of their capacity to perform such serving functions effectively affirms the difference itself: *I need him or her to do those necessary things that I cannot do myself.* By reflecting in one's own behaviour the complementary 'Otherness', one further confirms the duality and, of course, affirms the evaluation: *The things I can do provided I have this servicing are things that he or she could not do.* The actual evaluation of the attributes rests on what is taken as the standard. If male attributes are the norm, then servicing of those attributes by the female confirms that her strengths are strengths only in the service of his weakness; they do not have an independent value. If I am male, what I do is important, and I need her to support me; but if I am not doing important things, or if she is not supporting me, then her activities have no purpose. Jean-Jacques Rousseau expressed this in his contrasting prescriptions for the education of Emile and Sophie:

> A woman's education must therefore be planned in relation to man. To be pleasing in his sight, to win his respect and love, to train him in childhood, to tend him in manhood, to counsel and console, to make his life pleasant and happy; these are the duties of woman for all time, and this is what she should be taught while she is young.[9]

Today, even the least sensitive reader can see flaws in Rousseau's concept of a proper education for women, and fault his views on male–female relations. Over the last two hundred years the concept of wife as companion has emerged, a relationship which surely offers more than the oriental submission implied by Rousseau – though the recent scandal of the trade in Filipino women to be wives for Western men suggests that in some pockets the older prototype remains. But in fact, what has changed is the object of woman's natural, essentialist talent for total care and attention; the child has replaced the husband as the being to be serviced. During the nineteenth century the importance of mothering increased; motherhood became a significant role in its own right. By the twentieth century the skills of motherhood were seen to need enhancement through formal education. The servitor relationship between woman and man was replaced by a servitor relationship between woman and child.

Valerie Walkerdine and Helen Lucey describe the rhetoric of motherhood underlying much writing in developmental psychology.[10] The ideal or prototypical set-up is a committed relationship between the 'sensitive' and caring mother and the child. The contrast is made with the 'egocentric' mother. The prototype of motherhood becomes embedded in social order; the 'dire consequences' of failure affect society. Earlier in this century it was the duty of the good mother to rear sons for the benefit of the Empire; daughters were rarely mentioned, but if they were, it was in a supportive role to the family – and therefore to the nation. This rhetoric was still in place when Beveridge planned the welfare state in 1943: 'During marriage most women will not be gainfully employed.'[11] 'The attitude of the housewife to gainful employment outside the home is not and should not be the same as that of a single woman. She has other duties.'[12] 'In the next thirty years housewives as mothers have vital work to do in ensuring the adequate continuance of the British race and of British ideals in the world.'[13] Today it is 'the child' rather than 'the son' whom mothers are advised to tend, but as the journalist Jill Tweedie has pointed out, good mothering of boys produces good citizens who are capable of autonomous decision-making and independent lives, but good mothering of girls produces . . . good mothers.[14]

The difference in discussion of the effects of good and bad mothering on sons and daughters reflects the way the hierarchical nature of caring and serving relates to gender. John Bowlby, for example, argued that an outcome of maternal deprivation was the 'affectionless personality' which, he claimed, was at the root of various forms of male pathology and delinquency.[15] So the caring woman who would cosset Emile became the caring mother who gave her offspring the sense of being cared for, which would be a defence against antisocial behaviour. Note that the rhetoric was not that good mothering produced *caring* boys, but that the absence of good mothering produced boys *who did not feel loved*. It was the absence of being loved, not the absence of loving, which caused delinquency.

So the relationship of serving is not merely a matter of who does what to whom, but what is implied in what is needed to be done; it is one partner meeting a deficit in the other. The meaning of this relationship is illustrated by the guilt and obligation it engenders. The prototype of masculinity includes the ability to provide for and protect one's family; this is defined as a relationship between a person and his 'dependants' – a term which implies weakness, inferiority and immaturity. The male lives at the nexus of public and private worlds; he has power in relation to both. Femininity is identified with serving emotional and physical demands; woman's own needs are subsumed by her definition as need-meeter to others. Her function is to exercise her talents in dealing with those demands, rather than in developing her self. Masculine self-definition is through efficacious production of goods and services for a family economic unit; feminine self-definition requires sensitive responsiveness to the family's emotional needs.

Me active, you passive

There are innumerable metaphoric examples of feminine passivity and masculine activity. Above I considered sociobiologists' assumption that active males pursue passive females – and asked what would happen if we assumed that the females were active.

I remember being shocked by a male gay pin-up magazine – not because I am prudish or homophobic, but because it confronted me with my own unquestioned assumptions. There have been attempts to produce underclad male pin-ups for women. These pictures tend to come in two kinds: raunchy men with good physiques – conventional beefcake – who look directly and provocatively at the viewer; and dreamy, romantic males who are usually more slightly built, tender and less assertive – their gaze is directed off-camera, and expresses a troubled soulfulness. These two styles are precisely those to which we were accustomed in fully clothed film stars. The first style suggests desire for the viewer, and certainly hints at sexual prowess. The second implies sensitivity, and a preoccupation with something other than the viewer. The former image (clothed or unclothed) shows the model either doing or about to do something active. Halla Beloff has pointed out that the metaphor of the male image requires him to be doing something apart from merely being looked at. If what he is doing is symbolically phallic (but never autoerotic), so much the better.[16] The latter image is more cerebral: he would be a sensitive lover, but he needs to be cared for – if only one can attract his attention.

As the failure of the commercial efforts shows, it seems to make little difference to the female viewer whether a man is clothed or not; indeed, assertive raunchiness would be distinctly undermined by a limp penis. The romantically preoccupied figure may potentially be erotically exciting, but if he is not looking at the viewer, he has not connected with her sexually – yet; so an erection at this stage would be inappropriate. In fact, to my knowledge pin-ups for women never (at least in the publicly accessible literature) included erect penises. Recent, more sophisticated material exploits the erotic appeal, for many women, of the firm-toned buttock. But naked pin-ups seemed, if anything, less appealing than clothed pin-ups; one explanation is that women rely less on visual cues than men, and more on fantasy. Alternatively, women decode different signals about sexual potential; the message can be expressed effectively by posture, facial expression or style of dress (rather than undress).

The subjective reality of this became clear when I saw the gay magazine. The males were naked or nearly naked, and they mostly had at least partial erections, sometimes escaping from their brief clothing. Some were photographed from the back, showing muscular buttocks to the camera. I wondered why they did not excite me, and were in fact not even as sexually interesting as men on a beach. I also asked myself why I knew immediately that these were homosexual, rather than heterosexual, pin-ups. I realised that it was because they contravened what Beloff calls the appropriate metaphors for male self-presentation. These figures were passive even when they were doing active things. Their stance was as object of another's gaze; they were not controllers of the image. While many presentations of the male form are designed to attract attention and, indeed, admiration, they are to be admired for the action they are performing, or because the action implies strength or heroism, or because their physical beauty is the product of their body-building efforts. The gay models, in contrast, revealed their excitement as a titillating partial exposure, a half-accident. Their expressions were bland and vacant, or receptive, rather than challenging or self-contained. They were also autoerotic, surprised in the act of self-caress, or in narcissism. In other words, the visual metaphors they enacted were exactly those conventionally required of women in front of the camera or the palette.

John Berger's writing on the relationship between active and passive in the field of visual presentation has been very influential.[17] Women are objectified through the role they play in presentation; or as objects of men's (the voyeur's) gaze, whether as artist's model or the final image. This passivity is a pervasive metaphor in art, as activity is of the male role. It is the metaphor of woman as plaything or possession, the object or prey of the male in sexual pursuit; woman is eroticised because passivity expresses sexual receptiveness. So any act performed when she is in the voyeur's lens becomes, by definition, erotic. A voyeur is someone who has illicit access to what he sees through guile or accident. Or he may have licit access, because she is 'on view'. But even when she is on view, she *receives* the viewing rather than defining what image she wishes to present; she is defined even by the action of others painting or photographing her. So she still remains an image to be made as he wishes. Soft porn, but also even less salacious imagery like advertising, trades on the male voyeur having privileged and gratuitous power over the object of his gaze. This metaphor has its mirror in romantic literature, where women are preoccupied with being constantly fit to be seen, in case He appears. The message is that she should permanently be on guard – always presentable for this moment in dress, appearance, gestures, stance.

The artist who paints the maiden at her toilette, the porn merchant who photographs the model stroking her labia in front of a mirror, affirms to the male viewer that he controls the unlicensed invasion into such delicious privacy, and that the woman is passive and, by definition, in his control. Such imagery also confirms the idea that women are vulnerable to invasion of their privacy. Woman's control of her world depends on her ability to maintain her private boundaries; if she fails, she has no defences. However, I think there is something missing from this analysis. The assumption throughout is that women are vulnerable and helpless, rather than that they are participating in the enactment of their passivity. Shirley Ardener has pointed out that when women are accidentally interrupted in their private places, or when they want to shame men who wish to invade them, they do not necessarily 'close the door' – an act which would affirm the metaphor of male control. They may choose instead to present themselves openly, brazenly offering to view what had been covert, and discovered only through the power of male cunning. In this way the relationship becomes reversed: the woman has now defined her own representation, even if she is blatantly naked.[18]

Bel Mooney's novel *The Fourth of July* explores the idea that if a woman chooses to reveal herself to the camera she may be in fact in control, rather than being exploited.[19] A number of glamour models have also argued in this way. The problem is that this really works only if the image she represents makes this clear. The representation of coquetry in art – in other words, the representation of woman inviting sexual advance – differs from voyeuristic 'accidental discovery' in that it is apparently less passive. The woman is, after all, manifesting sexual interest in the viewer of the picture, the audience. But in fact the active–passive relationship is not reversed. The voyeuristic model presumes that any surprise of privacy is erotic, even if the actions being surprised are not necessarily erotic in any way; it is part of the rhetoric that private equals sexual when it concerns women's privacy. The coquettish gestures merely imply that the model is aware of her viewer, and of the effect she has upon him. A voyeuristic perspective can accommodate the idea that a woman can actually enjoy being 'surprised'. The coquette is saying, 'Come and get me', or 'I am available for your attentions'; she is playing her part in the active–passive rhetoric, encouraging his action by her compliance in it.

There is one example which illustrates a real reversal of the active–passive relationship. Mae West turned coquetry upside down by making it quite clear that she was neither 'receptive' to the male advance, nor aroused only in response to it. Her coquetry was defined in terms of her own desires and intentions, not the male viewers'; in other words, she was sending a demanding, not a receptive, message. Coquetry is passive when the woman responds with the cues she knows are expected in the male script; it is active when she defines the terms of reference. Mae West's shift to an active mode, yet using the same basic gestures and behaviours, had enormous rhetorical power. Like the women who present their naked parts to males as a protest against voyeurism, Mae West turned the rhetoric upside down, and changed the whole meaning of the situation.

It follows from the equation of sexuality and eroticism with activity and passivity that if women are in a position of greater power than men, or if they take the initiative, this will have an effect on sexual performance – either literally or symbolically as a threat to masculinity. Animal behaviour again came to the rescue in support of the prototype.

Males in some species deal with aggression by adopting the posture of female sexual presentation. This provided support for the assumption that there was inevitable conflict between eroticism and power. If eroticism defuses power conflicts, then it follows that confrontation of power disturbs eroticism. It is part of the prototype that women behave inappropriately and ineffectively if they attempt to use power in response to male power assertion. If female power lies in eroticism, and male power lies in assertion, there is balance; it also confirms women in a primarily erotic role. The passivity of the female in relation to the activity of the male is confirmed by her own emphasis on her erotic role – or rather, by her acceptance of and collusion with his definition of her erotic role.

The active–passive metaphor is partly the heritage of Darwin's metaphors. Ruth Hubbard has demonstrated how Darwin's ideas of sexual selection reflect his peculiarly nineteenth-century assumptions about the different sexual feeling of males and females, and the pattern of activity and passivity implied in this.[20] Hubbard argues that the consequence is that even in the twentieth century, when metaphors of human sexual relationships have changed somewhat, ethologists are still prone to look for active–passive difference and models of pursuit and response amongst animals – as we have seen in our discussion of sociobiology. This is an example of an explanation where the metaphor makes sense of what is taken for granted, but comes apart – and reveals the rhetorical assumptions – when the expected behaviour does not occur, or when it occurs in the 'wrong' sex. So, as Hubbard says, when male sheep act passively as a way of dealing with being the loser in a fight, they are interpreted as 'behaving like females', or female sheep 'behave like males' when they are active. Given that such behaviours are presumably entirely normal for those male and female sheep, it is the observer's lay social theory about 'normal' and functional patterns of activity and passivity which defines the situation, not the sheep's.

Mapping and engendering: rationality and science

Active versus passive is only one cultural duality that maps on to gender. Other examples are light and dark, hard and soft, sun and moon, public and private, rational and intuitive, nature and nurture. Each of these evokes a parallel with male and female, or masculine and feminine. In many cultures the parallels are drawn even more strongly, and with greater ritual and rhetorical explicitness. Once the metaphoric frame is established, the natural dualities of gender, the daily cycle, moral poles and other dualistic phenomena become entwined in cultural thought. It is a moot point, of course, whether the experience of naturally occurring dualities like day and night is partly responsible for metaphors of dualism, but there still remains the question of how far any culture highlights the dualistic metaphor. In the case of gender, the need to justify and make sense of masculinity and femininity contributes to the mapping. We need Apollo and Diana to be male and female not only because we need a clear differentiation of the sun and the moon in our mythology, but because that makes sense of our conceptions of masculinity and femininity.

The mapping of gender metaphors on to other domains has been particularly interesting in the history of ideas about the human being's relationship to the natural world. I have already described the changing perspectives in the seventeenth century, when the organic model of the universe, of nature and of the human being's place in it, was replaced by a mechanistic model. The equation of nature with femaleness creates problems for male-centred world-views. The Earth Mother image which prevailed until Elizabethan times attributed great power and wisdom to the female force. But an alternative view was of the earth as mother or wife to man; the caring role diminished her overwhelming power, placing her in the position of service. The questing scientist may have to cajole, but it is nature's function to serve mankind – to nurse it. The metaphor of an Earth Mother imbues all things with life – and has profound implications for the prototype of the feminine. A female-dominant principle underlying the universe implied holism, organic relationships between things, and life everywhere. Organic relationships gave the male principle a function as a catalyst in the generative process. The alchemists, for example, saw knowledge and scientific developments as the outcome of a fusion, a coition, between male and female principles.[21] Once there was a shift to a mechanistic model, the organic function of the female principle was overthrown and – more importantly – the idea of dualism and conflict, as opposed to holism and functional harmony, became ascendant. As we have seen, a dualistic model *per se* can imply *either* a functional complementarity between different principles *or* hierarchical relations between two things which therefore become, by definition, antithetical.

The equation of mechanism with masculinity appears to have emerged from the Aristotelian definition of the soul, and Aristotle's assumptions of sex differences in rationality, but also from the Platonic view of knowledge being gained through the communion of equals. Plato conceived of nature as being permeated with Mind.[22] In his view, knowledge of nature was analogous to the communion of men who were equals – a communion that eschewed the material and the physical. Such a communion, by definition, excluded the feminine; therefore, the female could not be part of the knowledge-creation process. Aristotle started from the premiss that the soul has two parts, the rational and the irrational. The rational should govern the irrational – so already there is the possibility of conflict, and the need for a hierarchy. If women are less rational beings, it is therefore natural that they should be governed by men. But there was another element also: the Greeks did not fully understand the role of sperm in conception; it was assumed that semen provided the spiritual input, and menstrual blood the material input: yet another metaphor.[23]

The Platonic influence excluded the feminine from the processes of mind; actions of mind, and knowing, become the province of the masculine. The Aristotelian influence presupposed a dichotomy and a hierarchy which equated the masculine with rationality and femininity with irrationality, and imposed a model of governance of one by the other. Thus, irrational forces (such as fortune) become equated with femininity. Furthermore, woman was supposedly closer to nature, both because nature herself was female and because women were less equipped with those things, such as rationality, which distanced them from nature. This made them more unruly and subject to forces outside their rational control.

For extended historical periods, views of sexuality fuelled this distinction. Women's lustfulness was deemed considerably greater than men's. This made them less predictable, prone to victimising men, and also prone to consorting with devils, which in turn led them to become witches. The *Malleus Maleficarum* of 1486 claimed that 'All women have insatiable desires and to satisfy them they consort with devils'.[24] The point about witchcraft is that witches have special powers to summon each person's personal 'spirit' – and thus control them. Witches, in other words, had power over nature; and witches were women who gained this power as a consequence of unholy congress with devils, itself a consequence of unholy lusts. Women's 'weakness' came not from their lack of general strength but from their lack of moral strength in relation to their sexuality. Like nature herself, women had considerable powers, but they were not controllable.

A mechanistic metaphor facilitated the belief that nature and other wild forces could be controlled. If nature could be understood, she could also be changed. The 'perverseness, violence and forwardness' of matter could be controlled. For Descartes, this was to be achieved through mathematics and explicitly mechanistic processes, which conceived of the universe as a clockwork model.[25] For Bacon, it was still metaphorically a struggle between Man and reluctant (and organic) Nature. This struggle was expressed in metaphors of quite explicit sexual congress; however, in contrast to alchemical models of the fusion of male and female principles, this metaphor is sometimes not far from rape. Certainly in Bacon's metaphors, and those of his contemporaries, the struggle between Nature cast in a stereotyped feminine role, and Man cast in a stereotyped masculine role of activity and control, is obvious:

> By art and the hand of man she is to be forced out of her natural state, and squeezed and moulded [to yield] the many secrets of excellent use.[26]

> [Aristotle left] nature herself untouched and inviolate [being unwilling] to lay hold of her and capture her.[27]

> [It is a mistake to assume that men were] on such familiar terms with nature that, in response to a casual and perfunctory salutation, she would condescend to unveil to us her mysteries and bestow on us her blessings.[28]

Bacon effectively changed not only the metaphor of man's relationship with nature, but also the underlying mechanisms of that relationship. He identified three states of Nature:

> She is either free and follows her ordinary course of development as in the heavens, in the animal and vegetable creation, and in the general array of the universe; or she is driven out of her ordinary course by the perverseness, insolence and forwardness of matter and violence of impediments, as in the case of monsters; or, lastly, she is put in constraint, moulded, and made as it were new by art and the hand of man; as in things artificial.[29]

The first model is the standard organic model. The second model, as Merchant says:

> was necessary to explain the malfunctions and monstrosities that frequently appeared and that could not have been caused by God or another power acting on his instructions. Since monstrosities could not be explained by the action of form or spirit, they had to be the result of matter acting perversely.[30]

Here were anomalous phenomena which needed explanation. A model of 'perverse matter' provided such an explanation, and would itself be strengthened by any evidence of matter as perverse. It was also necessary to find something to control 'perversity' and unruly forces; emerging at this time was the concept that man could operate upon nature to *change*, not merely to understand.

It is interesting that these developments of Bacon's thought retained the organic metaphor, in contrast to the Cartesian clockwork metaphor. Bacon – at least in those of his metaphors which very explicitly contain models of mechanism – continued to think of Nature as an organic, female force even when it was being subjected to mechanical constraint.

Nature remains female and organic; matter itself has the qualities of the feminine and the characteristics of an organic thing. ('Matter is not devoid of an appetite and inclination to dissolve the world and fall back into old Chaos.') The action of man, through technical arts, first causes Nature to yield her secrets and also makes it possible to change matter. But as long as Nature and matter remain organic and female, if Bacon wished to talk about control and force he was almost bound to use the metaphors of sexual assault.

The masculine was mapped on to the mechanistic, yet there is no necessary *a priori* connection between mechanism and masculinity. If, however, nature is defined as feminine, and that which is natural is less rational, unruly and to be controlled by the rational, then that which controls the antithesis of this must perforce be rational and masculine. If the mechanistic model opposes the organic, then the mechanistic will be masculine. Clockwork is not inherently masculine; it may become so by association with the rationality deemed characteristic of a predictable mechanical object, so mapping on to the rational–irrational distinction that parallels masculine and feminine. But if organic nature is subdued in a metaphor of sexual assault, this necessarily presupposes the action of male upon female. The starting point of the changing metaphor of the relationship between the human being and nature was to have a measure of control over the universe, but the end point was the mapping of masculinity and femininity on to a whole range of intellectual, technological and scientific processes.

My own studies of images of different fields of knowledge show that this still survives. A decade ago, British adolescents mapped gender on to science.[31] Two pieces of background information are useful; first, British school students were then obliged, at the age of fourteen, to select a course programme which favoured a more science-based, or a more humanities-based, curriculum. Effectively, this choice excluded certain future options for ever: a child who dropped sciences at fourteen could never hope to take science at tertiary education level, or train in a scientific or technological field. Secondly, university education in Britain is highly specialised, with students taking at most two closely related subjects. So university students identify quite closely with their discipline of study, and there is a sense of subcultural differences between 'science', 'social science' and 'humanities' students.

My study asked undergraduates and school students to rate a range of disciplines on a series of scales. I found a clear relationship between subjects perceived as *scientific* and subjects perceived as *masculine*; physics, mathematics, chemistry, engineering and medicine were both masculine and scientific. Perhaps more surprising was the fact that masculine/scientific subjects were also seen as having attributes associated with males in our culture; science subjects were seen as hard (rather than soft), as complex or difficult (rather than simple), and as thinking-based rather than feeling-based. We cannot explain the association between science and maleness as simply due to young people believing that more boys than girls take science subjects. The relationship is between science as an activity and a form of knowledge, and culturally defined masculinity.

The other surprising finding tells us something about cultural definitions of the feminine. While there was a cluster of definitely masculine disciplines, there were no strongly feminine disciplines. Most disciplines clustered around the centre of the masculine–feminine scale. The positive conclusion one may draw from this is that some areas of knowledge, at least, are perceived as gender-neutral. An alternative conclusion is that there is no such thing as 'female knowledge' – that knowledge and femininity, at least in the formal context of academic education, are not compatible concepts. John Archer replicated this study recently and found some diminution of the stereotyping, but girls still see subjects they regard as more masculine as 'difficult', and boys see subjects they regard as feminine as 'less interesting'. There is an implied hierarchy here: girls may aspire unsuccessfully to 'masculine' subjects, but boys dismiss 'feminine' subjects as boring.[32]

'Her indoors'[33]

Gender also maps on to the public–private dimension. I have referred to the 'privateness' of women's lives in relation to eroticism and passivity. The need for female privacy and its equation with the erotic is assumed in the metaphors which presuppose male intrusion on the female. The privacy and secrecy of Nature was presupposed in Bacon's metaphors. Why does the cultural theory presuppose the privacy of the female, but not the male in the same way? The different view of male privacy is partly due to the active–passive metaphor: women do not pursue; they await pursuit. To enter the male space would be an agentic act which is contrary to the metaphor of the female role. It would occur only where women wished to assert power over men, or to disrupt the male world.

The exclusion of women from male clubs, male institutions and male professions is often justified by an appeal to a hierarchical model. The qualities required for the performance of particular tasks and the roles required for membership of the institution are male characteristics; to include the female would be impossible, because she would not pass the tests. More usually, however, exclusion depends upon a metaphor of *pollution*. The practice of male exclusion and taboos on females entering male space does occur in cultures which see the female force as either polluting to the male – usually under special circumstances such as puberty ceremonies or preparation for war – or see femininity as a potential threat: the presence of females will impede or adulterate masculine qualities. This may be material pollution – for example, bringing a person of ritual status into contact with menstrual blood – or pollution because the antithetical female qualities dilute the male qualities. Many a gentlemen's club over the last decade has confronted the issue of women members; at least one heard in opposition the argument that 'the voices of women in gossip in the public areas of the Club would inhibit serious reading and research'. The raising of the noise level is a metaphor of pollution; the assumption that women 'gossip', rather than engage in reading and research like male members, is a pollution of rationality.[34]

This pollution metaphor is about the danger of antithetical qualities. But pollution may be through the weakening effect of distraction or temptation. The presence of women as a distraction to men, and a source of possible sexual rivalry and even violence, has long been an objection to women working with men on British boats, oil-rigs and similar isolated structures – other nations do not seem to see their males as so vulnerable to weakness. Here privacy creates defences against male frailties, and entry of the female into the male's private space violates those defences. The monastic life is obviously based on the same principles and, to an extent, so is single-sex education. Some of these 'frailties', however, are more mundane. In discussing the entry of women into the Garrick Club, the columnist Peregrine Worsthorne objected on the grounds that it would constrain the male members from snoring after dinner with their clothes undone and their mouths open.

Male privacy protects the male world from contamination of various sorts. There are some paradoxes about this privacy. On the whole, the strengths which need protecting from contamination are strengths perceived to be necessary for the performance of public duties. Even when males privatise themselves in relation to other men – for example, in the creation of secret societies or in groups – these exist ostensibly for the more effective performance of males' public duties: in government, warfare, the pursuit of knowledge or religion. Men's secret societies tend to apply the same rhetorical boundaries to male outsiders as they do to females, often by rituals and metaphors which define the in group as pure and the out group as polluting.

Mapping the private world on to the feminine and the public world on to the masculine is a direct consequence of prototypes of masculinity. The public world is the arena of action and the masculine self; one retreats from this into a haven or private place. Christopher Lasch entitled his book about the family as the private domain *Haven in a*

Heartless World, a metaphor which precisely expresses all the associations of the conflict of public and private.[35] The private haven is a place inhabited by women, and it is with his womenfolk that man is permitted intimacy, and the expression of feelings and thoughts which cannot be shown to the public male world. Thus personal male privacy is associated with the female world. Man can symbolically shut out – by closing the door – the external world. The movement from public to private world takes place via certain symbolic actions, including setting boundaries on what can be talked about, and what emotions and thoughts are permitted to be seen in public. Men who enter therapy or groupwork in middle life suddenly realise that they know nothing of other men's lives apart from what is presented publicly.[36] How much is what is in the private domain presumed to exist but to be out of view, and how much are certain behaviours simply deemed not to exist: do men not cry just in public, or do they not cry at all?

Traditionally, for men, women are equated with privacy, partly because they represent the domain where man's secret life is kept; as long as he can rely upon female collusion in setting his boundaries, he can maintain his public self-presentation. The presumption that women neither have nor understand the symbolic boundaries and rules for being 'private' in public places is implied in objections to their becoming club members. Women's natural private status in men's eyes makes them already part of a private world. They are assumed neither to move between the public and the private worlds, nor to move into a further private world of their own – except into that world which is eroticised because 'private' means 'covering one's nakedness' rather than the solitary exploration of one's inner life. The privateness of the female world is defined by the terms of reference by which male life is divided into public and private, and any female is located within the private domain. Her own 'privateness' is primarily a consequence of the definition of the public–private boundaries in the male world; as keeper of man's secret life, she is herself a secret being. She enters the public domain as a man's adjunct, reflecting his public status.

Female 'secretness' arises partly because until recently there has been a lack of public discussion of female experience. Women have been 'another country', not to be understood. Freud admitted that he did not understand women. Woman's Otherness is a mystery, disturbing and incomprehensible. This may be threatening, because it may be seen as polluting, but it may also confer power. If femaleness cannot be understood in the terms of reference of male experience, this enhances woman's private and secret status. This was Bacon's metaphor. Nature's secrets were of value to masculine knowledge. His solution was metaphoric seduction or rape – not an uncommon male reaction to female power and threat.

Even traditional female discourse does a great deal more than passively reflect the male definition of females as belonging in private space. The female version of the idea that privacy protects, excludes the outside world, and especially male intrusion, but whereas male discourse defines the female inner self as erotic and to be protected (or violated), female discourse has never accepted this fully. Women in general set different kinds of symbolic boundaries to public and private. Within the boundary of the private world there is much more acceptance of and desire for intimacy and exchange of confidences, and of mutual emotional support that acknowledges rather than hides the emotion. The complex friendship-making of young adolescent girls hangs on the keeping and sharing of secrets, the break-up of friendship on the betrayal of secrets. It is not what is told to the other, but the fact that it is defined as 'secret', that is important. The interaction is defined as highly privatised, but in fact it involves considerable sharing of knowledge.

There is a problem: while functionalist and hierarchical models are different interpretations of sex difference and gender role, they are not entirely separate. The hierarchical model defines the masculine pole as the epitome of the human, and the feminine pole as its antithesis, a deficit or a support. The functional model perceives the two sexes' roles as mutually dependent and reciprocal. But this reciprocity is subsumed into a hierarchy when the masculine pole is evaluated as 'really' more important. The functional necessity of the 'feminine' pole is then interpreted as servicing a deficit. What could, in principle, be the free exchange of roles between persons, irrespective of gender, becomes instead contaminated with the metaphors of greater and lesser, and of pollution.

Notes

1. S. J. Gould, *The Mismeasure of Man*, Harmondsworth: Penguin, 1981.
2. S. Shields, 'Sex and the biased scientist', *New Scientist*, **80(1132)** pp. 752-4, 7 December 1978.
3. E. Jones, *The Life and Work of Sigmund Freud*, Harmondsworth: Penguin, 1966, p. 168.
4. M. Ruse, *Sociobiology; Sense or nonsense?*, Dordrecht: Reidel, 1979; G. W. Barlow and J. Silverberg (eds), 'Sociobiology: beyond nature/nurture', *AAAS Selected Symposium No. 35*, Boulder, CO: Westview Books, 1979.
5. E. O. Wilson, *Sociobiology: The new synthesis*, Cambridge, MA: Harvard University Press, 1975; E. O. Wilson, *On Human Nature*, Cambridge, MA: Harvard University Press, 1979.

6. H Cronin, *The Ant and the Peacock*, Cambridge: Cambridge University Press, 1991, especially ch. 9.
7. T. H. Clutton-Brock, F. E. Guinness and S. D. Albon, *Red Deer: Behaviour and ecology of the two sexes*, Edinburgh: Edinburgh University Press, 1982.
8. Richard Gregory, personal communication.
9. J. J. Rousseau, *Emile*, trans. B. Foxley, London: Dent, 1974.
10. V. Walkerdine and H. Lucey, *Democracy in the Kitchen*, London: Virago, 1989.
11. W. Beveridge, *Report on the Social Insurance and Allied Services*, Cmnd 6404, London: HMSO, 1943, para. 111.
12. *ibid.*, para. 114.
13. *ibid.*, para. 117.
14. J. Tweedie, 'Mum's rush', *Guardian*, 3 November 1975.
15. J. Bowlby, *The Making and Breaking of Affectional Bonds*, London: Tavistock, 1979.
16. H. Beloff, 'Ecce Homo; towards a new focus for the female gaze in psychology', Paper presented at the British Association for the Advancement of Science Annual Meeting, Plymouth, August 1991; R. Dyer, 'Don't look now', *Screen*, **23(3)**, pp. 61–72, 1982.
17. J. Berger, *Ways of Seeing*, Harmondsworth: Penguin, 1972.
18. S. Ardener, 'Sexual insult and female militancy', in S. Ardener (ed.), *Perceiving Woman*, New York: Wiley, 1975.
19. B. Mooney, *The Fourth of July*, Harmondsworth: Penguin, 1989.
20. R. Hubbard, 'Have only men evolved?', in S. Harding and M. B. Hintikka (eds), *Discovering Reality*, Dordrecht: Reidel, pp. 45–69, 1979.
21. C. Merchant, *The Death of Nature: Women, ecology and the scientific revolution*, San Francisco: Harper & Row, 1982.
22. Plato, *Timaeus*, in B. Jowett (ed.), *The Dialogues of Plato*, New York: Random House, 1937.
23. Aristotle, *De Generatione Animalium*, trans A. Platt, Oxford: Clarendon Press, 1910.
24. H. Institor and J. Sprenger, *Malleus Maleficarum* [1486], New York: Bloom, 1970.
25. R. Descartes, 'The meditations', in *Meditations and Selections from the Principles of Philosophy*, La Salle, IL: Open Court, 1952, p. 98.
26. S. Warhaft (ed.), *Francis Bacon: A selection of his works*, London: Macmillan, 1982, 'The Great Instauration', p. 320.
27. B. Farrington, *The Philosophy of Francis Bacon*, Liverpool: Liverpool University Press, 1964, p. 83.
28. F. Bacon, *Works*, ed. J. Spedding, R. L. Ellis and D. D. Heath, London: Longman Green, 1870; 'De Augmentis', vol. 4.
29. J. Spedding, R. L. Ellis and D. D. Heath, *Works of Francis Bacon*, London: Longman Green, 1870, p. 294.
30. Merchant, *The Death of Nature*, pp. 170-1.
31. H. Weinreich-Haste, 'The image of science', in A. Kelly (ed.), *The Missing Half: Girls and science education*, Manchester: Manchester University Press, 1981.
32. J. Archer and M. Macrae, 'Gender-perceptions of school subjects among

10–11 year olds', *British Journal of Educational Psychology*, **61**, pp. 99–103, 1991.

33. This refers to the popular British television series *Minder*, starring George Cole and Denis Waterman. The character played by George Cole, Arthur Daley, has a wife who never appears on the screen, but exerts considerable power over Arthur. She is never referred to by name, simply as 'Her indoors'.

34. Personal communication, but see also B. Rogers, *Men Only: An investigation into men's organisations*, London: Pandora Press, 1988.

35. C. Lasch, *Haven in a Heartless World: The family besieged*, New York: Basic Books, 1979.

36. See C. Griffin and M. Wetherell, 'Open forum: feminist psychology and the study of men and masculinity', *Feminism and Psychology*, **2(2)**, 1992.

Chapter 4: Self and Otherness

Carol Gilligan argues that there is a distinctively female way of thinking about morality; it focuses on responsibility and caring, and contrasts with the male preoccupation with justice.[1] She claims that this comes out of different ways of thinking about relationships: girls grow up thinking of themselves as connected to others; boys grow up thinking of themselves as separate from others. An ethic of responsibility is concerned with maintaining relationships; an ethic of justice is important in resolving conflicts fairly. Evelyn Fox Keller argues that women go about scientific investigation differently from men; they are more concerned with detailed observation in context, less interested in grand theory.[2] Some French feminists are trying to develop a way of writing that is 'open, nonlinear, . . . fluid . . . incorporating the simultaneity of life . . . . Different also from preconceived, oriented, masterly constructs and didactic ("male") fiction'.[3]

Are there real sex differences in approaching discovery and knowledge, or are such assertions really part of a rhetorical challenge to the convention that rationality is couched in metaphors of masculinity?

The paradox of Otherness

Gender roles and models of sex difference are sustained by the central concept of 'Otherness'. The very concept of difference defines members of the other group as 'not-like' the self. 'Not-like' may mean different from, or less than, or antithetical to. Simone de Beauvoir was perhaps the first to point out the paradox of Otherness.[4] For males, the definition of self depends upon there being an Other who differs and, by differing, asserts the integrity and definition of the Self. This is not true for women, who appear, she thought, to accept themselves as being defined solely as the Other to Man – to have no identity as a group or category apart from the way they are defined by men and male discourse. Since de Beauvoir's time, several writers have argued that an alternative female discourse which offers self-definition for women has always existed. However, her perception is particularly valid for women like herself who operate primarily within the male world; subjectively, in the face of male discourse and male culture, woman is the Other.

If the model of differences implies that the male is the standard, woman is defined in terms of her lack of or antithesis to male characteristics and male qualities. In so far as she fails to meet those standards, she is perceived to be in deficit. In this perspective difference implies hierarchical evaluation; with certain exceptions, the quality ascribed to the male is superior to the quality ascribed to the female. The exceptions concern areas with clearly bounded roles, such as nurturance and family life.

There is also the dualism of thesis and antithesis. 'Not-male' is not only deficit, but *antagonistic*. The 'otherness' defines the self by negation: if I lack this negative quality, I am therefore positive. But if I lack this positive quality, if I am 'other-like', I am no longer self-like. Thus the possible Other is a potential threat. I must sustain my self-quality in order to avoid the dangers of the Other-quality. This conception has a built-in metaphor of pollution – particularly so for the male, because the Otherness is inferior as well as antagonistic. But womanhood may also be polluted, essentially womanly qualities may be destroyed, by taking on male roles or male attributes.

Crossing the boundary of gender may pollute the self, even if the acquisition of certain positively valued Other qualities is a benefit. Becoming more 'like a man' in the field of rationality or leadership may make one less 'like a woman' – potentially a positive situation, if a woman wishes to be taken seriously in male discourse. But there may be internal leakage; one's rationality or leadership skills, though evident and proven, may be perceived as vulnerable to the polluting effect of one's other female essences. Similarly for males, acquiring the positive qualities of nurturance or peacemaking skills – again, valued in certain professions – may be seen as polluting to one's other masculine essences, or may themselves be seen as untrustworthy because one's basic masculinity may leak across the boundaries – hence the fears people seem to have about male nursery nurses.

Positive female qualities come in two versions: the *carer* and the *neutraliser*. For the self as carer, the Otherness of the male defines the self by functional reciprocity rather than negation: for me to care, someone must need caring for. The qualities of nurturance and sensitivity are valued in women, and attributed to women as essences. Neutralising qualities work differently. There are negative male characteristics which women either do not possess, or for which they possess an antithetical quality. Qualities such as aggression and certain forms of irresponsibility are perceived as essentially male, and are negatively valued; their manifestation in males may be deplored, but this does not detract from their masculinity – in fact, it may be enhanced. Because of this paradox, the relevant qualities of women are not so much positive as neutralising. Women's presumed lack of aggression is a positive quality *per se* – whether it is expressed in compromise, peacemaking skills or whatever – but it is valued because it enables women to *neutralise* the negative male qualities. Thus its value, like that of nurturance, rests on its relationship to male behaviour and male needs – I am fortunate to lack those unpleasant qualities which men have; or, alternatively, I must use my female talents to make peace among my menfolk.

Resolving Otherness leads down many paths. One route is to find an authentic description of the female self, a definition which is more than merely the negation of the male self, one which takes proper account of female experiences. Another route is to make sense of actual sex differences – whether subjective or objective. The conventional picture of gender differences did not necessarily match the subjective sense of difference – it distorted the significance of difference and gave explanations of the origins of difference which often merely reflected a simple polarity of positive and negative. An example is the thought process called 'intuition'. This has been unambiguously bounded as a female characteristic. Rather than being considered a useful additional skill, it has frequently been the negation of logic and rationality, and regarded as dangerous and misleading. So in the pursuit of a more authentic picture of the female and the feminine, we may reconsider formerly devalued qualities – for the benefit of both sexes. If differences in thinking and problem-solving are really to do with gender, the outcome would be, first, a re-evaluation of the feminine; and second the establishment of an authentic Otherness based on valid differences rather than distortions or illusions.

But there are other ways of looking at this. What is invented or discovered in seeking to validate the feminine may in fact be a long but submerged tradition of alternative conceptions of rationality – not necessarily always associated with femininity. A number of movements in current Western thought exemplify this. Jane Flax suggests that feminism is a part of post-modernism.[5] The rejection of modernist conceptions of rationality, of what has been seen as the primary orthodoxy, draws upon the same sources, rediscovers the same hidden alternative traditions. There are parallels with Green politics, with Humanistic psychology, with holistic medicine and with organicist models in biology, all of which are posing the same kinds of challenge to orthodox traditions.

The very interesting question is: Why should alternative models of rationality be associated with the feminine, and why should women seeking an authentic sense of Otherness feel in tune with these alternatives?

Some feminist theories deal with difference by minimising it, and in particular by arguing against 'essentialism'. Their objection is that even to acknowledge difference, particularly if it is as complex as an alternative model of rationality, tempts the commentator either to search for a biological or physiological essence, or at the very least to accept that there is functional utility in the difference between male and female roles. But there are ways of avoiding essentialism, while at the same time recognising that there is a valid link between a hidden culture, and female experience and consciousness.

There are several ways to explain different perspectives or different styles of approaching knowledge. One argument is that the dominant culture attributes to any non-dominant group an antithetical position, or set of (negative) attributes. This polarisation affirms the attributes (and superiority) of the dominant group. A possible response from the non-dominant group is to accept the classification – but turn its meaning and evaluation upside down. So one may accept the mind–body split, the emotion–reason split, of masculine Cartesian rationality, but *invert* the value placed upon it by the dominant culture. In effect, the subordinate group is saying: *Yes, I accept that description of the world and our differences, but who would want to be like a man (or white person, or whatever)? My qualities are superior, and much more useful.* But the non-dominant group may be so alienated that they reject the dominant perspective entirely, and seek alternative schemas. So they may look to traditions and lay social theories which offer a more authentic definition and explanation of their experience. These may be hidden or undervalued strands of the mainstream culture, or come from a different culture or historical period. In effect, the subordinate group is saying: *Your picture of me and my world is completely wrong – you have no knowledge of the reality of my life. There are historical traditions of my group of which you know nothing, or that you have suppressed.* A third type of response acknowledges that there are some specifically female experiences which make certain issues salient, and predispose women to select some metaphors, schemas and lay social theories rather than others. These include experiences tied to the body; metaphors of cyclicity, embeddedness or enclosedness, and wetness.

Women (like other subordinate groups) also experience being on the margins, being the spectator who sees most of the game. As the servicers of men, women watch how the game-players operate; they see the rationalist system failing. Women are reared to be aware of the mainstream, and to participate in it through formal education, but in some ways they are less constrained by it. If women are free not to play the game according to the rules of the mainstream, they can explore other possibilities – though women who do participate in the game *may* be constrained to be very mainstream in order to be accepted. So not only may women sometimes be freer to innovate and seek alternative solutions, they are also able to entertain the *idea* that there can be more than one solution.

An important question is whether experiencing inauthenticity and alienation makes certain attributes necessary. Is cooperation actually more useful to the oppressed than to the oppressor? Does the capacity to take the point of view of many arise from being constantly at the margins? Lynne Segal, for example, in discussing Carol Gilligan's view of a female moral perspective, says:

> Perhaps this moral sensibility would disappear . . . if women were as socially valued and privileged as men. It is well known that those with less social power and confidence are more likely to develop a greater attentiveness, watchfulness and desire to please in their relations with others. These are typical characteristics of all subordinated peoples – at least, as Frantz Fanon would say, until the point of resistance. Such capacities are a necessary protection against the greater vulnerability to discrimination or abuse.[6]

The question then is: Does one join the mainstream and take on its attributes when one has successfully 'resisted', or does one choose to undermine the mainstream by promoting an alternative evaluation of one's former 'subordinate' attributes?[7]

Selfhood and culture

These problems of the connection between alternative models of rationality and gender raise wider questions about culture. Focusing on women and men in Western society ignores the fact that virtually all these issues are routinely raised by anthropologists. Should we treat women and men as if they occupied different cultures? Cross-cultural material can tell us quite a lot about Otherness. One's subjective sense of self is how one experiences oneself *within a particular culture*. Cultures vary considerably in how they define the self. Clifford Geertz describes the male self, in several cultures, as it is subjectively experienced – or at least, as it is accounted for in ways that are comprehensible within that culture.[8] The metaphors vary dramatically, but what is interesting is what is taken for granted, not in need of explanation, and what is not. Different things are salient; different things need control, management, and enhancement. Most important, the *boundaries* of self are different.

Western male – particularly American male – self underlies most of Western psychology and most of Western writing about self, whether this be literary, artistic or psychological. It certainly underlies what we understand to be the ordinary, subjective experience of the Western male. Self is conceived 'as a bounded, unique, more or less integrated, motivational and cognitive universe, a dynamic centre of awareness, emotion, judgement and action, organised into a distinctive whole and set contrastedly against other such wholes, and against a social and natural background'.[9] For Western Man, the boundaries are between the inner self and the outer, other selves, or the external material world; the public versus the private domain. We extend the boundaries of selfhood to include others 'like' ourselves, and certain physical objects and spaces which are identified with our self – our house, our car, our clothes. Such boundaries are made explicit by what we find disgusting; we find our own bodily fluids perfectly pleasant and 'part of' us as long as they remain within the boundaries of the body, but repellent once they have left. We happily swallow the saliva in our mouth, but cannot do so with the same saliva after it has been spat out.[10] In relationships, we have access to the bounded space of others – their homes, and their bodies.

The boundaries for Javanese Man are set differently. There is a sharp division between Inside Self and Outside Self – not quite the private and public domain of Western self. The Inside Self is subjective and emotional, it is what is experienced as Self. The Outside Self is observable behaviour. It is not just a question, as it were, of 'how I feel privately' and 'how I feel publicly', it is the Self as experienced versus the Self as perceived by others. For both aspects of Self, what is important is balance:

> The outside and the inside are regarded not as functions of one another but as independent realms of being to be put in order independently. It is in connection with this proper ordering the contrast between *alus*, a word meaning pure, refined and smooth, and *kasar*, the word meaning impolite, uncivilised and coarse comes into play. The goal is to be *alus* in both the separated realms of the self.[11]

In Bali, life is a stage; the self is conceived in dramaturgical terms, defined in terms of roles:

> There is a systematic attempt to stylise all aspects of personal expression to the point where anything idiosyncratic, anything characteristic of the individual . . . is muted in favour of his assigned place in the continuing,

never-changing pageant that is Balinese life. It is *dramatis personae* not actors that endure . . . indeed, that in a proper sense really exist.[12]

In the Western model the public Self is the presentation of a different aspect from the private Self; in Javanese culture public and private Selves are distinct, but the Balinese Self does not appear to acknowledge a private existence. These examples show how *different things need to be explained* about the Self. Where the Self is 'public', particularly in Bali, any deviation from the role performance would be problematic; how could one have experiences that were not constrained and defined by rules and roles? In a role one does not exist independently, only in relation to others who play the reciprocal roles.

In contrast, Western Man – and I use the word Man advisedly – has a highly individualised conception of himself as a unique being separated from others, creating a coherent, internal self which contrasts with other selves. The individual in Western society is highly self-directed, highly self-conscious. What is problematic for Western Man is anything which appears not to fit into this coherent Self, not under its control. The Self is threatened by things which *disturb* – for example, by too much emotion, even by too much awareness, by things which *threaten the boundaries* and make the Self more permeable to the influence of others. It is also threatened by *ideas which reduce individual autonomy*. The model of rational, autonomous being is central to the model of Western Man, able to organise and control all those areas of life which fall within his own bounded universe of self.

The metaphor of Western Self helps to make sense of the link between rationality and masculinity. A central metaphor of rationality is *mastery* – over the environment, over others, and over ideas. This emerged in seventeenth-century models of relationships between the human being and the environment. I have explored how new technological rationality became mapped on to masculinity, and now the dualism of male rationality and female irrationality goes back to Aristotle. There was a resurgence of the synonymity of masculinity and rationality in the nineteenth century, with the emergence of a major new metaphor which came to dominate lay social theories about a very wide range of issues: the metaphor of evolution.

Evolution theory and the threat of the feminine

Darwin's evolution theory fuelled beliefs about sex differences – partly through his own writings on the scientific basis for gender differentiation, but partly because the evolution metaphor implies certain conceptions of masculinity. The same threat to masculinity which had existed for several hundred years was extended, through the evolution metaphor, to new areas.

The idea that Man was in a state of biological evolution was a new and important metaphor in the nineteenth century. In a sense, the 'perfectibility of man' moved from being the task of the soul to the task of the species – or 'race' in contemporary terminology. By the latter part of the nineteenth century it had became important in a vast number of areas of life. Evolution implies progress and change, towards a positive improvement and a higher state. Negative consequences come not from the wrong kind of change, but from impeding the process of evolution. Change occurs as a consequence of creating the optimal conditions for evolution. The concept of 'natural selection' and 'survival of the fittest', the metaphor which Darwin took from reading Malthus, enabled him to transform evolution into a working theory.[13]

This metaphor gave a cutting edge to the popular idea that progress happened only to those who deserved it. Not only was man in evolution, but he had an obligation to pursue activities which furthered this. This concept was reflected in art and literature as well as social and natural science. It fitted well into emergent capitalism and imperial expansion, and the exploitation of natural and human resources. There were certain key elements in the schema of Man's – specifically the male's – continuing evolution to the highest state. One was rationality, which transcended emotion to an extent, but particularly transcended sensuality. A second was masculinity, which contrasted with femininity; the masculine self could not 'evolve' if it had the trappings of the feminine.

The logic of this is complex. It arose from something Darwin said about sex differences.[14] He argued at one point that beings were originally hermaphrodite, and sexual differentiation emerged in the course of evolution, as part of the survival of the fittest. It seemed to follow – cautiously in the hands of Darwin, crudely in the hands of popularisers of Social Darwinism – that further evolution depended upon increasing sexual differentiation. Social engineering should encourage rather than impede this. So the prototype of woman which already prevailed in the mid nineteenth century was strengthened by the justification that femininity should be in sharp contrast to masculinity for the *benefit of the species*; crossing gender boundaries was going against evolutionary progress. By the beginning of the twentieth century a highly rational self came to be seen as the heritage of evolution – a self which, to survive, had to deny areas of non-rationality, and inevitably to deny the feminine. Such a model of the self depends on the assumption of a bounded, unique and integrated universe, and the belief that the self can be defined and controlled.

This prototype of the masculine had been developing for two hundred years; it was given an additional dimension by the metaphor of evolution. Other nineteenth-century metaphors – imperialism, for example – enhanced the idea of the male's control over himself, and mastery over the environment. What is problematic – what has to be explained – within this model are deviations from the prototype, and threats to the rational self. A major threat was the feminine, and woman. There were issues of woman's natural qualities, of men's relationship with women, and how to deal with men who did not fit into the prototype of the masculine super-hero. Finally, and most difficult – how to deal with one's own behaviour and feelings that did not concur with the ideal?

One way to deal with woman's Otherness was in terms of her natural difference and inferiority. Above, I explored two models of difference. One was *hierarchy*, where the antithetical quality is inferior; so one is rational only by fighting the irrational, one is strong only by fighting one's weakness, one is masterful only by fighting one's submissiveness, one is active only by fighting one's passivity. The antithesis defines by negation, but it also constitutes threat. The other model of difference was *functional complementarity*, where both characteristics are necessary for the effective working of the team, but they are assigned to one or other partner. Though in principle functional complementarity need not assign tasks on the basis of gender, in practice they tend to be aligned on the basis of essences. In both these models, man perceives woman as Other and as different. By being in contact with woman, man risks being contaminated by her femininity; in relating to a woman, there is always a danger that her femininity will rub off and dilute the masculine.

There was a general feeling around the turn of the century that boys needed protection from the dangerous influences of the feminine in order to maintain their masculine selves. The reciprocal was true: girls might be contaminated by masculinity. A separation of the sexes, especially in education, prevented each from being polluted by qualities of the other. This accords with the idea that sexual dimorphism is essential for evolutionary progress. But much of male terror of the female derives from sexuality. If rational man required the taming influence of female submission and female virtue, then if, in turn, women had strong sexual feelings, this would constitute a threat. Women who expressed sexual desires distracted men and detracted from their rationality.[15]

That this issue really was problematic is obvious from the enormous amount of literature arguing that women who were not naturally 'feminine' were pathological. The natural state of womanhood was submission to her husband and lack of sexual autonomy. Anything that deviated from this was seen as dangerous to the species and destructive to social order. This was a complex picture. Sexually predatory women were defined as ill and degenerate, but women who were deviant in other ways – who did not submit to the power of men – also became tagged in this way. So feminists in that period, who largely presented themselves as rational beings and not sexually demanding, were cast in the same light. The 'virago' was not using her 'natural' sexual feelings – those designed solely for reproduction and submission to her mate; her sexual feelings had been twisted and contorted. Her attempts to be equal to men could be ridiculed as not consistent with nature and, in fact, were also highly dangerous because they upset the natural order of things and the natural evolution of man.

So, paradoxically, the feminist virago, whose stereotype was an unattractive, middle-aged woman, was aligned with the nymphomaniac, that creature who epitomised degeneracy in the female. The underlying concept was that all females had the potential for slipping into violence, lust and sinfulness, but most females who had evolved normally did not show these characteristics; all women who displayed 'unnatural' characteristics were suspect. These paradoxes – and their reflection in both 'high' and 'low' art – are explored in Bram Dijkstra's stimulating book, *Idols of Perversity*.[16]

Women and feminine symbols posed a threat to the rational man's image of himself, but homosexuality was worse. There is a deep paradox of homosexuality. On the one hand truly evolved men are heterosexual, they are masculine, they reject the feminine in themselves, they reject the influence of women. They also reject men of those other races that are perceived as having feminine characteristics. These characteristics are associated with degeneracy, which, in the imagery of the immediate post-Darwinian period, was manifested by hairiness and similarity to the apes, but also by sensuality. Jews, Negroes and others fitted various categories under this heading.

Male purity and the threat of the feminine

The paradox is that one way to avoid contamination by the feminine is to live in an exclusively masculine world. Many writers advocated this and even, in certain cases, homosexual relationships as a means of preserving the truly masculine, truly evolved self. Contact with woman was best avoided in order to prevent sexual feelings – certainly heterosexual feelings. Thus man might be free both from the physical self and from the feminine self. The paradox has always been that anxiety about homosexuality arises because it is associated with an effeminate image, yet that very terror of effeminacy is also manifested in avoidance of women and seeking an exclusively male world. This Platonic position has been a powerful undercurrent in Western thought. It rests upon a spiritual ideal, which in the nineteenth century became conflated with a evolutionist ideal. Man attains his true purpose only in communion with the divine. This entails transcending the material and the sensual, and possessing the capacity for reflection, rationality and consciousness. The first-century Hellenistic philosopher Philo of Alexandria argued that 'Man realises his true nature by forsaking the transient, ephemeral, material world, giving himself wholly to the quest for virtue, and opening himself completely to receive the grace of God.'[17]

The relevance of a first-century mystic to thinking about metaphors of masculinity and femininity two thousand years later becomes clear when we see how Philo conceptualised the struggle for communion with God, and how his concept became mapped on to popularisations of evolution. For Philo, the first man was androgynous, made in God's image and not subject to sexual desire. But man's soul is divided into a higher rational part, which is indivisible, and a lower irrational part, which is subdivided into masculine and feminine. This creates a problem. The higher self is not necessarily masculine/male; indeed, females can attain communion with God. But Philo equated the senses with the 'feminine', and classified natural weakness and susceptibility to temptation as feminine, characteristic of women as people. So the attributes which lead to attaining the ideal state are 'masculine', even if both sexes may possess them – and obviously it is more dificult for females to do this. Salvation meant breaking away from the power of the female, both the feminine in oneself and the emotional and sensual power of actual women; this was typical of Gnostic thought.

Philo's gender metaphors were very explicit: 'manly reasoning schooled in fortitude'; 'Progress is indeed nothing else than the giving up of the female gender by changing into the male, since the female gender is maternal, passive, corporeal and sense-perceptible, while the male is active, rational, incorporeal and more akin to mind and thought.'[18] Therefore, 'It was fitting that man shall rule over immortality and everything good, but women over death and everything vile.'[19] A fascinating manifestation of this, showing how deep the metaphor of gender went, is Philo's discussion of the symbolism of the Number 7:

virgin among numbers
essentially motherless
begotten by the father of the universe alone
ideal form of the male with nothing of the female
the manliest and bravest of numbers
well-gifted by nature for sovereignty and leadership
the opportune moment
the symbol of knowledge and perfection of mind[20]

This encapsulates the equation of masculinity and perfection – and, by contrast, casts the feminine as the negation, the antithesis, and the potential subverter of the masculine.

The most significant modern exemplar of this philosophy was Otto Weininger.[21] His *Sex and Character* was published in 1906, when he was twenty-three, and became a bestseller – its significance is that it reflected and fed into a *Zeitgeist*. It was a highly influential book, especially for writers attacking feminism. It is still quoted even today – most recently by Roger Scruton.[22] In Weininger's writings one hears echoes of all this century's quasi-scientific and spiritual arguments against woman; it is as though current male chauvinism is merely a footnote to Weininger.

Weininger drew heavily on contemporary popularisations and extensions of evolution theory (though he did strongly contest the idea that humans were descended from monkeys). He attacked feminism specifically on the basis of women's inferiority and lack of 'genius', but his arguments were more profound. The evolved male is in danger from the feminine in himself and in women around him. Sexual dimorphism was the outcome of true progress, so males became ever more rational and spiritual, females ever more materialistic and physical. There was a conceptual ideal of 'absolute' men and 'absolute' women – yet many people of both sexes had a mixture of characteristics; women who were talented and successful (and he did concede that such women existed) were possessed of many masculine attributes, both physical and psychological. They were 'intermediate types' – as were homosexuals and many talented men, especially in the field of music. A measure of the complexity of Weininger's position is that he saw such people as valuable, and to be encouraged. He was opposed to legal discrimination against homosexuals, for example; and he considered that the rare talented woman should be able to fulfil herself. It was women *as a whole* who could never achieve the heights of the masculine; this, for him, made a nonsense of feminism.

Weininger's gender metaphors, like Philo's, cast the feminine as the antithesis of the rational, noble and spiritual masculine:

> As the absolute female has no trace of individuality and will, no sense of work or of love, she can have no part in the higher transcendental life. The intelligible, hyper-empirical existence of the male transcends matter, space and time. He is certainly mortal but he is immortal as well . . . . The deepest will of man is towards this perfect, timeless existence; he is a compact of the desire for immortality.[23]

Weininger explicitly equated masculinity with autonomy:

The birth of Kantian ethics, the noblest event in the history of the world, was the moment when for the first time the dazzling awful conception came to him 'I am responsible only to myself; I must follow none other: I must not forget myself even in my work: I am alone: I am free: I am the lord of myself[24]

He saw women as wholly incapable of such autonomy – indeed, it was their 'nothingness' that was the antithesis of the male 'something': 'Women have no existence and no essence; they are not, they are nothing. Mankind occurs as male or female, as something or nothing.'[25] Therefore woman is wholly dependent on man, and seeks him as a mate; she is parasitic.

For Weininger the route to true destiny and genius requires rejection not only of the feminine but of sexual desire. He equated women with sexuality, and saw all women as pursuing sexual congress with men: 'To put it bluntly, man possesses sexual organs, her organs possess her.'[26] A man's attractiveness to a woman is entirely his sexuality: 'The qualities that appeal to a woman are the signs of developed sexuality; those that repel her are the qualities of the higher mind. Woman is essentially a phallus worshipper.'[27] The reason for this is partly that woman's destiny is to reproduce, but this is interwoven with Weininger's overriding dualistic model of the world:

The decision must be made between Judaism and Christianity, between business and culture, between male and female, between the race and the individual, between unworthiness and worth, between the earthly and the higher, between negation and the God-like. Mankind has the choice to make. There are only two poles, and there is no middle way.[28]

For man, love of women is impossible, for she has no worth. Therefore, when a man loves, what he is loving is a projection of himself:

Can any one believe that it is a concrete person who is loved? Does she not in reality merely serve as the starting point of incomparably greater emotions than she could inspire? In love, man is only loving himself. Not his empirical self, nor the weaknesses and vulgarities, not the failings and smallnesses which he actually exhibits, but all that he wants to be, all that he ought to be, his truest, deepest, intelligible nature, free from all fetters of necessity, from all taint of earth.[29]

It follows, also, that sexual desire is incompatible with love; sexual desire drags one down into the material, so by definition, if one has physical contact with the object of one's love, love dies.

This antipathy towards women, and the threat of the feminine to any higher level of thought, or immortality, means that men must avoid the feminine, and reject sex. It is clear that Weininger had very ambivalent feelings about women; he considered that 'woman's nude body is distasteful to man because it offends his sense of shame'.[30] This, combined with his dualistic world-view, makes it unsurprising that he should say: 'I shall show reasons in favour of the possibility that homosexuality is a higher form than heterosexuality.'[31]

Weininger was that dangerous combination, an immature man and a genius. He wrote superbly and argued with wide-ranging scholarship. He killed himself at the age of twenty-three, but left the heritage of a tortured and unstable adolescent under the intolerable strain of asceticism and desire for immortality. His arguments fed anti-Semitism as well as anti-feminism; the characteristics of woman were seen as common to other races, especially Jews. Weininger considered that Judaism was 'saturated with femininity', and that Jews sought Aryans as women sought men, because without them they had no existence. He was Jewish himself.

As Dijkstra says: 'Weininger was clearly mad . . . .Yet . . . his contentions were simply one more step on the same road of dualistic extremism trod by the majority of turn-of-the-century intellectuals.'[32] Indeed, it was around this time that Rupert Brooke said, as I quoted above, 'This mixture of the sexes is all wrong . . . . Male is male and female is female . . . manliness is the one hope of the world.'[33] Weininger 's importance lies in the success of his book; it clearly spoke to, and affirmed, a prevailing lay social theory. Weininger also had great influence on Ludwig Wittgenstein. According to Wittgenstein's biographer, Ray Monk, Weininger's influence on Wittgenstein lay in his 'strict separation of love from sexual desire, . . . uncompromising view of the worthlessness of everything save the products of genius, and its conviction that sexuality is incompatible with the honesty that genius demands'. Furthermore, Weininger's interpretation of Kant's Moral Law implies that 'To acquire genius . . . is not merely a noble ambition; it is a Categorical Imperative'.[34]

Weininger was extreme, yet he distilled two of the popularisations of the evolution metaphor: beliefs about sex difference, and conceptions of the autonomous masculine self. The threats he confronted, and their proposed resolution, by their very existence affirmed the definition of what they threatened. This is an elaborated example of why we must take seriously the psychodynamic underpinnings of dualism. The problem is in the very definition of the masculine self. Because of the lingering equation of masculinity with rationality and evolutionary supremacy, assumptions of natural difference between the sexes will inevitably conclude with the inferiority of women in most areas of life, except those involving nurturance, because the areas of female 'superiority' are those associated with meeting male deficit, and providing back-up for the male in his publicly rational, nominally autonomous roles. A difference means *boundaries*. To deny the difference means denying the boundary. So denying differences between the sexes denies the particular qualities of masculine and feminine. Lack of difference undermines, feminises or emasculates – or masculinises and defeminises.

But there is another deep anxiety underlying beliefs about difference and beliefs about the feminine. If the feminine is potentially irrational, and possibly evil, because femaleness is closer to nature and therefore in conflict with culture, a woman may disrupt the carefully maintained balance between man's rational and emotional self. If females are fundamentally deeply irrational, allowing women social power will itself produce social chaos. Giving women access to that domain of rationality which is the traditional preserve of men would release chaos, and men would be dragged down into it. This may all sound fanciful, and even if it was widely believed a hundred years ago, one would imagine that this could not still be so. Yet it is clear that many men are deeply terrified of women's power over them, and the power of their own sexuality to override rationality. To change this state entails transforming the metaphors of Otherness. It requires more than the assertion of fact – it requires postulating an alternative which cannot just be absorbed into the existing antithesis.

Notes

1. C. Gilligan, *In a Different Voice*, Cambridge, MA: Harvard University Press, 1982.
2. E. Fox Keller, *Reflections on Gender and Science*, New Haven, CT: Yale University Press, 1985; E. Fox Keller, *A Feeling for the Organism*, San Francisco: Freeman, 1983.
3. C. Makward, 'To be or not to be . . . a feminist speaker', in H. Eisenstein and A. Jardine (eds), *The Future of Difference*, Boston, MA: Hall, 1980, p. 96.
4. S. de Beauvoir, *The Second Sex*, trans H. M. Parshley, London: Cape, 1953; G. Lloyd, *The Man of Reason: 'Male' and 'female' in Western philosophy*, London: Methuen, 1984.
5. J. Flax, 'Post-modernism and gender relations in feminist theory', *Signs*, **12(4)**, pp. 621–43, 1987.
6. L. Segal, *Is the Future Female?*, London: Virago, 1987, p. 148.

7. G. M. Breakwell, 'Women: group or identity?', *Women's Studies International Quarterly*, **2**, pp. 9–17, 1979; J. Williams and H. Giles, 'The changing status of women in society: an intergroup perspective', in H. Tajfel (ed.), *Differentiation between Social Groups*, London: Academic Press, 1978.

8. C. Geertz, 'On the nature of anthropological understanding', *American Scientist*, **63**, pp. 47–53, January 1975.

9. *ibid.*, p. 48.

10. P. Rozin and A. E. Fallon, 'A perspective on disgust', *Psychological Review*, **94**, pp. 23–47, 1987.

11. Geertz, 'On the nature of anthropological understanding', p. 49.

12. *ibid.*, p. 50.

13. R. M. Young, *Darwin's Metaphor: Nature's place in Victorian culture*, Cambridge: Cambridge University Press, 1985; H. Gruber, *Darwin on Man: A psychological study of scientific creativity, together with Darwin's early and unpublished notebooks transcribed and annotated by Paul H. Barrett*, London: Wildwood Press, 1974.

14. C. Darwin, *The Descent of Man and Selection in Relation to Sex*, London: John Murray, 1871. Facsimile edition, edited with introduction by J. T. Bonner and R. M. May, Princeton, NJ: Princeton University Press, 1981, p. 210.

15. Dijkstra, *Idols of Perversity: Fantasies of feminine evil in* fin-de-siècle *culture*, Oxford: Oxford University Press, 1986; E. Showalter, *Sexual Anarchy: Gender and culture at the* fin de siècle, London: Bloomsbury, 1991.

16. Dijkstra, *Idols of Perversity*.

17. R. A. Baer, *Philo's Use of the Categories Male and Female*, Arbeiten zur Literatur und Geschichte des Hellenistischen Judentums III, Leiden: E. J. Brill, 1970, p. 45.

18. *ibid.*, p. 46.

19. *ibid.*, p. 41.

20. *ibid.*, pp. 50–1.

21. Otto Weininger, *Sex and Character*, London: Heinemann, 1906.

22. R. Scruton, *Sexual Desire: A philosophical investigation*, London: Weidenfeld & Nicolson, 1986.

23. Weininger, *Sex and Character*, p. 284.

24. *ibid.*, p. 161.

25. *ibid.*, p. 286.

26. *ibid.*, p. 92.

27. *ibid.*, p. 250.

28. *ibid.*, p. 330.

29. *ibid.*, p. 243.

30. *ibid.*, p. 241.

31. *ibid.*, p. 66.

32. Dijkstra, *Idols of Perversity*, p. 221.

33. R. Brooke, quoted in C. Hassall, *Rupert Brooke: A biography*, London: Faber & Faber, 1964.

34. R. Monk, *Ludwig Wittgenstein: The duty of genius*, New York: Free Press, 1990, p. 25.

Chapter 5: Changing the scenarios

I own two books of cartoons – by different authors – entitled 'I'm not a feminist, but . . .'.[1] This widely heard expression signifies the concerns of ordinary women who encounter sexual inequality, yet reject the conventional image of feminists. A student of mine, Jane Baddeley, found that many women thought the Women's Movement had benefited them personally in a variety of ways, yet their image of feminists was 'fat people with hairy legs' or 'ugly, shouting, angry people'.[2] The ideas that come out of feminism have penetrated Western culture far more effectively than has the image of feminists. There is a clear division between people, of both sexes, for whom being feminist is an essential part of their identity, and those who regard feminism with suspicion and hold stereotypes about feminists. The backlash against feminism is profoundly defensive, reflecting deep antipathy and fear. Backlash writers stereotype feminists, and reject most of the ideas which have come out of feminism. But they hold an undifferentiated ragbag image of what feminism is actually about.

The recent feminist theories have a lot in common with previous efforts, despite different historical and cultural contexts, and different explicit agendas. One uniting theme of feminism at all times is the desire to change the power relations between the sexes in order to create greater equality. Different agendas for pursuing this goal reflect different interpretations of the causes of the situation. A major target has always been the legal constraints which directly or indirectly limit women's access to fields of work and public life. Another is financial constraints, whether they arise from legal rules about women's right to property, or out of a social structure which makes women the financial dependants of men.

These targets fuelled the setting up of the medieval beguines as much as they stimulated the Equal Rights Amendment. But all feminist movements rapidly discover that changing the law is not enough. It is rarely possible, in any case, to change a law effectively without eventually changing the underlying conceptions of gender roles that created and sustained that law. Even when the statute alters, it becomes obvious that there are still deep-seated lay social theories in place about gender. In principle, the American Constitution made it easy to pass an equal rights amendment; it was really only a matter of ratifying an existing statute. Yet American society has had no less a struggle than those European societies who needed new laws to create equality, to alter cultural beliefs about gender roles that govern nearly every aspect of everyday life.

Feminist theories are diverse, but the common agenda is relocating the definition of self – out of a male perspective into a female perspective. It is a claim for the right to authentic self-definition, rejecting both a male conception of female Otherness, and the narrow boundaries of cultural conceptions of female roles. Forms of feminism differ in how this is to be achieved, and in what is seen to be the problem.

Claiming an authentic definition has two strands. One is to gain freedom and autonomy for the self: freedom of movement, freedom of thought, freedom of self-development. It means affirming the capacity to live an autonomous life, to make autonomous decisions and to operate as a self-defining being. The other strand is to get women out of 'underclass' status. Practically, this means gaining *opportunity*, giving women access to the skills necessary to avoid dependency and deprivation. But symbolic changes are also needed, in explanations and in the lay social theories which justify defining women as inferior beings.

Feminism, in all its forms, creates an *anti-logos*. I have described the dominant *logos*: a view of male–female relations which asks certain types of questions, and takes certain things for granted. The very nature of the question defines the status of the issue. Questions about what is taken for granted seek explanations for why these states of affairs are normal; questions about what is seen as problematic seek explanations for why such problematic situations exist.

The first task is to make gender problematic in new ways. In traditional views of gender, the feminine was problematic in relation to the norm of the masculine. Women were 'not-men' – less than, or other than, men. But at the same time, such difference was seen as natural and normal, not needing explanation. Making gender problematic in new ways means questioning taken-for-granted assumptions about the nature and origins of sex difference, but it also means offering new ways of looking at actual differences, and at the meaning of difference itself.

There are several ways to create an *anti-logos*. Let us consider as an example a fictional company that has a policy of not employing women in one of its main manufacturing departments. One approach is to work within the existing *logos* but redefine the boundaries; the broad picture is accepted, but the implications need reinterpreting. This can be done by extending the range of exceptions – for example, accepting some natural differences, but considering how compensatory factors could overcome their limitations. The world-view remains essentially the same, but more flexible in its applications.

MANAGING DIRECTOR: We do not employ women in J Section.
QUESTIONER: Why not?
MD: Because they do not have the physical strength or the technical know-how to do the job.
Q: But there are some women who would be strong enough for the tasks, particularly with training, and surely there are a lot of women these days who have got a technical background. You might be right in general, but there are a lot of exceptions.

A second onslaught might point out where the existing *logos* is factually wrong, and therefore why both premises and conclusions are incorrect. If there are no real sex differences, then the whole argument is based upon an illusion – there is nothing to explain about difference, and similarity, not difference, has to be taken for granted and explained as normal. In order to correct the situation, there has to be some explanation of why the illusion of difference arose in the first place.

MD: We don't employ women in J Section.
Q: Why not?
MD: Because they don't have the physical strength or the technical know-how.
Q: But that's ridiculous. The skills you need in J Section are things like driving and operating machinery that women did all through the two wars, and are doing all over the country, and girls do just as well as boys in technical subjects.
MD: Well, we've never found many women interested in the work anyway.
Q: Maybe you ought to consider whether you're deliberately putting them off when you advertise.

A third approach is to replace the existing *logos* with a new *logos*, start again from scratch with a new frame of reference. This is not the same thing as undermining the facts. It is not a matter only of what are believed to be essences, but of what is believed about the functional interrelationship between male and female essence. Sweeping away an argument means removing beliefs about this interrelationship, not only beliefs about the differences.

The possible complexity of this may be seen in the way we deal with the contrast between female innocence and vulnerability, and male rapaciousness and lack of control. It would logically follow from this image that we should equip young girls with weapons to defend themselves. But until very recently efforts to control males emphasised that 'good' males should protect women against 'evil' males. It was also assumed that if women did not cultivate the aura of innocence and vulnerability, they would stimulate the bestial nature of males – and therefore be to blame for the consequences. These beliefs have long underpinned the interpretation of rape.

Another example is the tension between rationality and irrationality, where rationality seems constantly vulnerable to the forces of chaos. As we have seen, this was an issue during the seventeenth century; there was a resurgence at the end of the nineteenth. Rampant sexuality constitutes a part of this threat, corrupting, polluting and bringing chaos. Women are protected from their own potentially chaotic *alter egos* by a casing of innocence. If they lose their innocence they become corrupt and corrupting, both to themselves and to men. This argument has always been used to keep sexual material from the eyes of women, even as late as the *Lady Chatterley* trial in 1960. Mervyn Griffith-Jones, prosecuting counsel, asked whether this was 'a book that you would have lying around in your house? Is it a book that you would even wish your wife or your servants to read?'[3]

Creating an *anti-logos* to a view of male aggression and bestiality, barely controlled by a combination of rationality and female virtue, could just involve a factual critique – that women are not innocent even if they pretend to be, and that on the whole, rationality triumphs most of the time for most men. Unfortunately, this is an area of great subjective anxiety – for both sexes. Men fear loss of their self-control; women fear sexual assault. An effective *anti-logos* cannot deny either of these elements, but must instead break the model of relationship in which the illusory 'innocence' of women is used as a brake on the 'natural' unfettered violence of men. Removing the image of women's helplessness – without denying their genuine vulnerability – is the first stage of this.

In our hypothetical company, the argument might go like this:

MD: We don't employ women in J Section.
Q: Why not?
MD: Well, it's an all-male place with a lot of pressure, and the men tend to get tense and swear – not nice for the ladies to hear! But I'd also be worried that they'd get distracted by the women – you know –

especially the sexy ones, and this kind of thing can wreck a team of fellows. And the fellows would be worrying about the women getting hurt, as well; it's a tough workshop.

Q: You seem to have a rather strange view about women's sensibilities and helplessness. I think you'd find that both sexes of workers would just get on with the job together, working in teams effectively. It might be a different atmosphere from before in some ways, but I think your vision of a seething cauldron of repressed sex and resentment because the men can't swear is rather fanciful.

A fourth kind of *anti-logos* questions the premises upon which a model of dualistic relations is founded. It questions the questions themselves – in this case, the definition of difference itself. To start with our hypothetical company:

MD: We don't employ women in J Section.
Q: Why not?
MD: We don't think they've got the necessary physical or psychological make-up for the work.
Q: I've been down in J Section and I think there's a whole lot wrong there. What that work needs is a different style of management, more cooperative, more flexible. You've got a set-up which looks like the army. You rely on competition to get things done, you exaggerate the macho aspects of the job and don't give value to interaction and the sharing of ideas – it's all who can beat the other guy? and the one who does, gets to the top of the heap. It's a real hierarchy.
MD: Are you suggesting that if we hired women they'd run the whole show differently?
Q: Maybe, maybe not. What I'm saying is that you've set the place up according to some image of the male team and what 'men' are like. Then you employ only men and set up these expectations. Why not look at what the job needs, and then get the right people for that? You might find that women were more at ease developing certain of those skills than men are, because they don't have the same hang-ups about the macho role.
MD: But I would be worried about trusting women with decision-making; they don't seem always . . . well . . . rational to me – mind you, some men seem a bit feminine in their thinking too, in that way.
Q: Has it ever occurred to you that there may be more than one way to arrive at a solution?

This undermines the basic premises of the *logos*. It asks: Why are differences worth considering? But it also asks: Why do you take for granted the conventional definitions which lead you to ask that kind of question about difference in the first place? Feminist critics of social science objected that traditional research on difference reproduced the conventional stereotypes. This was partly an artefact of the academic game – one can publish evidence only of significant difference, not of similarity. But partly, the research questions were set in the terms of reference of conventional wisdom. So they found differences, or failed to find them, in well-trodden areas, but did not seek other differences which have subsequently emerged – differences which did not conform either to models of hierarchical relations between a male norm and a female deficit, or to models of functional relations between complementary instrumental and expressive gender roles.

The first three vignettes of our imaginary company adjust, marginally redefine, or deny the relational aspects of gender roles; the fourth reconstructs and reinterprets them. The major impact of feminist theory comes from this kind of *anti-logos*, deconstructing and changing the fundamental principles on which we base lay social theory and folk models of gender. A broad distinction is between policy changes and meaning changes. Changing policy may require a changing understanding of the situation – an appreciation, for example, that one's categories are too rigid, or that a principle (such as equal opportunity) is not being properly applied to certain categories of person. Changing policy may also alter meaning; it is undoubtedly true that certain legislation – for example, on homosexual rights, on abortion and on capital punishment – changed social norms as well as legal practice. But deconstruction and reconstruction start from the *symbolic meaning* of a phenomenon, and look at how this meaning is conveyed, sustained, and protected from questioning.

Redefining Otherness

The clarification of inauthentic self-definition has been a starting point for feminist critique, but there are several ways to challenge and reconstruct Otherness. Not all are confined to feminists. Indeed, some challenges are actually antagonistic to feminism. In Bea Campbell's book *The Iron Ladies*, she identifies two kinds of conservative women: traditional social conservatives, and liberals.[4] The traditional woman is very happy with the division of labour to which she is accustomed. It gives her considerable autonomy in the home and in areas deemed the female domain; these areas are claimed by women as female territory, not simply assigned as such by male society. This is a covert, but in many ways quite effective, way of dealing with the male perspective. These women do not wish to enter the public domain, but they are not submissive and compliant. Their conception of male–female relations is functional complementarity. Men have their world, men have their responsibilities. Men's talents are different from women's, but since no comparison between the two worlds is made, these women have no sense of inferiority. The female world is women's rightful territory, and males are not welcome. This female culture deals with the male's Otherness in a number of ways. Men, far from being superior, have a number of negative characteristics, including a potential for uncontrolled aggression and sexual irresponsibility. The image is of a rather unaware child who needs to be indulged and cared for and have his ego stroked, but is also capable, under certain conditions, of irrational violence and sexual assault.

In this interpretation of Otherness, 'control' means law and order, to prevent violent and licentious men from damaging innocent women. But even the conception of 'innocence' differs from that held by the men who share the rhetoric. These women do not see themselves as ignorant or unaware of reality, but they are vulnerable. They seek legal constraints to prevent the undercurrent of violence and licentiousness entering into their ordered lives. This view of Otherness gives women security of territory, and a sense of self in which they perceive themselves as more rational, mature, controlled and calm than most men. This female culture does not accept the male definition of Otherness; there are quite separate domains of male and female experience, and an alternative model of female experience flourishes.

A different kind of challenge to Otherness denies the premises of male superiority, and even denies significant sex difference. There is no barrier to female entry into the male world – women who are excluded from male privilege are those who have chosen to accept the myths and stereotypes of female frailty rather than proving their equality. This lay social theory sustained most efforts for equal educational and work opportunities, and until recently defined the self-image of most women who succeeded in professional life. Prior to the development of feminist theory, it was the most effective *anti-logos* to conventional theories of gender. It accepts traditional models of rationality, but excludes all the implications of a dark tension between masculine and feminine, between rationality and chaos. It rejects the dualistic metaphor, and claims all persons' right to membership of a rational, androgynous world.

A final response to Otherness is the one described by Simone de Beauvoir. It includes awareness of women's exclusion from a cultural heritage. Even if one can share knowledge and activity, one is never fully 'of' the culture. Women who acknowledge this alienation, while feeling themselves truly entitled to be part of the cultural heritage, frequently use the metaphor of a mirror. Virginia Woolf saw herself and other women being forced to be mirrors held up to reflect the male ego – with no reciprocal response from men to the female ego.[5] One could share in that world, succeed in it even, but have no schemas for making sense of those areas of female experience which did not lend themselves to androgyny. Because they could not – and would not – fit the conventional, traditional schemas of male–female relations, there was no way to legitimate their sense of the feminine.

These responses to Otherness predate recent feminist developments, and modern feminism has impinged upon them in very different ways. The traditional conservative women are in many ways the most interesting; these women do not feel any need of a feminist perspective because they already deal efficiently with the less congenial aspects of male–female relations. For those women whose rationalist strategy had been to deny or underplay sex differences, the first phase of recent feminism seemed to grate with self-preoccupation. It took a substantial injection of new understanding about social structure and institutional patriarchy to make them recognise that attacking oppression entailed that one first acknowledge that there were complex and deep-seated resistances to gender-role changes. In the responses to Otherness reflected in de Beauvoir and Woolf, however, were already the seeds of alienation and disaffection, and of the recognition that symbol and meaning are crucial to the cultural ordering of gender – and, therefore, to changing that order.

Modern feminist theory has evolved from several different traditions, and there are some profound differences of emphasis and interpretations – indeed, contradictions. One major distinction is between Enlightenment assumptions and post-modernist assumptions.

A heritage of the Enlightenment is the cult of rationality, and certain conceptions of human rights and human potential. These ideas have been beneficial in a large number of ways – not least in making the idea of rights central to lay social theory. One route of feminism has been to argue that women belong in that culture also. They are entitled to the fruits of the Enlightenment, and entitled to be recognised as rational beings – this was very much Mary Wollstonecraft's position.[6] It follows that we need to remove any justifications for difference which currently prevent women having access to that world of rationality, autonomy and natural rights. Women should be allowed to join the club from which they have been excluded – a club whose own principles should never have permitted such a thing to happen.

A second route is through a post-modernist critique of the Enlightenment. Jane Flax has argued that the Enlightenment model of rationality and truth took for granted certain principles:

the self is stable and has privileged insight into self and laws of nature
reason can provide an objective and universal foundation for knowledge
such knowledge is 'true'; real and universal

reason has transcendental and universal qualities and exists independently of the self's contingent behaviour
complex connections exist between reason, autonomy and freedom
claims of authority are grounded in reason, therefore conflicts can be
overcome, truth can serve power without distortion, and knowledge can
be neutral
science is the paradigm for true knowledge
language is merely the medium for representation of reason; language
makes things present to consciousness rather than constructing them.[7]

Much of the Enlightenment model can be traced directly to the Cartesian
tradition. A major objection to this model is that it ignores variation
in ways of understanding, variation in cultural experience, variation
in possible modes of explanation. The critique of this position asserts
that there are different perspectives from which one can experience the
world. There are different, but equally valid, explanations and accounts.
There is not only one form of truth but many forms of truth, and
many forms of knowledge. Flax proposes that feminist theory should
be an exploration of other authentic ways of experiencing the world
rather than an effort to gain credence within one monolithic model
of experience. Feminism can contribute to a pluralist perspective. The
monolithic model of rationality, authenticity and truth has been the
very model which has previously excluded women because of the
assumption that there is only one way of doing things. So post-
modernist feminism is not only a blueprint for policies to overcome
inequality; it becomes part of current philosophical debates about the
nature of rationality and epistemology.

I shall illustrate this debate by outlining the diversity of four emergent
theories of feminism: *socialist feminist*, *radical feminist*, *cultural feminist* and
liberal feminist. There are commonalities between them, but there are also
major differences. Each offers different explanations for sex differences,
both their nature and their origins. Each implies a different definition
of femininity and what it is to be a woman, and different definitions
of the relations between the sexes. The four theories see different
things as problematic; they see different boundaries to be drawn,
and they also offer different models of solution. Their commonality
is the goal of authentic self-definition, the right to autonomy and
independence.

Socialist feminism

What is broadly termed *socialist* or *socialist-Marxist* feminism is particularly prevalent in Britain and Western Europe. Its basic assumption is

that women's status, women's position in relation to men in general, are consequences of the pressures of capitalism and particularly of a definition of the family which arose out of the organisation of labour in the Industrial Revolution. Socialist feminism focuses on the economic and social system, and how it sustains unequal relations between the sexes in the personal domain and unequal opportunities for the sexes within the public domain. Socialist feminism tends to focus on structural issues, seeing the symbolic elements of gender roles as contingent, or as outcomes, rather than causal. But socialist feminism does attack, profoundly, conventional models of sex differences and their origins.

The argument of socialist feminism is that the Industrial Revolution broke up the pattern of a family unit which had hitherto combined domestic and production roles. In the new large industrial units man became the breadwinner – or at least the main labourer – and woman became to a large extent the support for his labour, even though there was extensive female and child labour during this period. This conception of the family treats the man as economic head of the household and widens the gap between public and private, requiring men to have talents and skills necessary for the work in the public domain, which were not required of women. The goal of feminist critique and feminist reconstruction within this framework is redefining the conception of difference which maintains women in this state of dependency.

The main arguments of socialist feminism are that conventional models of sex difference sustain the male as instrumental breadwinner and the female as submissive, expressive and domestic. The *anti-logos* is to minimise sex differences, and emphasise that most are the consequence of culture rather than nature. Socialist feminism mounts a sustained attack on 'essentialism', whether physical or psychological, but it also attacks existing rhetorical boundaries. The overarching concept is a model of natural justice where there is sexual equality at home, in the workplace and in economic rewards. In Flax's sense, socialist feminism fits the 'Enlightenment' model. The origins of socialist feminism lie in nineteenth- and twentieth-century socialism. The conception of class struggle, and the power of interest groups, is central. In tandem with some rather uneasy efforts to map gender relations on to a model of class relations, there have been somewhat more successful integrations of class and gender which analyse the different kinds of sexual oppression and power inequalities that different social classes experience.

Socialist feminism deals with sex difference by advocating a model of androgyny, where both sexes have the characteristics that are traditionally deemed feminine and masculine.[8] Relations between the sexes are ideally between two people who are fundamentally rather similar and certainly equal in terms of rights and abilities. This minimises difference, and argues that most difference is due to nurture. The dualistic dimensions of interrelationship, such as active–passive and public–private, are interpreted as the outcome of a patriarchal culture that is sustained by an oppressive relationship between the sexes in the private domain and discrimination against women in the public domain.

Until recently socialist feminism has largely failed to address the more psychodynamic aspects of fear of the irrational and the mapping of gender symbolically on to other dualities, perceiving these either as too intrapersonal to be relevant to the political dimensions of change, or as contingent manifestations of the ethos of patriarchy – the assumption has been that making structural changes which removed inequality would overcome these symptoms. The explanation of male violence towards women is that it is the consequence of a macho male image which fits the economic and competitive needs of society. Marital violence and active individual oppression are consequences of frustration arising out of this, or of a distortion of these already corrupt values.

The metaphors of socialist feminism draw upon Marxist models, applying systems from the economic and work spheres to gender. The categories derived by Marx from his description of a particular form of production of commodities are applied to all areas of human life, in all historical periods. Socialist feminism makes issues of production and the division of labour key elements in the explanation of gender difference; this makes labour itself a central activity. As Flax points out, this is not necessarily true of all cultures in the same way as it is true of capitalist society, and the extent to which labour is the essential basis of all human beings is itself questionable. To overcome this kind of objection, socialist feminism has widened the concept of production to include most forms of human activity – this is an example of *extending the boundaries*.

There are some differences between European and American socialism. As a generalisation, one can say that the major difference between the two traditions relates to the place of socialism in mainstream political culture. Socialism, in various forms, influenced reformist thought in Europe during much of the latter part of the nineteenth century, and by the end of the century socialist political parties were beginning to make an institutionalised impact in several countries. The suffrage movement in Britain had support from the fledgling Labour Party, and there has subsequently been continuous overlap between women's movements of various forms and rising socialist power in mainstream politics. For most of the twentieth century socialism has been a major force in European politics. Furthermore, in Europe the long tradition of class and caste struggle is reflected in pessimism about the possibility of social change, and belief in the power of the group rather than the individual. Despite the importance of anarchism in the development of aspects of democratic ideas, and belief in revolution as a means of social change, the main goal of the Left and the Liberal has remained the restructuring of oppressive institutions through pressure on the democratic system – a strategy which means changing the party in power, rather than destroying the system.

American socialism, in contrast, has always been marginalised. First, it is marginalised by the lack of any power base within the government; secondly, it is marginalised in its role in the history of political thought. The nineteenth-century movements out of which, or alongside which, feminism developed in the United States were concerned with the rights of the underprivileged and with equality and overcoming oppression, but they were couched in the rhetoric of the American Bill of Rights, the Enlightenment model of 'rights of man', rather than in structural class divisions which characterise the schemas of the Left in Europe. The American Revolution freed the people from a colonial yoke, a people who had already fled the home country to escape constraints on religious beliefs of various kinds. Anarchism – the protest of revolution against external masters or institutions – has always been more central to American lay political theory than the struggle of classes locked within the same social system. The socialist dimension of American feminist discourse therefore tends to favour schemas which focus on underprivileged groups, especially ethnic groups, more than schemas which see feminist issues as part of the wider class struggle. Revolutionary potential is there on both sides of the Atlantic – as Hester Eisenstein says, 'what would become of present social arrangements, in the capitalist west and indeed, in most societies, capitalist and communist, if all the demands of the women's movement were met with respect to all women?'[9]

The national difference is subtle but important. British women – notably at the History Workshop at Ruskin College Oxford in 1970, but predated by Juliet Mitchell's writing in the previous decade – saw the Women's Movement as a part of the wider socialist struggle which had its own, long-established rhetoric for analysing power.[10] American socialist feminism came out of the Students for Democratic Society and the Civil Rights Movement, much more marginal groups associated with protest for specific rights. While attaining such rights would require the restructuring of the social and legal system, the rhetoric of rights, rather than the rhetoric of class, was predominant.

Radical feminism

Radical feminism developed initially in parallel with socialist feminism, The main strand of the radical feminist position is 'woman-identified-woman'; the *anti-logos* goes straight to the core of authentic self-definition, and the rejection of male definitions of Otherness.[11] To identify oneself as a woman, and be identified in terms of other women, requires exclusion of the male from the definition of the self. This presupposes a female culture and, to some extent, the subjective exclusion of male culture. The consequence of this is that for many radical feminists heterosexual relations are impossible; in relations with a man one has no choice, given the present culture, but to accept his definition of one's Otherness, and society's definition of one's identity as 'his' woman. Thus, lesbian identification is not simply a matter of personal sexual freedom to choose one's partner and one's form of sexuality, it is a political protest against the cornerstone of male supremacy – compulsory heterosexual relations.[12] Only by creating an alternative culture can one truly create an alternative, authentic definition of femininity.

Radical feminism contrasts strikingly with socialist feminism in the way it confronts models and metaphors of gender differences. Whereas socialist feminists play down difference, ascribe it to nurture and to the social structures of patriarchy and capitalism, and aspire to a goal of androgyny and moral equality, radical feminists argue for essential sex differences, based in biology and life experience. Radical feminists do not view culture and economic factors as responsible for women's oppression, except in so far as culture is created as a prop and justification for men's fundamental nature. In some ways strikingly similar to Campbell's traditional conservative women, radical feminists regard men as fundamentally and irredeemably bestial creatures, their natural aggression to be controlled if possible but preferably avoided. Men control women through the threat of violence and especially the threat of rape. Many radical feminists argue that all men are potential rapists, though writers do differ in exactly what they mean by this, and whether they actually mean it concretely or symbolically.[13] But it is an important and central metaphor.

In some ways the radical feminist perspective shares with traditional conservative women a pessimistic model of males as subject to irrational forces, barely controlled and contrasting with the 'good' forces of the feminine. But whereas in the traditional model the balance is precariously held by a taming female, or tipped by a wanton temptress, radical feminists have severed the relational elements. Woman are morally superior because they lack these destructive tendencies, but they have neither the power nor the inclination to act as brakes on male chaos. Women's only optimistic course is to find common cause with other women.

Radical feminism is fundamentally utopian; indeed, it has generated a rich utopian literature, novels exploring worlds that reflect the ideals of a female culture either without, or confining, males. Radical feminism has also engaged in various reconstructions of history, mythology and prehistory, on the same lines. Historical studies create an *anti-logos* that can justify present lay social theories; 'lost' worlds of matriarchy or of a female priesthood and female religion directly confront the *logos* that patriarchy is inevitable and universal. Critics who argue that utopian schemas and fanciful reconstructions are unrealistic (or even proto-fascist) miss the point: radical feminism is primarily concerned with deconstruction and an assault on the metaphors and schemas of male-defined culture. The enactment of separatism may be more politically important as a symbol and as the creation of a concrete alternative schema than an effective onslaught on the social system. Some radical feminists have argued that they are politically subversive in the sense that their position is so counter to the male world-view that it destabilises men, and male institutions. To some extent this is the rhetoric of Greenham Common; confronting professional soldiers (the concrete) and the whole machinery of the military (the abstract) with a counter-masculine principle, counter-masculine symbols and an antithetical response to violence is designed to demoralise and cause confusion.[14] In this case, there has been some measure of success at least in getting the symbolic alternative noticed.

It is particularly in the area of language and metaphor that radical feminists have been active. Mary Daly, Dale Spender and Adrienne Rich, *inter alia*, have explored linguistic forms and metaphors and demonstrated the pervasiveness of masculine symbolism.[15] The argument is that metaphors are extraordinarily powerful in creating subjective meaning, and only by removing them can one create a new framework.

The differences between radical feminism and socialist feminism are profound. Radical feminism owes little, as far as I can see, to the traditions of socialist analysis or socialist models. Radical feminism is not an 'Enlightenment' model of feminism, it is, to a large extent, post-modernist in Flax's terms, in that it confronts the very essence of meaning and cultural definitions of gender, and redefines them in new terms. Politically it owes much more to the traditions of anarchism – especially the conception of unfettered freedom and self-determination. Commentators on the various crises in the uneasy alliance between radical and socialist feminism in the early years of the Women's Movement tend to focus on the tactical problems of radical feminism

– especially the lesbian dimension; Betty Friedan and others saw the extremism of radical feminism as off-putting to 'ordinary' women, and therefore as a handicap to reformist tactics. But Hester Eisenstein pointed out that this very extremism might be a tactical advantage; it made other quite radical demands look very moderate in comparison, and less threatening.[16]

Liberal feminism

A third model of feminism is normally termed 'liberal feminism'. This is conventionally associated in the United States with the National Organisation for Women, which was founded after Betty Friedan wrote *The Feminine Mystique* in 1963.[17] Subsequently the term has been used generically and pejoratively by feminist writers of all persuasions to mean reformist people of both sexes who believe that the problems of gender inequality can be solved by some tinkering with the law, and persuasive campaigns to change discriminatory attitudes. Such criticisms tend to reveal the lay social theories of the critics. Socialist feminists criticise the liberal position for lacking analysis of social structure and entrenched power groups and interests, and the naivety revealed by such optimism about the malleability of public opinion. Post-modernist feminists criticise the absence of an appreciation of the profoundly metaphoric basis upon which our understanding of gender is structured, and the deep-seated anxieties that lie behind the construction and maintenance of such metaphors. Radical feminists add that liberal feminists are far too optimistic about male nature.

Liberal feminism does not really have a voice in feminist theory, but it is very important in mainstream culture. Its expression is primarily in the pages of news media and policy documents of the mainstream culture, where acceptable versions of change and pressure for change can be presented. In many cases, those who say 'I'm not a feminist, but . . . ' are actually expressing the arguments of liberal feminism. A general objection to liberal feminism is that it is concerned only with entry into the domains of 'success' in the male-defined and male-inhabited world. Therefore it is both elitist, because it ignores women who are not middle-class or educated, and individualistic, because there is an underlying belief that one changes the system by adding increasing numbers of individuals to the club, rather than by tackling – or even understanding the workings of – the social system as a whole, which sustains discrimination.

Obviously, liberal feminism is quintessentially an Enlightenment model: women are entitled to natural rights which they have been denied. Rational processes of persuasion and pointing out the objective truths about discrimination will achieve the necessary changes. Liberal feminists see the tactical advantages of pointing out sexist language, and recognise how such language perpetuates attitudes, but they do not recognise the profound deconstruction desired by both radical and cultural feminists. In this they are similar to socialist feminists. One way to look at liberal feminism is to see it as a diluted version of other forms of feminism – a moderated and sanitised form, reformist rather than revolutionary. This gives it the interesting status of being a public opinion indicator; the views held by liberal feminists reflect how far radical ideas are getting into the popular mind. It is certainly true that in terms of sheer numbers, liberal feminists must be by far the largest group. However, if this were all there was to liberal feminism, it would not merit a separate discussion in this book – except in so far as I am talking about popular culture. I want to argue that liberal feminism is distinctively different from other forms of feminism, and may have profound implications for the way lay social theories of gender are progressing.

In her definitive summary of feminisms, Hester Eisenstein claims that all forms of feminism are 'left-wing'. She bases this claim on the fact that to achieve the aims of feminism would demand quite radical changes in society. She makes the caveat that a number of supposedly feminist positions either do not acknowledge a debt to socialism, or could even be accused of some non-socialist beliefs. Indeed, Jean Bethke Elshtain goes further and attacks radical feminism as highly politically dubious; the 'call for a future utopia . . . shares certain roots with what might be termed the antidemocratic impulse in politics'.[18] But for Eisenstein and others, it seems inconceivable that liberal feminism could be anything other than left-of-centre. There is also a strong body of socialist feminist opinion which argues that feminism *by definition* has to be left-wing, because in addition to being 'radical' it demands a structural analysis in terms of class or quasi-class structure.

Recent developments of New Right thought challenge this view. Bea Campbell's first category of conservative women, the traditionalists, held views on male–female differences and the nature of men which are remarkably similar to some of the rhetoric of radical feminists, yet they were deeply opposed to most of what they understood feminism to be about. They found common ground with feminists only on certain issues, one of them being pornography.[19] Campbell's other category, New Right conservative women, were very different. Other writers, most notably Rebecca Klatch, have identified the same phenomenon in the United States.[20] These women closely fit the picture of liberal feminists on all issues concerning equality of opportunity. They deny difference between the sexes and believe in the necessity and feasibility of rational reconstruction of relations between them, in order to achieve a more just division of labour. They campaign against sexual discrimination in work, social life and education. They are the inheritors of those who, in pre-feminist days, rejected the male definition of Otherness and fought for equality of opportunity. They are not even confined to the interests of an elite educated group; they can see the inequalities that affect working-class women. But they vote Conservative in Britain and Republican in the USA. They are also, in both countries, politically active, and they end up in political office and in positions of power in government and the business world.

I have data from a large sample of young people which includes a substantial number of women like this.[21] These data give us some insight into their apparently contradictory position, and also confront the myth that feminist theory is incompatible with conservatism. The key schemas concern equality of opportunity (which is a perfectly respectable conservative ethos), freedom and rights. These New Right conservatives are concerned with justice based on natural rights as a keystone in social order. They also take seriously the right to demand one's rights, as part of the democratic protest – they are therefore potentially activists, under the appropriate circumstances. They oppose too much state control or too much social service support because it undermines individual responsibility; nevertheless, they recognise that the achievement of natural rights requires some compensation for deprivation (a welfare state in some form, at least in Britain, and an enlightened form of safety net in the USA). In Britain over the last forty years all parties have come to regard state health care and certain other welfare provisions as a natural right for the citizen, rather than as state intervention.

Combining perfectly respectable right-wing principles – freedom, the maintenance of social order through the just recognition of natural rights, and the provision of equality of opportunity – enables these women to extend the boundaries to include gender, and so gives them a commitment to liberal feminism. At the same time – and consistent with the same rhetoric – they endorse a free-market economy, an ethos of individualism and entrepreneurship, and a belief that one has individual responsibility for one's own life. The New Right has particular appeal to the postwar generation who grew up believing in self-determination and self-fulfilment – the 'baby-boomer' syndrome. This has several roots, one of which is the Human Potential Movement of the late 1960s and early 1970s. These ideas fed into the early developments of feminism. A significant feature of the search for authentic self-definition was the idea that it was one's *duty to oneself* to be 'authentic', to take responsibility for one's own life and one's own self-definition. There were many parallels between the rhetoric of human potential and the rhetoric of feminism; the difference was that human potential was not gender-aware. Feminism injected a realisation of the Otherness of women's identity, but the justification for self-actualisation was already available.

The dimension of self-development is a major element of liberal feminism; it was initially largely absent from socialist feminism. The goal is wholeness and realisation of one's own full potential. Discrimination impedes this, brakes one's development. This, in various guises, appears in the lay social theory of liberal feminism and in New Right ideas. Not only does there appear to be no inconsistency between the New Right and many feminist ideas, the emphasis in liberal feminism on personal development maps perfectly on to central schemas of New Right thought.

Cultural feminism

I have called this perspective 'cultural feminism' because the term seems to me to pick up its key elements – specifically a concern with cultural meaning systems. It also includes what Elshtain calls 'psychoanalytic feminism', and a number of strands that Eisenstein includes under radical feminism. It is a label under which I want to consider the common themes of French feminists who are influenced by Jacques Derrida and Jacques Lacan, American feminists such as Dorothy Dinnerstein, Nancy Chodorow and Carol Gilligan, who draw on object-relations theory, and feminists from various nations who draw on cultural anthropology and literature as sources of alternative conceptions of female experience.[22]

Cultural feminism is closest to Flax's post-modernist perspective. It acknowledges the issues of social structure which socialist feminists consider central, but cultural feminists believe that the structural problem is deeper, embedded in language. Cultural feminism comes out of the philosophical and psychological position that thought can be considered meaningfully only in its communication through language. Language creates meaning, rather than being merely the vehicle by which ideas are conveyed. Therefore rhetoric and lay social theory are central to cultural feminism. By unpacking the genderedness of language one unpacks the genderedness of thought that underpins cultural frameworks and lay social theory. Partly this means decoding metaphors about difference and about the relations between the sexes, but it also involves analysing styles of communication and discourse. It involves syntax as well as semantics. The French cultural feminist Hélène Cixous says:

Everything is word, everything is only word . . . we must grab culture by the word, as it seizes us in its word, in its language . . . . Indeed, as soon as we are, we are born into language and language speaks us, language dictates its law, which is a law of death . . . you will thus understand why I believe that political thought cannot do without language, work on language.[23]

The main goal of cultural feminism is to find a framework for defining feminine experience more authentically. It is taken for granted that women's experiences are different from men's – partly as a consequence of biology and partly as a consequence of the cultural schemas which define experience. The emphasis is on giving validity to genuine difference and to re-evaluating differences rather than denying them.

Cultural feminism contrasts with socialist feminism in rejecting androgyny as a resolution of the problem of traditional sex difference. Like radical feminism, it takes seriously the need to restructure language. However, cultural feminists do not subscribe to the same essentialist beliefs about male and female difference. For cultural feminists, difference arises from cultural creation of meaning, and the reproduction of that meaning through forms of language and discourse. There are gender differences, but what is important is the experience of those differences, rather than some fixed quality or attribute. The 'essence' of gender is located in power relations; male culture controls the female, and the female body. The consequence is that the cultural context makes certain schemas available rather than others. The problem of Otherness is twofold. The form of self–other is in terms of the male definition, and – more profoundly – there is no cultural space for more than one schema. Deconstruction does not only provide a missing schema for female experience. It *extends the bounds of rationality*, rather than just legitimating women's participation in a traditional form of rationality.

In contrast to other theories, cultural feminism takes a psychodynamic model seriously. Psychoanalytic feminists have reconstructed Freudian and Jungian theory, shifting the emphasis away from the phallus to a positive and affirming view of female–male relations.[24] French feminists take the unconscious seriously.[25] Cixous, for example, argues: 'Poetry involves gaining strength through the unconscious, that limitless country where the repressed manages to survive.'[26] One route to authenticity is by getting in touch with experience and meaning that have been lost to the conscious self – or were never available. But it is not necessary to invoke an orthodox psychoanalytic model to recognise the dynamic nature of the conflict expressed in the dualities of active–passive, public–private and – most particularly – rationality–chaos.

Cultural feminists tend to create an *alternative logos*, rather than an *anti-logos*. They also explain how traditional forms of female culture counter the orthodoxies of the male world – whether as a parallel form of knowledge or as a subversive one. French cultural feminists of the *Politique et Psychanalyse* group challenge and disrupt the symbolic order, the bourgeois language, and belief in a coherent subject . They do this by dislocating syntax and subverting the usual forms of language, also using puns. This is also what the radical feminist Mary Daly does in her work in English. Challenge to the metaphors of male rationality and schemas of order go deeply into form of speech, and especially of writing.

But not all cultural feminists take such a radical view of the reconstruction of language. There are many cultural feminists coming out of anthropology, philosophy, psychology and history who take the same political and tactical view of language, culture and metaphor but concentrate more on schema and symbol than on syntax and form. Their anti-Enlightenment, anti-Cartesian approach is to open up the monolithic view of culture, to start from the premiss of pluralism and the coexistence of alternative perspectives which are not *sui generis* antitheses. The objections to traditional male models are that monolithic world-views – one route to truth – inevitably generate dualisms and negations. That which is, and that which is true or correct, is affirmed by the existence of that which is false, the negative, the opposite. By taking the pluralist perspective, in contrast, the Other becomes an authentic different thing, an alternative, not a reflection or negation.

This plea for pluralism is found in another very different domain. Critiques of scientific method challenge the objectivist heritage of Cartesian orthodoxy about the ways in which science 'should' be done and 'is' done. The claims for an alternative, feminine, way of approaching science are epitomised by Evelyn Fox Keller's study of Barbara McClintock (see below, p. 232), but these claims are not exclusively feminist; they are embedded in alternative models of science which can be traced back to Vico and the Humanist rejection of Bacon and Descartes.[27]

Another interweaving of a feminine/feminist alternative form of rationality and a post-modernist argument for pluralism is work in moral philosophy and psychology. Carol Gilligan has challenged what she considers to be the dominant moral rhetoric of male culture – that morality is based on justice. The principle of justice appears to be a route to objective truth, and to impartial and universalisable fairness between persons. Her own findings suggest that reasoning in terms of justice is embedded in a model of self–other relations which assumes separation, conflict and the search for balance. She presents an alternative moral rhetoric which focuses on relationships and their obligations, and generates responsibility and caring as moral principles.[28] This, she found, was more associated with women. These findings contribute to the key themes of cultural feminism: that monolithic conception of universals, singular objectivity and a particular view of logic are not adequate to encompass the range of possible ways of knowing, and the authenticity of women's experience is not met by the dominant male schemas for defining the range and limits of knowledge.

Dimensions of difference

The profoundly different assumptions about meaning that underlie different feminist theories become clearer when we look at critical discussions between feminists. There are many ways to cut a typological cake; I am going to focus on three themes. The first is the *focus of change*; social cultural structure or individual behaviour and beliefs? The second is *male–female relations*; are they perceived to be conflicted and dynamic? Is this fundamental to the theory, or are conflicts mainly an outcome of the present system of inequality or oppression? Thirdly, *how optimistic* is the theory about successful change, and how large is the task of reconstruction seen to be? Radical feminists are the least optimistic about change (as reflected in their utopianism) and liberal feminists the most optimistic.

The opposition between cultural feminism and socialist feminism has perhaps been most extensively debated. It is a useful illustration of the issues. Socialist feminists criticise approaches which appear to undermine the primacy of social and economic conditions in the origins of oppression. For socialist feminists, issues of culture and meaning are subordinated to this, because they are the consequence of power relations. A particular concern is the exploration and re-evaluation of sex differences. This is seen as leading to a return to 'essentialism' – whether psychological or biological. Socialist feminists see gender differences as the outcome of oppression and deprivation, and symbolic of the divisive myths by which capitalist forces have sustained power and justified discrimination. For some socialist feminists, any acceptance of difference is deemed to be a return to the old categories of patriarchy; any attempt to reaffirm 'feminine' qualities can only, they argue, lead to support for old-style differentiation.

This is partly tactical; it is better to deny difference until the traditional position has been undermined, because this will have more effect on institutional sexism, and any attempt to create a more subtle categorisation will be misunderstood. There is, indeed, some justification for this; the backlash against feminism has seized with relish on some of the arguments for difference presented by cultural feminists. But another objection stems from the theoretical underpinnings. If difference is a consequence of patriarchy, then it can be explained either as a *creation* of patriarchy to meet traditional sex-role demands (for example, the special training of girls in nurturance, or boys in competition) or as a *defensive response* to an oppressive situation. Some writers argue that women's greater sensitivity to relationships is the consequence of being always in a marginal, vulnerable position, and that such awareness is shared by other oppressed groups. Therefore, ascribing difference to something 'essential' confirms and institutionalises something that arose out of oppression, rather than equipping women to escape that trap.

The socialist feminist Lynne Segal criticises cultural feminist concern with language because, she argues, a search for 'essential' female experience and authenticity, and the analysis of language and culture as male creations within which women are powerless and passive, are ahistorical approaches, and both assume the impossibility of change. Segal argues that 'women's experience' and the language available to make sense of it vary over quite short historical time periods and, most particularly, between social groups.[29]

Socialist feminists certainly recognise the possibility of changing lay social theories and schemas for making sense of women's lives that justify and reproduce gender differences, but they regard power struggles between subcultures of class and ethnicity and the wider culture as the main arena for change. Here they differ from cultural feminists, who look to a longer-established tradition of cultural ideas and see how these are grafted on to gender at specific historical periods. Segal objects to Gilligan, for example, on the grounds that she ignores 'every detail of social context' apart from sex. This is true, but Gilligan is attacking a tradition of thinking about morality that comes down from Plato via Kant; it is not merely the product of post-industrial social conditions, even though it may serve them.

Cultural feminists criticise socialist feminists for their overuse of the metaphors of Marxism to explain power and, therefore, meaning. Jane Flax argues that there has been too much emphasis on labour and production. Pregnancy and child-rearing, or relations between family members, cannot be comprehended merely as property relations in action, sexuality cannot be understood only as an exchange of physical energy with the surplus potentially flowing into an exploiter. Such concepts also ignore or obscure the existence and activities of other persons. Children, at least for their formative experiences, have nothing to do with production. The metaphors for a lay social theory of Marxism are geared to the idea of an exploitative capitalist class, oppressing the working class and depriving them of the fruits of their labours. This does not work terribly well in explaining areas of women's lives that are specifically in relation to men in the role of husband, or concerned with family tasks. It might work in relation to women serving men as workers, and it certainly works where women are regarded as a reserve army of labour, and where women workers are treated less favourably because of their family obligations.

But cultural feminists' main objection is that socialist feminism accepts the rationalist tradition; it is couched in terms of natural rights based upon similarity and equality. It does not attempt to *redefine the culture* but is concerned about *exclusion from the culture* – a concern which accepts the definition of inequality and achievement in the terms of reference of the dominant culture. The goal of socialist feminism is to remove the argument for difference, and thus to remove the rhetoric which legitimates exclusion of women from the fruits of rational culture. Cultural feminists argue that this is not enough. Material changes will not necessarily erode the underlying models of gender relations, nor provide more authentic definitions for the self (of either sex). Also, socialist feminism does not take into account the psychodynamic underpinnings of male culture which motivate the exclusion and compartmentalisation of women. There is no room within the socialist feminist *logos* for a proper recognition of this psychodynamic process.

Notes

1. C. Roche, *I'm Not a Feminist, But . . .*, London: Virago, 1985.
2. J. Baddeley, *Conservative Women's Perception of Feminism*, Dissertation for the Degree of BSc in Sociology and Psychology, University of Bath, 1990.
3. C. Haste, *Rules of Desire: Sex in Britain, World War 1 to the present*, London: Chatto & Windus, 1992, p. 178.
4. B. Campbell, *The Iron Ladies: Why do women vote Tory?*, London: Virago, 1987.
5. V. Woolf, *A Room of One's Own*, London: Hogarth Press, 1929.
6. M. Wollstonecraft, *A Vindication of the Rights of Women* [1792], Harmondsworth: Penguin, 1978.
7. J. Flax, 'Post-modernism and gender relations in feminist theory', *Signs*, **12(4)**, 1987, p. 624.
8. J. T. Spence and R. Helmreich, *Masculinity and Femininity: Their psychological dimensions, correlates and antecedents*, Austin: University of Texas Press,

1978; S. L. Bem, 'The measurement of psychological androgyny', *Journal of Consulting and Clinical Psychology*, **42**, pp. 155–62, 1974.

9. H. Eisenstein, *Contemporary Feminist Thought*, London: George Allen & Unwin, 1984, p. xvii.

10. J. Mitchell, 'Women: the longest revolution', *New Left Review*, **40**, Nov.–Dec. 1966, pp. 11–37; J. Mitchell, *Women: The longest revolution*, London: Virago, 1984; J. Mitchell, *Women's Estate*, Harmondsworth: Penguin, 1971; J. Mitchell and A. Oakley, *The Rights and Wrongs of Women*, Harmondsworth: Penguin, 1972; S. Rowbotham, *The Past Is Before Us: Feminism in action since the 1960s*, Harmondsworth; Penguin, 1989.

11. See H. Eisenstein, *Contemporary Feminist Thought*, London: George Allen & Unwin, 1984.

12. C. Kitzinger, *The Social Construction of Lesbianism*, London: Sage, 1987; C. Kitzinger, 'Lesbian theory', Paper presented to the British Psychological Society London Conference, 1988; M. Wittig, *The Straight Mind and Other Essays*, Hemel Hempstead: Harvester Wheatsheaf, 1992.

13. See for example, A. Dworkin, *Woman Hating*, New York: E. P. Dutton, 1974; and *Pornography: Men possessing women*, New York: Perigee/G. P. Putnam, 1981.

14. B. Harford and S. Hopkins, *Greenham Common: Women at the wire*, London: The Women's Press, 1984.

15. M. Daly, *Pure Lust*, London: The Women's Press, 1984; D. Spender, *Man-made Language*, London: Routledge, 1980.

16. H. Eisenstein, *Contemporary Feminist Thought*, London: George Allen & Unwin, 1984.

17. B. Friedan, *The Feminine Mystique*, New York: Dell Publishing, 1963.

18. J. B. Elshtain, *Public Man, Private Woman*, Princeton, NJ: Princeton University Press, 1981, p. 205.

19. Campbell, *The Iron Ladies*.

20. R. Klatch, *Women of the New Right*, Philadelphia: Temple University Press, 1987.

21. H. Weinreich-Haste, 'The English woman undergraduate', in S. Acker and D. Warren Piper (eds), *Is Higher Education Fair to Women?*, Slough: NFER-Nelson, 1984; H. Haste, 'The dissolution of the Right in the wake of theory', in G. M. Breakwell (ed.), *Social Psychology of Political and Economic Cognition*, London: Academic Press, 1991.

22. E. Marks and I. de Courtivron, *New French Feminisms*, Brighton: Harvester, 1981; N. Chodorow, *The Reproduction of Mothering: Psychoanalysis and the sociology of gender*, Berkeley: University of California Press, 1978; D. Dinnerstein, *The Mermaid and the Minotaur*, New York: Harper & Row, 1977; C. Gilligan, *In a Different Voice*, Cambridge, MA: Harvard University Press, 1982; C. Gilligan, 'Remapping the moral domain: new images of the self in relationships', in T. C. Heller, M. Sosna and D. E. Wellberry (eds), *Reconstructing Individualism*, Stanford, CA: Stanford University Press, 1986; C. Gilligan, J. V. Ward and J. M. Taylor, *Mapping the Moral Domain*, Cambridge, MA: Harvard University Press, 1988.

23. H. Cixous, 'Le sexe ou la tête?', *Les Cahiers du GRIF*, **13**, October 1976, p. 7, trans. D. C. Stanton; D. C. Stanton, 'Language and revolution; the

Franco–America dis-connection', in H. Eisenstein and A. Jardine (eds), *The Future of Difference*, New Brunswick: Rutgers University Press, 1985, p. 73.

24. J. B. Miller, *Towards a New Psychology of Women*, Boston, MA: Beacon Press, 1986; J. Sayers, *Mothering Psychoanalysis*, London: Hamish Hamilton, 1991; J. Mitchell, *Psychoanalysis and Feminism*, Harmondsworth: Penguin, 1974; Dinnerstein, *The Mermaid and the Minotaur*.

25. H. Cixous and C. Clément, *The Newly Born Woman*, trans B. Wing, Manchester: Manchester University Press, 1986 [*La Jeune Née*, Paris: Union Générale d'Editions, 1975]; L. Irigaray, *Speculum of the Other Woman*, trans. G. C. Gill, Ithaca, NY: Cornell University Press, 1985; L. Irigaray, *Ce Sexe qui n'en est pas un*, Paris: Minuit, 1977, trans. C. Porter and C. Burke, Ithaca, NY: Cornell University Press, 1985.

26. H. Cixous, 'The laugh of the Medusa', trans. K. and P. Cohen, *Signs*, **1(4)**, 1976. Reprinted in E. Marks and I. de Courtivron, *New French Feminisms*, p. 250.

27. E. Fox Keller, *A Feeling for the Organism*, San Francisco: Freeman, 1983; H. Haste, 'Legitimation, logic and lust: historical perspectives on gender, science and ways of knowing', *New Ideas in Psychology*, **6(2)**, pp. 137–45, 1988.

28. Gilligan, *In a Different Voice*; Gilligan, 'Remapping the moral domain: new images of the self in relationships'; Gilligan, Ward and Taylor, *Mapping the Moral Domain*.

29. L. Segal, *Is the Future Female?* London: Virago, 1987.

Chapter 6: New consciousness

Psychologists have illustrated precisely the everyday workings of taken-for-granted assumptions, and explanations of the unexpected. An example is how behaviour normally associated with one sex is interpreted differently when it is appropriated by the other – when women succeed it is attributed to luck or effort, but when men succeed it is natural talent; conversely, male failure is attributed to lack of effort or bad luck, and female failure to lack of talent.[1] Characteristics generally perceived to be mentally healthy and socially desirable in an 'adult person' of unspecified sex were the same as those of an adult male, but characteristics regarded as healthy or desirable in an adult female were deemed unhealthy or not socially desirable, in an 'adult person'; on both counts, women were seen as *inadequate adults*.

These are examples of stereotyping which show how people draw on conventional schemas of gender to make sense. In the first example there is an anomaly, something contrary to expectation. Female success is still apparently as surprising as it was for Samuel Johnson. The explanation must fit the unusual into expectations. The more natural or innate explanation of talent fits the expected; the add-on factors of luck or effort explain the unexpected. In the second example, the stereotype is that 'adulthood' is generalised from the male; the female is either anomalous or irrelevant. But what is really interesting is that we happily lived with this for so long, either unaware of the contradictions or implicitly recognising that different rules apply to different sexes. The practising clinicians (of both sexes) who apparently fell into the trap of identifying adult mental health with the male, and accepted the paradox that the characteristics of a mentally healthy woman were in many cases those of a mentally unhealthy 'adult', were probably not so rigid in their actual interactions with patients. But in responding to the questionnaire they subconsciously adopted the received practice that the male mode is the norm. In real life, what actually happens is that double standards apply.

The problems arise when people want to step outside those norms. Then the paradoxes of the dual standards and categories become apparent, and it becomes necessary to redefine the ways we make sense of gender, explain sex differences and use language, imagery, rhetoric and metaphor to affirm and reproduce lay social theories of gender. This is necessary only when there is a change of consciousness. The exceptional case, the category of recognised deviance, can always be accommodated. The existence of the 'honorary man' – whether in the British or American business world, or in Middle Eastern countries where Western women leaders are treated as men – does not undermine the category system. As long as such women enact the male role effectively, they do not pose a threat to the boundaries.

Even when roles are exceptional for prolonged periods it does not upset the status quo unless an explicit reformulation of lay social theory makes the contradictions and paradoxes explicit. In two world wars large numbers of women entered the workforce in 'male' jobs, creating the need for child-care provision. Government propaganda changed traditional ways of looking at female skill and at the role of women in family life, in order to fill the labour gap. Films challenging traditional stereotypes and assumptions were produced to help the 'war effort'.[2] Large numbers of women experienced a sense of competence in 'male' jobs, and recognition of that competence from colleagues and from the establishment. Yet after both wars – especially the second war – it was as if the waters had closed over again. Briefly, advertisers catered for the raised level of competence. In 1945, Main gas cookers appealed to technical skill: 'She's been using the finest equipment in war – she'll want the best equipment in peace.' But by 1948 cookers were selling on simplicity, lack of technical demands, aimed at 'the Home-lover'.[3] The stereotype of female technical incompetence had returned. The war was 'exceptional', time-out-of-life; now it was time to return to normality, traditional gender roles, and a world exemplified in Britain by a welfare state whose benefit system explicitly assumed the family unit of working male breadwinner with dependent wife and children.

It would be a mistake to imagine that feminism and consciousness about gender died out just because the prevailing ethos did not express it. There was a continuing undercurrent of feminist awareness that had fed into the lives of many women – especially professional and politically active women. The recent wave of feminism may be dated in the United States to the mid 1960s, and in Britain to the History Workshop conference at Oxford in 1970, but feminist thought had survived – indeed, flourished – since the suffrage movements of the early part of the century. But something did happen twenty-five years ago that had a major impact on the culture of the West; it was more than legislative changes to improve work opportunities and rewards. The re-emergence of feminism as a political force has affected the lives of everyone; it has changed the framework within which people think about gender. It has changed lay social theory about gender, even though actual economic and legal gains may be less impressive.

Relatively few women consider themselves self-conscious feminists, and amongst those who do, there are several different versions. Outside this circle, the effect of feminism has been to make people confront their own construction of gender, even if only to affirm it. Objections to feminism reveal explicit reconstructions of lay social theory about gender. In an editorial in the *Salisbury Review* in 1987, the Conservative philosopher Roger Scruton referred to feminism as 'A spectre haunting the Western world'.[4] He picked on aspects of feminist thought which he considered undermined two things he holds dear: freedom of choice and family life. His objection was based on ignorance of feminist theory, and much of his ire was about a single event: the exploration of lesbian identity within a consciousness-raising group of heterosexual women. What is significant is that Scruton's objection shows that he has been forced to make explicit his lay social theories of gender, to develop a consciousness which may not have existed before the rise of feminism. Basic attitudes may remain the same; what has altered is consciousness about them.

The same is true to a lesser extent of what one might call the passive opponents and also the passive supporters (the people who say 'I'm not a feminist, but . . .'). For these people, ostensibly, feminist theory and even feminist goals are outside the framework of their lives and attention. They may consider the whole topic irrelevant, or even objectionable. Yet the issues raised by feminists form part of the common discourse of everyday life. The rhetoric of feminism (or of anti-feminism) may not be explicit, but the recognition that there are issues about gender roles has permeated the media.

This has progressed further in the United States than in Britain. In 1983 Betty Friedan spoke in a debate at the Cambridge Union, at the University of Cambridge in England. This was reported in the *New York Times* – with considerable sympathy for Ms Friedan.[5] It was not the objections to feminism that distressed her, but the terms of reference in which the debate was conducted. The 'foppish young men' of the opposition, with their extravagantly laid-back Cambridge style, clearly did not consider the issues to be serious. These young men lacked consciousness about gender and felt untouched by the issues – they were not even fired into opposition and the articulation of a substantive critique. Trivialisation is an effective form of attack – and is, indeed, a characteristic weapon in the armoury of the British satirist – but it is also a symptom of disengagement. What surprised (and angered) Betty Friedan was that these young men did not recognise the implications of feminism for their own lives – even enough to perceive it as a threat. During the 1980s the level of consciousness moved apace in Britain; young men may reject feminism, but they do so with defensive anger and more awareness.

The Women's Movement made people aware of the gendered self as they had not been before: either critically reflecting upon it, or defensively redefining and reconstructing it. For many women, 'consciousness-raising' has been a liberating process; the experience was an education in the gendered symbols, metaphors and rhetoric both in their own behaviour and in their relations with others. The early years of the Women's Movement produced a lot of very personal writings; it was a painful process for women to realise how they had accepted, and cooperated in the construction of, views of themselves that inhibited their growth and development, and defined them in terms of their functions *vis-à-vis* men in the workplace and the home. They became aware that on those dimensions which mattered in the male-defined world, women were inferior, and on those dimensions where female superiority (or at least equality) was conceded, the cultural evaluation of their importance was either diminished or marginalised. The writings of that time were raw, they were painful, and they were angry.

The novels and personal writings from this time portray the heightened sensitivity to symbolic behaviour, to language and metaphor; newly aware women could perceive the patronage and sexism, yet were unable to provide a strong counter-model. I remember discussions where we sought social theories that would give us a framework for explanation and reconstruction. These were interspersed with efforts to find a new and coherent liberated identity. Some of these were seemingly trivial but symbolically significant. If I shaved my legs and armpits, was I simply conceding to a media-created image of my body – lying to the world about its reality? Should I treat men's little courtesies, such as opening a door or giving up a seat, as a symptom of mindlessly conditioned formal good manners, or the reflection of a patronising view of women as either physically weak or unreal idols? And if so, did I ignore the action or lecture the poor man on his thoughtless patriarchy?

One became aware of every action and interaction; it was an extraordinary education in the symbolic and rhetorical nature of all behaviour and language. It remains with the women who went through that period, even though they have long established a more complex and secure – and also realistic – theoretical perspective on gender roles. The critics, the scoffers and the plain bewildered never could understand why such things as door-opening, 'chair*man*', 'girls' (applied to adult women) engaged us so – when the real problems were supposedly more serious, and concerned with legal rights and discriminatory practices.

There is a paradoxical event which never actually occurred but became a worldwide symbol for women's liberation: the mythical bra-burning. The tabloid journalist who invented that story intuitively understood what was going on – that women were struggling to redefine their role, and to do so they had to question those trappings of that role which most non-consciously but most powerfully reproduced it. No one was ever going to ask 'Why do you want equal pay?' Both the reasons for and the objections against equal pay were within the rational discourse of the culture – self-evident truths, or at least self-evidently acceptable arguments, even if one disagreed with them. But people asked why women should want to burn their bras – or not have doors opened for them, or not be flattered by being called 'girls' – *because it was unexpected; it had surprise value*. It was an anomaly which created a new consciousness, a consciousness that made it possible to explore – and eventually to construct – new frameworks for analysing and interpreting, and ultimately changing, the social construction of gender. At the time, the bra-burning issue was considered – rightly – to be a damaging media trivialisation which confirmed the worst masculine suspicions about deviant and unnatural feminists; I argue, however, that it was paradoxically consistent with the deconstruction process in which feminists were engaged.

Consciousness-raising groups were significant in the deconstruction of the prevailing lay social theory. The majority of British women who became feminists in the early 1970s were already committed to many of the feminist ideas of the last forty years. They expected equality and belonged, often, to political groups whose ideology endorsed fundamentally feminist principles. Yet many socialists and communists, including Simone de Beauvoir, considered that a preoccupation with women's rights detracted from the broader socialist struggle. Or they genuinely felt that they were personally 'liberated' and had equality with their menfolk and in their work; they did not need the Women's Movement. From the broad groundswell of feminist consciousness a wide variety of different feminist theories emerged, founded on a range of lay social theories of gender; but the ideals of feminism, non-sexism, and equal opportunity existed already within the liberal Left of the political spectrum. So what happened?

Historians of recent feminism identify certain key events in the 1960s and early 1970s in Britain, the United States, Germany and France as the beginnings of the Women's Movement, and of a fundamental change in consciousness. In the United States, Betty Friedan's *The Feminine*

Mystique appeared in 1963.[6] This book defined 'the problem that has no name'. It analysed the trap of postwar educated woman, the 'happy housewife' purveyed by the media and generally accepted by women. Friedan's recommendation was that women redefine themselves, reject the 'feminine mystique' – particularly by finding a career. It is a measure of how far we have progressed that in 1963, that seemed a revolutionary suggestion. A parallel development in England was the 'graduate wife' syndrome, particularly discussed in the pages of the *Guardian*.[7] On both sides of the Atlantic, there was a groundswell of personal discontent and feelings of being unfulfilled – indeed, to some extent cheated – by the lack of opportunities available to put into practice years of professional training. By definition this was a middle-class problem, concerning underachievement. By implication, the problem would not apply either to working-class women or to women who had careers. This self-conscious reappraisal of woman's role was happening concurrently with the new Human Potential Movement. This movement affirmed that it was legitimate to recognise one's own needs, to take responsibility for one's own self-definition. It meant questioning roles, and the power constraints of relationships. This applied to males as well as females.

Much of what Friedan said about the feminine mystique had been said fourteen years earlier in French (ten years earlier in translation) by Simone de Beauvoir. De Beauvoir drew upon a wider range of examples from literature and culture, and a more sophisticated analysis of symbol and meaning. Friedan made only one reference to de Beauvoir, acknowledging her importance and pointing out that an American critic had greeted *The Second Sex* as irrelevant to the lives of American women. In 1971 Germaine Greer wrote *The Female Eunuch*, which pushed the analysis of the feminine mystique (and its dialectic with the masculine world-view) further.[8] By that time feminism had progressed apace; indeed, many 'politically educated' feminists dismissed *The Female Eunuch* as lacking in analysis and being too glib and popular. Greer herself objected to the political inefficiency of the feminist style of action, which involved workshops and consciousness-raising. The book did, however, have an enormous impact on both sexes, and undoubtedly precipitated many women into liberation workshops, where they began to develop feminist theory. It also put feminist consciousness into the public domain in Britain.

There were two routes to the stirrings of feminist consciousness in the postwar era. For one group, consciousness meant questioning the interpretation of personal experience. It was associated with taking responsibility for the definition of the self. It facilitated the development of analysis which, eventually, made sense of the feminine mystique in terms of the symbolic structures of patriarchal society. It became 'political'. The rallying cry of all feminists at this period – stirring, because it was a new and illuminating concept – was 'The personal is political'. When women did try to unite in order to gain mutual support for the redefinition of the female role, they encountered opposition, and the realities of discrimination in law and the workplace became apparent. They realised that matters concerning their personal lives were part of the political framework.

For socialists, 'the personal is political' meant something different. The traditional socialist framework of thinking about the individual in terms of their class or ethnic group experience, and of power relations in terms of the structures which located that experience, separated the personal from the political. Socialist thinking generally was suspicious of subjective and private experience, and of psychological analysis. So family allowances, nursery provision and issues associated with fertility control that affected women's position in the workplace were acceptably part of the political domain, but family relations and sexuality were not. Confronting the contradictions within left-wing groups, and between men and women apparently on the same ideological side, produced a consciousness that one's own experience could vividly illuminate the ways in which oppression operated. Furthermore, it rapidly became apparent that when women focused on the issues that concerned them as women, and saw them in these terms, they became considerably more engaged and motivated to participate in the political process.[9] So for the more individualistic feminist analysis, the emphasis was 'The personal is *political*'; for socialists, it was 'The personal *is* political'.

Early feminism in Britain was quite closely associated with socialism. Two volumes of writings produced in the early 1970s provide raw detail of British women's growing consciousness, and the ways in which they strove to find frameworks for making sense of their experiences and their growing understanding: *Conditions of Illusion* and *The Body Politic*.[10] These writings show the interweaving of personal consciousness and socialist discourse. In 1966 Juliet Mitchell wrote a much-quoted – and, as she says, much-pirated – article entitled 'Women: the longest revolution'.[11] This offered an explicitly socialist resolution, emphasising the need to transform *all* the structures in which women are integrated – production (work), reproduction, socialisation and sexuality. Changing only one could lead to the entrenchment of the others; changing only work would not necessarily change sexuality, and indeed, in some former socialist countries sexuality was considerably more repressive to women than it is in the West.

Mitchell's article was extraordinarily influential, not least because it enabled women (and men) trained in the orthodoxies and subtleties of the New Left to see how feminism, analysis and action arose from a socialist position. Also, because it dwelt upon the personal aspects of women's own experience, it made it easier for socialist women to recognise the political validity of their own experiences as women. And it made it possible for women who came to feminism through a personal crisis, rather than through political awareness, to understand that their experience could be interpreted in a theoretical political framework.

The movement in Britain is usually considered to have begun with the History Workshop conference at Oxford in 1970. That was the first time women had met to try consciously to formulate a theoretical and practical position. Over four hundred women turned up, more than four times the number expected – clearly the time had come. People writing of that period (and my own memories confirm this) remember that in the late 1960s visiting American women introduced us to Betty Friedan's book; they told us of the confrontations between men and women in the Students for Democratic Society that were so important in making explicit the sexism of male American radicals. They communicated to us the enthusiasm that the new movement was creating. There was a greater seriousness about the American political scene. Despite campus activism and occasional violence in Britain, we knew that in the USA people were seriously getting hurt, and being imprisoned in much larger numbers, for a wider range of causes. We met young men who gave false or incomplete names: young men who were fleeing to Europe to avoid the Vietnam draft.

Sheila Rowbotham also argues that the wives of the trawlermen who campaigned for better safety conditions, led by Lil Bilocca with courage and vigour, and the women who were on strike at Ford's for equal pay, were important role models for women of the Left who were struggling to feel the confidence to act. All this came together in 1970, and there began the slow building of a new framework for interpreting experience, challenging the received wisdom about sex differences and gender roles.

An impressionistic account of early consciousness-raising in Britain was written by Michelene Wandor,[12] presented as 'conversations' from twenty-four weeks of a group. We can see in these extracts the increasing awareness of the relations between the sexes, and the gradual acquisition of an alternative lay social theory. This includes explanations about social conditioning and the structural context of society, incorporating socialist rhetoric and metaphor and also a strongly libertarian, anti-control ethos:

Week 4
Lynn: At the school's Easter concert [that her children atended] all the boys sang a song about a dragon and a sword, and all the girls sang a song about pretty dresses and lovely smiles. How can you attack that sort of thing?

Angela: It's part of the whole system which says that mothers must look after their children completely till they're five, and then hand them over to a system of education over which parents and children themselves had no control.

Judy: I think it would be better if parents themselves weren't so fierce about their children . . . . Mothers always put up brick walls round their children.

Lynn: Well it's hard not to. If you've been told that having babies is a natural urge.[13]

Week 6

Susan: I really used to hate women. Well, I distrusted them really.

Ann: So why did you come to a Women's Liberation group?

Susan: I only realised I was disliking other women after I started coming to the group. Up to then I thought simply that men were more exciting than women. I suppose I came because I found it easier to talk to women on their own, without men around. As soon as men came in the entire atmosphere changed. It was as though the serious business only started when they were around.

Ann: I really resent the feeling that I'm not complete unless I'm with a man. You're a valid unit if you're a couple; if you're alone you're only half a person.

Susan: Make-up is another thing. I can't go around without make-up. It's a mask to hide behind.

Jenny: You're all talking like a lot of gossips; all those things are about how we've accepted men's view of us. How are we going to change this? That's much more important.

Susan: If you're aware of the ways in which you've been conditioned to feel inferior, you have a basis for realising that there is no need to feel that way, and that in order to change the situation you have to go into it in a different way. If men stare at you in a pub, they're expressing an attitude. By confronting them, perhaps by simply not looking frightened and being on your own confidently, you're affecting a change; it's slight, but still a change.[14]

Here are the beginnings of efforts to find alternative explanations, and guidelines for looking differently at the world. The topics on which the women focused – family role, control and possession of children, being the object of men's gaze, accepting male definitions of what counted as 'proper' discourse, recognising that one was conditioned and that awareness of that process was a significant part of change and redefinition – all are part of the deconstruction process. In such groups all over the world, women redefined the rhetoric of their lives.

Later in the same group's life (Week 10), after some time had been spent exploring possible alternative forms of family life – one of the group had actually joined a commune – the issue of theoretical frameworks began to emerge. The 'personal–political' interface became more explicit:

Jean suddenly got very angry. She said why were we talking about personal salvation? Moving into a commune wasn't working for the revolution.

Ann: What do you mean by 'revolution'? It's meaningless to talk about 'ologies' and 'isms' unless you understand the way in which they permeate your everyday life.

Jean: It's narrow and self-indulgent to think that starting a commune with a few privileged people is going towards the revolutionary situation.

Ann: But if one of the things you believe in is a revolutionary society in which private property has been abolished and no one is discriminated against for any irrational reason, if you believe such a society will bring about different relationships between the sexes, between adults and children, you have to start now. We all have a lifetime of conditioning to unlearn. You've got to start now otherwise you won't be ready in time for any revolution.

Jean: But you're all privileged people. What about women who haven't got enough money to live on?

Ann: Well, I'd think it was patronising to suggest changes other people should make in their own lives. Those are decisions we should all make ourselves. But in the office where I work some of us secretaries have had our teabreaks cut because the boss thinks we spend too much time doing make-up and chatting. We've decided to go on strike next week. We've also started talking about a lot of other things. I don't think changing your own life means you can't take part in bigger changes. Also I don't want to talk about 'theory' until I know who I am and how I got here. Then I'll discuss revolutionary theory.

Jean: You've got to have a theoretical framework to fit discussions into; just going on strike for ten minutes doesn't give any grounds for thinking that secretaries will go on to think about other things.

Ann: They'd be far more put off if I produced an immaculate theoretical analysis which didn't mention us, and which we didn't understand. We all understand what cutting down the teabreak means.[15]

After ten weeks of discussions, we see the beginning of some consolidation of the personal and the political. Jean, coming from a Marxist background, believes that the political analysis has all been done; it just requires study and application to make it relevant. This view was certainly prevalent amongst Marxists at that time; it ignored the fact that necessary motivation may come from personal experience of oppression – something which characterises all labour and revolutionary movements. Ann's experience is that the personal alerts one to the problem – and thus creates the conditions where some kind of explanation and analysis is sought and welcomed. The group went on to engage in more serious study of theory, having raised their awareness of the problems through the analysis of their personal experience.

This discourse encapsulates most of the theoretical debates which preoccupied feminists during the next decade. It illustrates how people generate new frameworks for making sense of their experience and their relationships. Most of the ideas expressed on that discourse were new; even though they can be traced back to various forms of libertarianism, Marxism or Humanism, they were being applied in a novel context. These women were trying to establish a framework for looking at the position of women in relation to individual men and to the structures of society as a whole. In struggling to make some kind of coherent, consensual ideological perspective, the discussion invoked a range of lay social theories about the following:

the relation between public and private power and possession in regard to parents' roles and rights
the process of conditioning
the nature v. nurture question
the definition of woman as a social appendage to, and defined by, her male partner
the ways that the discourse of the masculine world becomes the discourse within which women accept the definition of themselves and their experience
the public and private dimensions of marriage
the role of 'theory' in consciousness and in social change processes
the role of individual experience in political consciousness-raising.

These women recognised the validity of this discussion of their own liberation, and the liberation of women in general. Yet for them, the majority of these themes would be novel. Even where they were were familiar, as they were for Jean, the discussion forced a reappraisal of their terms of reference.

Wandor's account is probably typical of consciousness-raising in Britain at that time. The themes which emerged from it – or at least the themes which Wandor chose to make explicit – dominated feminists writings in the early 1970s. It is interesting to compare this with a study of American women at the same period.[16] Ann Micossi's interviewees recognised that activism and pressure within a democratic society come out of appreciating the collective nature of the problem and the necessity for collective action to change social structure. However, the American women talked more frequently about their conflicts around intellectual performance and self-fulfilment. They analysed more extensively their 'underachievement', and the expectations of family and social mores that they should conform to the housewife-mother goal. They saw themselves as trapped in the social definition of the feminine role, and this was responsible for their lack of self-fulfilment – the self must be redefined, and the social expectations and stereotypes challenged. This emphasises culture. Wandor's British account gives less attention to 'underachievement', but much more emphasis on being assertive and taking power in work situations and relationships. Necessary structural changes in society could come out of alternative ways of doing things – communal living, communal child care, changing attitudes to property, more involvement with the creation of unions and forging links with other activist groups.

This suggests that the early construction of a new political framework for interpreting women's experience, and the potential for change, in the United States were less enmeshed in the debates of theoretical socialism than they were in Britain. The early feminist writings of the two cultures confirm this. In British collections there are many more allusions to Marxist thinkers, and to economic factors such as work, unionisation in the workplace, the relationship between the family and private property, and of course the relationship between class politics and sexual politics. In American collections there is greater attention to the lay – and academic – social theories about gender roles and supposed sex differences, and how these perpetuated the traditional gender consciousness of both men and women. It was as though on one side of the Atlantic the new feminists were focusing on how the social structures at a macro level created the power basis of gender roles, while on the other side they were focusing on how the social construction of gender reproduced those gender roles at an individual and institutional level.

There are differences between the United States and Britain in lay thinking about democracy and the processes of social change which affected the development of feminist thought. The concept of democracy in the States has resonances with 'We, the People', a body of equal citizens, operating as a political unit. The tradition is that this body will speak out against overpowerful institutions, or social evils – whether as a pressure group in present-day Washington or in the Town Meetings of early New England.[17] In this tradition of collective action the voice of a 'free society' must be taken seriously in public opinion. While the law does not automatically change actions or attitude, the existence of law provides redress for the weak against the powerful. In Europe the concept of democracy has a somewhat different resonance. It is associated with class or group power, gained through struggles against the entrenched forces of tradition. The rights of the free individual in Europe, therefore, depend more on the rights of the group to which he or she belongs. So pressures for change require an analysis of the group's status within society, the pressures upon it, and the mechanisms which can alter those pressures. In Britain the law is not seen to be particularly effective in achieving such changes – though it certainly acts as a prod to institutions to alter their practices with regard to particular social groups.

This early period was the crucible of ideas. What the first new feminists brought into their discussions reflected what was available within the traditions out of which they had come. At this stage we can see the generation of new ways of interpreting experience. In Wandor's 'composite' group there is a range – which, perhaps, she presents deliberately in order to illustrate the spectrum of consciousness at that time. Typical or not, they express the reactions and consequences of twenty-four weeks of reconstruction:

Judy: The most important thing I've learnt is the process of connecting what has happened in my own life to abstract thought, and to a way of seeing society as a series of large and complex structures. I've got much more of an understanding of the meaning of the word 'political' and also of the direction I think we can go to change things most effectively. I think some form of socialism is the only answer.
Susan: The most important thing for me to accept was the business of identifying myself as part of a group of women. I've always thought of myself as isolated, on my own.
Ann: I've found that I can think, I mean I've got a mind as well as a body. I always thought that people who were educated and could quote things were intimidating. There's a lot we have to do: not only to work for more women to participate at every level in society, but also to work on things that other groups don't; people's total relationship with each other, as well as the structures in which we live.
Jean: I suppose I came from the strongest history of previous political activity, and a very tough training in marxist theory and method. [Group] has forced me to be a bit more patient than I used to . . . . I'm more convinced than I was about the importance of personal experience, but I think . . . there is a danger that the euphoria will give you strength to change just a bit of your life to make you more confident as an individual and possibly not necessarily more likely to work for more massive change with larger groups of people.
Jenny: I think that the small group structure – self-responsible, encouraging each person to contribute freely and work out her own responsible relationship to the group – is important not only in terms of political organisation. Not just so that decisions can be taken as democratically as possible, but also it shows the possibility of a real, widespread interaction between autonomous individuals who want and need to work together in a non-authoritarian way.[18]

These responses reflect different emphases, different schemas for thinking about gender. The women point up what, for them individually, had become salient aspects of the newly emergent feminist world-view. Yet they believed by now that they shared a common discourse, a common analysis and a common set of basic explanations. In these quotes there is no real indication of the effect of the new social theory upon their personal interactions. However, Micossi's real-life, American respondents do describe the effect of a new framework for interpreting experience; they focused more on personal growth and confidence, and more on redefinition of their relations with men. The experience of consciousness for American respondents is reflected in feelings like: 'I can hardly go to a movie anymore. I used to be able to laugh along with the dumb blonde and the dizzy housewife. But now it's clear that these ludicrous stereotypes are the justifications men use to keep women down.'

Again and again we see versions of the metaphor of 'shedding scales'. Behaviours hitherto regarded as normal become recognised as part of a symbolic relationship reflecting symbolic assumptions – hence the fuss over opening doors, giving up seats, and so forth. It is as though one had developed antennae, which tuned one into dimensions of the situation which were not apparent before; it was a new framework for decoding language, metaphor, non-verbal cues in interaction, and the behaviour of oneself and others.

These examples were drawn from the very early period when women were trying to formulate a new social theory of gender, drawing on a very wide range of different traditions of political and social thought, and looking to the whole range of social science and philosophy for models of explanation and analysis. Many of the issues already present by 1971 remained the dominant themes of discourse amongst feminists. The feminist theories that developed formalised these analytical frameworks. But for individual women it was not necessarily enough to acquire understanding at second hand; frequently, some personal event or crisis raised awareness of the need for the feminist perspective.

For me personally, it was a friend's abortion that triggered my commitment. I consider that I had been a lifelong feminist; I recall first defending equality between the sexes around the age of eight, and many times since. By the early 1970s I was established in a university post; I felt little need to make a time-consuming commitment to what I then perceived to be an interesting but rather inward-looking movement. Intellectually I was aware of the literature and the arguments which were coming from the movement, and personally I did not feel unliberated or unable to hold my own in relation to men. I was also a socialist.

My friend was a graduate who had become immersed in the domestic role, with two small children. Politically she was an uncommitted liberal. She presented herself as intellectually low-key, accommodating to the needs of others. When she became pregnant and decided to have the abortion, it seemed there should be no problems. This was 1971; abortion was legal in Britain and, depending on where one lived, either free or relatively inexpensive. But one had to demonstrate social or psychological need. As a consequence of the abortion, my friend became depressed and guilt-ridden. She joined a group of women with similar experiences to seek support, and through this she became tuned into feminism, socialism and a strong sense of self-direction. I sat on the sidelines of these changes in her, and became aware that my own position was untenable.

I became aware that intelligent and rational women, whose reasons for wanting an abortion were complex and equivocal, were obliged, in order to comply with the law, to play out a charade about mental instability, placing the doctor in the role of God and also, by implication, judge – of one's incompetence, if not one's morality. To me, this realisation suddenly epitomised women's position in society. I felt great empathy with the exchange between Malcolm X and the educated Black heckler who queried the uncompromising view of ethnic stereotypes Malcolm X was presenting. Malcolm X asked: 'What do they call a Black man with a PhD? Nigger!' I became aware that for the men who did not know me, the men in pubs or on building sites who whistled, I was just 'cunt' – my professional achievements were nothing to them. And I allowed myself to recognise just how many men of my own circle responded to my unbowed intellect and assertive discussion of things that I cared about with 'What's a nice girl like you doing in an argument like this?' – something I had chosen to ignore for many years.

My consciousness changed, and everything associated with gender became of symbolic importance and in need of appraisal and redefinition. Films, advertisements, news reports, were now seen through a lens which sharpened the focus upon implicit assumptions about sex differences, gender roles, and expectations of male and female behaviour. I decoded every metaphor and symbol, in every minute experience. My anger came only partly out of resentment of masculine oppression, and men's failure to realise the symbolic meaning of what they were either doing or endorsing others doing. Mostly it came from *not having realised it all before*. It was painful to realise that one had known-but-not-known, that one had chosen to deny or justify. This, in fact, is the situation of many women who have never been touched by feminist consciousness. The 'traditional' conservative woman is not blind to the faults of men, nor to their chauvinism and discrimination. It is just that she regards the sexes as inhabiting quite different worlds, and having different strengths and faults. According to her lay social theory, it does not matter; it does not impinge on her identity as a woman. The anger and the sensitivity to symbol for women like myself came, I now think, from having lived in a conceptual and rhetorical world which *assumed* an attitude of equality and liberal ethos, and a decent lack of exploitation. American women, even more than the British, subscribed to the belief that one could be whatever one wanted, and therefore that one had chosen one's fate voluntarily, whatever it was. The disjunction between that rhetoric and the sudden awareness of how gender is constructed within patriarchy created a major state of dissonance and disorientation. Reconstruction and redefinition were necessary, to fill the vacuum.

The women who were part of that first period felt that they were creating a whole new perspective on gender. Consciousness meant constructing and defining. For women (and men) who were not involved in that early period, the process of becoming 'conscious' of gender was different. The new consciousness filtered into general cultural awareness. Later involvement depended on how it touched a personal chord, whether it related significantly to one's own experience.

In April 1985 Lindy Wingfield and I interviewed four women, ranging in age from twenty-six to forty-five, who had spent time at Greenham Common. They came from very different backgrounds, in terms of both socioeconomic status and political commitment. Apart from their peace activities, all they had in common was that they had come into higher education as mature women. These women had not been feminists in the early 1970s; indeed, in so far as they now were, it was in different ways. The feminist rhetoric, the changing consciousness, had impinged on them at various times, only to be rejected for different reasons. When they eventually came to view the world through a feminist lens, it was through different routes of consciousness-raising, and in the context of different political discourses.

Laura had four teenage children, and had been married since her early twenties to a man with a high-powered job that frequently took him away from home. The children were close in age, which meant that she was often alone with demanding youngsters while he was working away. All her adult life she had been associated with radical Left groups, alongside her husband. Two things prevented her becoming involved in the women's movement: the impossibility of doing very much about her situation, and her political beliefs, which made it difficult for her to see women either as a separate group, or as an effective force in isolation from other groups.

> Laura: Yes [the Women's movement] did touch me, but in a curious way. I was aware that I was very oppressed during the sixties, I mean, I had four children and I was aware of all the inequalities and the fact that I was feeling all these strains and tensions and conflicts, that I wanted to be doing other things but physically couldn't. So the liberation sort of passed me by and I was slightly sceptical of it all, to be quite honest. I was sympathetic but because I was totally enmeshed in four children and the actual reality of having a husband who had a very fulltime job, which demanded everything of him, and demanded a lot of me in order to support him.... I couldn't see a way out of this dilemma that I was in –

and I still can't to be honest. I find it very difficult, even now. Of course I can see that women deserve more and obviously are equal, but I can't see a mechanism for achievement, with children.

Her response to offers from a supportive women's group reflected this dilemma:

I used to have lots of women come round and sort of say that I was the epitome of what they were trying to liberate! But I was actually quite sceptical and I suppose I was bloody-minded, because I knew I was in the hot seat but I couldn't see any way out of it, therefore I stayed there on my own.

So Laura appreciated the force of the feminist arguments; her own lay social theory of gender was sympathetic. However, her beliefs about the mechanisms of change included belief in the structural powerlessness of women – and therefore the impossibility of their actually achieving real change:

I haven't always been active, apart from going on demonstrations. I've always been aware of strikes that were going on – teachers and miners and whatever – I've always wished, actually, that I was a working class man, because then I would feel that I could do something in work, and I would be a Trade Union member, and I would be involved in strikes. But as a woman one can't.

The fact that Laura considered that going on demonstrations was not enough to qualify her as an activist reflects the relative concept of 'active' in the circles in which she moved. Laura saw the Greenham camp as ultimately ineffective for change (though it had other functions for her) because it was isolated. For her, the power of group action, solidarity between groups, was the effective political protest:

I don't actually believe in individualism. I actually think that individual action doesn't make much difference. I think that unless groups forge links, I don't think they make any difference. This is why the miners were defeated, because they were isolated. If they'd forged links with the teachers, the dockers, the railwaymen, they would have been a force, and they would possibly have won. And I feel the same thing about Greenham. Unless they forge links with other groups, they will make no difference at all.

Yet there is a schism; these comments reflect Laura's conceptions of effective processes of change, well integrated into her socialism and using the rhetoric of traditional class struggle, and the blacksmith metaphor of 'forging links'. But Greenham was an important part of her feminist consciousness, a consciousness that was also associated with her successful participation in higher education:

> It was essential that [Greenham] was an all-women protest. I think women have got a lot of learning to do, and it's a very good way of raising consciousness. I think we've got a long way to go, and I don't altogether think that people realise the extent of the problem. I mean you do actually deny your soul to such an extent, and have done for such a long time, that you forget you're a person, and I think that women have got to go through that struggle together so that they've got that support from one another without men.
>
> I think women have to go through this, where they make a lot of mistakes, but they've got to go through that before they find a way of doing it. I don't think Greenham's the answer, but it's an essential step.
>
> I suppose it's all to do with coming [into higher education]. I wouldn't have gone to Greenham because it was just too difficult. I wouldn't have gone because the reasons to not go stand out more than the reasons to go. But now I feel it's just something I can do, it's one thing I can do as a person, as me, rather than as a mother and wife.

It is interesting that Laura saw women as still in the process of redefining themselves, finding new frameworks for interpreting their experience, fourteen years after the groups described by Wandor and Micossi. She herself was caught between two lay social theories about social change. Her previous conception of class struggle, and her use of very traditional socialist metaphors, allowed her to conceptualise change only in terms of those parameters – solidarity, struggle with the powerful and antagonistic government, mass action. She saw this world as essentially masculine, a world which excluded her as a woman. Unlike many women from a similar political background – like Jean in Wandor's group – Laura did not make a distinction between the privileged middle-class woman and the underprivileged working-class woman. For Laura, women were oppressed as a consequence of their biological role. For her, there was no mechanism by which women's position could be improved. Women like herself, tied to family commitments, had no structure to engage in mass action.

Yet Laura did not express her growing consciousness of gender in the terms of Marxism or socialism, even though these terms of reference exist in quite a sophisticated form within feminist theory; she used the terms of *self-definition* and *self-confidence*. Laura was beginning to identify herself in terms of other women. She was particularly struck by the female symbols and metaphors which characterised the iconography of Greenham. Laura's lay theory of socialism has got in the way of her feminism, rather than providing an intellectual framework for it.

Fiona also had three teenage children, born close together in the 1960s, so, like Laura, she was occupied with child care during the emergence of feminism. She also had a physical handicap. One effect of this was that she had attended a special school where, in contrast to her own upper-middle-class background, the children were mainly working-class. This disjunction created an early alienation – she identified with her peers rather than her family. In adolescence she had lesbian feelings, but a counsellor 'explained' that they were temporary, and related in some way to her handicap – an explanation which, at the time, she accepted. She became an activist early. She left home at eighteen and lived in London, becoming involved in anti-racist groups and in pacifism. At that time she considered herself to be a Quaker. Then she married a man who had very different political views and a job which was at odds with her own beliefs. Of necessity, she dropped her political activities. Eventually, in 1980, she left her husband:

> Fiona: I had never thought of myself as a woman, which sounds peculiar, until I left my husband. I mean obviously I was a woman, functioning as a mother, but not as a woman in my own right. In 1978 I began a degree course and that started me off, and I suppose probably that's why I left my husband, not because I met anybody, but because I just began to realise that there was something I was missing out. I'd done all the political stuff and a lot of agitation for blacks and whites and peace, but I wasn't a woman. I didn't feel I looked at myself in my own right, for me.

A consciousness-raising group, and then a co-counselling group, gave her a chance to see:

> How I fit politically, how I am oppressed as a woman. I mean, one can carry it to ridiculous lengths, because I can say I am oppressed as a woman, a woman with a disability, a single parent – you can go on and on. But I think that out of that comes my strength, to think I am me, I can stand up, I am a strong woman, and I feel that I have claimed that now, and I feel good about it.

Fiona gained strength and autonomy, becoming able to identify herself as a woman, a person rather than a role. Her political activities were *moral* protests. Though she recognised the social origins of the oppression she experienced, nevertheless her terms of reference concerned individuals as members of social groups. Male oppression of women, for her, was a matter of economic power within capitalism, rather than the capitalist system as such:

> Men are the wage-earners, they have the money, we don't. We may individually have some money, but we don't as a whole. And therefore

they are in charge of us, because they are the workers and wage-earners. So they can't possibly be oppressed. But working class men are oppressed by middle or upper class men.

Fiona's analysis reflects the importance for her of power relations between individuals, and she saw the future in terms of changing the relations between the sexes:

> I get very angry over men's sexual assumptions. I think it's the powerlessness. I know I have a great sense of powerlessness around men. If a man used to demand sex, I would find it very difficult to say no, and I still haven't worked out quite why that was.

Greenham helped her to come to terms with her lesbian identity, because it allowed her to explore relations with women in a safe context: 'I think I felt the safety factor was there. Being with a lot of women felt safe, to explore around that area. There wasn't any sort of threat from men around me.' But she does not dislike men:

> They are the oppressors, but . . . in fact I rather like men, I like getting alongside men, and do a lot of work with gay men. In many ways I can easily see the separatist thing, of getting away from men, but that to me is defeating the whole object. We need to be getting closer to men to show them how they need not oppress us.

Fiona's feminist lay social theory of gender and of social change concerned self-definition, escape from socially defined roles, gaining personal strength, and effecting social change through interpersonal action. She sees change in terms of the products of culture (attitudes and roles) rather than political structures in a conventional Marxist sense. She has, however, a strong sense that there is powerful and ruthless government control.

Sandra was twenty-seven at the time of the interview, the mother of two children. The youngest of the group, she would have been in her very early teens when the Women's Movement began. She grew up in a very rural area, the fourth of five children. Her father was 'very Labour, very, so right from the beginning the whole working class bit was drummed into me'. She passed the eleven-plus examination and went to grammar school:[19]

> Sandra: They had this language that I didn't understand. They'd talk about things and I'd just say, 'yes, yes,' – I just didn't know what they were going on about half the time. Luckily after two years it joined the

Secondary Modern, went comprehensive. Most of them were middle class people – they were going on about the working classes and it was all Marxism. They were all talking about things that I thought 'They don't understand what it's all about – they don't know'. Dad would have one job after another because he'd been made redundant and he had five kids to bring up, and had to pay the rent .

So, after spending a couple of years unable to relate to her peers, Sandra came to a discourse that was comprehensible to her – but was conducted in a way that was at odds with her own practical experience and her own political consciousness.

She left school at sixteen, and within a year she married a soldier:

> I got married because everybody said 'No! No!' The more they said 'Don't do it!' the more I was determined this was what I was going to do. I remember when I got pregnant, and I went to Mum, and I thought she'd be so happy. 'O no, that's the worst thing.' She thought I'd be married for a year or two and then realise I'd made a drastic mistake. I just got on with being a wife and mother. And then after the first one went to school I felt, the other one's going to go, what am I left with? So I began my course with the Open University. I went to Summer School and I was myself again; they didn't care whose mother or wife I was, it was just fantastic. Then things started to go bad with the relationship – well they had been for a while. I realised that I was a person again in my own right and my husband said, 'What on earth are you doing all this studying for?' and I said, 'Well if I've got it, I want to do it' and things just got worse. I was just rebelling about everything I didn't like about my life. I started going to a peace group, and to get involved again with things politically. Everything I did my husband said 'O no!' He wouldn't babysit; if I was going to go out to one of these meetings, he wasn't going to stay in and look after the children. That was my job.

The gaps between her husband's 'conservative' Labour, pro-militaristic beliefs and her own peace activities grew wider. They divorced, and she continued her studies, feeling increasingly like a person rather than a role. Symbolically, she reverted to her maiden name: 'My mother says I've changed, dramatically. So much stronger, that I just feel that I could do anything – anyone can do anything to me and I can come above it.'

Sandra, like Fiona, saw her increased personal strength to be a consequence of shedding her role. She says little about the political dimension. Her activism, although genuinely motivated by a concern for peace, was also symbolically a negative gesture against her husband – and also, curiously, an affirmation of her family roots and being the person she was before she married. For Sandra, becoming a person – being identified as an individual, not a role – was the rhetoric of liberation; it was not overtly tied to feminist or political analyses.

The fourth member of the group, Melanie, became a feminist out of a combination of socialism and the alternative culture of the 1960s. Indeed, she thought the latter had delayed her feminism quite considerably. She left home at seventeen to become involved in the 1960s culture and the excitement of London. Through her alternative theatre activities she met the man who fathered her first child, and whom she eventually married before having two more children:

> Melanie: Whereas most of my friends tended to get involved with feminist theatre groups I was at home looking after my child, and in fact I thoroughly enjoyed it. I say that slightly ironically because a lot of people were getting very involved in being liberated, and the women's movement. I didn't get involved in it at all. I liked staying at home and making jam and bread and all this sort of thing. As far as feminist awareness goes, I didn't really get going until I started studying. I always argued about 'my lot' from that sort of angle but I don't think I felt really able to cope until I came [to study] and having my own thing. I mean I was aware of it, like if I went to a party and people said 'what do you do?' I got on a sort of feminist high horse and said 'I am a mother, because I choose to be'. But I don't think I really feel I was me, until I got into this course.

As with Fiona and Laura, it is clear that Melanie's world was permeated with feminism, and the expectation that women would be exhibiting the rhetoric of consciousness, or at least liberation. They were all affected by the message of feminist theory, and endorsed it, but chose for a variety of reasons not to take its implications on board.

Melanie did get involved in political activism again when she began to feel that parenthood was not enough, but it was Green politics that attracted her. However, her search for a unifying theory for her political beliefs left her disillusioned:

> I got disillusioned because I felt it was out of touch with the Labour Movement, and that you just had to get all these issues together. I didn't feel it was tapping that. So I left. That ties in with Greenham a bit, because I think the women's movement and the Green movement have a lot in common, because it's all life-affirming and non-violent. I haven't quite sorted out where I'm at.

Her political actions were done with her husband and children – so she did not feel wholly identified with the women of Greenham. Melanie considered that her lay social theory lacked coherence because she had sufficient training in socialism to be looking for a structural perspective, but she found a common theme, a unity, in the concept of 'life-affirming'.

In the first wave of consciousness, reflected in the reports of Wandor and Micossi, there was an awakening appreciation that the prevailing discourse of gender was inadequate. There was conscious struggle by ordinary women to achieve new forms of discourse, new lay social theories of gender. This meant reconsidering one's role as a woman, and a radically increasing awareness of the limitations that traditional sex-role expectations placed upon women's behaviour and opportunities. It also highlighted the problems of beliefs about what was 'natural' about sex differences and gender roles. It challenged received wisdom, and made it explicit that beliefs about gender were embedded in conceptions about the family's relation to the state. This reconsideration touched every aspect of women's lives: work, relations with children and husbands in the family, and – with men particularly – expectations of sexual behaviour. There were few theories available. Wandor's group, and the writings of the early period, show this struggle for definition and formulation.

By 1985 women were coming into those lay social theories of gender which developed in the 1970s, bringing with them different experiences and different interpretations of what mattered to them. They were not making theory, but they were meshing their life and changing consciousness into what was now a culturally available repertoire. Their individual experiences of consciousness-raising were no less painful, but they were engaging in an existing and constantly developing flow, contributing to it but not creating it. The metaphors were available; we see in Laura, Fiona, Sandra and Melanie the processes by which these metaphors and lay social theories came to shape their changing lives and give them meaning.

Notes

1. I. K. Broverman, D. M. Broverman, F. E. Carlson, P. S. Rosenkrantz and S. R. Vogel, 'Sex role stereotypes and clinical judgements of mental health', *Journal of Consulting and Clinical Psychology*, **34**, pp. 1–7, 1970; P. S. Rosenkrantz, S. R. Vogel, H. Bee, I. K. Broverman and D. M. Broverman, 'Sex role stereotypes and self-concepts in college students', *Journal of Consulting and Clinical Psychology*, **32**, pp. 287–95, 1968; S. Feldman-Summers and S. B. Kiesler, 'Those who are Number Two try harder: the effect of sex on attributions of causality', *Journal of Personality and Social Psychology*, **30**, pp. 846–55, 1974.
2. C. Haste, *Keep the Home Fires Burning*, London: Allen Lane, 1977.

3. Jon Nordheimer, 'Betty Friedan defies Britons, wins debate', *New York Times*, 25 April 1983, p. 38.
4. R. Scruton, Editorial, *Salisbury Review*, **5(2)** January 1987, p. 55.
5. M. Sherman (ed.), *The Duty Mail Ideal Home Book, 1948–49*, London: Associated Newspapers, 1949.
6. B. Friedan, *The Feminine Mystique*, New York: Dell Publishing, 1963.
7. M. Stott, *Women Talking: An anthology from* The Guardian *Women's Page*, London Routledge, 1987.
8. G. Greer, *The Female Eunuch*, London: MacGibbon & Kee, 1970.
9. S. Rowbotham, *Woman's Consciousness, Man's World*, Harmondsworth: Penguin, 1973.
10. S. Allen, L. Sanders and J. Wallis, *Conditions of Illusion: Papers from the Women's Movement*, Leeds: Feminist Books, 1974; M. Wandor, *The Body Politic,* London: Stage 1, 1972.
11. J. Mitchell, 'Women: the longest revolution', *New Left Review*, **40**, 1966, pp. 11–37.
12. M. Wandor, 'The small group', in *The Body Politic*. I am indebted to Micheline Wandor for permission to quote extracts from her chapter, and for her comments on my interpretation. She has clarified the description of the piece as an 'impressionistic account' as follows: 'I invented them, on the basis of my own experience in different groups and on the basis of what was going on around me and the women I knew at the time . . . The "women" in it may not be real, but they were, in a sense, typical of certain kinds of women, as all the issues are typical' (personal communication, 28 June 1993).
13. *ibid.*, p. 108.
14. *ibid.*, p. 109.
15. *ibid.*, p. 110.
16. A. L. Micossi, 'Conversion to Women's Lib', *Transaction*, **8**, pp. 82–90, 1970.
17. H. Weinreich-Haste, 'Morality, social meaning and rhetoric', in W. Kurtines and J. Gewirtz (eds), *Morality, Moral Behavior and Moral Development*, New York: Wiley, 1984.
18. Wandor, 'The small group', pp. 112–13.
19. Until the 1970s, in most areas of Britain, secondary education was divided between grammar schools and secondary modern schools. Grammar schools selected about 25 per cent of eleven-year-olds and provided a more academic education. During the Labour government of 1964-70 this system was largely replaced with comprehensive schools, which did not select.

Chapter 7: The next generation

In the long run, what counts is how the next generation thinks. How far new ideas permeate culture is not measured just by attitude change during one generation, but by what is taken for granted in the next. How far have people incorporated feminist issues into their ordinary everyday lives; how far are they using the symbols coming out of feminism, and rejecting the symbols of traditional gender theory? An example is household tasks: are they *shared*, or does he *help*? To find out would require more than attitude studies; one would have to ascertain what lay social theories of gender are brought into the negotiation of household tasks.

A fair indication of received wisdom is the way children think about sex roles. Very young children have clear sex stereotypes which are quite rigid. Five-year-olds believe firmly that only boys can be doctors and only girls can be nurses – even in the face of contrary experience with their own doctors. This rigidity, however, seems to be a temporary developmental stage of extreme stereotyping.[1] I made a radio programme on gender in 1981, and used this example. The producer was sceptical. He took a tape-recorder to a nursery school in North London attended by the offspring of supposedly enlightened liberal intelligentsia (including his own child) – and found exactly the same thing. The content of such beliefs is affected by culture; there were recently British children of this age who believed that only girls could be Prime Ministers.

By middle childhood this has changed. Boys remain fairly traditional, but two-thirds of the girls in one American study showed interest in non-sex-typed occupations.[2] By mid adolescence, however, there was a return to convention; secretarial work was still, in 1987, the most popular occupation in this sample. But all studies are showing considerably greater awareness of the issues, and an erosion of the old lay social theories of gender. This is still more true for girls than for boys. Sue Lees found in 1987 that the double standard of sex still applied amongst working-class adolescents. The language of sexual morality was that 'he was a stud', whereas 'she was a slag'. The ploys that boys engaged in to persuade girls to have sex with them, and the way they regarded the girls who did, have changed little.[3]

My own research with British adolescents and young adults, conducted over the last fifteen years, illustrates changing rhetoric, metaphor and symbols about gender. One study was about motivation and achievement. Female underachievement has always been a perplexing question. Discrimination accounts for a lot, particularly in the higher levels of power and promotion, and girls have traditionally been steered into less demanding and rewarding work, with less status and opportunity for advancement. But there seemed to be something else: even though girls performed at least as well as boys in the formal school context up to mid teens, girls set their sights lower, avoided high-flying. This was particularly facilitated in Britain by having a two-step system of public examinations, at sixteen and eighteen. In the public examinations at sixteen, girls consistently do better than boys, and take a larger number of subjects. At eighteen, students choose to take up to three specialist subjects; until fifteen years ago girls consistently chose fewer subjects, effectively cutting off any option to go to university. In the late 1970s, only a third of undergraduates were female. This has changed dramatically: now it is nearly half. But there was formerly evidence of striking underachievement which in no way reflected the actual academic performance of girls.

Success and failure

Beliefs about gender apply to oneself as well as to others; they do not affect only how one judges others, but how one feels about one's own behaviour. I mentioned above that success and failure were perceived differently, according to the sex of the performer. Psychologists tried to account for female underachievement by suggesting that stereotypes created anxiety, inhibiting motivation. At the University of Michigan in 1966, Matina Horner presented young men and women with a story: either Anne or John has come top of the class at the end of the first year at medical school. The students were required to continue the story.[4]

This scenario produced a great deal of anxiety amongst women students. They interpreted Anne's success as deviant, in conflict with femininity. Their stories found different ways out of the difficult choice between her feminine role and her success. Sometimes she went on to a successful career, but never married. Alternatively she was extremely unattractive, or in some other way bizarre or strange, and sometimes she met a peculiar fate. In one example, the story was denied: Anne did not exist, she was merely the code name used by four male students who did her papers. Sometimes Anne chose social success, doing badly in her examinations the following year, dropping out and becoming a nurse, then marrying the boy who came top of the class. Two-thirds of Horner's respondents wrote such stories.

Horner interpreted this as a disjunction between expectations and rewards; professional success was detrimental to social success. The situation evidently produced strong anxiety. Young men did not suffer the same anxieties; only 10 per cent wrote stories which reflected ambivalence towards John's success. Other research found similar patterns, particularly when success was in a sex-inappropriate field.[5] It was not just success *per se*; less anxiety was produced by Anne being a successful nursery nurse, teacher or social worker. Anxiety about success seemed to diminish somewhat during the 1970s. But was it that girls were no longer frightened of being successful in a male world, or did they now see it as a challenge? Or was it that success in a male world had become relatively normal?.

Things have changed, but what schemas replaced conflict between popularity, sexual success, and achievement? I did two studies in Britain in the late 1970s – some time after the effects of feminist consciousness were beginning to be felt.[6] The first was with undergraduates at the University of Bath. I presented both male and female students with stories about success or failure in psychology, which in Britain is a sex-neutral subject. An additional element was that the protagonist's girlfriend or boyfriend was in the same class, so success meant beating one's partner. In this study I did not restrict the cues to same-sex respondents; some male students wrote about a female student and some female students wrote about a male student. Half the students received story cues about success and half about failure.

We might expect differences between American and British undergraduate anxiety about success because undergraduates in Britain are much more highly selected. Only about 15 per cent of British eighteen-year-olds, compared with nearly half of American eighteen-year-olds, go on to university education. So the person who goes to university in Britain has probably already confronted anxieties about conflict between success and sexual popularity. In the postwar era it was part of British adolescent folklore that bright girls were not sought after by boys, and going to university was damaging to one's prospects of marriage –

despite the fact that there was a sex ratio of approximately 3:1 in universities at the time. But in United States universities the sex ratio has always been nearer equal, and there is a rather different ethos: that college education is a prerequisite for any professional career, which was not then the case in Britain.

British students did not find success problematic. They anticipated some difficulties. Girls particularly expected conflict if they were successful in competition with their boyfriends. About half of each sex saw female success in positive terms, about half saw it in negative terms. Male success was seen as unproblematic. The response to failure was somewhat different. I defined as a positive response the person being described as determined to do well in the future. Females generally were positive about both success and failure; they thought that success would lead to good things in the future, and failure would be compensated for: the person would try again, and do well. The male pattern was different. Male students were quite positive about both female and male success, and very positive about male failure: the student would pull himself together, and do well next time. In contrast, males were very negative about female failure; they had no schema for dealing with girls failing, but they did have a schema for dealing with girls succeeding. The relationship was affected little by either failure or success. The picture for these British students is that success as such, even in competition with one's partner, is not problematic – at least in a sex-neutral subject.

The second sample was younger, with a wider range of ability. The stories matched the sex of the respondents, and varied the cue of sex appropriateness or inappropriateness, success or failure. They were about a male or female student at a technical college who was training to be an engineer, or a male or female student who was doing pre-nursing training. The boyfriend or girlfriend of the main protagonist attended the same college, though not explicitly the same course.

Girls foresaw problems for the girl engineer, but they were positive about them. Almost all wrote stories in which the girl engineer fought against discrimination and the reactions of her parents and boyfriend, and went on to be successful. 'Julie' was the engineering student who was described as doing very well in class:

> Her boyfriend and her friends and her mother all thought the idea of a female engineer was the most stupid idea anyone could have. Julie's Mum kept trying to persuade her to get a job in an office, or as a waitress, but Julie wouldn't listen to her. She wanted to be an engineer and that was that. She told Mick of her success in the exams, Mick's face was serious again. 'When are you going to give up that engineering lark, Julie', 'Mick, don't be like that', said Julie, 'we have been through it 100 times before, you just can't see can you?' 'Say', Mick replied, going

quiet, 'have you been accepted for that job yet?' Julie felt better, he did understand, really, she thought.

Julie got the job, and in the end Mick asked her to marry him. So it ended happily, but Julie had encountered antagonism from all her relatives, and from her boyfriend. Here is another story about Julie:

> Her parents of course were not too keen on the idea of their only daughter amongst five sons being an engineer, but Julie twisted their arms and they didn't grumble. When Mick found out about her exams, he came in, he told Julie that she shouldn't have worried and he wouldn't be upset that she had passed and he hadn't; he could now work harder and try to get up to Julie's standards. 'Even if I don't do as well, I still love you for what you are, not what you do,' and then he helped her with the washing up.

These stories reflect a combination of determination to succeed and a very realistic recognition of the kinds of objection that Julie would encounter. There were somewhat more muted reactions to 'Joanna', who was described in the cue as not being successful on her engineering course:

> The teacher told Joanna how hard it was to become an engineer. He suggested she should change her mind and do a more ladylike career. Joanna was very annoyed, she enjoyed her work and liked being with her boyfriend all day. She went to talk to Andy about her career, he did not know what to say, secretly he agreed with the teacher. In the end Andy said she must do what she wanted. She talked to her parents and friends and decided to become a teacher, she had often thought to do that anyway. Andy was much happier and so were her parents, who had often thought engineering was not a suitable career for their daughter. Joanna wrote off to a couple of colleges and was accepted. After a few years she became a teacher in a secondary school, she married Andy and was very happy.

Joanna dropped out, but at least when she encountered antagonism she questioned it. She was battling against sex inappropriateness, and also against failure. Here is another response to her:

> Joanna thought very carefully and decided she would have to work harder, maybe she would even stop seeing Andy as a consequence. She thought in a couple of years she might be battling with him to get the same job, she decided she would tell him she wouldn't see him any more.

In another response, Joanna, although she failed her exams, was determined to return to the course:

Andy told her he thought she was a swot and if she was going to be like this he didn't want to see her. In the end she was successful, when she left college, she got a job almost straight away. Most of her friends in college never got a job, they didn't know all the things that they had to know, so in the end she ended up better off.

So despite initial failure Joanna succeeded, but at some cost to her social life. These girls are clearly aware of the difficulty both of becoming an engineer and of confronting the issue of gender role. In many cases, they were quite explicit about feminist schemas. Although few of them said that Julie or Joanna was a feminist, clearly they themselves were influenced by the arguments that girls could do as well as boys, and although they would encounter opposition from traditional parents and boyfriends, they could, with determination, overcome it. Boys, in contrast, had no such consciousness. The parallel story was about a trainee male nurse called Dave. Dave created a similar level of anxiety for these boys as Anne had for Horner's women respondents. He elicited bizarre stories: 'Dave was eight feet tall with stumpy legs and a stutter. In the last three weeks of his job at the hospital, Dave had broken two people's legs and one person's skull.'

In many responses, Dave was portrayed as having sexual problems, mostly associated with impotence or homosexuality. These were surprisingly explicit for fifteen-year-old boys, often with vivid and barely printable detail. Possibly this was aggression against the researchers forcing them to confront this anxiety-inducing situation. There was a high level of bizarre responses, yet little consciousness of an issue about changing gender roles: that Dave was doing something rather brave in breaking traditional gender boundaries. These boys responded with anxiety to a disjunction between their own gender theory and what they saw as a very odd and unusual situation. The story elicited the standard responses sanctioning unmasculine behaviour – sexual failure or peculiar appearance. A few boys did express some sensitivity to changing gender roles, and one boy did see a relationship between male nursing and the question of gender:

The nursing officer said to him that there wasn't much future for a male nurse, and that Dave should start looking elsewhere. The content of the meeting did not worry Dave very much because he knew it was an inevitable conclusion. This was because he believed that people who did not fit the norm were discriminated against. Dave's apparent coolness didn't help when it came to telling Jane what happened. He didn't have to, because Jane saw right through him. Fortunately for Dave Jane shared his views. Jane told him it was his right to do what he wanted, it was his right to remain a male nurse. Dave began to feel slightly unwanted, a bit of a freak. When Dave got home and told his parents about the meeting there were mixed reactions. His father said 'I told you so'. His mother was more understanding, and like Jane, highlighted his right to be independent. Filling his friends in on the occurrence was one of the least difficult things to do, since they had always upheld independence. So with the support of his friends, Jane, and up to a point his parents, Dave decided to fight for his job. First of all he went to his local union boss, the reaction of his union was one of elation, because they had found another reason to strike.

This boy cites a lot of rhetoric associated with feminism. He talks about independence, discrimination, right to do the job which he wished to do, and the recognition also that one has political power through working collectively. He sees the issue within a social context. This response is more like the girls' responses to Julie or Joanna.

The same sample took part in another study, which used the 'My life' measure. A number of researchers have found that asking young people what will happen in the future elicits short-term predictions about leaving school and beginning a job. The 'My life' technique encourages a life-span projection; the cue was: 'Imagine today is your 50th birthday, please say what has happened to you since you were 15'. It is clearly an enjoyable exercise; it is a reasonable assumption that what is elicited reflects ordinary descriptions of themselves, or their fantasies.

Boys tended to write more about work than girls. Girls wrote more about training and family life than boys. There were different ways of dealing with family life. On the whole boys mentioned getting married and having children as events in their lives, but they did not dwell on them. Girls were more likely to write: 'I had four children, Julie, Jackie, Tracy and Dave.' There was a general tendency for girls to write more extensively about emotion, in some cases giving very vivid accounts of how they fell in love, how they got married or pregnant, drawing very much on the language of romantic novels. Few boys wrote such detail about their emotional life. This undoubtedly reflects the resources available: girls have more access to popular romantic literature. Boys do not read romantic novels, and they write about love more in terms of sexuality.

There were differences in the style in which boys and girls wrote about their future achievements. Here is a fairly typical middle-class male account:

I left school hoping to become a teacher. I went to college, hoping to study for two A levels in Maths and one other. Then I would have to go on to study for a degree in Maths. If I got my degree I would study for one year for a teacher's certificate, and then I could become a teacher, hopefully in a junior school. This would fulfil my wish, then maybe I could settle down and marry. I would be about 26. Then I would become a headmaster in future years and become someone famous in teaching.

Until the last line, this reflects quite modest ambition, but very much focusing on a career path. He mentions getting married in passing, but essentially he is thinking about his career. A second example comes from a boy with a working-class background:

When I was younger my mother said I had said I wanted to be a doctor, but now I want to be a TV man because I like watching it and when it goes wrong I am the one that fixes it. About 25 I will decide to get married, but I want to have a bit of fun before I get married to the right girl, then I would like to have a good job to support my family and be happy through life. When my kids grow up I will understand what they are going through but I don't think I will show it.

This boy shows more of a mixture of work and emotional life. Here is another boy with ambition, but not expressed only through the usual route of qualifications:

At the age of 16 I took my O Levels and got eight. I then lazed about for about five years doing nothing and finally got a job with the Forestry Commission for ten years out in the open. During this time I did a lot of rock climbing and became famous for my climbing and mountaineering. I was asked to conquer Everest on an expedition. When I returned to Britain, I opened a mountaineering shop in London and have owned it ever since.

This is striking for the complete absence of any personal relationships.

These are fairly realistic stories. Quite a few boys wrote about the future in cataclysmic terms, envisioning catastrophes, and ecological or military disasters; very few girls did. Some boys, but few girls, became the best football star the local team had ever seen, president of the world, a billionaire, extremely successful in business, and so on. Their fantasies are those considered acceptable for boys. Girls rarely wrote wild fantasies, though they did write about glamorous careers. It was noticeable that they combined writing about success in their career with writing about their personal lives, in much greater detail than the boys did:

From the age of 16 I was still at school trying my hardest to do my best in my exams. I really wanted to get good results and for mother and father to be proud of their little daughter, and also get a job that I really wanted. I went to college and decided I wanted to be a fashion designer. I was on top of the world when I got the post. From sixteen to twenty-five I was designing clothes. Things were going quite well, then I met Gary. He was very popular with everyone, then it just sort of happened, he asked to have coffee in the canteen, then there were parties, walks, pictures. I soon fell in love with him. He asked me to get married, but I wanted to wait. I was thinking about my career, everything was going so well. From twenty-five to thirty, Gary started to get restless, that's when Sheila walked into his life. I couldn't believe it, I felt as though my world had fallen apart, but he told me he wanted to finish, he loved Sheila. I tried my hardest to get over him. I did but it took time. Kevin helped me, I had known him for a while. We got married and had two children, a boy and a girl. They both grew up and got married and had children of their own.

Although this young woman has a rather odd timescale, this is a mixture of genuine personal ambition, the achievement of success, and a detailed account of her love life. Even though it is couched in the clichés of soap opera, it reflects an appreciation of the significance of her emotional life in the future. And again it is different from the boys' account of the path to success.

Here are two girls who wanted to be actresses, a profession which is romantic for girls. No boys in the sample wanted to be actors. Again, not only the pattern of career and family life, but also the phraseology, are characteristic of girls:

It seems a century ago, 15, how young I was, how green, I remember I was a punk then, it took me about two years to grow out of it. I passed all of my exams, O Levels and A Levels, and I was accepted at RADA, much to my pleasure. I was very happy there, I learned a lot and it was there I first made friends with Thomas. When I left RADA I was accepted by Equity, and I joined the National Theatre. I played a succession of roles, Juliet, Isobel, Rosalind, Desdemona, Eliza Doolittle and others. I was acclaimed by all the critics, called England's Hope and Promise. Plays were written for me, I made six films and acted on television, my social life was hectic, I was at parties or holding them. When I was 24 I married Thomas, who was then a successful actor. We had four children, Kate, Sam, Julia and Louisa. I carried on acting, but when I was 36, Thomas was killed in an air crash and I was left desolate. Six years later I married a producer, Jake. I still act now, my daughters Kate and Louisa are also actresses, Sam is at art school and Julia is a photographer.

This contains something that other researchers have observed: girls tend to kill off their husbands after they have performed their duty as fathers. Boys, when they mention marriage at all, tend to talk in a low-key way about being happily married for the rest of their lives. Another, less optimistic potential actress expected conflict between work and family life:

Since I was very small I have always wanted to be an actress. I suppose I could have succeeded if it wasn't for my five children. Please don't think I resent them, because that is just not true, I love my children and always will. At the age of 21 I got into RADA, then I started to do part time acting and I remember it was at 25 I got my first big part in a film. While I was making that film I met my husband and we had five kids one after the other. By the age of 30 I had finished having kids but my marriage fell to pieces because my husband couldn't take the responsibility of 5 children. I have now given up my career of acting, as I would have to keep on travelling at the same time as looking after my children.

None of these examples explicitly refers to gender-role issues, yet these fairly ambitious girls are very much aware of the conflicts they will encounter between family and career. However, a number of adolescents of both sexes did show some gender-role consciousness. One boy wrote about women's changing roles in very negative terms; he combined eco-disaster with an attack on feminism:

Since I was 16 many things have happened, oil has run out and the ecology party has come to power. Advancement has come to a halt and we are now reverting for the better, backwards. Women have been put in their places, looking after the kids, no cars are on the roads, there are no planes, trains or large ships. Horses are used to plough the fields, pull carts and for getting around. When I left school I joined my Dad's business, putting in central heating, until we looked ahead to see the oil run out, so we put our savings together and bought 30 acres of good fertile soil and started to farm. Here I am today a farmer; everything has reverted back to nature, towns are disbanding into small settlements.

This young man appears to equate feminism negatively with other forms of progress; he sees the future as a reversal to a more primitive state.

A number of girls did explicitly use a rhetoric of gender equality, which was integrated into preoccupations about work and career:

When I was eighteeen I left school with moderately good qualifications. Since I have been fifteen my life has been really good. My family have been getting closer together, especially my Dad, lately he has been trying to help me with what I want to do. He is not like other fathers because some fathers still think a woman's place is in the home, not going out to work, I suppose he does want me to settle down, but when I like. I left school with a couple of CSEs, went for a two-year course training to be a receptionist/typist. After I had finished I went straight to this big place, a Health Centre in the City of London. I worked there for years and worked my way to the top. I did get married to a boy called Eddie, we had four kids, two boys and two girls. We were very happily married. I married Eddie when I was twenty and he was twenty-five. When we got married, he wanted me to pack up my job and I wouldn't. In the end he just gave up. I also worked when we had the kids. We still both worked and looked after the kids as well.

This girl had quite low aspirations, and wanted only a simple job, but was determined to keep her independence and her career, in spite of resistance from her husband, though by implication she had support from her father. She specifically mentioned women's role. A more ambitious girl said:

At the age of 16 I decided to carry on at school to do A Levels in languages. I went to university and then carried on with a career in teaching languages. I wasn't the kind of person to stay at home with the cooking and cleaning, I was definitely a career woman. I made it quite clear to the person I was going to marry, that I was going to carry on with my career and he would have to like it or lump it. Obviously I had to stop work when I had the children, but until then I carried on. At the age of twenty-seven, after four years of marriage, I had my first child, a girl. I carried on with my career for a couple more years until I had a second child, who was a boy, and a lot like his father. As my daughter grew up her thoughts about life were similar to mine at that age, she was going to carry on with a career and not become a housewife straight away. My son, however, thought very much like my husband. He said 'A woman's place in the home' and we used to have many family arguments about it. My daughter left home to go to university in Manchester, much to the annoyance of my husband. I was very pleased that she had chosen what she wanted to do and to become independent. My son became an accountant.

These stories indicate an appreciation not only of the rhetoric of feminism, but of the kind of conflicts which are addressed within feminist lay social theory. Many of these adolescents have integrated these ideas into their ordinary lives. Is there any evidence about what kind of child is more likely to use such schemas? We had information about social class background and the work pattern of mothers. Mothers' work patterns are known to affect children's motivation, aspiration level and general view of the world; the children of working mothers are more likely to have more egalitarian concepts of gender roles.[7] This applies to both sexes. Our results were consistent with this. Both sons and daughters of working mothers, particularly part-time workers, were more likely to have high aspirations and be generally more orientated to work. They were more likely to describe their careers, and to give more differentiated accounts of their future lives. They were more likely to talk of work, marriage and family, and also to discuss problems of conflict. The contrast was greatest for boys. The sons of housewives were preoccupied with work, and rarely mentioned family life. For the sons of working mothers, family life was more salient; they also tended to have a more differentiated perspective – they were more likely to mention their future children, and more likely to write in detail of their projected family life.

So it seems that overall, having a working mother provides a schema that work and life are interwoven. It is not necessary to assume that working mothers are more feminist, or more likely to instil into their children a particular social theory about gender. This may be true, but it seems more likely that what matters is the experience of an everyday relationship between one's parents in which there is necessarily a sharing of tasks, presenting a picture of more complex roles. Having a working mother also means sharing her attention with the other things in her life, and not having her solely preoccupied with one's own personal achievement. A differentiated, complex model of gender is daily enacted.

By the late 1970s, the terms in which these young people were thinking about their future already showed the effect of changing rhetoric and lay social theories of gender. These studies show different schemas about gender being interwoven into young people's ordinary thinking about their lives. But many, especially boys, were as untouched by the issues as the young men at the Cambridge Union debate whom Betty Friedan deplored.

New Right youth and feminist ideas

I argued above that there were distinct differences in the roots of feminism, contrasting socialism and libertarian anarchism. In Britain the recent resurgence of feminism was closely linked to analysis of society and patriarchy in the terms of socialism. Many British feminists would expect a strong correlation between socialism and feminism at grass-roots level. I have conducted three successive studies on political and social values, which also included aspirations for careers, preferred styles of interaction in work institutions, expectations about family life, and ways of dealing with a specific conflict between career and family. The first, in 1982, involved 2000 young British people aged between seventeen and twenty-one, in school or university. The second, undertaken in 1986, involved 1300 university students and young people who had recently completed their degrees. About 500 of these were followed up from the first study. The third study, in 1992, involved a smaller sample of 200 science undergraduates.[8]

The findings superficially produced the predicted relationship between beliefs about gender and the traditional Left–Right dimension. Generally, people who defined themselves as left-wing were more likely to endorse a range of issues associated with improving women's rights, and those who defined themselves as right-wing were less concerned about this. However, when we looked at differences *within* Left and Right, an interesting finding emerged. There were two kinds of Right. One was concerned about social order, social control and stability, and maintaining family life; the other was concerned about maintaining freedom in the market, creating opportunities for economic growth, and making use of experts. These were also differentiated on gender issues.

One looked very like the *laissez-faire* or entrepreneurial New Right conservative identified by Campbell in Britain and by Klatch in the United States. This person was libertarian on many issues, and concerned about equality of opportunity for women. Women in this category wanted career involvement, they were risk-takers, and they believed in autonomy both for themselves and as a basic principle. They believed that social order came out of individuals feeling autonomous and responsible. Men in this category were similar, but with an even stronger commitment to individual freedom. I dubbed these people informally 'Yuppie Entrepreneurs'. They contrasted with women and men who were traditional about sex roles. Traditional women saw themselves as more feminine; they were religious and wanted to avoid risk. They were in favour of increasing legal controls, and believed in clear rules and guidelines. Traditional men had similar views, but additionally they believed strongly in community ties.

The differences between these two strands of right-wing thought are considerable. One is clearly at least a liberal feminist, the other is definitely not. The pro-feminist group held conservative opinions on economic and political issues, but on social policy issues and on gender issues they were liberal. They treated their own and their partner's careers as having equal value. These women tended to be engineering and science students. The less surprising findings were about women and men who fitted the socialist feminist pattern. They were motivated to pursue their careers, they held a variety of feminist values, and their beliefs were consistent with socialism. However, the feminist versus traditional split operated on the Left also; a number of women who described themselves as Left were nevertheless concerned about social order, wanted more legal controls and clear rules. These women were less concerned about their own careers, and more concerned about family life. (I dubbed these women Bedmates and Teamakers to the Revolution.)

These findings show that grass-roots thinking about gender bears some relation to different feminist theories, but they undermine the assumed relationship between an awareness of gender issues and socialist theory. One might argue that New Right feminists were compartmentalising; they do not have feminist consciousness – what they have are liberal feminist values associated with their own personal ambitions and lifestyle. Their belief in equality does not include analysing the situation in terms of patriarchy. They endorse an ethic of individual responsibility and self-determination into which the feminist rhetoric of self-determination fits. Issues concerned with gender are linked to personal fulfilment and personal responsibility, not to an analysis of patriarchy and capitalism. But in my view any account of the diffusion of feminist lay social theory should include a recognition of this perspective, which is quite widespread.

These studies show feminist ideas diffusing through society. At least some schoolgirls, and young women about to enter professional life, have extracted, from the complexities of feminist theory, schemas and explanations concordant with their own needs. The message is self-determination and autonomy, and refusal to be subject to conventional stereotypes, or to the pressure of male traditionalists. Whether in practice these young women will be able to live up to their beliefs we cannot know, but it is clear that they have the lay social theories about gender which equip them to do so. In all these studies we can see the diffusion of liberal feminist ideas of autonomy and self-determination, as well as the consolidation of feminism within socialist values and explanations.

Notes

1. L. Kohlberg, 'A cognitive-developmental analysis of children's sex-role concepts and attitudes', in E. E. Maccoby (ed.), *The Development of Sex Diffferences*, Stanford, CA: Stanford University Press, 1966; D. Z. Ullian, 'Why boys will be boys: a structural perspective', *American Journal for Orthopsychiatry*, **51(3)** pp. 493-501; D. Z. Ullian, 'Why girls are good – a constructivist view', *American Journal for Orthopsychiatry*, **54(1)**, pp. 71–82, 1981.

2. L. S. Liben and R. S. Bigler, 'Reformulating children's gender schemata', in L. S. Liben and M. L. Signorella (eds), *Children's Gender Schemata*, New Directions for Child Development, 38 (ed. W. Damon), San Francisco: Jossey-Bass, 1987.

3. S. Lees 'How boys slag off girls', *New Society*, **661(1091)**, pp. 51–3, 1983.

4. M. S. Horner, 'Femininity and successful achievement: a basic inconsistency', in J. M. Bardwick (ed.), *Feminine Personality and Conflict*, Belmont, CA: Brooks/Cole, 1970.

5. D. Tresemer, 'Fear of success: popular but unproven', *Psychology Today*, March 1974, pp. 82–3; G. Sassen, 'Success anxiety in women: a constructivist interpretation of its source and significance', *Harvard Educational Review*, **50**, pp. 12–25, 1980.

6. H. Weinreich-Haste, 'Sex differences in fear of success among British students', *British Journal of Social and Clinical Psychology*, **17**, pp. 37–43, 1978; H. Weinreich-Haste, 'Cynical boys, determined girls? Success and failure anxiety among British adolescents', *British Journal of Social Psychology*, **23**, pp. 257–63, 1984.

7. L. W. Hoffman, 'Effects of maternal employment on the child – a review of the research', *Developmental Psychology*, **10**, pp. 204–28, 1974; L. W. Hoffman, 'The effects of maternal employment on the academic attitudes and performance of school-age chldren', *School Psychology Review*, **9**, pp. 319–35, 1980.

8. H. Weinreich-Haste, 'The English woman undergraduate', in S. Acker and D. Warren Piper (eds), *Is Higher Education Fair to Women?*, Slough: NFER–Nelson, 1984; H. Haste, 'The dissolution of the Right in the wake of theory', in G. M. Breakwell (ed.), *Social Psychology of Political and Economic Cognition*, London: Academic Press, 1991.

Chapter 8: Sexuality: The real battleground

Many cultures spend an inordinate amount of energy trying to suppress sexual behaviour in that narrow time period between puberty and marriage. After marriage sex is required, but it is defined and controlled by convention, and even by law. In patrilineal family systems this is partly because of property; the control of sex before and outside marriage supposedly ensures the legitimacy of offspring. But that is only one aspect of the explanation. The sex drive is powerful and unpredictable; this presents a problem to civilisation. Certainly in Western society, considerable tension surrounds the power and threat of sexuality. Sexuality is a threat because it undermines rationality; the feminine is a threat to men because it embodies the temptation of sexuality. In the dualistic view of mind versus body, the tension between rational and emotional is closely interwoven with sexuality. This problem was vividly illustrated in the discussion of Philo and Weininger above.

The tension can be resolved in different ways. The struggle between rational self and emotional self is heavily laden with the concept of sin; the 'good' head, the 'bad' body, the rational head, the emotional and irrational body. I choose the words 'man' and 'himself' here advisedly. These models apply primarily to men rather than to women, and they are really ways of dealing with the pressures of male sexuality. A resolution is through a synthesis of rational and emotional. In such a synthesis, sexuality has benefits. The concept of karma, the concept of ecstasy, and other similar models suggest that the person is whole only when the two parts of himself are integrated. This has periodic resurgences, the most recent being in the Human Potential Movement of the late 1960s. But as it retains the metaphor of duality, it contains the seeds of its own reabsorption into the harsher ethos.

Fear of the irrational sustains a fear of women. But sexuality itself is the real battleground; the symbols and schemas surrounding sexuality constitute different kinds of threat to a fragile model of rationality. The extent of the threat to rationality depends upon how male sexuality is conceptualised, and how it can be controlled in the face of female sexuality. How sex is problematic for men is reflected in cultural images of female sexuality. Ideas about the nature of female sexuality depend upon premises about the power that men can have over individual women, and over women as a whole. The female appears as Other. Yet though it would seem logical for conceptions of male sexuality to have some complementarity with conceptions of female sexuality, they have a curious autonomy: there is a curious sense of man's *internal* struggle. Many images of male sexuality appear to arise out of the individual male contemplating his problematic desires, rather than his relations with women.

In one version of this, the primary relationship is between man and his penis. This was benignly caricatured in the cartoon book, *Man's Best Friend*.[1] These cartoons portray the simple sensuality of the penis-homunculus ('Wicked Willie') in conflict with the complex motivations – and pressure to social acceptability – of the man. But there are malign versions in which the terror is more explicit. The conflict between rationality and sexuality is seen as destructive, and generates a preoccupation with control. Anything that triggers off the conflict becomes defined as part of the conflict. So feeling desire for a woman gets turned inwards; she is just the third figure in the eternal 'existential triangle' of Man, Penis and Other.

A number of ways of resolving this conflict and legitimising desire defuse Woman's power to trigger the conflict. Through *idealisation*, man may relate to her only with his head, not his hormones. Alternatively, he can detach his head, and allow only a penile relationship with her – all women become sex objects. The fundamental conflict remains, but privatised inside himself. He manages to convince himself that real women need not intrude, but can be held at arm's length. For many men, of course, a 'real' woman or two slips under their defences, and somehow the problem of conflict goes away. For others, the conflict is never resolved; they remain alienated, resentful and non-comprehending of woman and the feminine – at least defensively chauvinistic, at worst potentially violent towards women.

Compartmentalising women – the triggers of conflict, threateners of balance and stability – into roles reduces their power. Wife, mother, whore, daughter, sister are all ways of defining women solely in terms of their relationships with men, and in each relationship, social conventions contain – or remove – sexual potential. These role compartments are buttressed by appropriate stereotypes of 'necessary' and 'natural' attributes of maleness and femaleness, attributes which make sense of man's difficulties in relating effectively to women. There is even an acceptable status for women who do not fit into these roles: they are honorary men, and provided that they do not threaten by asserting their sexuality, or bringing other female roles into the interaction, they can be accommodated.

Major intellectual edifices have been created out of such unresolved conflicts, which have made substantial contributions to Western thought. St Augustine, having for much of his early life enjoyed fully the exquisite torment of the existential triangle, chose to reject the world inhabited by the flesh of others and to devote himself to the struggle between his own flesh and spirit, elevating it to the status of an enduring treatise on sin's inevitability. Plato found another solution. Giving priority to the head, he allowed – indeed, greatly valued – the communion of beings of equal intellectual status. Provided that the condition of equality was met, the communion of the flesh could be an extension of intellectual communion; the existential triangle was in balance when the Other is not other but a reflection of the self. The Others excluded were women, and men of social or intellectual inferiority.[2]

So we find two enduring traditions in Western thought which accommodate the conflict: celibacy (the internalisation of the conflict through the exclusion of the Other) and homophilia (the integration of the Other into the self because the Other is like the self). These are states of mind, not necessarily states of life. Married men may lead lives of psychological celibacy, detached from their female partners, or lives of psychological homophilia in which their partners are wholly irrelevant to their real concerns, which are shared with other men. At all levels of society there is institutional support for both these forms of life.

The misogyny that arises out of the existential triangle is different from macho chauvinism. The macho stud figure is trapped in a particular image of sexuality – crude scoring, and performance – but he is not guilt-ridden; he does not reflect upon the problems of dualism, nor does he deny the pleasures of the flesh. Feminist ideas may challenge his simple world-view, but macho studs saw the benefits of the permissive society, and misinterpreted the message of feminism as an opportunity for even more free-and-easy sex. Such chauvinism is unthinking, sexist and exploitative, but it is fuelled by at worst indifference and incomprehension towards women, not fear and hatred.

Beliefs about the nature of female sexuality are central to the relationship between rationality and sexuality. There have been important historical changes. We tend to take the standpoint of the late twentieth century, with a very short historical vision. We are aware of the Victorian image of 'good' women, lacking sexual drive. In practice the predominant image of women's sexuality in the history of Western civilisation has been that women are highly sexed, closer to nature than men by virtue of their greater sexual drive, and sexually demanding. In some periods of history these images did not apply to 'nice' women, even though an undercurrent of women's potential for rampant and destructive lust always remained. This ideal existed during the period in the Middle Ages which coincided with the cult of the Virgin Mary, an innovation which contrasted with the previous iconography of Christianity as entirely male. This was also the period of chivalry, when chastity had a high value. An ideal of chastity is possible only if it is believed that women are not driven by overwhelming sexual desire. But apart from the Victorian period, and a period around the twelfth century, women have primarily been seen as more sexually motivated than men, and thus creating problems for men.

Anthropological evidence also reveals widely differing views of female sexuality. A culture's theory of female sexuality, myths about women, sex and the relationship between male and female sexuality, appear to be closely related to the kind of threat experienced by men in that culture. For example, cultures in which women have social power tend also to have myths like the *vagina dentata*.[3]

Our culture deals with female sexuality in many ways. One casts women as passive and without autonomous sexuality, aroused to sexual feeling as a consequence of male attention or the drive to have children. Women's sexuality is responsive and receptive. Sociobiology has taken this as a model for females of all species, even though, apart from humans, female sexuality is governed by the oestrus. If women are sexually passive, it defuses their power, because if their sexuality is aroused only by male action, it is in the control of the male.

Female sexuality is more threatening when women are seen to be actively seductive – indeed, female sexuality may be *defined* as seduction. Women have immense power to turn men's heads away from rationality, but eliciting sexual arousal in men does not necessarily imply that women themselves are sexually autonomous. Their power lies in their capacity to distract and undermine men's reason, rather than in their own sexual drive. This is an important distinction; it is the image in the more tortured writings of celibates. The demonic woman is intolerably tempting, a problem for the virtuous man. Versions of this view are held even today. At a conference session on anorexia nervosa which I attended a few years ago, a male psychologist expressed the view that a young girl's anxiety about her 'emergent sexuality' was a contributing factor. He did not mean her own sexual feelings, only her capacity to attract male attention.

Most threatening is woman being sexually autonomous, and sexually demanding beyond the power of men to satisfy. Such a woman does not respond to men on their terms; she makes her own demands. This is reflected in the image of the *vagina dentata*, and in its analogue in European culture, the 'castrating bitch'. This is threatening for individual men, but it is also threatening to a culture, because if women's sexuality is unbounded, then society's power to control it is very limited. The forces of darkness, the forces of the irrational, could so easily be released. Medieval rhetoric about witchcraft reflected this. If women consort with devils to satisfy their lust, as the *Malleus Maleficarum* claimed, they have access to demonic powers.[4] The forces of good are in the hands of rational men; the forces of evil in the hands of insatiable women under the influence of devils. This gloomy picture makes even more sense of men's fears about women's insatiable sexuality.

Male sexuality

Conceptions of male sexuality tend to be fraught, and to be about balancing internal pressures. The dualistic model of the rational head and the irrational body allows for *separation*, so the rational mode, thinking, is dominant at certain times, the less rational mode of love and sexual feeling is appropriate at other times. But this works only for individuals who are able to compartmentalise head and heart. The negative aspect is the conflict of man beset and troubled by his base nature, in a constant struggle between his good self and his evil, undermining self. This is very much a Puritan model, exemplified most vividly by Weininger. Sex is sinful, sex is evil and should be avoided if possible, and if not, endured under very circumscribed circumstances.

Such a conception may place the burden of control on men, as Weininger did, because he believed that women were irredeemably sexual.[5] But if women are seen as asexual, the burden of control may fall on them. The philosopher Roger Scruton takes the second view. He argues in *Sexual Desire* that the real basis of female power is the ability to subdue male passion and lust. Male lust is destructive and inevitable – Scruton says that 'men have an overwhelming desire to relieve themselves upon a woman's body'.[6] He represents precisely the 'existential triangle' model of male sexuality. Women's desire is tied to the 'rhythm' of their bodies, their natural goal of child-bearing, which enables them to 'tame' the male. This is the source of difference in social role; if these social roles and differences were removed, women's power to tame what he calls the 'unbridled power of the phallus' would disappear.

Fraught in a different way, and equally distanced from sex as relationship, is the *equation* of sexuality with manhood. A man is not a man if he does not have sexual potency. Making potency central to masculine identity leads to a rhetoric of prowess and performance. Prowess is defined in a variety of ways; crudely, it is how much, how often, and with how many partners. Language is permeated with metaphors of prowess (in all areas of human endeavour) that are essentially sexual, metaphors of maintaining an erection and producing seminal fluid; 'thrusting success', 'lead in your pencil', 'keeping it up' being a few examples. The concept of prowess puts a positive premium on sexuality, but only if it is adequately performed. Anxiety becomes attached to success and failure in the control of one's body. As a model of actual sexual behaviour, it is about the extent and speed of erection and ejaculation, not about skill in satisfying one's partner. But sexual prowess can also mean conquest; the metaphors that Bacon used about science as sexual penetration express that performance theme.

A striking example of this is described by Carol Cohn, who spent a year at an American Center for Defense Technology.[7] She found that the language used by the 'defense intellectuals' was permeated with gender and sexuality. It particularly struck her that these men seemed unaware of the feminist critique that equated missile with phallus, and were quite unembarrassed about using explicit sexual metaphors in all aspects of their talk about weapons:

> American military dependence on nuclear weapons was explained as 'irresistible, because you get more bang for your buck'. Another lecturer solemnly and scientifically announced 'to disarm is to get rid of all your stuff' . . . the MX missile is to be placed in the silos of the newest Minuteman missiles, instead of replacing the older, less accurate ones, 'because they're in the nicest hole – you're not going to take the nicest missile you have and put it in a crummy hole'. Other lectures were filled with discussion of vertical erector launchers, thrust-to-weight ratios, soft lay downs, deep penetration, and the comparative advantages of protracted versus spasm attacks – or what one military adviser . . . has called 'releasing 70 to 80 percent of our megatonnage in one orgasmic whump'.[8]

But Cohn warns us not to see too glib a parallel between the individual motivations of the defense intellectuals (or even the military personnel) and the language used; as she says: 'the imagery itself does not originate in these particular individuals but in the broader cultural context'. What is significant is that the sexual metaphors map on to other areas of life as part of a frame for interpreting it; they are an acceptable and comprehensible bridge between different areas of meaning.

Thinking about sex

Models of female and male sexuality underlie lay social theories about the nature of sexual relations. One's theory about one's own, and the Other's, sexual nature permeates the metaphors of relating. The way people define sexual relations reflects the way they manage and control, express or suppress, their sexuality. A particular Western romantic ideal is *sex as love*. In its ideal form, the mutual sharing of sexuality springs from close personal relations. However, the schema of sex as love can also be turned on its head as a way of dealing with some of the conflicts of dualism; for example, sex is legitimised when it is defined as love. So love redeems the 'bestial' side of nature. This is quite explicit in the Church of England marriage service: 'Secondly, it was ordained for a remedy against sin, and to avoid fornication; that such persons as have not the gift of continency might marry, and keep themselves undefiled.' So sex as love is both an ideal romantic image and a controlling and sanctioning image. The conception of sex as love was considered an excellent mechanism for restraining girls' sexuality, allowing them to define sex as permissible only in the context of love. The strategy of any sensible young Lothario with seduction on his mind was to declare his undying love.

Less problematic, because it is less demanding of the self, is the hedonistic model of sexuality as *appetite*. Sex is a pleasurable activity, to be enjoyed. It is natural to enjoy sex, but it can be made bland and light-hearted by being treated at the same level as a good meal or a good cigar; as Kipling said, 'a woman is only a woman, but a good cigar is a Smoke.'[9] This defuses the power of sexuality by allowing its expression in a symbolically relatively unimportant way. It lacks threat. Women are the means of satisfying the appetite, but both they, and man's own sexuality, can be conveniently compartmentalised. In the context of a relationship, sex is one of life's pleasures along with drinking nice wine, going to nice places on holiday, and generally being a civilised person. A relationship is mutual enjoyment and mutual pleasure, satisfying mutual needs.

Sex as legitimate pleasure emerged as a product of the Human Potential Movement and the sexual revolution of the 1960s, but it also became part of feminist rhetoric, the right to a sexual fulfilment which had been denied by the Victorian double standard. Legitimate pleasure goes further than appetite; it includes the idea that passion – or at least intense pleasure – is a 'high', a level of experience and awareness attained through our biological equipment rather than from drugs, akin to the search for beautiful sunsets. Seeking sexual pleasure is a way of extending the boundaries of self.

There are two ways of looking at *sex as power*; both imply inequality. In one, males have greater sexual drive and physical strength, and impose themselves sexually upon women, penetrating them, symbolically being on top. The symbolism of the missionary position is particularly congruent with a model of sex as male power; indeed, any other sexual position may be highly threatening. An interesting example of this appears in an early sex manual by Theodore Van de Velde, published in 1928.[10] This was quite enlightened for its time; it did assume that both sexes should experience intense pleasure from sex. However, in describing the position of woman on top, the author points out that the symbolism of this might be disturbing to some couples:

> The main disadvantage in frequent practice of the astride attitude lies in the complete passivity of the man and the exclusive activity of his partner. This is directly contrary to the natural relationship of the sexes, and must bring unfavourable consequences if it becomes habitual.[11]

The version where sexual power lies with women might be called the 'headache model' – Lysistrata being a classical case. According to this, men have an unfortunate uncontrollable appetite, and need sexual expression. They are therefore in the hands of women, who can control the quantity of sex they get. The 'power' that women have is to withdraw their sexual favours. The assumption is that women have no great sexual desire, and can therefore manipulate men by the sanction of withdrawal of sex.

Sex as surrender of the self contains elements of both sex as love and sex as legitimate pleasure, but it has additional spiritual connotations. Surrender implies giving oneself to another through sexuality, or surrendering to one's own sexuality. This can be the ideal synthesis of body and mind, spiritual ecstasy. Sex as surrender of self in the mutual seeking of ecstasy is egalitarian and symbolically ennobled by having a spiritual goal. However, sex as surrender of self in an unequal power relationship implies the surrender of one person to the other who has the power. The unilateral surrender by a woman to her man implies abandoning her autonomy, her independence, out of love for him. The man who surrenders himself to the love of an idealised woman – on a pedestal – surrenders to a person who is not an equal but a goddess, a superior being, frequently also perceived paradoxically as a being who transcends sexuality.

Both these are metaphors in Western culture; woman surrendering herself to man is a common theme of romantic novels, quite often expressed symbolically as rape. A woman is able to surrender herself to a man if he shows himself to be worthy, or if he takes power over her in such a way that she can legitimately surrender herself. Rape or violent seduction occurs often in fantasy fiction. Woman surrenders to man's power, and it is his very power that legitimates the surrender. He has forced her, she is His Woman, she has surrendered herself in the entirely noble cause of his ego. So the paradox is that both mutual surrender and unilateral debasement are defined as spiritually ennobling.

Images of woman: wife, whore, waif, and witch – and the paradox of Madonna

Western culture offers four images of women which express different mechanisms of coping with their sexual powers. *Woman as wife* is relatively sexless; she desires children, and sex is for that purpose. She is a faithful helpmate to man, and she is also an object of adoration; the wife/Madonna images are closely related. The young woman moves from being a virgin to being a wife, from purity to Madonna. Her sexuality is defused and related to her fecundity. She does not threaten man; she is not interested in his sexuality, only in the means by which his sexuality attains her goal of reproduction. His adoration of her as Madonna legitimates his making love to her as a form of worship. This model seems to dominate popular sociobiology, even when it is applied to lowly fruit flies. The female wishes to breed and requires the male for stud purposes and, in some species, for support. So the picture of the natural world is full of wives/Madonnas in various shapes and forms. Certainly the wife/Madonna pair-bonding bird or primate seems to be expected to do everything she can to make sure her mate sticks around, including being receptive to his sexual needs – which strengthens bonding.

Woman as whore does not have autonomous sexuality, but she is arousable and she is a seductress. She is available for men's pleasure. She presents herself as sexually attractive, but very much as a marketable fantasy object. She is sexually responsive, but on man's terms; her attractiveness builds his ego and arouses him, for his satisfaction. The woman as whore has reactive sexuality; she is controllable because essentially power lies ultimately with men, who can, as it were, stop paying for the product. Woman as whore is an extremely potent media image; she allows the expression of male fantasy while being safely constrained. Even the fact that she often comes to a sticky end in the drama assuages his basic anxieties about the sinfulness of sex.

Woman as waif is very problematic. Superficially, the woman as waif is woman as child. She is unthreatening because she is a dependant. Her waif-like qualities render her helpless in relation to man, because she lacks the maturity or stature to compete seriously with his social and sexual power. She is, however, sexually responsive, because a powerful man has created her sexuality. Whereas the whore is an experienced woman who will give sexual pleasure to any man, the waif is owned by the man who has power over her sexuality. Literature and film have explored woman as waif – notably *Lolita*. Dora in *David Copperfield* is another – tragic – example. But there are also heroines whose quality of childlike innocence is not a freedom from corruption, but utter vulnerability to corruption. Victorian iconography was particularly rich in pictures of little girls in states of undress. The child's pose expresses innocence, yet that innocence is open to being interpreted as an invitation to sexual fantasy.

Woman as witch is by far the most threatening image. Considerable defensive effort goes into dealing with her in narrative and metaphor. The witch has autonomous sexuality, and makes demands on men. They do not have power over her. There used to be a popular proverb that the way to control a woman is to keep her well fucked and ill shod. The problem is that witches cannot be kept well fucked because they always want more – and they tend to have the wit and wherewithal to find themselves shoes as well. The witch does not have only sexual power; she has social power, and she also has magical power. Partly this is because magical explanations are ways of dealing with the incomprehensible and the mystifying; it is an essential quality of witches that they are mystifying and incomprehensible to men. Efforts to defuse the witch in popular narrative, drama and film usually either transmute her into a whore, or else she is destroyed. The transmutation of witch into whore is particularly common for very powerful or successful women. There have been several films about Cleopatra, the archetypal witch who wielded power and also had enormous sexual presence. It should be enough to slake male anxiety, one might imagine, that she eventually died as a consequence of her great love for Antony. However, it seems necessary for Hollywood (though not for Shakespeare) to turn her into a whore, a woman who feeds men's fantasies.

Another witch was Mae West (see p. 72 above), who was sexy on her own terms. The plots of her films – which she wrote and directed herself – presented a woman who decided not only with whom she would sleep, but also how she would define her sexual attraction and the social power she wielded.

The witch image tends to be associated with some women who do have real power. The iconography associated with Margaret Thatcher was interesting. Although she did not present herself as sexy, she did present herself as attractive, in contrast with powerful women who have eschewed eroticism in favour of other metaphors of female power, such as mother or grandmother like Golda Meir or Indira Gandhi. Margaret Thatcher's witchhood is problematic. Some iconographers tried to turn her into the ultimate nanny or mother-figure, but she is not caring enough to be a mother, and she certainly fits neither wife/Madonna nor whore. She remains a witch in the terms I am using; British culture has not yet found a defusing metaphor for her, even after her fall from power.

Someone who deliberately confuses these categories, and has become an object of fascination for the public and the intelligentsia alike, is the singer Madonna. Blessed already by being christened with a name of enormous iconic symbolism, she has generated an extraordinary amount of controversy about her symbolic meaning for sex roles and stereotypes. Indeed, Kate Muir headed an article about Madonna in the London *Times*[12]: 'The face that launched a thousand theses', and captioned a photo with 'Intellectual icon: if the Madonna created in the heads of academics existed she would have to carry Foucault in her handbag.' Much has been written about her subversive effect on middle-class and Catholic values, and the explicit eroticism in her music, her act – and most recently – her book. According to Kate Saunders, writing about Madonna's 1990 London tour:

> Madonna's penchant for pornography, her mocking use of religious imagery, and the fact that she trades under the same name as the Mother of God have not endeared her to the Roman Catholic Church. Earlier this month, the Italian Episcopal Conference tried to ban her concerts, and condemned her for blasphemy.

Furthermore, the parish priest in her own home town fumed: 'Madonna is an infidel and sacrilegious. She is a woman who transmits and spreads evil.'[13]

But shocking the Catholic Church by being sexually provocative and unchaste is nothing new. The disjunction between wife and whore has a long history, and a familiar place in cultural controversy. Many media stars have run the gauntlet of Vatican disapproval, but pose no serious threat to existing cultural categories. Where Madonna is innovative – and the reason why she creates such interest amongst feminists and cultural studies experts – is that she confuses *whore* and *witch*. Twenty years of feminist discussion has argued whether presenting oneself as sexy sends out the wrong signals, conforming to male expectations; at the same time, asserting autonomous sexuality as part of one's liberation should permit self-expression. Madonna's self-presentation as a porn star, in both her clothes and her behaviour, is deliberately confused with her vociferous self-presentation as a sexually liberated woman. A whore should be controllable by men, she is a fantasy figure; a witch is a threat.

Male reactions to Madonna are interesting, and show that she has successfully confused people. Sophisticated male journalists show a distinct distaste for her 'dick' jokes, and some anxiety about her assertiveness. William Cash, for example, writing about her in Cannes in May 1991, said: 'I did admire her energy. But if her dancing is anything to go by, then going anywhere near her bedroom would be highly dangerous.'[14] He is responding to her witchness. Some male journalists have expressed their revulsion at her over-the-top sexual aggression more vividly; Ray Kerrisson wrote:

> She will do anything, say anything, wear anything, mock anything, degrade anything to draw attention to herself and make a soiled buck. She is the quintessential symbol of the age; greedy, self-indulgent, sacrilegious, shameless, hollow.[15]

Other male journalists see the whore. One described her bra as 'titillation. It certainly does look easy to wrestle off.' This article also made a side-swipe at feminism in a way that suggested a favourable sexual response: 'Madonna . . . poses a problem to feminists – as feminine women always do.' For what the writer calls 'those clinging to traditional feminist dogma' Madonna is to be despised 'because, like strippers and prostitutes, she uses the stereotype of female beauty to pander to male lust'. The same article later even tried to rehabilitate Madonna as 'wife', talking about her desire for motherhood and a stable relationship.[16] In summer 1991 I gave a public lecture in which I mentioned Madonna and the arguments of this chapter; it received extraordinary national and international press coverage. Informal responses from men at the time showed the same kind of split, compartmentalising her into *either* sexy whore *or* threatening witch.[17]

Feminist discussion about Madonna does not make the same distinction. Women often respond positively to her deliberate confusion of whore and witch, and to the conscious ambiguity of her stance. They also comment favourably on her being in control of her life and her work, and asserting her own definition of sexuality. Julie Burchill[18] sees her as 'the first big female icon who doesn't have a man behind her'. This refrain runs through much of what is written about her. But the more profound analysis – of which there is now a great deal – picks up the disjunction between whore and witch, and how this is a major challenge to traditional gender-role compartmentalisation. Ann Kaplan, for example, considers that Madonna subverts dominant gender hierarchies because of this disjunction.[19] Camille Paglia, who comes out of the same Catholic American culture as Madonna, defines herself as a feminist, but is a savage critic of what she sees as traditional feminism, celebrates Madonna because 'she exposes the puritanism and suffocating ideology of American feminism . . . . She shows girls how to be attractive, sensual, energetic, ambitious, aggressive and funny.'[20] The debate on both sides acknowledges the ambiguity of Madonna as witch/whore, and its symbolic importance.

Reclaiming authentic female sexuality

All feminist theories share the view that redefining sexuality is part of authenticity and self-determination. The culture has defined female and feminine in terms of Otherness to the male and masculine. In none of the definitions of male or female sexuality that I have described so far is woman's perspective taken. The construction of sexuality as I have presented it is androcentric – which is why the discussion of Madonna is so illuminating. Whether women are perceived to have sexual desires or not, the implication is constructed in terms of the effect upon men. Only the witch category might allow some space for female self-definition, but her image is suffused with its threat to men. Much feminist writing and thinking about the deconstruction and reconstruction of sexuality questions male power in sexuality: male power to impose sexual demands upon women – whether in response to male desire, or as a brake upon them; male power to control women's sexuality by defining her sexual needs, and constraining how and with whom she satisfies them; male power to eroticise and define women's personhood in purely sexual terms.

Part of the feminist challenge is claiming authentic female sexuality. One way is the demand for equality, recognition of equal sexual needs. The denial of sex difference in this area, as in others, is an attempt to redefine the concept of essence; denying difference is a claim of equal need, and equal obligation to meet that need. Another challenge claims not equality but new definition. Women need to discover their own sexuality in order to escape the inauthentic definition they have grown up with. For many heterosexual feminists, personal discovery has involved exploring autoerotic and homoerotic sexuality in addition to – or as an extension of – heterosexuality. For others, freedom from patriarchal definition is possible only within lesbian relationships.

In a sense, any claim to female sexual self-definition challenges male orthodoxy. Confronting male sexual power also means claiming the right to refuse to be defined indiscriminately as a sexual being. The right to define one's sexual demands gives the right to refuse others' sexual demands. The challenge to male power also includes the right to define oneself as not a sexual being at all. But a more profound challenge is to the symbolic basis of male sexual power, which can be seen as an edifice to protect the uneasy balance of rationality against the forces of the irrational. Male sexual power may be sustained by economic power, but it also comes out of the cultural need to find checks and balances for sexuality. So challenges which deny men's right to impose sexual power do not necessarily tackle the symbolic underpinning; that requires a challenge to the meaning of sexual power, and the link between sexuality and rationality. For example, strengthening laws against rape may not necessarily affect beliefs about the *meaning* of rape.

In the last three decades, feminist consciousness has interwoven with other changes in lay social theories of sexuality. Chronologically, the first issue was the development of the contraceptive Pill. The contraceptive Pill was seen as liberating. It is received wisdom – reiterated even by backlash writers – that the 'sexual revolution' which predated the rise of feminist consciousness was a consequence of the contraceptive Pill. Why should the Pill have a significant effect – not just on sexual behaviour, but on the whole theory of sexuality? The usual answer is that it made sex free from consequences. But contraceptives have been available for a very long time; a reasonably well-organised person could have had non-reproductive sex for quite a long period. The contraceptive Pill was easy to use, and did guarantee freedom from pregnancy, but it was not just a matter of physical freedom, it was a matter of psychological shift.[21] Cate Haste describes this in *Rules of Desire*.

First, the contraceptive Pill was in the hands of women; it gave them control over their own fertility. It also freed men from that particular responsibility; it permitted them an irresponsible attitude to sex. Secondly, the Pill was taken all the time. A woman was a 'conception-free zone' at all times, not just when she prepared for sex. This made women *publicly* non-fertile. Threat of pregnancy was no longer a deterrent to sex, nor an excuse to avoid it. This was a major rhetorical shift away from the traditional objections which young women had been taught to use both in controlling their own sexuality, and in defending themselves against the attentions of men. The public excuse had gone. There was no longer a strong reason for not having sex if she wanted to – or, at least, if he wanted to. What was important was the symbolism of the contraceptive Pill, rather than its actual effectiveness. In fact, the statistics indicate that the Pill was used by only 7 per cent of unmarried women in 1970. Now there are anxieties about its side-effects, but the rhetoric of female control of contraception, and the separation of sex from fear of pregnancy, remain an essential part of our lay theory of sexuality.

The contraceptive Pill contributed eventually to feminist consciousness because it put symbolic responsibility and control of fertility in the hands of the woman. But initially its effect was associated with the misnamed 'permissive' climate. The so-called 'permissive society' – a paradoxical term in its own right – symbolically reduced social sanctions against sex. There was a shift from sex as love, or sex as surrender of self, to sex as appetite and legitimate pleasure. The main consequence of the 'permissive society' was increased public discussion of sex and increased presentation of symbols and images of sexuality as fun, as readily available, and as socially acceptable. Some feminists see the permissive society retrospectively as opening the floodgates to exploitative male chauvinist sexual fantasy, because it made it possible for men to objectify women even more than before, to treat them as sex objects legitimately, and to confuse sexual freedom – which would enrich the lives of both sexes – with sexual exploitation, which benefited only men. To some extent the primary effect of permissiveness was to enlarge the range of male fantasies about women, to cast women primarily in the role of whore, and to build up a stereotype that all women have to be sexy all the time – to legitimate the eroticisation of women even further.

However, the change that allowed – indeed, required – sex to be a pleasurable game was important for feminism. At one level, sex is fun, sex can be an irresponsible, transient pleasure, play. But at another level, treating sex as a game frees it from its traditional context. Sex could now be like any game – pretence, defined in whatever way one wished. Hitherto, the definitions were laid down: sex was *pleasure*, or sex was *love*, or sex was *power*, and the culture very clearly defined these distinctions in representations of good women, bad women, moral sex, immoral sex, acceptable behaviour of various sorts. Making sex a game enabled the separation of sex and love, but more importantly, it opened up the possibility that sexuality *could be redefined*.

The redefinition of sex in the 1960s had little to do with feminism. It came out of a combination of things, including libertarian influence in the artistic and literary world. A key element, however, was the Human Potential Movement, which came out of Humanistic psychology. As part of the search for routes to self-fulfilment, this defined sex as legitimate pleasure; indeed, elevated it to a spiritual plane. The experience of intense enjoyment extended the boundaries of self. These developments had little to do with challenging patriarchal society, but a great deal to do with libertarian ideals. They fed eventually into feminist consciousness through the ethos of self-determination.

The relationship between feminist consciousness and symbolic changes in conceptions of sexuality should be looked at in the context of sexuality's rhetorical role in revolutionary change. Revolutionary social and political writings often deal with the question of sexuality and sexual relationships. The ideal of harmonious and mutually satisfying sex appears in several rhetorics of revolution. Social and political revolution will make it possible for people to love each other as equals, and to have satisfying sexual relationships. The argument is that it is impossible to have egalitarian and harmonious relationships between the sexes because society is structurally corrupt. Incidentally, both the Right and the Left endorse versions of this. The right-wing version is that in the current decadent moral climate, proper relationships between the sexes are not possible because sexual freedom exploits and degrades individuals. In an ideal world of moral reform, sexual problems would diminish, because sexuality would be confined within marriage. Left-wing changes would remove structural inequality and exploitation for capitalist profit; right-wing changes would remove the artificial stimulation of unhealthy sexual appetites, enhance family values and fidelity, and reduce preoccupation with sex.

Some argue that freer sexuality can be *the route* to revolution. Symbolically casting off the constraints of society through the enactment of sexual freedom undermines society, and therefore brings about major social change. Feminists around the period of the Russian Revolution, like Alexandra Kollontai, argued that sexual freedom undermined capitalist society, because the conventions of bourgeois sexuality are so powerfully rooted in it.[22] Some strands of the Human Potential Movement took the argument further into the individual domain. One achieves revolution through sexual exploration, even sexual excess. One might argue that this is an alternative to revolution: if the goal is a personal utopia, then the attainment of a personal utopian orgasm may be a perfectly adequate substitute for creating the social conditions under which a utopian orgasm may occur. But it is also argued that sexuality interferes with revolution. If revolution is concerned with a rational reconstruction of the social system, sexuality should be constrained and controlled because it is a personal preoccupation which distracts from the serious public things of life. Left and Right rhetorics are very similar. It is not possible to achieve a perfect society if one allows rampant sexuality, so one controls sexuality in order to achieve the desired world.

Symbols have been especially important in creating feminist per- spectives on sexuality. The symbolic objections to the missionary position are that it enacts the symbolic power of man, being on top, penetrating the woman; when a woman climbs on top of a man, she is making a political statement. Another feminist objection was ostensibly practical: for many women, stimulation during intercourse in the missionary position is not adequate to produce orgasm. If the missionary position does not produce sexual pleasure for women, it is inequitable and exploitative. Furthermore, missionary-position sex is not likely to challenge conventional beliefs about women's lesser sexual drive.

The power of symbolism is obvious if we rethink the meaning of the missionary position. The predominant interpretation is that it symbolises male power – for chauvinists and feminists alike. But one can also interpret the missionary position in terms of an 'Earth Mother' model; the man is not so much 'on top of' as 'enclosed by' the woman. He has not 'penetrated' her; he has been drawn into her and enfolded by her. The act is identical, the symbolism utterly different, the subjective experience completely different. Such reinterpretations can undermine and reconstruct conventional lay social theories of sexuality, and fundamentally alter subjective experience.

Sexual harassment: redefining access

Sexual harassment is another area, rich in symbolism, where there has been considerable change. It has now been formally made actionable, despite the problems of defining it. Sexual harassment symbolically means that men are doing things to women against their will. Objecting to this is a recognition of women's right to define their own sexuality, so the new legislation is a blow for authenticity and female autonomy. But one can also interpret sexual harassment as proof that men are more interested in sex than women are. Men are more likely to take the initiative, men are the aggressors, both sexually and in other ways. It is a part of their base nature that needs to be controlled. So the symbolic threat of sexual harassment may be interference by men, their intrusion into women's personal space. This also sustains the schema – shared by some feminists with some very conservative non-feminists – of bestial man and virtuous woman. The possible symbols are wide-ranging. It is not surprising that there has been considerable public support for legislation to outlaw sexual harassment.

Sexual harassment is part of another area that is laden with symbolism: sexual initiative-taking. The dominant cultural model is that men take the initiative and women respond. What this means in practice is that men enact certain behaviours which look like initiative-taking, and women enact certain behaviours which look like being pursued. In fact both sexes are equally active in taking the initiative; it is the symbolic way in which they express it which differs. The failure to recognise the reality underlying the symbolism is undoubtedly responsible for naive assumptions about non-human sexual behaviour. How far is it true, for example, that the female fruit fly merely passively awaits persuasion by the male?

Taking the sexual initiative is problematic because it is tied up with power relations. Raising consciousness has not reversed the nexus of pursuer–pursued roles, but it has facilitated more egalitarian negotiation processes. The challenges to male power have undermined the assumption that he had a right to ask, whatever she felt like and even whatever messages she transmitted, and she had the obligation not just to refuse, but to find a legitimate excuse which did not hurt his ego, however distressed she might be by his advances. Furthermore, if she chose to accept his advances, she was still required to protect his ego by pretending that it was his idea.

Common to all these issues is the question of self-definition; defining oneself as a woman, defining one's own standards of beauty, one's own sexual performance, one's own sexuality, not having them defined by the patriarchal culture, the requirements of men. The symbolic features of orgasm were early appreciated by feminists.[23] The violent rhetoric produced in response to early manifestations of feminism was deeply shocking to anyone who observed it. Clearly it was a response of very deep terror on the part of some men, and part of the threat came from the idea of women defining sex in their own terms.

Evidence in support of equality of sexual feeling came from solid scientific research. The publication in 1966 of Masters' and Johnson's book *Human Sexual Response* just predated the rise of the Women's Movement.[24] It demolished beliefs about physiological difference between the orgasms of men and of women. Even more encouraging, the research showed that women were capable of multiple orgasms. This report was highly legitimating to alternative definitions of female sexuality. A rather more extreme position was taken by Mary Jane Sherfey, based on ethological studies. She argued that not only women, but also other primates, were sexually insatiable and, were it not for cultural constraints, would spend their entire time in orgasmic delight.[25] Such writings were disturbing to both sexes; either they felt they were missing out, or they felt confronted with the impossible task of helping their partners to that degree of pleasure. Even before the emergence of feminist consciousness, therefore, there were utopian views of orgasm, which became a key rhetorical issue in women's self-definition.

Rape rhetoric

Conflict between traditional assumptions and reconstructed assumptions continues with regard to rape and sexual assault. Here are all the problematic issues surrounding Otherness, and the equally problematic issues of potential chaos and sexuality. Rape is a peculiarly symbolic crime. At each point it depends upon interpretation, and interpretation derives from lay social theory – which may also be enshrined in professional theory. The act itself may occur as a consequence of misunderstanding cues. Not only may the perpetrator misunderstand the situation, but the criminality of the act stands or falls upon his claim; it is legitimate to claim misunderstanding. The victim's interpretation is crucial. A major issue in reconstructing the interpretation of rape has been to shift its symbolic meaning from being an extension of sexual intercourse to being an act of violence using the penis as weapon.

Finally, and symbolically very important, is the judge's summing-up. Here so much about cultural meaning of rape is made explicit. Here the judge also symbolically stigmatises the culprit – and frequently the victim. Punishment usually includes stigmatisation; this is part of retribution. But in the case of rape, it seems that the crime also needs to be *publicly explained*. Theft, after all, is theft – it may be compounded by violence or pain, but this is an add-on. Because rape depends so much on interpretation, the judge needs not only to castigate the culprit publicly but to explain the nature of his crime. This explanation makes explicit what is deemed natural, what is taken for granted, and what is deemed deviant and problematic.

The complexity of this is made apparent in a recent article by Barbara Amiel, a writer who is frequently critical of feminism:[26]

> Curiously, the feminists have managed to sell the idea that until they came around, society did not regard rape as the heinous crime it is. The evidence for this is entirely to the contrary; rape, together with murder, was virtually the last offence in a civilised society for which a man could be executed.

In my view, this entirely misses the point; what is problematic is *why* rape is perceived to be 'heinous'. Not surprisingly, objections to the rhetoric of the judge's summing-up will be louder when this is accompanied by a light sentence rather than a heavy one – but the same beliefs about natural essences and relations between the sexes which lead to a light sentence may also lead, on other occasions, to a heavy one. The objection is to that set of beliefs about relationships, not to the light sentence *per se* – and it is here that change has occurred.

The gap between rhetorics still yawns. In a television programme in 1989 on rape within marriage, a commentator argued that rape inside marriage was not as bad as rape outside marriage because honour was not involved in the former case. This is an extraordinary assumption about the nature of woman's relationship to man inside marriage, and woman's relationship to her sexuality. In *Misogynies* Joan Smith cites a number of similar examples.[27]

> A 19 yr old man raped a 12 yr old girl who went back with him to his bedsit for a cup of coffee. Sentencing him to three years' youth custody Justice John Evans said 'It was foolish of her to go'. He also remarked 'In other days you would have said she was asking for trouble'.[28]

The phrase 'in other days' indicates that he acknowledges the fading of that view. A magistrate, handing down a conditional discharge to a man accused of kerb-crawling, suggested that any woman out late at night was likely to be a prostitute. He asked: 'Are you trying to suggest that these women, walking in that area at 1.25 a.m., could be there for any other reason than prostitution?'[29] This incident occurred near a busy station. A woman raped by a man she met in a pub said she submitted because she was afraid of being hurt. In his summing-up, Judge David Wilde said:

> Women who say no do not always mean no, it is not just a question of saying no, it is a question of how she says it, how she shows and makes it clear. If she does not want it she only has to keep her legs shut and there would have been marks of force being used.[30]

Several assumptions here are worth drawing out. One is 'natural innocence' – that a woman's virtue is located in her chastity, but also, perhaps, that less 'privacy' has been breached when something happens inside marriage and the home. But it is significant that attention is directed to the effects upon the woman's status in the world, her 'shame', rather than the experience of violence or the significance for her relationship. In the second example the judge attempts to invoke the model of women's innocence and prudence as the only bastion against ungovernable male lust, though he appears to recognise that this is no longer legitimate – or perhaps not legitimate in the case of a child of twelve?

The third example draws upon the view that the world can be divided into two kinds of women: those who are virtuous and innocent, and avoid provoking men, and those who are corrupt, dishonoured, and a danger to male control. This also maps gender categories on to night and day, and public and private. Daytime is legitimate public space for both sexes. Daytime is also a time when rational forces prevail, and lightness rules. Night-time is private time – time when women, in particular, should be private, at home, because this is the time of dark forces and lack of control. A woman who is 'in public' at that time does not protect her innocence and, by definition, does not restrain men's passions; she is part of the dark forces of the night. This example presumes the eroticisation of women; a woman who is in a 'public' place at a time not designated as public for women is presumed to be making a statement to all men present – an eroticised message that she must be offering herself for sex.

In the last example, the issue is interpretation. If one means 'no', one must symbolise it in body language; verbal communication is not enough. This draws upon the assumption that rape is 'really' only an extension of intercourse unless demonstrated by evidence of force. It also explicitly refers to the schema of 'woman as temptress'. 'Not always meaning no' suggests teasing, and also implies that men cannot distinguish between erotic games, coyness, and a forceful refusal. Surely this could be true only if men regard women's interaction as *always* erotic, whatever the circumstances.

There is evidence of some change. One enlightened judge, Mr Justice Rougier, said in 1988: 'Women are entitled to dress attractively, even provocatively if you like, be friendly with a casual acquaintance and still say no at the end of the evening without being brutally assaulted.' Jailing the offender for eighteen months, he added: 'This sort of brutal violence particularly to women has got to be dealt with severely, you broke her jaw just because she wasn't prepared to go to bed with you.'[31] This illustrates a major shift in schemas about male–female relations, and sexuality generally. It is also a move away from seeing men as possessors of women, and women as ever vulnerable to male assault, yet presumed to be culpable when it happens.

The debate about the meaning of rape in the context of privacy has resurfaced in the discussion of marital rape, and recent changes in the law. In March 1991 English law caught up with Scottish and made rape within marriage a crime. This brought out some useful statements which acknowledged, for example, as Lord Lane said, that 'the idea that a wife by marriage consents in advance to her husband having sexual intercourse with her whatever her state of health or however proper her objections . . . is no longer acceptable'. It was, he said, 'not the creation of a new offence. It is the removal of a common law fiction which has become anachronistic and offensive.' The point was made by objectors, however, that the case would be very difficult to prove, and that in fact a man who raped his wife was almost certainly doing other violent things to her – for which he could already be charged by law, and might be more successfully prosecuted because the situation was clearer and less likely to be lost under a haze of ambiguity and jurors' uncertainty.

The creation of *anti-logos* means new metaphors. In rape we see metaphors and symbols of male possession of women, of men's ownership of women with whom they have relationships, of men's legal domination over women. But women are also temptresses, provokers of sexual assault – victims, but not blameless. Men dominate women on the grounds that men are naturally more powerful than women. This is part of the natural order of things, and does not carry with it connotations of morally reprehensible 'oppression'. Dominance implies leadership, superiority, greater rationality, and so on. In a *logos* where hierarchy is both natural and part of good order, dominance does not necessarily imply exploitation and violation. One of the first tasks of feminism was to reconstruct the concept of domination as illegitimate oppression.

Progress?

From the perspective of the early 1990s, what has changed? Clearly the theories of sexuality which I described at the beginning of this chapter have been considerably undermined and, at the very least, become differentiated. The most significant change is the growing recognition that women are sexually autonomous beings who have their own sexual needs and their own sexual desires. The positive consequence for men has been liberation from the need to pursue and to perform Olympically, and freedom to seek mutual sexual enjoyment and a more fulfilling and satisfying egalitarian sexuality. The feminist message is that sexual stereotypes impose constraints that are equally oppressive to men's emotional life, and that a man's fully developed sexuality requires integration of sex into the whole of his life. A man should be able to relate to a woman not as a sex object only, nor by denying that she is a sexual being, but by seeing her sexuality integrated into her self.

But many people have been unable to redefine sexuality. The feminist challenge poses a deep threat to men who are fighting the battle of the existential triangle. Most obviously, feminists have challenged men's right to define them and to determine the expectations of how they should behave. The man trapped in the existential triangle needs the conventional categories in order to cope. Without those categories his only choices are psychological celibacy or psychological homophilia – forms of flight, in other words. More subtle – and less often stated – is the far greater threat: the demand that men come to terms with their own sexuality. Such messages are highly threatening to a man who has dealt with his sexuality by a combination of denial, isolation and rationalisation. He will rush to re-establish the impermeable categories of different kinds of woman, casting feminists as witches and demons. Feminism seems to be removing an external force which keeps his internal conflict in a state of balance. Man is required to take responsibility for his own sexuality, as well as acknowledging it.

Notes

1. G. Jolliffe and P. Mayle, *Man's Best Friend*, London: Pan Books, 1985.
2. Plato, *Symposium*, in B. Jowett (trans.), *The Dialogues of Plato*, New York: Random House, 1937.
3. M. Eichler, 'Power and sexual fear in primitive societies', *Journal of Marriage and the Family*, **37(4)**, pp. 917–26, 1977.
4. H. Institor and J. Sprenger, *Malleus Maleficarum* [1486], New York: Bloom, 1970.
5. O. Weininger, *Sex and Character*, London: Heinemann, 1906.
6. R. Scruton, *Sexual Desire: A philosophical investigation*, London: Weidenfeld & Nicolson, 1986; R. Scruton, 'The case against feminism', *Observer*, 2 May 1983, p. 27.
7. C. Cohn, 'Sex and death in the rational world of defense intellectuals', *Signs*, **12(4)**, pp. 687–718, 1987.
8. *ibid.*, p. 693.
9. R. Kipling, 'The Betrothed', in *Departmental Ditties and Ballads and Barrack Room Ballads*, New York: Doubleday, Page & Co., 1913.
10. T. H. Van de Velde, *Ideal Marriage: Its physiology and technique*, London: Heinemann, 1928.
11. *ibid.*, p. 158.
12. K. Muir, 'The face that launched a thousand theses', *Times*, Tuesday 4 August 1992, 'Life and Times', p. 1.
13. K. Saunders, 'Sister superior', *Sunday Times*, 15 July 1990, p. 7:1.
14. W. Cash, 'Dancing with the queen of Cannes', *Times*, 17 May 1991.
15. Cited in [Unsigned], 'More like a tomato than a virgin', Profile, *Sunday Telegraph*, 19 May 1991.
16. *ibid.*
17. Described in H. Haste, 'Sex and dinosaurs', in C. Haslam and A. Bryman (eds), *Social Scientists Meet the Media*, London: Routledge, 1993.
18. In Saunders, 'Sister superior'.
19. E. A. Kaplan, 'Madonna politics: masks or mastery?', in A. Schwichtenberg (ed.), *The Madonna Connection*, Boulder, CO: Westview Press, 1993.
20. C. Paglia, 'Madonna I: animality and artifice', in *Sex, Art and American Culture*, New York: Vintage, 1992; C. Paglia, 'Madonna II: Venus of the radio waves', *Sex, Art and American Culture*.
21. See C. Haste, *Rules of Desire; sex in Britain: World War I to the present*, London: Chatto & Windus, 1992, especially ch. 8.
22. A. Kollontai, *Sexual Relations and the Class Struggle: Love and the New Morality*, Bristol: Falling Wall Press, 1972; A. Kollontai, *Communism and the Family*, London: Pluto Press, 1971.

23. A. Koedt, 'The myth of the vaginal orgasm', in A. Koedt, E. Levine and A. Rapone (eds), *Radical Feminism*, New York: New York Times Books, 1973.
24. W. H. Masters and V. E. Johnson, *Human Sexual Response*, Boston, MA: Little, Brown, 1966.
25. M. J. Sherfey, *The Nature and Evolution of Female Sexuality*, New York: Vintage, 1973.
26. B. Amiel, *Times*, 14 September 1990.
27. J. Smith, *Misogynies*, London: Faber & Faber, 1989.
28. *ibid.*, p. 2; report from *Independent*, 13 January 1988.
29. Smith, *Misogynies*, pp. 2–3.
30. *ibid.*, p. 3; report in *Sunday Times*, 12 December 1982.
31. Smith, *Misogynies*, pp. 1–2; report in *Daily Telegraph*, 4 March 1988.

Chapter 9: Reclaiming the symbols

The message of this book has been that real changes occur only when there is a profound change in the underlying metaphors of gender. Beliefs about the nature of sex difference map on to much more extensive beliefs that are framed by metaphors of dualism. Where we identify something as masculine or feminine, we are not only talking about the affinities between that phenomenon and our images of gender-linked characteristics, we are assigning to it the *metaphor* of masculinity versus femininity. We see in that phenomenon all the interrelationships between its parts that we ascribe to the interrelation of the masculine and the feminine. Therefore, to change the metaphors of masculinity and femininity as we apply them to stereotypes of human behaviour and attributes, we have also to challenge the principles of dualism on which so much of our thinking rests. But that dualism itself, and the mapping of it on to gender, does not reflect only mental organisation, convenient frameworks for categorising the world; it also reflects profound anxieties. We construct 'either–or' categories not just for convenience, but because by defining one pole as the negation of the other, we assert not only what it is, but what it is *not*. The world is in balance because by asserting, or supporting, or endorsing, A we are denying, or suppressing, or devaluing B. Yet we also define A *in terms of* B; without the negation of B, A does not have the same force. Innocent has meaning precisely because it is not guilt. Hardness has no real significance unless we see it as negating softness.

This is not only conceptual usefulness. We have seen in earlier chapters that those areas on to which the masculinity–femininity polarity is mapped are often areas of anxiety and uncertainty. This merely reinforces the obvious point that masculinity and femininity themselves are problematic and fraught. This has always been true, but it becomes particularly explicit in periods when issues of gender are a matter of public debate. As various writers have pointed out, the period around the end of the nineteenth century has many similarities with our own time, and much of the rhetoric of that time is echoed in today's discourse. Indeed, it is surprising how familiar the current backlash against feminism sounds. But I have argued that certain strands of feminism have failed to appreciate the extraordinary power of that anxiety, and the need to understand this and challenge it if any real change is to be made.

What characterises all forms of feminism is the challenge of authentic self-definition. Whatever the theoretical stance, and whatever the beliefs held about the nature, origin or importance of sex difference, the agenda is to claim an authentic voice for women in their own destiny. Not only an authentic voice, but an authentic view: to perceive the world through women's eyes rather than holding a mirror up to men; to see the self as one experiences it rather than as it is experienced through men's perceptions. If there are 'mysteries' of the female, then let these be mysteries that women recognise and define, not those that men describe and endlessly strive to 'uncover' – and, through uncovering, control. The idea of the 'authentic voice' is more than the 'right to be heard' – to take part in the discussion, or to sit at the policy table. These are rights of access to power within the system. Real authenticity comes from saying, 'This is not how things are; this is not how I experience them' – and providing a new perspective.

This goal has been conceived in several ways. For some people, the goal of feminism has been equity, overcoming discrimination. If one believes that inequality and discrimination are founded upon mistaken theories about gender difference, the strategy for achieving the goal is to challenge those beliefs, to generate counter-evidence. Mostly, this has led to a concerted attack on lay and scientific misconceptions and distortions about the nature and extent of sex difference, emphasis on the social and economic conditions which create discrimination, and analysis of why the perpetuation of discrimination serves cultural needs. If the locus of concern is social context, individual psychological dynamics (such as anxiety about the boundaries of gender roles) are seen as the product of social and economic forces. Equality would be achieved by changing the underlying social and economic conditions. Behind such a conception is a fundamental belief in the possibility of rational change, and the eventual implementation of rational justice. In principle, justice should not depend on the absence of differences between groups; equal treatment can be accorded on the basis of citizenship alone. But in practice a great deal of the discussion about discrimination has hung on perceptions of difference, and of lesser worth or relevant talents. One should not have to believe that people are the same in order to treat them equally, but in effect this has been the case.

For this reason, the process of reconstructing gender and arriving at greater authenticity (for both men and women) within this model has emphasised the equal talents of men and women. A great deal of work, especially in psychology and anthropology, has been directed to undermining the myths of difference, demonstrating the biases in the research in many fields which have perpetuated difference. The effect has been to narrow down the areas in which there are established differences; one outcome has been discovery of differences which were not evident before. In other words, in the past science and social science largely confirmed conventional prejudice about gender; later work has undermined the stereotype and clarified the reality.

The important message of the rationalist search for authenticity is that differences are few. If they are not created by environmental factors, they are certainly exaggerated by them. They can be explained in terms of the social forces and economic conditions to which they serve a useful function – and they are amenable to modification. These are partly strategic positions, based on the premiss that inequality of treatment, whether justified or not, will continue unless there is a major cultural change in common beliefs about sex difference. The message that differences between the sexes are minimal is seen as the most effective *anti-logos* to the present orthodoxy.

A plea for *androgyny* emerged from this position. Stereotypes not only deprive people of opportunity and reward by virtue of their sex, but also constrain them as human beings. There are two versions of androgyny. One is that real differences between people are based on personality traits rather than gender, and there is enormous overlap of traits between the sexes. Gender plays a minor part in individual variation, though labelling may distort the way people are perceived. The concepts of 'masculinity' and 'femininity' are largely irrelevant. A second version of androgyny is exemplified by the work of Sandra Bem, and of Janet Taylor Spence and Robert Helmreich, though it also echoes some popularisations of Jung. 'Masculinity' and 'femininity' are recognised. In Bem's work they reflect exactly nurturance versus agency. But the 'healthy individual' has a balance of both these characteristics. So androgyny is possession of both, rather than the denial of either.

Both versions of the androgyny model challenge a *logos* which is propped up by apparently 'scientific' evidence for sex difference. Using scientific evidence to counter this *logos* is a rational move. The rhetoric of 'rationality' is a useful strategy in a public discourse where this is the dominant and accepted mode. The argument for minimal difference has been quite effective in creating an ethos of anti-discrimination, and in changing policy and legislation in many countries. However, this supposed rationality is in fact underpinned by profound anxieties about gender roles and sexuality. It also flies in the face of some subjective experience which, even if it is only a consequence of social construction and social conditioning, is nevertheless a profound part of ordinary personal identity. Rational arguments for androgyny fail to take account of the power of gender metaphors across most areas of life, culture and thought. Nor do they begin to tackle the emotional and defensive functions which masculinity and femininity serve.

Nor does the strategy of minimal difference take account of the possibility of distinctive female (and male) experience. The battle to 'own' one's perceptions of one's body, and of the peculiarly female experiences of menstruation, childbirth and the physical changes of illness and maturation, was first fought in the context of the medicalisation of women's experience. Medical expertise controlled not only the transition through these events, but their symbolic meaning.[1] This battle continues and remains lively, partly because it affects all women, irrespective of their social position or beliefs. Scandalous examples are still occurring.[2]

Here, authenticity would mean recognising the validity of women's experience and women's interpretation. This is not overtly feminist; women have always recognised areas of separate knowledge and awareness, and have excluded men either explicitly or by the tacit charge of 'not understanding'.[3] The issue for feminists has been the culture's treatment of this exclusion. 'Women's worlds' or 'women's ways of knowing' are at least marginalised and at worst denigrated. The Otherness of woman is *reinforced* by recognition of her special knowledge or her special understanding. It increases her alienation from the 'masculine'; confirms the difference between the masculine and the feminine, and the impossibility of bridging it. This feeds anxieties about maintaining rationality and control – which are closely tied to certain definitions of masculinity. Women's 'other' ways of knowing, or women's 'special' world of experience, become a threat because they appear inaccessible to the male. The frequent metaphors of 'uncovering', 'disclosing' and 'penetrating' the mysteries of the female psyche – and the female body – are expressions of this male unease.

The darker side of this is the anxiety that underlies Otherness. The problem is not that men deny women's experience, it is how this experience is dealt with in order to reduce its threat to the masculine world. Claiming authenticity requires that the Other be a valid alternative, to coexist with masculine experience, rather than 'alien to, a threat to, the antithesis of'. This task requires demystifying female Otherness – women are not such secret and bewildering creatures about whom nothing can be truly known. There needs to be recognition of complexity, but a complexity defined through women's own authentic appreciation. At the end of the last century, the female poet George Egerton 'vowed to reveal the terra incognita of the female psyche, to "unlock a closed door with a key of my own fashioning"'.[4] This is the message of both cultural and radical feminism, whether at the hands of Carol Gilligan, the French school of Cixous, Irigaray and Kristeva, or the radical feminist Mary Daly.

'The key of my own fashioning', or Gilligan's 'different voice', represent a female perspective rooted in shared female experience. It does not necessarily assume that all women experience everything in the same way, only that it is legitimate to claim a valid voice, to challenge the masculine perspective which casts the feminine as alien and antithetical. This, at the very least, gives women the right to a privileged interpretation of their own lives. Indeed, feminine discourse about female experience has always flourished, privately and amongst women. But it is not enough to give women privilege with regard to their own experience, or even the right to an alternative perspective on the world at large. *The real challenge is to an orthodoxy that there is only one way of interpreting the world, only one model of reasoning.* The challenge is a plea for a pluralistic perspective; it has implications for all domains of knowledge. It is not the replacement of a masculine perspective with a feminine one, but the implication that if there is more than one valid alternative perspective, a monolithic or absolutist position is untenable.

Why is this different from the androgyny ideal? Androgyny denies the force of metaphors of gender by presuming that the tensions can be overcome by a rational challenge. If one takes seriously the argument that there is a hidden perspective to be brought out, to coexist with the dominant current perspective, then one has to understand the forces and anxieties which have cast that alternative as 'hidden'. To do this it is necessary to reconstruct the previous dichotomies. So it is not enough to say that women have the same kind and degree of rationality as men. Nor, even, is it enough to say that they have a special kind of knowledge that we call 'intuition'. Instead, the message is that knowing requires *both* 'rationality' *and* intuition. Saying this undermines the dualistic metaphor, the antithesis of logic versus intuition.

In her provocative book *Sexual Personae*, Camille Paglia distinguishes between the 'Apollonian' and the 'Dionysian' modes, contrasting and conflicting streams within Western culture.[5] She sees the Apollonian mode as the triumph of reason in the struggle against the chaos of nature and the Dionysian. To achieve the changes for which I am arguing, we must not only redefine both the attributes of the Apollonian and the Dionysian, but we must also stop thinking of them in terms of a desperate struggle. To do this, we must recognise that there is something to be redefined, not merely denied. Masculinity and femininity are mapped on to these grand dualities because they serve important metaphorical purposes, but the concepts of masculinity and femininity themselves are trapped by just those metaphors on to which they are mapped. They need to be challenged and redefined. This is a very profound challenge to our present concepts of culture and civilisation, because the current metaphors both create anxieties and resolve them.

'Authenticity' in this context, therefore, means two things. It means deconstructing and reconstructing the various metaphors of the relationship between masculine and feminine, both symbolically as mapped on to other metaphors of dualism and, specifically, with regard to male–female relations And it means finding new and more authentic conceptions of masculinity and femininity as human characteristics. In the last two decades, moves towards such authenticity have been made through the attack on symbols. Consider the problem: we have inherited at least two thousand years of metaphors of gender. These include actual beliefs about and 'scientific' justifications of sex difference, but they also include an enormous system of metaphors and symbols, covering everything from cosmology to the electric plug, on to which the duality of masculine and feminine has been grafted and become an inherent part of the meaning. In some of these areas (like the electric plug) this is little more than a simple physical analogy. In others (like the dichotomy of rationality versus chaos) a vast edifice has been constructed, a complex theory of control and mastery.

Such edifices are enshrined in the dominant ethos of the culture, which, on the whole, is the ethos that is explicit in the main cultural institutions – religion, literature, art and the mainstream media. Conceptions of what constitutes science, medicine, and education are distilled through it. This culture has numerically been dominated by men, particularly men of learning who were well trained in the subtleties of theory construction and rationalisation. It has further been dominated by the preoccupations of the male psyche, the anxieties surrounding masculine experience, male biological cycles and the crises of male life.

Yet this is not entirely a monolithic history. The voice of woman, and the voice of the feminine, has not been wholly absent from the construction of culture. Woman's role has not only been as a fantasy figure of threat or of private succour to men. Furthermore, there have been many diverse strands within male culture, and successive waves of very different, and competing, belief systems. Even though each wave may be replaced by another, these alternatives do not die out; they remain hidden or low-profile, or confined to non-powerful groups. Therefore, in reconstructing metaphors, there is a vast resource of these other cultural strands to draw upon. Such mining of hidden culture has been a favourite occupation of reformers and reconstructors.

Strategies for change

There are a number of possible strategies for change. Existing schemas and models can be challenged and proved untenable – either because they are based on inaccurate data, or because they are no longer necessary as defences against anxiety. One example is the way scientific evidence has been used to challenge former science-backed beliefs about sex difference. A more practical example can be drawn from campaigns for birth control – equating masculinity with the siring of numerous sons is still a problem in many cultures. This can become less important if there are alternative symbols of masculinity (the level of success achieved by those sons) or if one of the justifications for large families, provision for old age, is removed by welfare systems. In these cases, 'masculinity' is not challenged, only its manifestations. Both these examples are ostensibly about appeals to logic and reason, but in fact they work because the old symbol is replaced with a new one and the anxiety is defused.

A second strategy is to redefine the meaning or significance of the symbol or metaphor. This is being done to some extent to concepts like 'mastery' and 'control' – not only through feminist thought, but particularly in the Green Movement. The equation of control metaphors with assault upon the environment, and attempts to replace the metaphor of mastery with the metaphor of harmony and holism, are far wider than the explicit debate about gender, yet the metaphor of mastery is deeply implicit in masculinity.

Frequently redefinition comes serendipitously out of research itself, but needs overt acknowledgement of its implications. Herman Witkin, a cognitive psychologist, found sex differences in ability to focus on one stimulus and exclude the context.[6] The task was to find figures (such as geometric shapes) embedded in a confusing background. Those described by Witkin as 'field dependent' took longer to find the shapes than those who were described as 'field independent'. There are significant rhetorical implications attached to the words 'independent' and 'dependent'; they resonate with the American ethos of individualism and masculine no-nonsense getting to the point. Witkin found that males were more likely to be field independent, and females, field dependent. But when the research team later looked in greater detail at just how respondents scanned the pictures, it emerged that field-dependent people were systematic, taking into account the whole picture before arriving at their conclusions; whereas the field-independent respondents zoomed in on the target.[7] If they were successful, they solved the problem fast, but if they failed to spot it quickly, they had much greater difficulty in finding alternative strategies. The original interpretation was that women (and field-dependent people) have difficulty in focusing on one singular problem. An alternative conclusion is that men (and field-independent people) can focus on only one aspect of the problem, and have difficulty in taking into account other things that might be important. Some tasks need 'field independence'; others need 'field dependence'.

There is another, real-life example of the need for different strategies for perceptual tasks. During the Second World War, scientists of various kinds were drafted to interpret aerial photographs. In a discussion of the relative merits of what he termed the 'hard' and 'woolly' sciences, Beverly Halstead wrote:

> This was a task for which mathematicians, physicists and chemists had no aptitude, whereas geologists, botanists and zoologists excelled at it. They were trained to view the whole scene and their eyes were trained to spot changes, minor inconsistencies in pattern. It is the ability to take on board a vast array of seemingly unrelated data and then grasp connections, usually missed by the exact sciences, that gives the woolly sciences their great vitality.[8]

The dichotomy of hard versus woolly science was a deliberate challenge to the assumption that there is only one 'correct' method in science. Halstead's challenge parallels the masculine–feminine distinction. In these examples the value of the poles is inverted, but this does not profoundly challenge the polarity itself; the feminine, and the woolly, become as valued as the masculine and the hard, but the meaning of the metaphor remains the same.

Redefining and reclaiming metaphors includes *mining the hidden traditions* – and again, inverting their evaluation. Some radical feminists have embraced the traditions of witchcraft, have turned into positive terminology the traditional negative epithets 'hag' and 'crone'.[9] The search for a lost matriarchy of the past proved ill-conceived for a variety of reasons, but it drew attention to the hidden role of women in many political systems. More significantly, it has drawn attention to the powerful metaphor of the Earth Mother in her many forms, both good and destructive, and alerted us to the deep anxiety about femininity which explains some of the defensive aspects of masculinity. In the mythological image of a benign and powerful Earth Mother, the reasons for male fears become rather more obvious.

Matriarchies may be myth, but religions which are 'earth'- as opposed to 'sky'-based either accord power to the female principle or, more often, require both male and female principles to function in balance, to maintain harmony with the forces of nature. This tends to remove the metaphor of struggle between masculine and feminine which is such a profound element of sky-god cultures. Marion Bradley's novel *Mists of Avalon* is a fictional treatment of this. The Arthurian legend is recast as the early history of conflict between the Roman influence that brought the male religion of Christianity, and the traditional Celtic faith of the Earth Mother and the Horned God.[10] Other Westerners have turned to the mythologies of Hinduism or the American Indians, looking for ways of building a cosmology around a different version of masculine–feminine relations. In a controversial search for a new definition of masculinity, Robert Bly, author of *Iron John*, has turned to Teutonic fairy tales.[11]

Reclaiming the organic metaphor as a counter to the mechanistic is a central part of Green thinking, finding its expression perhaps most fully and lucidly in the Gaia hypothesis of James Lovelock.[12] The rejection of a mechanistic model of science and technology as control and mastery is about much more than being nice to the environment. It is a challenge to the whole relationship between the human being and the object of investigation, replacing a relationship of separated objectivity with participant observation. The Gaia hypothesis also argues that a model of evolution based upon successful development of competitive attributes may be wrong; instead, cooperation may be the characteristic mode of successful adaptation. This is hardly new; Petr Kropotkin proposed a cooperative model of evolution in 1902.[13] It is not only the idea that is interesting, but the context out of which it arose, and this context is a particularly good example of the role of culture in the generation and acceptance of metaphors that influenced scientific thinking. For Western Europeans, Malthus's spectre of disastrous overpopulation, which led Darwin to the concept of natural selection, resonated with their experience of an overcrowded and increasingly industrialised world. Marx wrote to Engels in 1862: 'It is remarkable how Darwin recognises among beasts and plants his English society, with its divisions of labour, competition, opening up of new markets, 'invention' and the Malthusian 'struggle for existence'.'[14]

But for Russians like Kropotkin, the world was large and empty. As Halstead argued:

> The struggle for existence, the idea of competition, the very idea of population pressure were seen as evidence of the inseparability of science and cultural values and related to the experience of English schoolboys brought up on competitive sports. Darwinism was seen by Russian scientists in particular as a purely English doctrine expressing

the English preoccupation with practicality and competition. The sparsely populated Russian Empire with its enormous wealth of natural resources, made it virtually impossible for Russian scientists to grasp the notion of overpopulation with its consequent pressures on natural resources. Such ideas seemed fanciful and flew in the face of the Russian scientists' own experience. Other aspects of Russian life such as a preference for group activities led to the theory of mutual aid as a key factor in the process of evolution.[15]

There is a fine line between rediscovery and innovation. In claiming or reclaiming ancient metaphors and symbols of relationship, feminists and Green thinkers alike are self-consciously challenging the dominant metaphors of the culture. But they are not just returning to an earlier, or hidden, mode. Challenging a metaphor with its antithesis, or with a new metaphor, undermines its meaning. When the women at Greenham Common weave webs on the wire, or use flowers and toys as symbols of protest, they are affirming feminine symbols to challenge the masculine hierarchy expressed in the power metaphors of war, but they are also offering an alternative way of looking at the world. In the search for new definitions of masculinity and femininity, therefore, the first task is to challenge received wisdom, received symbols and the metaphors which explain and justify the traditional patterns. This exercise reveals just how extensive and profound are the anxieties underpinning our conceptions of gender.

Fear and the limits of rationalist change

Let us postulate for the moment that there do exist the sort of people, and the sort of cultural tradition, in which the ideals of a truly post-feminist, rational-androgyne world are possible. Such people have been raised without strong sanctions against sex-inappropriate behaviour, they have never learnt to worry about failing in their masculinity or femininity, and they have acquired a rounded view of the human person which acknowledges the coexistence of masculinity and feminity within every balanced individual. The ideal model of sexual relationships is the merging of essentially similar selves who have equal power in a relationship. Discrimination against people on the grounds of sex would be anathema, and furthermore, because work and family life (and all their ramifications) have equivalent importance, the necessary accommodations to family responsibilities are made, rather than being seen as a handicap to full efficiency in the work context. Such people, and such a world, are the goal of much writing within the socialist and liberal feminist tradition – for example, that of Lynne Segal and Ann Oakley.

It is a world which some people even do inhabit, cushioned by education and the right professional situation. It is a world that is represented as attainable once two things have been achieved: changing the social and economic conditions that emphasise work, marginalise family life and discriminate against women in terms of both economic rewards and a voice in policy-making, and changing the attitudes which equate masculinity (and maleness) with power – over women, over subordinates and between men.

However, as soon as this rationalist goal became public currency, it was clear that most people had not grown up free of anxieties about gender, and that these anxieties would not be assuaged by economic change. Furthermore, it became explicit that there was a common belief that many aspects of culture and civilisation depended upon a struggle between the forces of rationality and the forces of chaos. The darker side of human passion, whether general emotion that disorganised the intellect, or specifically overwhelming and destructive forces like sex and aggression, constantly lurked below the surface, and was potentially more powerful than the forces of reason. To defend against this requires constant control and vigilance.

This is a direct mapping on to the internal life of human beings, of the metaphor of Man trying to control the powers and chaos of Nature. It is indeed the world that Freud describes, but it is also the world of the Judaeo-Christian tradition, the sky-god (equated with intellect) who battles against the dark forces of the earth, in the form of the flesh. Camille Paglia uncompromisingly states that 'Sex is daimonism' and that 'Western love . . . is a defense mechanism rationalising forces ungoverned and ungovernable. Like early religion it is a device enabling us to control our primal fear. Sex cannot be understood because nature cannot be understood.'[16] The dualism she describes – and to which she subscribes – is Apollonian reason in conflict with the Dionysian appeals of nature and the flesh. For her, as for others in this tradition, civilisation and progress in science and culture depend upon the triumph of the Apollonian over the Dionysian. There seems to be no space in her perspective for shifting between the Apollonian and the Dionysian, for *integration*. There is constant battle, yet the Apollonian can never fully win.

Paglia's thesis about culture rests upon the assumption that men fear the female and the feminine, the cyclic and the natural, and are constantly trying to esape both the feminine and the power of their mothers. It is through this struggle, and the symbolic phallic ejaculation and erection (and urination standing up, though she is wrong to believe this is universal[17]), that creativity and conceptualisation are possible: 'Male projection of erection and ejaculation is the paradigm for all cultural projection and conceptualisation.'[18] So culture is *necessarily* both masculine and male-dominated, and women have access to it only in their 'Apollonian' mode, in which they are hampered by being closer to nature and to the Dionysian forces. For Paglia, women do not have an alternative culture but, by definition, no culture.

Paglia's position is uncompromising; indeed, one might say extreme. But it expresses a long tradition of profound anxiety experienced by individual men, and manifested in a cultural perspective associated with Catholic asceticism and, in a different form, Puritanism. The theory of conflict on which it rests reproduces anxieties in generations of people. Paglia is right, of course, when she argues that the kind of feminism that I describe as a rationalist ideal has taken absolutely no cognizance of these forces. She herself is using the metaphor of rationality versus chaos, and the mapping of male–female relations on to it – and she endorses it. Within this cultural tradition, the only way to change gender roles must be to challenge the whole basis of the model of rationality. Paglia accepts the model; I dispute it; but we share an appreciation of the same metaphors. Paglia presents a total picture, within which she explains decadence in art and literature. But elements of her world-view can be seen in less apocalyptic visions of society, which nevertheless feed the anxieties about gender that sustain many current metaphors. Many writers who do not share Paglia's gloom do acknowledge the widespread fear of the feminine and the belief that masculinity is equated with personal autonomy, even if it is not seen as a power.

Here we can return to the mythology of the Earth Mother. This is ambivalent; the enveloping, caring female force may be a haven into which one can sink, but it may also smother, devour or reject. For some reason this is seen as a major problem for men, but hardly considered in relation to women. The tension is expressed in the conflict between the pressure on little boys (and later men) to be tough, independent and self-sufficient, yet reliant on maternal approval and affection – especially in cultural contexts where adult males do not express warmth to their sons. In *Men in Love*, her book on male sexual fantasies, Nancy Friday concludes:

> Inside every male is a denied little boy . . . . He loved his mother, but feared her power. The male principle in society says he is expected to be tough and domineering with women, always in control, and sexually voracious. The female principle is the opposite; when he approaches women, he carries with him all his unconscious memories of mother's awesome powers of retaliation and rejection.[19]

Friday argues that male fantasies are the means for men to create women as magic beings who do not possess this threatening power.

Such men might greet with relief a changing gender scenario in which they do not have to be all-powerful, and can welcome women who will give them love and acceptance without overtones of mother-power. Again, in the ideal rationalist world there are people who have achieved this in their relationships and in their self-image, but the cultures which generate myths of Kali, Lilith, and Babi Yaga do not have such a rationalist basis. And while these are not the myths of Anglophone Western culture, nevertheless in this culture we see the flight from the feminine in a host of different ways: the ethos of manliness that requires rejection of the feminine in all its forms and, to achieve this, severs the ties between the little boy and his mother in order to toughen him – the symbolic as well as actual separation of the boy from that which is female – defines, by antithesis, that which is male. Power, strength, autonomy, rationality, control and self-assertion are equated with symbols of phallicism, erection and ejaculation, all of which are, by definition, denied to females.

In this model, the male gains his adult/male status through the rejection of everything symbolic and concrete about his ties to his mother. The fear is not explicitly, in this metaphor, that she will devour him, but that her femaleness will sap his masculinity, and therefore his strength, and therefore his identity as a person. He must escape from the feminine and all its metaphors. Paglia talks of 'slime' and 'swamp' – especially the oozings of the female body, which the male encounters again when he begins sexual life with women. Male 'oozings' are 'outside' the body by the time they are evident, and can be washed away quickly. Such oozings are both a concrete and a metaphoric contrast with the purity of the masculine. For men, but not for women, they can be confined to periods of infancy, illness and the eventual decrepitude of old age. The association of menstrual blood with taboos in many cultures, and particularly with the pollution of male figures in religious roles, reflects this metaphor. It is still true that advertisements for sanitary towels and tampons on television in Britain and the States can only be very coy about either the product or its purpose. Even as recently as January 1993 the British Advertising Standards Authority was besieged by – and conceded to – objections to the advertising of a sanitary towel on television.

The fear is of the feminine as sapper of masculinity, weakening and polluting through her very femaleness. Woman is mother who devours and smothers, preventing the separation that leads to strength and autonomy (and may be manifested in woman-as-wife who controls). Woman is a terrible powerful judge who may reject the boy in childhood; she is symbolic in every little girl who giggles with her friends, and may grow up to ridicule the adult male. To escape this, the male must find ways either to pretend that women's opinions are unimportant, or to exert power to suppress women.

Finally there is woman, and the female, as the representative of temptation away from the path of Apollonian purity and transcendence of nature and chaos. Woman tempts because she causes Man's thoughts to stray to the fleshly, the carnal, the natural, and away from cognitive control. Yet into this is also woven the Good Mother, Roger Scruton's ideal, who has the power to control the little boy's passion and to restrain his potentiality for chaos and destruction. So the female represents both the domain of chaos that masculinity can transcend through reason, and also at the same time, because she has less passion of her own, she can exert restraints upon the male. She is both Superego and Id, between which the frail male ego struggles to survive.

These scenarios seem to underlie the dualism of masculine and feminine in the culture we have inherited. They belong to different strands, but the individual within the culture has access to all the myths. Some will be more salient than others. Characteristic of all these myths is the idea of struggle and conflict between the feminine and the masculine. One is defined in terms of the Other, usually as a negation, but sometimes as a force which must be kept in a fine balance of control: enough feminine force to support and praise, or to act as a brake, but not enough to swamp uncertain and fragile masculinity.

So, many anxieties underlie the force of gender as a framework for meaning. The least emotionally problematic is simple cognitive categorisation, learnt early and confirmed through the individual's own use, and through constant cultural affirmation. En-gendering is the result of continual exposure to a dualistic category system which frames so many areas of thought. Threat comes when a boundary is challenged, and comfortable certainty is replaced by ambiguity. The emotional power of dualistic metaphors is greatly increased when they map on to gender. More anxiety-inducing are metaphors of gender that presuppose conflict between the masculine and the feminine, especially where the masculine is defined by a negation of, or escape from, the feminine. To remove the underlying anxiety which creates that categorisation requires not only a redefinition of the masculine but a different conceptualisation of the feminine, in balance rather than antithesis. But most difficult to deal with are conceptions of masculinity which arise out of a fear of being devoured or overwhelmed by female emotional power. The motivation is escape from that power, rather than denial of the feminine *per se*. Such metaphors of gender see the power of the female force, and deal with it by translating it into something Other and dangerous.

There is a difference between, on the one hand, fear of being overwhelmed by feminine power and, on the other, aligning masculine with reason in a confrontation with the threat of chaos and the feminine to one's identity. The former is a statement about external forces that may smother or overwhelm me – without necessarily trying to change what I am. The latter is a statement about that-which-I-am versus that-which-I-am-not. Men may fear women having too much power over them through emotional ties, without that implying the fear of being feminised or weakened in their identity. The distinction is evident in different responses to the threats of changing gender roles. For those who fear female power, the power of women as persons/mothers to overwhelm, to change gender roles would give women power in areas which have hitherto been denied them, and extend their arena of emotional action. Here the idea of androgyny is threatening because it undermines little boys' strength to resist the power of women; it is general 'weakening'. But for those who hold an image of warring factions of reason and chaos, of the Apollonian and the Dionysian, androgyny is the dangerous leakage of the feminine, the polluting of the pure, the undermining of the good, which comes from confusing the boundaries.

It is tempting to claim that the threat of overwhelming female emotional power exists only in the fevered imagination of a few men. This is manifestly not true; for many women trapped in the traditional role of life lived through her male, emotional control, however limited, is the only strategy – the tyranny of the weak. The powerless woman, dependent financially and for social status upon men, had no alternative but to manipulate the Other role to her best advantage, to enhance those aspects of her personality and body which reassured male anxieties (by enhancing the feminine, by playing down the emotional power, by building up the male ego) and guaranteed her the only kind of security available in that culture. Within this model the success of the maternal role will be measured by the outcome, so the effort to praise the male child for masculine behaviour endorses those very strivings for 'manliness' which the male culture prizes – so reinforcing also the mother who both loves and rejects, reproducing just that very culture which is ambivalent about mothers. Early in the century, Ambrose Bierce, in his *Devil's Dictionary*, expressed this fear. He defined Weakness as 'Certain primal powers of Tyrant Woman wherewith she holds dominion over the male of her species, binding him to the service of her will and paralysing his rebellious energies'.[20]

It has been said that boys walk a constant knife-edge of failure, always pushing the limits of their skills and often failing as well as often succeeding, continually reinforcing their uncertainty. The vulnerability of the male ego – that very vulnerability which generates defensive masculinist strategies – is well recognised by women. Yet the traditional sex-role pattern reinforces that vulnerability by encouraging the young boy's 'dicing with failure', his testing the limits – the reward being approval from females. Little boys learn that females will provide the necessary sympathy and praise for their behaviour; little girls learn to provide that sympathy and praise. So little girls learn to sustain their own egos through nurturing others, while little boys learn to be uncertain and constantly in need of proving themselves. The cycle continues thus.

Notes

1. B. Ehrenreich and D. English, *For Her Own Good: 150 years of the expert's advice to women*, Garden City, NY: Anchor Press/Doubleday, 1978.
2. I describe a case in Chapter 10.
3. See, for example, D. Tannen, *You Just Don't Understand: Women and men in conversation*, New York: Morrow, 1990.
4. Quoted in E. Showalter, *Sexual Anarchy: Gender and culture at the* fin de siècle, London; Bloomsbury, 1991, p. 156.
5. C. Paglia, *Sexual Personae: Art and decadence from Nefertiti to Emily Dickinson*, New Haven, CT: Yale University Press, 1990.
6. H. A. Witkin, R. B. Dyk, H. F. Faterson, D. R. Goodenough and S. A. Karp, *Psychological Differentiation*, New York: Wiley, 1962.
7. H. A. Witkin, D. R. Goodenough and S. A. Karp, 'Stability of cognitive style from childhood to young adulthood', *Journal of Personality and Social Psychology*, 7, pp. 291–300, 1967.
8. B. Halstead, 'The hard and woolly sciences', in A. Berry (ed.), *Harrap's Book of Scientific Anecdotes*, London: Harrap, 1989, p. 127.
9. M. Daly, *Pure Lust*, London: Women's Press, 1984.
10. M. Z. Bradley, *Mists of Avalon*, New York: Knopf, 1983; J. Rowan, *The Horned God: Feminism and men as wounding and healing*, London: Routledge, 1987.
11. R. Bly, *Iron John*, New York: Addison-Wesley, 1990.
12. J. Lovelock, *Gaia: A new look at earth*, Oxford: Oxford University Press, 1979.
13. P. Kropotkin, *Mutual Aid: A factor of evolution*, Boston, MA: Porter Sargent, 1902.
14. K. Marx, 18 June 1862, *The Letters of Karl Marx*, selected and translated by S. K. Padover, Englewood Cliffs, NJ: Prentice Hall, 1979, p. 157.
15. B. Halstead, 'Revolutions and colonisations in the history of life', in S. Osawa and T. Honjo (eds), *Evolution of Life*, Tokyo: Springer Verlag, 1991, p. 32.
16. Paglia, *Sexual Personae*, p. 5.
17. C. S. Ford and F. A. Beach, *Patterns of Sexual Behaviour*, Westport, CT: Greenwood Press, 1980.
18. Paglia, *Sexual Personae*, p. 20.
19. N. Friday, *Men in Love: Men's sexual fantasies: the triumph of love over rage*, New York: Delacorte Press, 1980.
20. A. Bierce, *The Devil's Dictionary*, New York: A. & C. Boni, 1926.

Chapter 10: Finding a female voice

The search for authenticity, and ending Otherness, requires a new framework for looking at the female self. This search means deconstruction, demolition, of many of the ways in which women view their selves, and many of the ways in which men view women. A new conception of the feminine, necessarily, will not be complementary to old conceptions of the masculine. The invention or discovery of new forms of the feminine may be an 'add-on' to the male – adding a lacking dimension, enlarging and extending – but it may even replace the concept of masculinity as it currently exists. It is arguable that the dominant culture depends upon defensive dualism for the very basis of meaning – so it cannot accommodate an alternative perspective because any alternative, by its very existence, challenges the monolithic view of truth.

Here I want to make a personal statement. It seems to me that there are different routes available for homosexual women and heterosexual women in reconstructing the metaphors of gender. Lesbian women have generated the concept of 'woman-identified-woman', the woman who draws upon the community of women for her self-definition and her metaphors, and withdraws from the male world in order to do this. Those lesbian women who are radical feminist separatists may cut themselves off from the male world altogether, free from the need to negotiate with men, but many lesbian women live in a mixed society where social and work relations with men continue.[1] For heterosexual women like myself, there has always been the problem of finding an identity in the midst of a culture which ignores, actively denies, but covertly constantly reaffirms and reproduces, the state of Otherness. Also, most heterosexual women feel responsible at least for some involvement in the reconstruction of masculinity amongst those men with whom they have close personal relations – lovers and sons in particular. This is partly self-defence, necessary for the survival of one's relationships during one's own reconstruction of self, but it is partly that heterosexual women find it very difficult to see femininity as something that can be isolated completely from masculinity – however it is conceptualised.

It is for this reason, perhaps, that the rational androgyny model appeals to many heterosexual women. It can take the positive aspects of oneself and one's partner and merge them; it is also a positive model in which to rear children of either sex. Yet many heterosexual women feel the need for a model which redefines the feminine in a way that identifies its separateness and difference from the masculine, but at the same time expresses the tension between masculinity and femininity, and allows for the coexistence within one being of both masculine and feminine characteristics.

My own perspective is that the several strands of what I call 'cultural feminism' are trying to do this. The most definitive statement of a female voice that deliberately confronts the masculine world comes from Mary Daly.[2] Her work is a *tour de force* in the creation of a positive female identity. It is a wide-ranging attack on the masculine, phallic metaphors which pervade all areas of thinking and experience. She takes the many terms of abuse directed at women who fail to conform to male efforts to control them. She does not just turn them into positive terms, but elaborates their meaning so that the male version is inverted and the word becomes imbued with vitality and with her definition of Lust – the desire for change. She describes women as Hags, Nags, Prudes, Viragos, Shrews, Scolds, and so on. These terms express rejection of male hegemony, the assertion of female autonomy and the rich expression of female elemental energy which, she argues, the Phallic State desperately tries to control, suppress or tap into for itself. Daly sees women as having great power – a power which is a threat to men, a power which men are constantly attempting to curb. Furthermore, she identifies women with the elemental forces of nature, in touch with the basic life forces and possessing – if they are not subjugated by the Phallic State – a memory of an archetypal past shared by all women.

Mary Daly's work is a treat to read, and a wonderful example of playing with metaphors in the deconstruction and reconstruction of meaning. In fact, she is doing the classic thing: turning some very old traditions upside down, keeping exactly their terms of reference, but changing their significance and meaning. It is striking how much similarity there is between Daly's and Paglia's world-views: both come out of a Catholic tradition; both see a struggle between being in touch with elemental forces and the forces of reason and control. Both agree that male progress is gained at the cost of intimate contact with life forces.

They differ *absolutely*, however, in their interpretation of that struggle, and in the location of good and evil within it. They also differ in their location of the forces of creativity. For Daly, all creativity (at least that of women) comes from the elemental forces and from women's Wonderment and Lust. For Paglia, creativity is gained through the *transcendence* of nature and elemental forces – something males can achieve far more easily than females, because females have more of a 'burden' of nature to overcome. For Daly, there is a glorious scenario for women's self-assertion and self-definition, but virtually no role for the transformation of men, and no discussion either of the possibility that the wonderful femininity she describes might be joined in passionate discourse and union with some kind of recon-structed male. For Paglia, there is a terrible scenario of unsuccessful struggle between the Apollonian and the Dionysian, in which the latter always gets through a little, in some distorted form, because it cannot be wholly suppressed, and men can progress and achieve, but only through pain and suffering. Women are even worse off: their only options are fulfilment through acceptance of the natural role which leaves them with no human-ness – almost, one might say, no 'soul', but no Catholic would concede that – or through a pale imitation of the male Apollonian. And she specifically says that doing this 'must limit eroticism, that is, our imaginative lives in sexual space'.[3]

Mary Daly writes a counter-mythology using puns just as Freud argued that puns emerged in defence mechanisms – words that sound like something else: realise/real eyes; luster = one who lusts/luster = American spelling of lustre. She invents words which again, in true metaphoric fashion, carry meaning across from one domain to another, creating new interpretation by so doing: Nag-Gnostic, Crone-logical. She argues – though less strongly – that the language of the Phallic State, the Cockocracy, which tries to submerge the female and the feminine, also operates by such puns. Again, she echoes Paglia in seeing the cultural force of metaphors of erection, ejaculation and urination as the metaphors of progress and creativity.

Daly has tackled the history of struggle between two powerful forces. Other seekers after the female voice are the French school associated with *Politique et Psychanalyse*, and with the debates around Jacques Lacan.[4] In this tradition, as with Daly, language is central to concepts, but that language has been utilised for the expression of a male world-view, based especially on the metaphor of polarity and dualism: 'The world is the word; it is experienced phenomenologically as a vast text which encompasses the sum total of human symbolic systems. Throughout the history of Western thought, that text, the Logos, has been founded on the structure of the binary, the dichotomy.'[5] The strategy of the French cultural feminists – notably Julia Kristeva, Hélène Cixous, Luce Irigaray and Monique Wittig – is to subvert the tradition by subverting the form of the text as well as its content. (Donna Stanton uses the metaphor of wild grass growing between, and eventually loosening, concrete slabs.) This is to be achieved through forms of language and syntax that are open, non-linear, unfinished, fluid, exploded, fragmented, polysemic and attempting to 'speak the body' – including the use of silence. There are, inevitably, problems of communication, but the goal is the creation of a form of writing especially which breaks away from the masculine mode. This emphasises not only the content of language but how its structure reflects the masculine mode of thinking and dealing with thought. The metaphors of the alternative, eschewing traditional forms and in particular eschewing linearity, boundary and atomism, are the metaphors picked up by others seeking a female voice. (Deconstructing language to break through the conventional frameworks for thinking is not, of course, confined to feminists. The classic literary exponent was James Joyce, but innumerable modern poets have experimented with syntax and form.)

The challenge is to find ways of authentically defining oneself in a world where the dominant metaphors and forms are defined in terms of the male, the phallic. It is the constant reiteration of the need to find a voice for one's self – to 'write one's self', as Hélène Cixous says in her important essay 'The laugh of the Medusa'. Cixous argues, like others in this tradition, that we as women must find those aspects which are different from the masculine, in order to reject the phallic tyranny of our self-definition. There is little in Western culture which 'inscribes' femininity, so woman's authentic experience has been denied her because it has been expressed in male language, from the male perspective, and serving male needs – including the reduction of male anxieties – and is therefore distorted and exaggerated for this end.

Yet the very exclusion of woman from male culture and male language has in some sense protected her from the fate of Western male: fragmentation and conflict between mind and body. Cixous says that when women speak in public they use their whole bodies to express themselves, whereas men hold themselves in a way that shows the dominance of their mind and reason. Because men constantly fear the loss of their erection/phallic power, they exercise more control over their bodies. Women are freer to get in touch with their bodies, yet they are made guilty for doing so, and are also made guilty for trying to express their selves in the male way – for example, through writing. The plea that Cixous is making is for women to get in touch with that self that has survived the masculine culture, and to find a way of expressing and inscribing it. In contrast to

Daly, Cixous does not separate the masculine and feminine within women; the authenticity of women involves the coexistence within them of the two principles. She also argues that men must find their own ways of being in touch with their masculine and feminine parts.

The invention or discovery of a mythology, and the search for new ways of finding expression and authenticity, are exercises which move somewhat uncertainly between the symbolic order and claims about true gender difference. Both cultural feminists (like Cixous) and radical feminists (like Daly) start from the position that women must seek authenticity and self-expression through a thorough critique and rejection of the masculine perspective which has dominated the way women and the feminine are represented in the culture. Men in general draw upon certain images and metaphors of women and the feminine, shaping their identity by negation of them, and so assuaging their anxieties about masculinity.

The search for an authentic self-expression does not, *per se*, require us to assert that a difference has remained undiscovered as a consequence of the masculinist framework, but it does require us to redefine and re-evaluate that framework. It is therefore both discovery and invention. How are women different? How is our customary mode of explaining ourselves to ourselves different from the orthodoxies of the public/masculine mode? These are discoveries, which have to be made not only by proper observation of the 'alien tribe' but by trying to understand a language which contains different concepts. The process of invention entails making up a new language which incorporates the new concepts and their implications. But this invention also feeds back into the dominant framework; not only are there more, new, concepts not previously available (the 'add-on' effect), but these new concepts change the meaning of the old ones.

If the old language is based on an assumption of unity or absoluteness, new concepts, alternative perspectives, may profoundly undermine it. If a culture believes in monotheism, the existence of other people's gods can be taken as additional – in effect, parallel – information, but it can also be a challenge to the concept of monotheism and to one true religion. It can even be taken as an alternative and truer religion altogether – this, in fact, is what happened when Christianity replaced the earlier pagan faiths. Feminists are rediscovering (or inventing) new gods because the old gods did not reflect the female experience except as adjunct to or antithesis of the male. Finding an authentic voice means generating the concepts of a plurality of voices. What remains uncertain is whether the new gods, the new voices, are useful to male experience also. Is male experience, the conception of masculinity, better served by non-masculinist voices and gods? Is the betrayal of authenticity as great for men who are denied voices other than those of the masculine world? Cixous noted that the exclusion of women from male culture protects them from some of its problems, including some of the fragmentation of mind and body. The affirmation of that holism is part of female authenticity, but it is also an alternative perspective which could enrich all human experience.

Morality and the different voice

Carol Gilligan's search for authenticity through different metaphors and symbols of morality shows just such a transition.[6] Her work began with a straightforward question: Do women think about moral issues in the same way as men? The history of this question is a classic sequence: the assertion of a dominant framework, its outcome in terms of the interpretation of sex differences, the challenge to the authenticity of the dominant framework for making sense of experience of the non-dominant group, the assertion of an alternative and, finally, the challenge to a monolithic view, with implications for both men and women.

To appreciate the discussion about gender and morality, we need to look at the context of Gilligan's critique and the development of her alternative position. There are many philosophical positions on the nature of morality, and psychologists ask a wide range of questions about individual moral development. Qualities of the person, virtues or behaviours, are not our present concern, nor is the role of emotions in morality. The contentious domain of morality for models of rationality is *moral reasoning*. The Kantian tradition of thinking about morality emphasises the role of reasoning, and justice as the principle for arriving at solutions to moral problems. Modern Kantians include John Rawls and Lawrence Kohlberg. Some objections to this position come from people who just do not like the rationalistic emphasis;[7] others are happy to focus on reasoning, but would want to consider other principles as well as justice.[8]

Lawrence Kohlberg first interviewed nearly seventy adolescent boys in Chicago in the mid 1950s; he followed them up at intervals over the next twenty years.[9] He presented hypothetical situations in which there was a conflict between principles; for example, should a husband steal medicine that he could not afford to buy for his dying wife, or should he obey the law that forbids stealing? This is a conflict between the principle of saving life and the principle of obeying the law. In such interviews, respondents reveal the reasoning behind their solution, and what they consider important in the situation.

Kohlberg and his collaborators identified five stages of development in the young men's reasoning. Each stage is an increasingly complex organisation of understanding of the situation, and of the moral principles to be applied in resolving the dilemmas. Kohlberg saw this progess as increasingly more integrated understanding of the principles of justice. More points of view were taken into account, and wider social and moral implications of the decisions considered. So a stage 2 reasoner (usually in his early teens) would see the problem of the husband in terms only of the man stealing to meet his wife's needs, or the man in conflict with the drug inventor who would not sell the medicine at a reasonable price. In his twenties, now using stage 4 reasoning, the respondent could see that the husband's problem was part of the wider social context: a free market in medicines, exploitation, conflict between the man's obligations to his wife and his obligations as a citizen, the precedents set by his punishment. Robert Selman has shown that underlying the moral stages is progression in the ability to take the perspective of others in the situation, moving from egocentrism, through the perspective of the dyad, the community, and society, finally to a viewpoint which can consider hypothetical perspectives that are not tied to just one culture.[10] This means that moral reasoning development is not just a matter of getting better at a particular kind of moral philosophy. Moral reasoning is about understanding relations between persons, and between the person and society.

Kohlberg's theory of morality expressed a mainstream philosophical position in which justice is the basic concept of moral reasoning, the keystone of resolving moral dilemmas. Despite considerable variation in the way his sample tackled the dilemmas, this was seen to be subsumed under different aspects of justice reasoning. The first indication that there was some problem with justice as the underlying principle for moral reasoning came from cross-cultural studies. It appeared that non-Western cultures manifested lower moral stages than respondents from industrialised countries. The first explanation of this was that more complex societies required more abstract reasoning about social issues, and a greater appreciation of concepts like 'society'. Latterly, some critics, most notably Richard Shweder and Carolyn Pope-Edwards, have argued that the problem lies in making justice the basis of moral reasoning for non-Western cultures.[11]

When the measures were applied to female respondents, some studies appeared to suggest that women and girls were less able to think in abstract terms of wider society, that they focused more on concrete community and individual relationships. Other studies, however, showed no sex difference.[12] The findings of sex differences in scores suggested a bias in the measure, and this generated strong criticism. There seemed to be echoes from other debates; both Sigmund

Freud and Jean Piaget had suggested that girls seemed to have a lesser sense of justice. G. W. F. Hegel had written: 'Women regulate their actions not by the demands of universality but by arbitrary inclinations and opinions. Women are educated – who knows how? – as it were by breathing in ideas, by living rather than by acquiring knowledge. The status of manhood, on the other hand, is attained only by the stress of thought and much technical exertion.'[13]

In fact careful analysis showed that sex difference in *level* of moral reasoning was an artefact; women did not score less well than men when education was taken into account. But the issue alerted researchers to another question – not about *level* of reasoning but about *kind* of reasoning. Gilligan found that female respondents were reluctant to focus on who had 'rights' in the situation. Instead, they wanted to change the emphasis to the *responsibilities* of both the husband and the chemist to help the wife. Her respondents wanted to talk about negotiation and cooperation, rather than about forming contracts to resolve competing rights. Gilligan identified a different ethos, a different basis for thinking about morality. Whereas Kohlberg's male respondents worked within a lay moral theory of rights, contracts, the resolution of competing interests and the search for an equitable (and universalisable) solution, Gilligan's female respondents emphasised responsibility to others, mutual obligations and involvement with the other, and the principle of care.

It became apparent to Gilligan and her colleagues that the key issue was the relationship between moral orientation and conception of self–other relations. The difference lies in whether the self is seen as being *connected to* others, and therefore of necessity cooperating and negotiating to achieve harmony, or *separate from* others, and therefore in conflict and needing to find mechanisms to establish contracts, rules for fairness and justifications for assigning rights. The justice orientation seems to come out of seeing the self as separate from others, in conflict with others. Justice schemas are based on the balancing of rights and the formation of rules for conflict management. They reflect a view that relationships between persons are conflicted. The responsibility and care orientation seems to come out of seeing connection between the self and others; the moral schemas concern cooperation, participation in the experience of others, and sharing. However, even if there is a link between conception of self and moral orientation, Gilligan is still also dealing with two distinct issues: the dominance of an ethos of justice, and a mainstream conceptualisation of self–other relations in terms of separation and autonomy.

Gilligan's claims for a female perspective on self and morality initially appeared to explain the discrepancy in moral scores. She challenged the validity of the dominant cultural mode by demonstrating that 'deficient' scores were due to a different perspective rather than incompetence. Debate developed the issue of sex difference – for example, Nancy Chodorow argued that boys have to make an early separation from their mothers in order to establish their gender identity as 'different' from the primary caretaker, whereas girls experience connection and similarity with the primary caretaker.[14] Recently, however, there has been an important shift. Data have emerged showing that women and girls can use justice/separate reasoning as well as connected/responsibility reasoning, and that boys and men can also – albeit less frequently – switch their reasoning orientation.[15] Kay Johnston presented children with fables – the Porcupine and the Mole, and the Dog in the Manger – which are about conflicts of interest. She found that girls were likely to produce a connected response – negotiation and perspective-taking; whereas boys were likely to produce a separate response – confrontational or rule-making; though there was more mixture of response amongst girls than amongst boys. But when children were asked to consider other possible solutions, both sexes were able to generate them – though again, girls found this easier than boys. In other words, it seems that both sexes have access to each orientation, but their preferences tend to go along gender lines.

The only explanation for this must be that both modes of thinking, and both ethical systems, exist within the culture, but that the sexes either have differential access to them, or strong constraints on the use of one style of thought. The evidence of gender overlap leads to a pluralistic conclusion: *there is more than one way of looking at moral issues*. Connectedness, responsibility and caring may more authentically reflect women's moral thinking, but they also represent an alternative, additional approach; they enlarge the scope for the moral. It may seem surprising to many people that there should be any problem about there being multiple principles upon which to base moral thought. Many male philosophers have indeed questioned the emphasis on justice.[16] The point is that the claims made for justice include the idea that there is a 'best, most rational solution' on which all could agree. The evidence of more than one basis for moral judgement is truly a challenge to the dominant cultural perspective. So pluralism is not just the adding-on of an additional and more authentic dimension which more accurately reflects (many) women's thinking. It is of itself a challenge to a unitary model.

There is, however, more to Gilligan's arguments for reclaiming a feminine symbol than moral ethos. She writes of the female 'voice' not only with the implication of an alternative voice, but with the recognition that 'voice' is itself a metaphor that women use rather than men – hence the title of her first book, *In a Different Voice*. A key aspect of connectedness is *listening*: participating in the dialogue between persons in a receptive rather than a combative manner. The 'different voice' is also a metaphoric pun; the metaphors that women use in describing relations with others frequently refer to 'voices being heard', and to 'listening'. To listen is not only to hear; the act of listening is itself an act of connecting. The 'listening ear' is a key metaphor of the caring process (whether conducted by men or women). *Prima facie*, the listener accepts the perspective of the speaker, rather than analysing or imposing an interpretation upon what is said. The listener is *receptive*.

Gilligan developed her analysis of the female self in another study with Mary Belenky, on women who were contemplating abortion.[17] One issue here was the extent to which women feel able to take responsibility for themselves, to give themselves nurturance. Women who define themselves within the conventional schema of Otherness characteristically focus on the needs of those whom they serve and with whom they relate. They have no schema of permitting a self that has rights; one's own needs and wishes have secondary status in one's identity as nurturing others. One of the most powerful adjectives of sanction is 'selfish'. For some women, the dilemma concerned which others (including the foetus) were making the strongest claims on them: whose needs should they meet? For others there was the voice of the self, asking the question about their own integrity and wholeness, taking responsibility for the decision and for the place of the decision in their lives. Gilligan and Belenky saw this as a more integrated and mature response, being able to transcend the role of nurturant server of others, and taking charge of one's own identity.

The metaphor of voice was traced through its developmental sequence by Mary Belenky, Nancy Goldberger, Blythe Clinchy and Jill Tarule, in a study of 135 women.[18] The sequence began with a state of silence, powerlessness, obedience to male definitions and needs. This was followed by 'listening to the voices of others'. The individual now has some power if she can listen to the right message. But she is still receiving; she is not an active agent. The third level is 'subjective knowing': having a sense that one's intuition is valid as a source of truth. 'Subjectivism is for women a position from which they can redefine the nature of authority . . . . This interior voice has become, for us, the hallmark of women's emergent sense of self and sense of agency and control.'[19]

The next level, 'procedural knowledge', is transition beyond the subjective to an understanding that there are ways of arriving at answers through reasoning and judgement that involve taking others' points of view on board. It has two forms: knowing-through-doubting and knowing-through-believing – or knowing from the outside versus knowing from the inside. Women who used the former became adept at the rhetorical task of anticipating the doubts of others in constructing their discourse. Those who used the latter needed to understand what is behind a reason, and had difficulty in taking a critical stance, because they wanted to be sure that they knew the whole situation, and when they did, it often seemed to make sense from both persons' point of view, so a critical stance became unnecessary.

The most integrated level was called 'constructive knowing' – an integration of separate and connected knowing, and characterised by a sense of self as effective, taking responsibility for one's evaluations and assumptions:

> They noticed what was going on with others and cared about the lives of people about them. They were intensely self-conscious, in the best sense of the word – aware of their own thought, their judgements, their moods and desires. Each was ambitious and fighting to find her own voice . . . wanted her actions to make a difference to other people and in the world.[20]

How far is this sequence linked to sex? Belenky and her colleagues studied only women; their goal was to see what emerged from a female sample, to establish the range of perspectives amongst women. Males may indeed use similar ways of knowing, but the point is that this is not recognised formally. What alternative authenticity of Otherness does this work offer? It asserts that there are differences, but differences fully recognised within the traditional framework; furthermore, these differences positively evaluate the feminine. Gilligan and Belenky have given authenticity to women's ways of approaching moral and personal issues. The enormous success of Gilligan's book *In a Different Voice* is testimony to how her perspective resonated with women's experience. Gilligan herself was voted Woman of the Year by *Ms.* magazine, and her work is widely known outside academic circles; I once heard her being discussed enthusiastically on a transatlantic flight by a group of American women who were not even college graduates.

Extending the domains of separateness and connectedness

Working with Lindy Wingfield, Barrie Lipscombe and Jane Baddeley, I have found a similar pattern of separate and connected thinking amongst British adolescents, extending further than the moral and personal domains that Gilligan found. We interviewed adolescents of both sexes, aged between twelve and seventeen.[21] We covered a wide range of topics, moral and personal dilemmas and issues such as responsibility, promise-keeping, loyalty. We asked questions to tap understanding of society and social order. To measure understanding of political systems, we used a modified version of Joseph Adelson's story about how a thousand marooned Islanders might set about governing themselves.[22]

We did not set out to look at connection and separation, but we found that it emerged from the data. A significant point is that we did not use Gilligan's coding methods, but found a parallel picture. Our data were similar to Gilligan's: girls showed greater mixture of styles, and boys showed more separate thinking. The interesting findings from our study were how extensively the styles were applied. In response to the question: Why keep promises? we identified as *separate* answers such as this:

> If you say you're going to do something and you don't do it, then it's not going to make people want to trust you, or believe you, or rely on you at all.

This answer sees trustworthiness as an attribute of the person rather than the relationship. The connected response, in contrast, reflects trust as a quality of the relationship, rather than the person:

> I think [trust] is something that shouldn't be lost, because there's not really that much that you can give to someone, that doesn't cost anything, that doesn't require anything in return, so I think it needs to be there, just to have.

Trust is *between* persons rather than *of* persons. To destroy trust is to destroy a relationship rather than a reputation.

We also presented a story of divided loyalty. The scenario involved two same-sex best friends, and the boy- or girlfriend of one of them. When that person went on vacation, the boy/girlfriend asked the other friend to a disco. The dilemma concerned whether they should accept the invitation and, later, whether they should respond to the offer of a kiss. A clear example of separateness was:

> Well at least if he can go, there's always the chance that he can keep an eye on her, and if he's a really good friend he can refuse her advances, but if she goes on her own there's no telling who she's going to pick up.

Here the girlfriend is the possession of the absent boy, and it is the best friend's duty to take care of that possession. There is no suggestion of any relating between the friend and the girl, and relating between the two male friends implies rules of loyalty, codes of behaviour.

A contrasting picture comes from a girl's connected response:

> If Mandy [the absent girl] knew it would be all right. But not if she didn't know. Then I wouldn't do it because she's my best friend. And that's hurting her. They'd argue and that would split the two up, and Debbie wouldn't want to go with Kevin because that would only cause arguments.

This implies negotiation with the friend ('If Mandy knew') and implies also that friendship means not hurting the other. But also in this response is the idea of managing and maintaining relating; she refers to 'arguments' rather than to Debbie breaking a code which might lead to Mandy rejecting her, which would be the rhetoric of separation. The outcome foreseen is the breakdown of relationships.

These findings are very similar to Gilligan's. The novelty of our study was that we found separation and connection in non-personal areas, in political and social reasoning. In the Islanders story, we asked about the kinds of problems the Islanders might face, the possible solutions, and the form a governing council might take. The separate responses to these questions conceived of a world of potential conflict, which needed either strong rules and powerful forces, or the imposition of an ordered system to remove the source of conflict. There were two versions. In one, respondents foresaw unbridled greed and violence, requiring laws and strong control. In the other, the problem was unequal resources and bad planning, which needed order and organisation, particularly by experts. Both solutions implied a 'top–down' model of organisation. Here are examples of the 'chaos and control' scenario:

> [the problem]
> Violence and things. Stealing all the stuff they've got to make their things.
> Rivalry, almost a civil war. Some groups wanting other resources so that they overpower other groups.
>
> [the solution]
> Be organised and form little parties and say, 'We're going to have law and you have got to abide by this law.'
>
> Divide up the land into equal sections and give a certain plot of land to every person or family, to stop the rivalry, maybe splitting the groups apart.

The scenario associated with 'order and planning' implied contracts and rights, rather than the imposition of strong rule by fiat:

> Better off organised together, with one or a group of leaders, people with leadership qualities, skills, knowledge – say there'd been a captain, somebody who had authority beforehand.

Laws; how much food to take, because you don't want to use it all up. Council to say not to cut the trees down because you need some in the future.

The connected orientation focused on forming and maintaining relationships. Problems arose because people did not have the skills or the facilities to negotiate. There were two types of response. One emphasised relationships between persons, and saw the qualities needed for running the Island as the same as those required in a successful relationship:

> People were starting to have arguments . . . they needed someone to take responsibility and sort out arguments, someone who is good with other people. People that can understand others' feelings.

The other type of response emphasised community. Both these types are 'bottom–up' models of organisation, based on cooperation and negotiation, and the mutual appreciation of others' needs. The controls needed are those which prevent conflict by meeting needs, rather than being imposed in order to deal with problems once they arise:

> Jealousy could probably creep in . . . . I wouldn't have thought that they'd made any laws if there were just a thousand of them . . . you'd feel you could trust each other and if somebody started something just because they couldn't make as much use of the material resources as others, it wouldn't be right.

> If people were becoming too competitive over what was there, and trying to build themselves up . . . organise in the manner of a cooperative where everyone has equal opportunities . . . . Some sort of monitoring service . . . not keeping tight controls, just making sure that nobody is suffering because of somebody else wanting too much.

The argument for pluralistic perspectives

The attack on the masculine model of the rational self comes from re-evaluation of differences, but it also comes from affirmation that there can be an alternative *per se*. To present an alternative is a challenge to the *logos*, if inherent in the *logos* is the idea that there is only one way of doing things. The paradoxes and problems of pursuing the question of a different way of knowing, a different voice, become apparent if we consider the age-old question: would the world be different if women ran it? Those who say *no* argue that the structure of societies and the inevitable conflicts of interest would lead to exactly the same constraints on women as they do on men. So patterns of behaviour, styles of negotiation and policy-making arise out of the situation rather than the gender of the leaders. Those who say *yes* include the biological argument that as women have less physiological tendency to aggression (i.e. secretion of testosterone) they would be less warlike. A more complex argument is that the upbringing of males instils in them a strongly competitive streak, a fear of losing face, and the need for conquest and success. These are translated into public policy and relations in the public domain. As long as women lack this background, they would not have the same motivation.

But the assault on the dominant world-view does not come from either of these appeals to individual psyche, it comes from the underlying difference in processes that are implied. The model of negotiation and the model of interaction which underlie 'male' behaviour in public make only certain outcomes and strategies conceivable. The assertion of a 'female' style is a challenge to this way of dealing with interaction which happens to be associated (for whatever reason) with female experience. It is the challenge of a different way of *doing* things arising out of a different way of *thinking about* things: a change of metaphor from the presumption of conflict to the presumption of cooperation and negotiation. To assert that it is 'female' (when manifestly many men, especially in certain professions where negotiation is crucial, are tuned into this) is really an assertion that it is a challenge to a pervasive masculine world-view rather than a claim that women necessarily have epistemological privilege or psychological advantage.

There have been two kinds of objections to Gilligan's claims for a qualitative difference in reasoning. How far are differences distributed according to sex, and therefore 'gender-related', and how far is an ethic of responsibility and care truly an *alternative to*, rather than a *subset of*, an ethic of justice? If women can use separate ways of knowing as well as connected ones, as the data strongly indicate, this can be explained by their immersion in the dominant culture – an inevitable consequence of formal education. But if men use connected ways of knowing, does this not undermine the notion of female culture and an authentic female voice? One explanation is consistent with my suggestion that women are freer to use a hidden tradition, so men who use connected ways of knowing would, in fact, be tapping into that alternative tradition. In that case, this work is making explicit, rediscovering and validating, an existing cultural alternative which the dominant culture has attempted to deny, hide, and denigrate by labelling it 'feminine'.

Kohlberg argued, for example, that responsibility and care are ultimately aspects of 'respect for persons', which is fundamentally about justice but may be expressed in terms either of rights or of responsibilities.[23] An attempt to bring the alternative under the umbrella of the *logos* is, of course, a plea for a unitary model. Another way of dealing with an alternative is to argue that it is a different kind of phenomenon, a different class, not an alternative at all. Owen Flanagan, for example, argues that what Gilligan is 'really' talking about, and what her respondents are really talking about, is the good life, rather than justice.[24] 'The good life' requires different qualities from justice, and is much more related to being a certain kind of person, rather than principles for deciding between conflicting interests. This neatly allows a different ethos, but leaves the unitary model of justice intact, because each ethos is applied to a different kind of issue.

Philosophers are not hamstrung by the need to produce data and to demonstrate the existence or otherwise of differences. Several feminist philosophers have tackled this question, and they are just as divided as anyone else about whether one should take the Enlightenment or the post-modernist course. Those who support the latter tend, even more than psychologists, to be concerned that a 'female point of view' undermines the dominant model of rationality. Morwenna Griffiths argues that what is missing from most male philosophers' accounts is any effort to see emotion as important in experience, rather than something that interferes with reason, or something that can be explained as a part of reason:

> Feelings are a source of knowledge and should be treated seriously as such since both need to be taken into account in coming to understand the world . . . . In other words, a rational agent is required to reflect on feelings, not to attempt to control them, except insofar as a rearticulation of feelings might be appropriate in the light of reflection.[25]

Griffiths considers that only feminist theory seems to be able to confront the dominant rationality ethos, and to break the Cartesian mind–body bondage.

Nel Noddings takes a similar view.[26] She argues for a relational approach: one does not 'care', one 'cares-for', and the activity has meaning only if it includes the one who is 'cared-for'. This relational approach contrasts with principles of 'ought' applied to separate beings. In other words, the aim is not to topple a dominant ethos by another competing ethos, but to plead for a more pluralistic perspective which can allow the relational nature of the human condition to be taken on board in discussions of ethics. Noddings also makes a further point about authenticity.[27] Most conceptions of evil, she argues, rest on a negative view of women – either as disobedient to the patriarch, or as temptresses who lead to chaos. But she is concerned that confrontation with evil has used the metaphor of the warrior, and of attack. Noddings considers that the warrior metaphor underlies a morality of rights and rules – codes for conducting oneself *vis-à-vis* others rather than in relation to others. These traditions affect both philosophers and laypersons – precisely because the model of evil is so pervasive in lay social theories of the feminine. We are back to that same message: *authenticity is attainable only when the underlying fear of the Other is understood.*

The claim for women's special nurturance has been made by people of all persuasions. For traditionalists it marks out the special territory of woman in her relation to man, the functional interdependence in which men's effectiveness in the public domain requires the private care of the female. In the 'rational androgyne' model, caring and nurturance are characteristics that both sexes may have: the denial of male nurturance is a consequence of the pressures on young boys; excessive female nurturance is a manifestation of the female role as mere adjunct to the male. The desired outcome is a balance, which relieves the actual and psychological burden on women to be the primary carers.

The reclamation of caring as feminine is tied up with a number of issues to do with authenticity – the acknowledgement of a real difference, but its interpretation in a novel way. In Gilligan's and others' hands, caring becomes embedded in a wider set of cognitive and affective issues, including the actual processes of interaction. Thus caring is the concomitant and outcome of a different way of approaching the self and social relations; it is not just a matter of more affect, or even of greater sensitivity.[28] But the assertion that women are more caring is also an assertion that there is an ethos based on caring which is lacking in the dominant cultural perspective, and that the moral world-view is incomplete unless it is included. This again is a challenge to a monolithic perspective which comes out of recognising special and authentic female experience.

Notes

1. C. Kitzinger, 'Lesbian theory', Paper presented to the British Psychological Society London Conference, 1988. See also M. Wittig, *The Straight Mind and Other Essays*, Hemel Hempstead: Harvester Wheatsheaf, 1992.
2. M. Daly, *Gyn/Ecology: The meta-ethics of radical feminism*, London: The Women's Press, 1979; M. Daly, *Pure Lust*, London: The Women's Press, 1984; M. Daly, *Outercourse: The be-dazzling voyage*, San Francisco: Harper & Row, 1992.
3. C. Paglia, *Sexual Personae: Art and decadence from Nefertiti to Emily Dickinson*, New Haven, CT: Yale University Press, 1990, p. 9.
4. See, for example H. Eisenstein and A. Jardine (eds), *The Future of Difference*, Boston, MA: G. K. Hall, 1980; V. A. Conley, *Hélène Cixous*, Hemel Hempstead: Harvester Wheatsheaf, 1992; M. Shiach, *Hélène Cixous: A politics of writing*, London: Routledge, 1991; M. Whitford, *The Irigaray Reader*, Oxford: Basil Blackwell, 1991.

5. D. C. Stanton, 'Language and revolution: the Franco–American disconnection', in H. Eisenstein and A. Jardine (eds), *The Future of Difference*, p. 73.
6. C. Gilligan, *In a Different Voice*, Cambridge, MA: Harvard University Press, 1982.
7. R. S. Peters, 'The place of Kohlberg's theory in moral education', *Journal of Moral Education*, **7**, pp. 147–57, 1978.
8. See, for example, R. Shweder, 'Cultural psychology: what is it?', in J. W. Stigler, R. Shweder and G. Herdt (eds), *Cultural Psychology: Essays in comparative human development*, Cambridge: Cambridge University Press, 1990; H. Haste, 'Morality, self and sociohistorical context: the role of lay social theory', in G. Noam and T. Wren (eds), *Morality and Self*, Cambridge, MA: MIT Press, 1993; H. Haste and J. Baddeley, 'Moral theory and culture: the case of gender', in W. M. Kurtines and J. L. Gewirtz (eds), *Handbook of Moral Behavior and Development, vol. 1: Theory*, Hillsdale NJ: Lawrence Erlbaum, 1991.
9. L. Kohlberg, *The Psychology of Moral Development*, San Francisco: Harper & Row, 1984; A. Colby and L. Kohlberg, *The Measurement of Moral Judgement*, Cambridge: Cambridge University Press, 1987.
10. R. Selman, 'Socio-cognitive understanding', in T. Lickona (ed.), *Moral Development and Behavior*, New York: Holt, Rinehart & Winston, 1976.
11. C. P. Edwards, 'Cross-cultural research on Kohlberg's stages: the basis for consensus', in S. Modgil and C. Modgil (eds), *Kohlberg: Consensus and controversy*, Lewes: Falmer Press, 1986.
12. L. J. Walker, 'Sex differences in the development of moral reasoning: a critical review', *Child Development*, **55**, pp. 677–91, 1984.
13. G. W. F. Hegel, *The Philosophy of Right*, trans. T. M. Knox, Oxford: Oxford University Press, 1952, pp. 263–4; see also L. A. Blum, 'Kant's and Hegel's moral rationalism: a feminist perspective', *Canadian Journal of Philosophy*, **12(2)**, pp. 287–302, 1982.
14. N. Chodorow, *The Reproduction of Mothering: Psychoanalysis and the sociology of gender*, Berkeley: University of California Press, 1978.
15. D. K. Johnston, 'Adolescents' solutions to dilemmas in fables: two moral orientations – two problem-solving strategies', in C. Gilligan, J. V. Ward, and J. M. Taylor (eds), *Mapping the Moral Domain*, Cambridge, MA: Harvard University Press, 1988.
16. See, for example, essays in S. G. Clarke and E. Simpson, *Anti-theory in Ethics and Moral Conservatism*, Albany, NY: SUNY Press, 1989.
17. G. Blackburne-Stover, M. F. Belenky and C. Gilligan, 'Moral development and reconstructive memory: recalling a decision to terminate an unplanned pregnancy', *Developmental Psychology*, **18**, pp. 862–70, 1982.
18. M. Belenky, N. Goldberger, B. Clinchy and J. Tarule, *Women's Ways of Knowing*, New York: Basic Books, 1986.
19. *ibid.*, p. 68.
20. *ibid.*, p. 133.
21. L. Wingfield and H. Haste, 'Connectedness and separateness: cognitive style or moral orientation?', *Journal of Moral Education*, **16**, pp. 214–25, 1987; H. Haste and J. Baddeley, 'Moral theory and culture', in W. Kurtines and J.

Gewirtz (eds), *Handbook of Moral Behavior and Development*, vol. 1, Hillsdale, NJ: Lawrence Erlbaum, 1991.

22. J. Adelson and R. O'Neil, 'The growth of political ideas in adolescence,' *Journal of Personality and Social Psychology*, **4**, pp. 295–306, 1966.

23. D. Boyd, C. Levine and L. Kohlberg, 'The return of stage 6', in T. Wren (ed.), *The Moral Domain*, Cambridge, MA: MIT Press, 1990.

24. O. J. Flanagan, *Varieties of Moral Personality*, Cambridge, MA: Harvard University Press, 1992.

25. M. Griffiths and M. Whitford, *Feminist Perspectives in Philosophy*, London: Macmillan, 1988, pp. 148–9.

26. N. Noddings, *Caring: A feminine approach to ethics and moral education*, Berkeley: University of California Press, 1984.

27. N. Noddings, 'Do we really want to produce good people?', *Journal of Moral Education*, **16(3)**, pp. 177–88, 1987.

28. H. Haste, 'Why thinking about feeling is not the same as feeling about feeling, and why post-androgyny is dialectical not regressive: a reply to Philibert and Sayers', *New Ideas in Psychology*, **5(2)**, pp. 215–21, 1987.

Chapter 11: Science and rationality

When I talk about the 'masculinity of science' to practising scientists (of both sexes), most of them claim that there is no such thing as male or female science, only good and bad science. Then they admit, when pressed, that the image of science which reflects the orthodoxy (specifically the oversimplifications of Popper's views) would be bad science, and good science would include just those elements which Keller and others have attributed to the 'feminine' – at least in addition, if not in substitution. Keller argued that a holistic, discursive discovery mode contrasts with an atomistic, linear, analytical and conquering mode, and that the latter is associated with a general view of the appropriate way to deal with knowledge and with masculine mastery.[1] The assertion that the dominant mode is male/masculine is a major challenge because it says that the normal is gendered, not neutral, and that it is flawed by utilising only limited frameworks for interpreting the world. Debates about scientific method have become entwined with the issue of gender and rationality, and somewhat similar issues arise in relation to both science and morality.

How is rationality conceived? In Chapter 2 I discussed the two competing traditions of Cartesian dualism and Humanism. I also described the recent revival of interest in rhetorical, as opposed to logical, models of knowing. Logical models imply a unitary mind, engaging in linear analysis, deducing solutions, using an atomistic approach to isolate the phenomenon under investigation, to treat it as much as possible uncontaminated by its context. It is 'objective' and passive, 'out there'. Discovery requires gradual accumulation of such isolated bits. Communicating knowledge within this process means transferring these bits of information to others. The assumption is that such communication is a logical process, that knowledge exists, in a sense, separately from those who know it. There is a long-standing distinction between the Socratic method and the Adversary method. The Socratic method depends on convincing others, engaging with them and creating disequilibrium in their beliefs, so that they become more open-minded. The aim of the Adversary method is to demolish the position of the other person, to show how they are wrong, rather than negotiating with them to find agreement.[2]

Within the rhetorical mode, knowing requires involvement and participation. One can know something only in the context which gives it meaning, so ideas are constrained by social and historical context, and they are constrained also by being part of the shared culture, because only that which can be communicated can be known. Communication is not the transfer of information bits from one mind to another, but the negotiation of meaning between people who share common frameworks of understanding. 'Knowing' effectively means participating in that which is known, becoming conversant with, rather than imposing from outside.

These two traditions have existed side by side for the last two millennia. What has differed has been the evaluation and truth status of each. In many areas of philosophy and social science, the rhetorical mode of knowing has been reviving. Many feminist critiques of rationality are consistent with the rhetorical model. The same applies to the Green critiques of science and technology. The challenge of the Green critics – the reclamation of the organic metaphor – is, like the challenge of feminists, to the metaphor of 'mastery' and 'conquest' in our dealings with nature.

Images of science

I was personally alerted to the issue of science and gender by the study I mentioned in Chapter 3.[3] Fifteen years ago people became aware of a great imbalance in scientific education. Girls failed to opt for science at school, and were very underrepresented at university level. Less than 2 per cent of engineering students were female. Biology was the only subject where there was any degree of equality. The concern expressed at that time was that by missing out on science, girls were cutting off opportunities for future careers at a time when technology was expanding into ever larger areas of our lives. Even housewives would need technological skills which they were showing no sign of acquiring. Policy-makers realised that there was going to be a skill shortage, and that women represented – classically – a reserve army of talent, if only they could be trained. The practical message was:

get more girls into science. But the underlying message was more complicated. It was obvious that girls were put off science by many things, not least a constellation of images which associated science, and especially technology, with masculinity. At this period television programmes, drama and advertising alike still took for granted male technical competence and female incompetence – despite the fact that in the DIY boom, many women were acquiring the basic skills of home improvement.

Several initiatives were designed to make young women aware of opportunities available in technical jobs, and in graduate science careers. This undermined the assumption of difference: girls could do it too. So if science was seen as masculine, this was clearly an error, because both sexes could do it. The image of science needed to be de-sexed. There were efforts to make textbooks and teaching examples either sex-neutral, or sex-balanced. Teachers, long conditioned to an assumption that boys were interested in science and girls were not, perpetuated expectations of sex differences in the classroom, so they needed to become aware of their non-conscious sexism.[4]

My study contributed to this picture. The image of masculinity was not just to do with science versus arts; there was a cluster of adjectives which linked these subjects – a cluster which patterned masculine characteristics of our culture: hard, intellect-based, difficult. But as well as asking about images of subjects, I also asked my school respondents about their image of scientists – how they felt about becoming scientists, and about marrying scientists. This replicated an earlier study by Margaret Mead and Rhona Metraux.[5] Girls were interested in living things, but put off by 'dead' mechanical things. They were more worried than boys about the dangerous consequences of scientific advance. Both sexes saw scientists of either sex as very bright. Both sexes also differentiated between the 'mad scientist' stereotype and the kind of scientist they might become themselves. The image of the scientist, of both sexes, was cold, rational, hard-working, intelligent, and not very sociable. Some comments about the advantages and disadvantages of marrying a scientist:

> She would be logical in her approach to life and would not be prone to irrational outbursts of temper.
> He would be intelligent and quick-minded and could make decisions, I hope.
> They seem too wrapped up in their work, only seem to bother with their experiments.
> I'd get sick of his persistent braininess and solitude.
> She might be cleverer than me and show me up.
> He would always bring up science when I am trying to talk about things in everyday life.

John Archer's recent replication of my study shows that 'difficult' still applies to girls' view of 'masculine' subjects, and 'boring' to boys' view of (relatively) 'feminine' subjects, but suggests some reduction in the stereotyping of science amongst schoolchildren.[6] There has, indeed, been an increase in girls' participation in science, and an increase – to about 12 per cent – in the proportion of female engineering students. Over the same period there has been a general increase in Britain in the proportion of female undergraduates, and worldwide, in the number of women working in science and technology at all levels.

There is plenty of evidence, however, that the growing child picks up the old image. Studies of children working and playing on computers show that girls actually enjoy the task and have taken to the actual person–machine interface well. The problem is boys, both on their own and particularly in interaction with girls. Boys treat computers as an extension of masculine technology; they claim expertise and tend to denigrate girls' failures in terms which clearly indicate a presupposition that this is a male domain. They tend to cast a girl partner in a secretarial role in any joint activity, and give her instructions rather than treating her as an equal. This may reflect normal behaviour for boys of this age. In middle childhood concepts of sex roles are well established, and boys' beliefs in male superiority are probably at their peak. But many observers argue that computers, like sports and craft technology classes, remain the domain where the technology-masculinity-mastery-control ethos is enacted and affirmed by pupils and, often, by teachers. Most computer games are of the 'warrior' or the 'competitive sport' variety, again perpetuating the association of information technology with masculinity.

A recent study by Paul Light illustrates the problem.[7] He presented eleven-year-old children with a computer-based task involving the search for a king's crown, in which pilots pitted their wits against bandits and pirates. This task mirrors many of the standard 'Dungeons and Dragons' computer games, and boys did better than girls. However, when the substantive topic (but not the underlying form) of task was changed to a fairytale mode, in which teddy bears on a picnic had to retrieve their honey while avoiding honey monsters, the sex differences disappeared; clearly, in the first task girls cued into a sex stereotype which demotivated them.

The metaphors which link science with masculinity, rationality and control need to be set in the context that science, for most people, is a remote activity. Its knowledge is esoteric, and accessible only to the privileged few. This belief is held by both sexes. The effect is compartmentalisation: there are things a person 'needs to know' with regard to those aspects of science and technology that impinge upon them. As one of my respondents said: 'Science is very unfeeling and the physics/chemistry side of it pretty useless. It doesn't make any difference whether you understand Newton's laws of gravity – gravity still exists whether you know about it or not.' This lay view contrasts somewhat with a positive image of science as controlling and powerful. Indeed, even when my respondents saw science as powerful, this was a possible danger – it might get out of control. Much of science fiction plays on exactly that theme.

The 'need to know' principle operates quite extensively in relation to science. Government efforts to educate people about the nuclear industry have found that there is resistance to acquiring knowledge that is not seen as essential to ordinary life. Mike Michaels and his colleagues, working on attitudes to nuclear power in a sensitive geographical area – Sellafield – found that people's resistance did not seem to depend on pro- or anti-nuclear attitudes, but on the boundaries of what they deemed 'necessary knowledge'.[8]

Professional scientists often become very agitated about the perseveration of incorrect and even dangerous beliefs, and wonder at the irrationality of laypeople who do have access to popularised versions of science. Such castigations miss the functional importance of knowledge. People tend to make sense of the world using whatever resources are available, and seek additional information only if it meets a need – a need such as the realisation that one's existing schemas don't work.[9] This explains why folk models and beliefs coexist benignly with scientific explanation. This is much more explicit in countries where traditional medicine still exists as an institution. People use the traditional system, and go to the 'Western' doctor only if the traditional system fails. If folk models work, why get more complicated?

Less benign is the *anti-science* position. Objections to science, and suspicion of it, seem to spring from two main sources. The first is that science *covers only certain areas of life,* and many important things are outside its purview. So religion, ethics, personal emotion and even natural processes may be deemed outside the realm of science. Science has no business to interfere, or has nothing to offer. Or it has the wrong perspective in the first place – in thinking that things are open to rational analysis, when they really demand a less intrusive, more contemplative approach. The second objection sees science as *dangerous.* Science has been responsible for most man-made [*sic*] disasters; scientists as a group seem determined to preserve their illusions of rationality, detachment and objectivity, and to ignore their ethical responsibility until it is too late. Alternatively, the whole project of science is dedicated to interfering with nature, to upsetting natural balance, with catastrophic consequences. This is a re-emergence of the 'Nature as Chaos' metaphor of the pre-Baconian era.

There has recently been a spate of books and discussions on this topic, essentially addressing the question of whether science and 'humanitarianism' are compatible.[10] Is the pursuit of science necessarily a denial of the spiritual? Is the spiritual dimension of life subject to rational analysis? Have we even lost, or are we in danger of losing, that dimension as a consequence of our rational search for scientific truth? Or should we just recognise that there are different domains with different truths? There are indeed scientists who simply compartmentalise; their faith in a god is not subjected to the same kind of experiential criteria, or truth tests, as their science.[11] For others, the findings of their field lead them – like the nineteenth-century geologists who saw evolution as a manifestation of the Great Creator at work – to a sense of wonder at the divine complexity of the universe. Much of this has been sparked off by Stephen Hawking's closing remarks about 'knowing the mind of God' in his *Brief History of Time*.[12]

Feminist perspectives

There are several feminist perspectives on science. One is simply pressure for more women to be engaged in the activity of science. This perspective tends to be less concerned with the basis of scientific activity, and more with changing the images currently associated with science to facilitate easier access for women. It is a rationalist approach. A more profound feminist objection to traditional science concerns attitudes to women as both practitioners and customers of science. These apply particularly to medical-related fields. The tendency of medical scientists and medical practitioners to regard women as reproductive systems whose effectiveness could be improved by various forms of 'technological fix' has been widely criticised. It is an area where the authenticity of woman's voice has been long ignored, and the role of the 'doctor-expert' is particularly rife.[13]

As recently as summer 1992, a British gynaecologist, Ian Fergusson, removed the uterus and ovaries from a woman of fifty-one who had gone into hospital for a minor operation (an endometrial resection) *without even waking her from the anaesthetic to consult her, and without any histological analysis*. He did it purely on the basis that he thought he detected a swelling on the side of the uterus. He subsequently wrote to her general practitioner: 'I carried out a hysterectomy and bilateral salpingo-oophorectomy [removal of ovaries and Fallopian tubes]. Both the ovaries were normal, but I thought that at her age it was the wiser thing to remove them.' The clear implication is that a woman of fifty-one has no sexual life, and that she does not need to be consulted before undergoing a major – and in fact quite unnecessary – operation which has had severe effects on her physical and psychological welfare.

The woman discharged herself from hospital and complained to the police that she had been assaulted. At the time of writing – a year after the operation and after extensive police investigation – Britain's Director of Public Prosecutions, Barbara Mills QC, has yet to decide whether the surgeon should face prosecution. Perhaps fortunately for the future of a more humane gynaecology, the patient is a prominent medical journalist.[14]

The systematic removal of medicine from the hands of women, as medicine became more professionalised, meant the denial, and the loss to orthodox science, of a multitude of skills which women had carried as 'wise-women'. That was a practical outcome of discrimination,[15] but it also reflected the emergent scientific metaphor of medicine. Women's medical activity had tended to be tied to an organic model of nature, the person and the person's relationship with nature; they were less likely to use intrusive methods in the pursuit of control. Certainly there have always been many male doctors – especially in general practice – who retained such an organic model, but much of medical science became caught up in the same mechanistic, progress-orientated, rationalistic metaphor as other fields of science.

Some social scientists have consciously sought a 'feminist' methodology.[16] A key element is the relationship between researcher and respondent. Psychologists have conventionally spoken of 'experimenter' and 'subject', which exactly reflects the assumptions of objectivity, and relative activity and passivity, in the traditional controlled experiment. Feminist methodologists create a collaborative situation in which both parties are involved in the discovery process; the researcher is a participant observer, non-intrusive, at best facilitating. All parties are active in the process. This is not only a question of method; it presumes that people are active in constructing their own meaning, and that research should investigate such real processes. The traditional experimentalist model of research in psychology identified variables which affected outcomes, or group differences, and manipulated these experimentally. Feminist methodology has developed alongside other critical developments in methodology, such as action research, which challenge traditional models.[17]

The real *anti-logos* to the orthodoxies of masculine science has come from writers who are not concerned only about the absence of women in science, or about the rejection of female traditional skills. This critique sees science as dominated by the unitary rationalism of Descartes and Bacon, which is bad not only for women, but also for science. It considers how science is actually done, and contrasts this with prescriptions of how it should be done. It is a critique which argues that the metaphors of science distort the actual activity of science, and that science cannot fail to reproduce masculine rationality because it is the essential expression of it. The argument is not just that this leaves women actors out – that is, it is unfair – but that it leaves out, just as other forms of orthodox rationality leave out, anything that is perceived to be antithetical to the careful edifice of analytical rationalism.

The objections and alternative options take various forms.[18] First there is the *factual*: real scientists don't behave like that, and what they write in journals as accounts of proper scientific activity are selective, sanitised reconstructions. Then there is the *methodological*: by questioning the prescribed way to do science one may loosen up the possibility of exploring innovative methods, or recognising existing methods which are not officially acknowledged. There is the matter of *what questions are asked*: what is investigated is what is deemed problematic. The taken-for-granted either is not investigated, or is investigated in a different way. If one challenges the assumptions behind the questions, one may get different – and better – answers.

There is also *metaphor*; we have already seen that the metaphors of the human being's relationship with nature, and the metaphors of the natural world itself, are crucial in one's understanding of the scientific process. The activity of science is riddled with metaphors which not only reflect descriptions of what is believed to go on in science, but prescribe, by their very evaluation, the 'proper' way to do science – a classic example is the pejorative concept 'hard' versus 'soft' science. Finally, there is the way in which scientific activity is embedded in rationality. While all the foregoing is about rationality, there is also the question of explicit parallels between scientific activity and the model of logical analysis itself.

Sociologists of science point out that the way scientists actually do science bears little relationship to the Popperian model of careful deductive reasoning and falsification of hypotheses. Science tends to be a team effort, involving a great deal of discourse within shared tacit knowledge, which takes for granted what 'counts' as an interesting question, an interesting finding and a proper proof. It is a collective grope towards some acceptable solution. Lonely scientists do exist, but again they seem in general to lurch from small insight to small insight, with occasional large insights which shift perspective. It is not so much a matter of 'discovery' as a less fuzzy picture of what is going on, a better explanation of the mess/mass of data. Many scientists make a distinction between 'technicians', who do systematic testing and controlled experiments, but who rarely innovate, and 'real scientists', who are passionate, intuitive people.[19]

The grist of this material for the feminist *anti-logos* is mainly recognition of the intensely social nature of science, and the implications of this for women scientists. There are reports of women scientists – Rosalind Franklin in particular – who were not part of the social life of their team, either because of direct discrimination (Franklin was not permitted, as a woman, into the coffee room of the college where she worked) or because some women find the camaraderie style of males, which is often designed to exclude women, difficult.[20] But while many women may have the same experience as Rosalind Franklin, there may also be many who function perfectly well within a male team. The wider issue is that the image – indeed, the prescription – of rational science does not include this crucial social part of the process, and to acknowledge it might threaten the model of how science 'ought' to be; analytical rationality relying on individual logic rather than consensus.

Science as rationality

Science is tied to a model of rationality by certain assumptions about falsifiability and deduction. The philosopher Karl Popper is the prophet of this, and he has been widely criticised – not only by feminists. The key elements are the construction of theory, the generation of hypotheses, the testing of hypotheses to falsify them. Built into the method are assumptions about objectivity, experimental controls, replicability and generalisation, which imply either large sampling (in the human sciences, where one is looking at averages and differences between means) or replication (where one is looking at recurrent events).

The main problem about this view of science is that it is unworkable, and it excludes a number of sciences from its purview. It also has the dangerous effect in social sciences of making superficial measures with large samples more 'scientific' than detailed and careful studies of small samples. It rules out the historical sciences, such as palaeontology and archaeology, and it rules out a number of areas where inference is explicitly necessary – Popper has argued that psychoanalysis is not amenable to scientific investigation. In fact, it also rules out much biological science which requires careful observation of probably unique events, and even much of modern physics now deals with events that can be inferred only from mathematical calculations. It also fails to take into account the reality of scientific progress, which happens through modification, adjustment and the evolution of ideas, rather than refutation or falsification. The definitive experiment is rare. Popper, of course, excluded social science from his purview, thus in effect condemning it to 'non-science' status; those who wish to reinstate the social sciences have all too often tried to reconstruct them in Popperian terms – with sorry consequences.

Evelyn Fox Keller's study of Barbara McClintock (who died in September 1992) is now a classic.[21] In this book, evocatively entitled *A Feeling for the Organism*, Keller shows how McClintock developed her own methods for studying corn genetics. McClintock resisted the pressures of her male colleagues, who were involved in generating grand theory in the newly emergent field of microbiology. Instead, she concentrated on detailed study of the data, at source. This painstaking study was not just a matter of objective note-taking – the routine of the technician style of scientist. She became involved in her corn stalks, she got to know them individually so that she was aware of changes in them. Her 'way of knowing' was involvement and sensitivity to the data; she metaphorically 'listened' to them.

Keller argues that this style of working can be considered a paradigm of 'feminine' science – in the sense of being the antithesis of 'masculine' science. It has the qualities of participation, contextualisation and 'listening' in order to understand, rather than imposing a template upon what is to be investigated – whether such a template is theory, or a particular code of rigour. There are other examples of women scientists who approach their work in this way – Lilian Moller Gilbreth, who was engaged in time and motion studies in industry and on the conditions of work, particularly women's work, is another.[22] Again, however, the fact that it is a 'paradigm of feminine science' is not a statement that men do not do it, nor that all women do it. It is its metaphorical status in relation to the orthodoxy that is at issue.

Biology as destiny

Sociobiology has developed roughly contemporaneously with feminism, and sociobiologists have addressed some similar areas to those addressed by feminist thinkers – but they have provided rather different models. We can track the emergence of metaphors and models within the same timespan, and see how cultural traditions overlap between the two areas. Sociobiology presented a biological model at a time when biological models were not fashionable. It has been subject to distortion by both its supporters and its critics. A number of feminist critics regard sociobiology as the desperate and doomed last stand of the theory that 'biology is destiny'; however, while popularisations of sociobiology have certainly been used to shore up masculine world-views, there are nevertheless many critics who allow a biological dimension of behaviour, even amongst humans, but question the lay social theory that underlies it.

Sociobiology has been criticised because it has applied animal research as a model for human behaviour, but it is even more interesting that the analogy goes the other way: assumptions about human behaviour have been applied to non-human organisms. The two key issues in sociobiology are the dissemination of genes and the successful rearing of offspring so that they, in their turn, can disseminate their genes. Some critics reject any assumption that social behaviour is grounded in biology. A more moderate criticism is that the theory places too great an emphasis on only three areas of behaviour, all of which have been incorrectly interpreted: competition, dominance and female sexual behaviour. Behind much sociobiology is an assumption that relations between the sexes, and patterns of male and female behaviour serve evolutionary purposes. In fact, as Michael Ruse has pointed out, males do not emerge particularly nobly from sociobiology, and the argument that sociobiology props up male superiority does not stand up strongly. The best one can say is that males may not be very nice, but their behaviour has survival value.[23]

Not all feminist critics reject sociobiology. Sarah Blaffer Hrdy considers that one can leave intact the assumption that there is a biological basis for behaviour, but question some of the assumptions made by male sociobiologists about what is natural and unproblematic. They make inappropriate assumptions about human and non-human behaviour.[24] She draws attention to two in particular: that social systems are founded on male competition, and that females are sexually passive. The picture of submissive, receptive females is accurate for very few primate groups, and female initiation of sexual activity is common. She questions whether females are excluded from the behaviours which stabilise social groups. Traditionally, sociobiological models emphasise male dominance hierarchies and male behaviour, and assume that female behaviour depends on the status of males. In fact, careful observation of primates indicates that females independently have ways of maintaining social groups.

Several assumptions which lend themselves to extrapolation to human society are wrong. The first is that having a dominant male as central figure ensures the group's existence over a long time – in other words, it is a beneficial system for the group. In fact, in primate groups 'dominance' carries none of the connotations of 'leadership' that it carries in human terms, and refers mainly to the pecking order of males in one-to-one confrontations – and mostly it is relatively short-lived. The argument that competition is peculiar to the male sex is also wrong; both sexes are highly competitive amongst themselves. It is also incorrect to argue that female hierarchies are less stable, or that a female's status tends to change to reflect the status of her male consort while she is in the mating phase of her cycle. Indeed, observers have largely ignored the specifically female dimensions of hierarchy, which play an important role in female social behaviour and in cooperation in rearing offspring.

Ruth Hubbard similarly notes that Darwin's assumptions about the 'greater passion' of males have come down in studies of animal behaviour, so that *all* behaviour tends to be embedded in a metaphor of male activity and female passivity – even amongst algae and *Drosophila*.[25] This emphasis on competition and sex means that sex and aggression are taken as the primary explanatory behaviours across the phylogenetic scale. This is not only selective perception – focusing on only part of the behaviour – it is in fact wrong; Hubbard argues that there is little evidence that dominance does improve one's chances of access to food or sex. Recent work in animal behaviour suggests that cooperation is a rather more effective strategy than competition.

Many women anthropologists and ethologists have noted that when one actually looks at what is going on in the human or animal group, different things become apparent from those which caught the eye of their male predecessors. Donna Haraway spells this out in her excellent and provocative book *Primate Visions*, which describes how primatology has both reflected and reproduced a particular, masculine view of the development of humans, and of relations between primates.[26] One aspect is that females (of whatever species) are cast in the role of 'effective reproducers' and carers rather than cultural innovators, and that evolution itself is seen in terms of technical advances. This has led to particular views of male–female differences, and social and sexual behaviours. The rise of female/feminist perceptions and approaches in primatology has led to a rather different perception.

These women scientists are consciously aware that their perceptions of female primate behaviour are informed by their own female experience. This has made even more explicit the extent to which male primatologists' perceptions were directed not, as they imagined, by a neutral perspective, but from the point of view of the males they were observing, and from the point of view also of a particular conception of the role and function of social and sexual behaviour. As Haraway says:

> It is not simply coincidental that the reworkings of what counts as female in primate studies since the early 1970s have been accomplished in concert with worldwide reworkings of what the differences and similarities within and among women might be . . . . A large part of the shared problematic has been the effort to reconstruct descriptive practices. Seeing women and females differently does not come easily to those raised with the visualising technologies of universal man.[27]

The outcome of these efforts has been the discovery that:

1) females are competitive and take dominance seriously, 2) females too wander and are not embodiments of social attachment and conservatism; 3) females too are sexually assertive; and 4) females have energy demands in their lives as great as those of males.[28]

But Haraway is careful to point out that it is female *experience*, rather than female biology, which creates this lens:

> these matters concern both men and women, males and females, as actors, authors and subjects of the stories. That women usually took the lead in the reconstructions was not a *natural* result of their sex; it was an historical product of their positioning in particular cognitive and political structures of science, race, and gender.[29]

These examples illustrate how a scientific theory can be contaminated by cultural expectations and lay social theories, making the observer selective both in what is seen and how it is interpreted. Conceptions of human male–female relations, and of male dominance, influence the observation of non-human species. These more sophisticated critiques of sociobiology have become incorporated into, and reflect, an emergent feminist *anti-logos*, which does more than naively question 'biology as destiny'. It shows how a subtle appreciation of sociobiology can bring into question premises about what is 'normal' human and animal behaviour – premises that have sustained traditional views of gender.

Style or gender?

One must be wary of claiming too much for gender specificity. Here we return to the key question about whether we are talking about men and women doing science differently, or masculine and feminine science being done by either or both sexes. Very good scientists of either sex are able to shed the shackles of their training, and to utilise innovative methodologies. For example, most psychologists of merit recognise the fact that despite what undergraduates are taught about sampling, experimental design, control of variables and replication, real advances in the subject have always been made through insightful observation. The innovative psychologist is a Gestalt primate rather than a Hullian rat.

After attending a discussion on gender and science at the British Association for the Advancement of Science meeting in 1985, the palaeontologist Beverly Halstead said he suddenly felt that he understood his own approach to science, having always felt ill at ease with the conventional models of scientific activity.The discussion of 'feminine' science illuminated for him his own feelings about his work; he translated this into the language of 'hard and woolly sciences'. He talked about 'snuggling up to' a subject, as the way he thought many biological scientists actually approached their work. As he wrote:

> I, at least, am proud to be a woolly scientist. There is a sense of becoming one with the natural world, almost snuggling up to it to understand it, in contrast to the hard version where you bash the world into shape and are concerned with ordering nature about. Until you really understand nature in all her ramifications, if you just go barging in, you will come unstuck and deserve all you get.[30]

A tale from palaeontology elaborates the conflict between these approaches. The famous debates about the impact hypothesis were precipitated by the claim that the major extinctions of life associated with the end of the dinosaurs were caused by a meteorite. The significance of the story is that a physicist entered this palaeontological field and attempted to impose the methods of physics, and the 'hard science' scientific philosophy of physics, in a domain which used very different approaches and had very different kinds of data. In brief, it was reported in 1980 that there was a layer of iridium in boundary clay, at a level of deposit which would be consistent with meteorite impact around the end of the Cretaceous era, approximately 66 million years ago. To Luis Alvarez, a Nobel-prizewinning physicist, this looked like 'hard' data, refreshingly better than the 'soft' approaches normally adopted by palaeontologists who rely on observation and interpretation of the whole picture. Alvarez and others utilised complex statistical methods to establish patterns and cycles of extinctions. The debate began, and it rested not only on the nature of the evidence, but on how one should go about doing science.[31]

The problem with palaeontology is that it depends upon the interpretation of partial material, not on replicable experimentation. Inevitably, much is missing; therefore, it is particularly important to consider what is absent, as well as what is present. As the sociologist of science Elizabeth Clemens writes:

> Palaeontological field work involves establishing the relative position of faunal and floral remains in the context of a geological structure which is often complex. In a sense, this type of analysis is more akin to the interpretation of a text (with nine out of ten pages missing) than to the ideal of a repeatable laboratory experiment.[32]

On similar lines, Beverly Halstead writes:

A mathematician, physicist or chemist seeks to eliminate as many extraneous areas as he can, ending up with a simple, clear, elegant solution, backed up by some sophisticated number crunching. The Alvarez scenario was a classic of this . . . . We [palaeontologists] do not in fact spend our time looking for the answers, instead we try to find as many pieces of information that need to be taken into account before any theory can be formed . . . . We try to discover ass many facts as possible that might be connected, the more the better. We let the problem become complicated. We want to know all the factors that must be taken into account, so we let the difficulties accumulate.[33]

Alvarez's response to such resistance to his approach was exasperation. He called palaeontologists 'stamp collectors' and asserted the 'hard science' view thus:

The field of data analysis is one in which I have a lot of experience. Such great computing power has never before been brought to bear on problems of interest to palaeontologists. I'm really quite puzzled that knowledgeable palaeontologists would show such a lack of appreciation for the scientific method. I'm really sorry to have spent so much time on something the physicists in the audience will say is obvious.[34]

The problem, of course, was that the approach was fundamentally flawed, but his method did not pick up the flaws, whereas the palaeontologists did. For example, only some species actually died out at around that period, and they took several million years to do it. Furthermore, the evidence for the iridium layer is highly suspect, and in fact it seems very likely that the event causing it happened somewhat later than the mass extinctions.[35] There are obvious parallels between this saga and the career and work of Barbara McClintock.

Green critics, Gaia and cooperative evolution: reconstructing the organic metaphor

Gaia, in many ways an archetypal Green construct, does not necessarily offer a different metaphor of male–female relations. Lovelock's view of nature still retains man as the wise and caring agent who protects nature and facilitates her 'wisdom'. This is a very different concept from a metaphor where nature is herself the fount of wisdom, or has a particular kind of wisdom of which the human being is a part.[36]

Why should this be perceived, and claimed, as feminine? The metaphor of connection and holism has been assigned to the feminine domain since the Cartesian revolution, and even groups who are not self-consciously gendered, like the Greens, identify it as feminine. The common claim is that the masculine world, *qua* dominant culture, must be challenged not only at its overt level, in its explicit metaphors, but across the range of associated metaphors. Claiming that mastery and destruction are characteristics of the masculine world automatically pits an alternative metaphor – the feminine – against it. Furthermore, it implies that there is a dynamic interrelationship between this domain and other domains where 'masculinity' and 'femininity' are more obvious.

Eco-feminists in particular make an unambiguous link between the female and the living, and the male as destroyer. In 1983 Ynestra King wrote:

> We're here to say the word ECOLOGY and announce that for us as feminists it's a political word . . . [it] stands against the economies of destroyers and the pathology of racist hatred. It is a way of being which understands that there are connections between all living things and that indeed we women are the fact and the flesh of connection.[37]

Here again there is interweaving between the assertion of a metaphoric relation (feminine as life-affirming, masculine as destroying) and the assertion of male and female essential qualities. For some eco-feminists, as for some radical feminists, the link feminine–female is explicit. But for others in the various strands of the Green movement, what is asserted is a *metaphoric* masculine–feminine dichotomy, the conscious adoption of the feminine style as an alternative, an *anti-logos*, and a challenge to the dominant world-view, rather than claiming the epistemological – or biological – privilege of a female person.

Various developments in biological science are consistent with the conception of connection, organicism and holism. The Gaia hypothesis, proposed and developed by James Lovelock, conceives the earth as a living thing, an organic and interrelated whole, governed by the principles of interconnection and symbiosis. The system is goal-seeking (but not purposeful) and self-regulating. In describing Gaia, Lovelock hesitates to use the old concept of 'Mother Earth' or 'Earth Mother'; indeed, he says that he is using the pronoun 'she' only in the sense that a ship is conventionally 'she':

> Occasionally it has been difficult to avoid talking of Gaia as if she were known to be sentient. This is meant no more seriously than is the appellation 'she' when given to a ship by those who sail in her, as a recognition that even pieces of wood and metal may achieve a composite identity distinct from the mere sum of its parts.[38]

Lovelock slips into an interesting metaphor of male–female relations regarding Gaia, which is somewhat distinct from the conception of 'feminine science' described analytically by Keller and fervently by eco-feminists. At one point he shifts into what seems like a benign version of Bacon's view of Man cozening Nature to reveal her secrets – but here it is Man (he uses the male pronoun) who has facilitated Nature's own advance:

> Gaia is no static picture. She is forever changing as life and the Earth evolve together, but in our brief life span she keeps still long enough for us to begin to understand and see how fair she is. The evolution of *Homo sapiens*, with his technological inventiveness and his increasingly subtle communications network, has vastly increased Gaia's range of perception. She is now through us awake and aware of herself. She has seen the reflection of her fair face through the eyes of astronauts and the television cameras of orbiting spacecraft. Our sensations of wonder and pleasure, our capacity for conscious thought and speculation, our restless curiosity and drive are hers to share.[39]

Lovelock seems unclear exactly what relationship 'we' have to the earth; are we part of it/her, or do we have a separate existence? Can 'we' know earth only through participation and 'sharing', or do 'we' know through our 'restless curiosity and drive' in some separate sense? In fact, Lovelock presents the issue as a changing perspective on the part of *Homo sapiens* – as though the relationship between us and Gaia has actually altered as a consequence of changing ideologies and beliefs about nature – rather than, as eco-feminists and others suggest, that we are only now discovering the real nature of our relationship with the earth after centuries of dangerous mechanistic self-delusion:

> This new interrelationship of Gaia with man is by no means fully established; we are not yet a truly collective species, corralled and tamed as an integral part of the biosphere, as we are as individual creatures. It may be that the destiny of mankind is to become tamed, so that the fierce, destructive, and greedy forces of tribalism and nationalism are fused into a compulsive urge to belong to the commonwealth of all creatures which constitutes Gaia.[40]

Lovelock's metaphor here is political, not gendered, yet each of the characteristics he uses applies equally to gender. It is also interesting that he identifies the changes as the 'losses' perceived by many as the dangerous path to feminisation, the surrender of manliness and rugged individualism.

Another biologist whose work is closely associated with the re-emergent organic metaphor is Lynn Margulis. She is the main exponent of the *symbiotic metaphor*, challenging profoundly the traditional Darwinian interpretation that evolution depends upon competition and the survival of the fittest:

> Competition in which the strong wins has been given a good deal more press than cooperation. But certain superficially weak organisms have survived in the long run by being part of collectives, while the so-called strong ones, never learning the trick of cooperation, have been dumped onto the scrap heap of evolutionary extinction. If symbiosis is as prevalent and as important in the history of life as it sems to be, we must rethink biology from the beginning.[41]

She describes a pattern of predatory organisms 'invading' other organisms, becoming parasitic upon them initially, and then being absorbed into the eco-system:

> Symbiosis – the living together in intimate association of different kinds of organisms – is more than an occasional oddity. It is a basic mechanism of evolutionary change. Some plants and animals would long ago have become extinct were it not for the help of their partners: blind shrimps are led around by sighted fish, flowering plants need to be pollinated by specific insects, cows and other ruminants cannot digest grasses without the aid of gut bacteria.[42]

The implication of her metaphor is that cooperation is necessary for understanding life:

> In the traditional view of a cutthroat Darwinian world, merged life forms have always seemed a bit odd, aberrations from the law of the jungle that the poet Tennyson characterised as 'red in tooth and claw'. Yet it now seems plants and animals never would have evolved at all were it not for attacks and defenses followed by symbiosis and reciprocity. Uneasy alliances are at the core of our very many different beings. Individuality, independence – these are illusions . . . . It is in this light that we are beginning to see the biosphere not only as a continual struggle favouring the most vicious organisms but also as an endless dance of diversifying life forms, where partners triumph.[43]

Neither Lovelock nor Margulis, in these extracts, explicitly assigns gender to their position, yet it is clear that Margulis is confronting a certain Western view of male individualism – the metaphor described by Geertz for 'Western self'. But Margulis shows that 'good' science depends on a better model of what is going on, a better basic metaphor. As she says: 'Our concept of the individual is totally warped. All of us are walking communities. Every plant and animal on earth today is a symbiont, living in close contact with others.'[44]

Only with a metaphor of cooperation could she have understood the evolution of mitochondria. Mitochondria depend upon both symbiosis and conflict; thus Margulis integrates the two metaphors:

> a new kind of cell formed, larger and more complex than bacteria. . . . It had parts called mitochondria; dark bodies providing the cell surrounding them with energy derived from oxygen.[45]

> When they were first invaded, occupied hosts . . . probably couldn't survive, and when they died they took the invaders with them. Eventually some of the prey evolved a tolerance for their predators, which then remained alive and well in the food-rich interior of their hosts. As they reproduced inside the invaded cells without causing harm, the predators gave up their independence and moved in for good . . . . Invaded victims and tamed mitochondria recovered from the attack and have lived ever since, or 1000 million years, in dynamic alliance.[46]

But to integrate such metaphors, Margulis had first to challenge the unitary model, the image of struggle and conflict: she had to add a new metaphor. Margulis spent many years on the fringes of her science, without a tenured position, but she now has a thriving laboratory and a flourishing research team. Has the fact that she is a woman been important? A critic of her 1970 book *Origin of Eukaryotic Cells* wrote – presumably pejoratively: 'It has to be a young scientist and a woman who dared to challenge the scientific establishment by writing such a book.'[47] This is a comment about the importance of marginality in innovation, but commentators on Margulis, like Keller, see her ultimate success as due to her single-minded pursuit of an idea rather than her sex – just like any other scientist.[48] Yet her concept, organicist and cooperative, is part of the challenge to masculine metaphors and the traditions of unitary models.

Notes

1. E. F. Keller, *Reflections on Gender and Science*, New Haven, CT: Yale University Press, 1985; E. F. Keller, *Secrets of Life, Secrets of Death: Essays on language, gender and science*, London: Routledge, 1992.
2. See J. Moulton, 'A paradigm of philosophy: the Adversary method', in S. Harding and M. B. Hintikka (eds), *Discovering Reality*, Dordrecht: Reidel, 1983.
3. H. Weinreich-Haste, 'The image of science', in A. Kelly (ed.), *The Missing Half: Girls and science education*, Manchester: Manchester University Press, 1981.
4. A. Kelly (ed.), *The Missing Half: Girls and science education*, Manchester: Manchester University Press, 1981.

5. M. Mead and R. Metraux, 'Image of the scientist among high-school students', *Science*, **126**, pp. 384–9, 1957.

6. J. Archer and M. Macrae, 'Gender perceptions of school subjects among 10–11 year olds', *British Journal of Educational Psychology*, **61**, pp. 99–103, 1991.

7. P. Light, 'Thinking in context: collaborative learning', Paper presented at the British Association for the Advancement of Science annual meeting, Southampton, 1992.

8. M. Michael and B. Wynne, 'Misunderstanding and myth: the case of radiation', Paper presented to the General and Psychology sections of the British Association for the Advancement of Science annual meeting, Sheffield, September 1989.

9. See for instance, S. Sutherland, *Irrationality: The enemy within*, London: Constable, 1992; L. Wolpert, *The Unnatural Nature of Science*, London, Faber & Faber, 1992; H. Gardner, *The Unschooled Mind*, New York: Basic Books, 1992.

10. M. Midgley, *Science as Salvation: A modern myth and its meaning*, London: Routledge, 1992; B. Appleyard, *Understanding the Present: Science and the soul of modern man*, London: Pan Books, 1992.

11. There was a debate in the Correspondence columns of *Nature* in 1986 (vols 322–3) involving several scientists who expressed Christian and atheist positions.

12. S. Hawking, *A Brief History of Time*, New York: Bantam Books, 1988.

13. See for example, H. Rose, 'Hand, brain and heart: a feminist epistemology for the natural sciences', *Signs*, **9(1)**, pp. 73–90, 1983; Brighton Women and Science Group, *Alice Through the Looking Glass*, London: Virago, 1980.

14. Caroline Richmond, personal communication.

15. B. Ehrenreich and D. English, *Witches, Midwives and Nurses: A history of women healers*, Old Westbury, NY: Feminist Press, 1973.

16. L. Stanley and S. Wise, *Breaking Out: Feminist consciousness and feminist research*, London: Routledge & Kegan Paul, 1983; W. Hollway, *Subjectivity and Method in Psychology*, London: Sage, 1989.

17. P. Reason and J. Rowan, *Human Inquiry: A sourcebook of New Paradigm research*, Chichester: Wiley, 1981.

18. See, for example, H. M. Collins, *Changing Order*, London: Sage, 1985.

19. I. I. Mitroff, *The Subjective Side of Science: A philosophical inquiry into the psychology of the Apollo Moon scientists*, Amsterdam: Elsevier, 1974; M. J. Mahoney, *The Scientist as Subject: The psychological imperative*, London: Ballinger, 1976.

20. J. Watson, *The Double Helix*, London: Weidenfeld & Nicolson, 1968; A. Sayre, *Rosalind Franklin and DNA*, New York: W. W. Norton, 1975; S. Ruddick and P. Daniels (eds), *Working it Out: 23 women writers, scientists and scholars talk about their lives*, New York: Pantheon, 1977.

21. E. Fox Keller, *A Feeling for the Organism*, San Francisco: Freeman.

22. M. M. Trescott, 'Lilian Moller Gilbreth and the founding of modern industrial engineering', in J. Rothschild (ed.), *Machina ex Dea*, Oxford: Pergamon Press, 1983.

23. M. Ruse, *Sociobiology: Sense or nonsense?*, Dordrecht: Reidel, 1979.

24. S. B. Hrdy, *The Woman that Never Evolved*, Cambridge, MA: Harvard University Press, 1981.
25. R. Hubbard, 'Have only men evolved?', in Harding and Hintikka, *Discovering Reality*.
26. D. Haraway, *Primate Visions*, London: Routledge, 1989.
27. *ibid.*, pp. 285–6.
28. *ibid.*, p. 291.
29. *ibid.*, p. 303.
30. B. Halstead, 'The hard and woolly sciences', in A. Berry (ed.), *Harraps Book of Scientific Anecdotes*, London: Harrap, 1989, p. 127.
31. L. Alvarez, W. Alvarez, F. Asaro and H. V. Michel, 'Extra-terrestrial causes for the Cretaceous–Tertiary extinction', *Science*, **208 (4448)**, pp. 1095–108, 1980; W. Alvarez, E. G. Kauffman, F. Surlyk, L. W. Alvarez, F. Asaro and H. V. Michel, 'Impact theory of mass extinctions and the invertebrate fossil record', *Science*, **223 (4641)**, pp. 1135–41, 1984.
32. E. Clemens, 'Of asteroids and dinosaurs: the role of the Press in the shaping of scientific debates', *Social Studies of Science*, **16**, pp. 421–56, 1986 (p. 440).
33. B. Halstead, 'The hard and woolly sciences', pp. 126–7.
34. R. Jastrow, 'The dinosaur massacre', *Science Digest*, **151,** September 1983, pp. 51–3, 109.
35. W. A. S. Sarjeant, 'Astrogeological events and mass extinctions; global crises or scientific chimaerae?, *Modern Geology*, **15**, pp. 101–12, 1990; H. Haste, 'Dinosaur as metaphor', *Modern Geology*, **18**, pp. 347–68, 1993.
36. J. Lovelock, *Gaia: A new look at life on Earth*, Oxford: Oxford University Press, 1979.
37. Y. King, quoted in J. Porritt, *Seeing Green: The politics of ecology explained*, Oxford: Basil Blackwell, 1984, p. 46.
38. J. Lovelock, 'Mother Earth: myth or science?', in C. Barlow (ed.), *From Gaia to Selfish Genes*, Cambridge, MA: MIT Press, 1991, p. 3.
39. *ibid.*, p. 19.
40. *ibid.*
41. L. Margulis and D. Sagan, 'Microcosmos', in Barlow (ed.), *From Gaia to Selfish Genes*, p. 59; see also D. Sagan and L. Margulis, 'Cannibal's relief: the origins of sex', *New Scientist*, **115(1572),** pp. 36–40, 6 August 1987; C. Mann, 'Lynn Margulis: science's unruly Earth Mother', *Science*, **242**, pp. 378–81, 19 April 1991.
42. Margulis and Sagan, 'Microcosmos', p. 64.
43. *ibid.*, p. 66.
44. *ibid.*, p. 50.
45. *ibid.*, p. 61.
46. *ibid.*, p. 62.
47. Quoted by E. F. Keller, 'One woman and her theory', *New Scientist*, **111(1515),** pp. 46–50, 3 July 1986.
48. *ibid.*

Chapter 12: Redefining masculinity

The Gulf War in 1991 was a watershed in certain aspects of gender symbols and metaphors. It particularly disturbed metaphors of the public–private dimension, which maps so clearly on to masculine and feminine. Women moved from being protected, behind the scenes, mourners (or victims), to being in the front line, but there were many striking contrasts of imagery. Especially in the early stages, television presented the war as a technological exercise, an achievement of precision engineering. Yet at the same time, male soldiers wept openly and expressed their feelings to the media. The Gulf War played out the rhetoric of modern masculine conceptions of battle, while at the same time overtly undermining some masculine traditions.

At first the most remarkable feature was the way the television studio turned into a 'command control' headquarters. For twenty-four hours a day it was an information centre, with continual reporting of 'strikes'. Men all over Britain were glued to their sets. Their partners complained that they were behaving as though they were part of the action; to leave the couch for a meal, or even in some cases to go to work, would be an unpatriotic act. Two things characterised this early reporting: no human being was involved in the action, just technology, and no women appeared anywhere.

Again and again we saw the famous shot of high-precision targeting of an 'installation', which gave the illusion of streamlined success – *and cleanliness*. Two women with very different viewpoints on war were united in their response to this techno-fix depersonalisation. Rabbi Julia Neuberger, a liberal feminist, wrote: 'The day war began, I listened to the radio all day and didn't hear one woman's voice. It was as if men had taken over.'[1] Lady Olga Maitland, a Conservative who has consistently opposed the Greenham Common women's protest, and runs a pro-NATO organisation called Families for Defence, wrote after the incident in which a lorry with an Iraqi driver was dramatically demolished: 'I don't want Saddam to win, but I felt uncomfortable about the way the lorry was talked about as if it were a mechanised toy.'[2] Only later – much later – was the full extent of death and destruction amongst Iraqi civilians made known to the public. Even during the shelling of Israel, the reporting emphasised the accuracy or otherwise of the weaponry. I gained a picture of what it was like from phoning Israeli friends, rather than from press reports.

Yet alongside this was the changing public face of the soldiery, a new willingness to express feelings and admit – even in front of the television cameras – tears and strong emotion. The journalist Chris Peachment quoted three soldiers in *The Times*: 'It's clinical, it's terribly clinical. There is a constant awareness that in a few seconds' time you may not exist. You train to control your emotions, and when it really matters you can' (at which point he broke down in tears). 'I was in tears when I got back, essentially because we had lost a wingman. At the moment I am going through the full range of emotions, from elation right down to dread and the fear of flying.' 'We went in that far and survived, but we came back in tears.'[3]

No one ever pretended that men did not deep feel emotions in war. What differed here was the *public* expression, the admission that beneath the laconic style, the stiff upper lip, the joking, there are such 'unmanly' responses. It is not clear whether the military are so confident of their masculinity that it is permissible to show feelings nowadays, or whether there is a genuine change in the conception of masculinity. After all, in other undeniably masculine contexts, like football, men have publicly embraced and wept for some time.

The greatest symbolic change, however, was the involvement of women on active service. There were several intersecting discussions. First, it was consistent with – and the outcome of – American legislation for equality, a practical effect of changing gender roles. But the debates ran through all the traditional rhetoric. Could women be effective soldiers? This debate hangs on matching strength, stamina and endurance, under the strains of war – including courage. This was about sex difference. A second debate was about pollution: could women be team players, or would they distract men – either sexually or because men would tend to be more protective towards female colleagues – from making the 'right' military decisions?

The public–private metaphor was particularly aired. Does fighting take away from women's 'proper' function of rearing children and caring for them and for men? Should war in fact really be about men – who are expendable – protecting women to bear children and raise the next generation? A rather different question was protecting women from the nastier aspects of war. This ties into male images of women as delicate creatures who are easily 'degraded'. A vivid example came from Field Marshall Sir Nigel Bagnall:[4]

> Stomachs will still be ripped open and the unsupported entrails exposed; what were once limbs will be reduced to mutilated stumps, and corpses will be blackened by fire. All this is horrific enough when endured by men, but do we wilfully wish it to be inflicted on women as well? It is no argument to say that women and children will suffer such a fate anyway from bombing and missile attack.

Nor, presumably, was it an argument that female nurses, doctors, and war correspondents have coped with this for eighty years.

The moral argument about women's inherent pacifism came from both sides. It was picked up with glee by some anti-feminists, who saw feminists caught between the desire for equality and the argument for the moral superiority of women as pacifists. Nicholas Farrell crowed: 'Feminists are trapped by their own warped logic. Now their sisters are in the Gulf, they fight for Western defeat at home.'[5]

It was interesting that the discussion was about women *in the front line*, not about women in support positions; that battle was won in the Second World War. Nor was there an issue about women war correspondents. Several articles commented on the courage, professionalism and skill of women war correspondents, both past and present.[6] But what was interesting were the grounds on which the discussions took place. They rehearsed the symbols and metaphors of masculinity and femininity, essentialist sex difference versus cultural expectations, and whether women have a special or privileged position with regard to the moral dimensions of war and the search for less belligerent modes of conflict resolution. The Gulf War aired these issues in a real-life, practical context, where the outcomes of any decisions might have had a real effect. The discussions pushed back a few myths, but they also updated the debates.

New Men?

Men are changing, challenging in different ways the entrenched assumptions of masculinity, trying to find ways to escape the anxiety – and different responses to that anxiety. Some men, anyway. Many men who are trying to change are responding to the socialist feminist analysis. They are trying to escape from the pressures imposed on them by traditional patriarchy, taking a greater share of domestic tasks and self-consciously reflecting on how their upbringing has fostered damaging masculine values and traits. This includes cultivating a more androgynous selfhood, and involves getting in touch with nurturance and affectivity.[7] Such men can see the benefits of being more caring and expressive, spending more time on relationships with each other, with women and with their children, and being less obsessive about their careers. They are aware of the extent to which women have been discriminated against, and the victims of violence and sexual aggression. They have become sensitised to the way conventional expectations of sexual behaviour have treated women as sex objects, fantasy figures.

This is a large generalisation, but it is true enough – at least amongst educated Western men. The problems lie in implementing such a change. It is easy to argue that men are reluctant to give up the privileges of their traditional role, such as power, or that they are reluctant to take on board (or even recognise the need for) some of the more mundane aspects of domestic life. The classic question 'Yes, but does he clean the loo?' still lurks, in a world full of keen cooks and buggy-pushers. Studies of the changing patterns of household tasks indicate an increase of male participation, but still it remains a small part of the total.[8] It is not only reluctance to take on less pleasant tasks: the difficulty is confronting the deep anxieties about selfhood. The symbols of masculinity sustain this profound anxiety, while at the same time they assuage it. Tackling this requires more even than cleaning the loo. It certainly requires more than trying to please the new Great Feminist Mother. New Man, as conceptualised within a rationalist framework, is trapped, in a sense, in the new task of pleasing a different mother-figure from the one who made him stand up for himself, and take risks to prove that he was a real boy.

This anxiety about masculinity is expressed in stereotypes about fear: fear of failure, fear of weakness and loss of control – over self and over the world outside – and fear of the female, the feminine, in oneself and others. Since formulating my four images of women – wife, waif, whore and witch – which our culture has constructed as a defence against the fear of female sexuality, I have been drawn into finding parallel male categories. The categories that emerged, however, are not reciprocal. They are not products of female anxieties about males, but descriptions of male responses to relationships with women. I found myself thinking in terms of different styles of male coping and defence, rather than of men as Other as created by women. My categories are *worthy, warrior, whizzkid* and *warlock*.

The *worthy* tries to fulfil the proper obligations of husband and father, responsible and caring. At different periods of history, different qualities are required of him. So the Victorian patriarch, strict in his dealings with his children, responsible as a provider, and protective of his womenfolk to the point of oppression, has much in common with a 1990s New Man who tries to behave according to the role expectations of today's caring, sharing, compassionate and egalitarian husband and father. Both are conforming to what is demanded of a Good Man, a humane being within the terms of male domestic and public roles.

The *warrior* (who also includes the wanderer and the wife-beater) cannot relate to women, but seeks support in the company of other men, often in challenging tasks that continually affirm manhood in and through camaraderie. Warriors fear the cloying emotional demands of women, and they also fear the sapping threat of femininity. The hardness, the toughness and the resilience needed for the warrior role are threatened by the feminine, by family ties and by gentleness. For warriors, other men (either explicitly or implicitly homophile) are the source of security and affirmation. Women are best kept for brief and non-committed contact. Because warriors lack the skills for dealing with the feminine in themselves or in others, they may be driven to violence against women, or to flight. Yet it is not wholly a negative role; aspects of warriorhood, like the role of Man the Hunter which is part of it, are heroic, courageous and engaged in pushing back the frontiers.

The *whizzkid* believes that the world can be controlled by technology and gadgetry. He delights in making things work, in solving problems. For the whizzkid, women are approving mothers, or playmates. The whizzkid believes that there is a rational solution to crisis, including challenges in relationships, once the problem has been presented clearly and simplified. The problem for the whizzkid is not fear of women, or even of relationships as such, but a strong defence against getting out of one's depth; it is control that is at issue. Women upset whizzkids when they demand too much emotional complexity, or undermine their rational world-view.

The *warlock* sounds the most positive of the categories, as the witch sounds the most attractive of the images of women. He is able to explore and accept his and others' emotions, and also to tolerate the ambiguities and strains that relationships entail. A warlock is an integrated being, able to deal with the feminine and the masculine in himself and in others, rather than being threatened by it. The danger of warlocks is that they can become seduced by the power which such integration gives them. Wisdom, or its appearance, can generate guru status, and the temptation to exercise charisma.

These are styles of dealing with the world rather than categories of person – strategies for dealing with the threats posed by the feminine and by relationships. But each is a culturally recognisable response, available within male socialisation. One can see already in children the potential at least for worthies, warriors and whizzkids; eight-year–old warlocks are rare. I have not subjected these categories to empirical testing, factor analysis or large-scale surveys; like the observations about the stereotypes of women, they arise from looking at text and narrative, from jokes and from media – and from life experience. I present them as dynamic scenarios for coping and defence, rather than typologies. They underline the basic point of this book: that the metaphors of gender reflect ways of constructing the world, and ways of coping with it.

Changing men: a reluctant road paved with good intentions

Men's efforts to change the masculine from within reflect a widespread realisation that women have a problem, but a common male response is distancing, which allows acknowledgement of the immorality or injustice of men's treatment of women, without them personally being held responsible.

Roberta Sigel, in a study of 250 American men, identified five such mechanisms.[9] 'Distress and redress' is the most engaged, involving efforts to change one's own behaviour and to enter into empathic understanding of women's problems. She found this amongst relatively few men in her study. It characterised those who are self-consciously attempting to change, the ones who join men's groups and write the scripts for new male roles. But also relatively uncommon was the other extreme, denial of discrimination – what Sigel called 'see no evil'.

Many men recognise that there may be problems 'out there', but fail to see, or to acknowledge, inequalities in their own back yard or workplace. This can be a defensive denial. However, there are also many open-minded men who are persuaded that there is an issue by *prima facie* evidence such as statistics, yet cannot imagine the extent of subtle discrimination until they personally witness it. The organisational psychologist Cary Cooper said on a television programme that he realised the extent of sexual harassment in the workplace only when he made films of body language in offices. I have a friend with impeccable credentials as an aware person concerned with justice. Yet he realised the full nature of the problem only when he had a junior woman assistant in a corporation, under conditions where he daily witnessed the little manifestations of prejudice and discrimination that she experienced. Second-hand accounts, apparently, are not enough to capture the empathic imagination. One of Sigel's respondents expressed it clearly: 'I would have to say . . . maybe it's my naiveness or whatever that I haven't really seen discrimination in the way people describe it.'[10]

Another strategy that Sigel describes is 'inflated deservingness'. One's own rewards (or those of one's group) are justified by some criterion, such as the job being dirtier, more hazardous or demanding different skills – without recognising that this constitutes discrimination. The person denies, and rationalises, unfairness by removing the comparison from the arena of equality. 'Why punish me?' absolves the individual from society's sins – particularly if the person genuinely feels that they have not personally perpetuated unfairness – but removes from them any need to be personally involved in redressing legal or policy imbalances. Finally, 'recourse to lofty principles' is often used to justify traditional gender roles; Field Marshal Bagnall wanted to avoid 'degrading' women by exposing them to mutilation and gore. And women have a 'higher duty' to care for children.

Appealing to higher principles like justice can, of course, be an impetus to change – for example, to legislate against discrimination. But this is not the same as changing symbols. There have really been three waves in men's own efforts to change, each involving self-awareness and some pain. All have their roots as much in the Human Potential Movement as in feminism. Some are guided by a sense of injustice and guilt for the past sins of self or other men. The most recent are guided by a deep sense of a need to redefine masculinity and challenge traditional metaphors.

Before the Women's Movement properly began, the Human Potential Movement – exemplified by encounter groups, Rogerian therapy groups and analysis of mental illness which focused on pathological family dynamics – did two important things. It made it acceptable for people of both sexes, but particularly for men, to acknowledge and express emotion, to be in touch with feelings (including aggression and pain) and to engage in self-analysis. No longer need there be a mask of control, blandness or coping. It made self-integration and personal growth worthy goals that would be achieved by greater access to one's inner self and feelings. Freedom from unnecessary guilt, attained by working through one's hang-ups, was part of this. At the same time there came a new responsibility – for one's own selfhood, one's own decisions and one's own feelings. No longer could one blame parents, or partner, or teachers. One had control of one's own fate, but through self-knowledge rather than the exercise of power and control over others.

This framework emerged shortly before – and in parallel with – feminism and was not initially tied in with challenging the symbols of masculinity, except in so far as it overtly recognised men's particular difficulties in moving towards this better state of mind. Human potential meant, for men, coming to terms with one's own feminine side, shedding one's sexual hang-ups and one's latent homophobia and, indeed, exploring one's sexuality to the full. But it did not, at that point, mesh into an appreciation of women's oppression, or of the oppressive nature of sex roles in general. However, it laid the groundwork of self-awareness skills, working in groups, and men being able to let down the barriers and relate to one another.

A great deal of the literature on men's efforts to redefine the symbols and metaphors of masculinity, and to tackle the anxieties that these have created in their upbringing, stems from this language and these exercises. The redefinition of the masculine began with writings which explored the mechanisms by which boys are made into 'men' – and the harm this does to them as human beings.[11] The big message for men was that their masculine socialisation had turned them into less-than-complete human beings, limiting their fulfilment as fathers, lovers and friends. The Women's Movement brought, for receptive men, the message of guilt and the demand to acknowledge not only how masculinity limited personhood, but how it also led to oppression of women. Many men tried to be nicer through self-discovery as well as by doing more household chores. Understanding the subtlety of the need to sustain masculinity through putting women down was more difficult. A somewhat tongue-in-cheek account of men being self-consciously anti-sexist comes from Mick Cooper, a historian of the Men's Movement:

> I was at a conference once discussing 'The way forward for men' and I think what happened is fairly common for what happens at a lot of these events. Someone stands up and says 'we need to challenge sexism!' and everyone nods their heads furtively and mutters into their woolly beards and the room goes quiet. And then someone says we need to run more creches and people begin to look around a bit nervously because they've got crochet evening on Wednesday night and the anti-sexist rugby group on Fridays and every other Tuesday Pat comes round for a drink and the idea of wiping a few smelly behinds isn't very appealing. So everyone nods nervously and hopes the idea will go away. Which it does. And then someone says that men are always *doing* things and that the idea of doing political work is just so typically male and everyone breathes a sigh of relief . . . someone says that doing creches is just a product of male guilt and that if men really want to challenge sexism what they need to do is sort themselves out and learn to live with and feel ok with other men. So someone suggests a game of sardines as an all-out attack on patriarchy . . . . OK, so maybe that's a bit of an exaggeration, but what I'm trying to get across is that for us as men, it's not a pleasant business to talk about the way we oppress women. It's a lot easier to play touchy-feely games and to talk about the ways we're hurt by patriarchy.[12]

One way to tackle the damage of a patriarchal education is by learning to relate more effectively to other people, especially men. Another reconstructor, Vic Seidler, goes more deeply into how rationality and masculinity are equated, and how this creates an illusion of freedom that impedes men's recognition of the true nature of inequalities – and at the same time generates misogyny: 'The historical identification of masculinity with reason and progress has led men so readily to speaking for others, creating a blindness around the particular experience of heterosexual men.'[13] But the link with 'freedom' and its illusions is the heritage of Kant and the Enlightenment:

> Our emotions and feelings are seen essentially, at least by Kant, as 'inclinations' which are attempting to determine our behaviour externally, and so as sources of unfreedom. Only when we act from the inner voice of reason are we acting independently of influence and determination.[14]

Misogyny arises because:

> If sexuality is to be recognised as a 'natural need' it is only through its suppression and control that we can set 'our minds to work' on higher tasks . . . we can so easily despise women we have sexual relations with. Because the very existence of our sexual feelings proves our own unworthiness.[15]

This vividly echoes Weininger.

Seidler concludes, as I do, that socialist and Marxist feminism fail to recognise that the illusion of freedom, the Enlightenment heritage, cannot overcome the deep anxieties which such tensions themselves create. The paradox is that if we believe we are free moral agents, we cannot understand the social processes that can undermine that freedom. The Left has fallen into the trap of voluntarism: duty and will can counter self-interest.[16] So Seidler, like others who are part of men's groups and associated with *Achilles Heel* magazine, seeks a more psychodynamic model which incorporates an awareness of the darker side of gender tensions. By beginning to bridge the gap between reason and desire, they are breaking the grip that reason has had upon masculinity, and therefore the antithesis of unreason and femininity.

Wilder and woollier

Others have gone further in reclaiming or discovering symbols for masculinity which tackle a deeper aspect of the anxiety. For Robert

Bly, Sam Keen and John Rowan, the quest is not to overcome the sins of the past, or to negotiate a more enlightened masculinity in the context of feminist insights and redefinitions, but to start from the basic problems of masculinity.[17] They do not ground the symbolism of masculinity in social conditions, or economic forces, but in the basic relationships of family life, and self–body relations. However, the failures of masculine symbolism and the problems of male identity arise from ways in which culture distorts these relationships. Bly talks about 'defective mythologies'. His book *Iron John* is the most vociferous of these statements; it is also the one which has drawn the most fire from critics, and has had most impact in terms of activity and action scenarios. Robert Bly is a professional poet; he is also a charismatic figure.

Through this rethinking of the masculine run the premises that we think in terms of metaphor and image, and that mythology, narrative and legend are a crucial part of conveying symbolic meaning, and scenarios for living and resolving problems, to the growing child; that there are some basic relationships between male and female, adult and child, old and young, which if allowed to flourish properly, would enable the full development of masculinity and femininity; and that in our distorted times, with the failure of these relationships, men must turn to themselves, not to women, for reconstruction. The message is that men must find their own authenticity. Another key element in Bly's reconstruction is being in touch with wildness, and energy.

Both Bly and Keen argue that modern man suffers from the absence of good fathers who will provide the right model, and the right tension of relationship, to growing boys. As a consequence of this absence, the role of the feminine is overpowering. This is not, however, just a rehash of traditional right-wing 'anti-Momism', attacks on the loss of old masculine values. For Bly, a necessary part of a young male's growing is separation from the mother, and initiation into the male world. Where there is no strong or facilitating masculine world of adult men, the boy never resolves the mother–son separation in a healthy way. Thus, Bly does not seek the rejection of the feminine in the assertion of new masculinity, but an empowerment of the male in such a way that he can accept the feminine, and neither fight against nor be overwhelmed by it. Bly sees the Women's Movement as giving women just this kind of empowerment and energy, but considers that men need to do this for themselves, by redefining the metaphors and rediscovering masculinity.

Bly expresses many of his concepts in metaphors. These metaphors are simultaneously the mythologies of the culture and of masculinity, and the way in which Bly symbolically conveys a new masculinity:

leadership energy (Zeus energy) in men
the mentor role
the movement from mother's realm to father's realm
concept of initiation
leaving family life
the 'dark side' of men is the exploitation of the earth, and the devaluation
of women, expressed also in tribal warfare.

Some of his metaphors of the latter have echoes of Green romanticism:

> The dark side of men is clear. Their mad exploitation of earth resources,
> devaluation and humiliation of women, and obsession with tribal warfare
> are undeniable . . . . We have defective mythologies that ignore masculine
> depth of feeling, assign men a place in the sky instead of earth, teach
> obedience to the wrong powers, work to keep men boys and entangle
> both men and women in systems of industrial domination that exclude
> both matriarchy and patriarchy.[18]

But Bly is not just seeking a new Jerusalem. He does not reject the sky
in favour of the earth. Whereas other new mythologies have asserted
the superiority of the female (earth) against the male (sky), Bly argues
that we have lost the sky-mother and the earth-father – leaving the
mythology incomplete and separated. Furthermore, in contrast to what
he sees as the New Age blandness, his new masculinity (and new
adulthood for both sexes) is challenging: 'We could say that the New
Age people in general are addicted to harmony. . . . a child will not
become an adult until it breaks the addiction to harmony, chooses the
one precious thing and enters into a joyful participation in the tensions
of life.'[19]

The route to growth for the young man is through 'releasing' – being in
touch with – the wild man. The wild man – the hairy man – of mythology,
in general incorporates sexuality, emotion, and being in touch with forces
that are not accessible to the rational self. The wild man may be seen as a
profound threat to rationality, to be conquered and tamed – a metaphor
we have seen throughout this book, in the form of man's access to his
dangerous 'wild' or 'savage' self through sexuality.

The mythological strand that civilised/rational/cerebral man (less often
woman) becomes complete through communion with – and integration
with – the wild man has a very long history. Before I consider Bly's
metaphor, I want to go back to a very old tale which incorporates
the same tension of wildness and civilisation, and of male search for
the symbols of masculinity. The epic poem *Gilgamesh* is five thousand
years old. This story contains many elements which resurface again
and again in Western myth, in the symbolism of masculinity, dualism,
culture and wildness, the pursuit of the divine and of immortality.

Gilgamesh was king of Uruk, in Mesopotamia. He was the symbol of human (masculine) perfection.[20] Gilgamesh's boundless energy and lust, however, created problems for the people of Uruk, and they begged their gods for respite: 'You made him, O Aruru, now create his equal; let it be as like him as his own reflection, his second self, stormy heart for stormy heart.'[21] Aruru created the wild man Enkidu: 'His body was rough, he had long hair like a woman's . . . . His body was covered with matted hair.' Enkidu lived wild, amongst the animals. Gilgamesh dreamt that he would find in Enkidu the perfect companion: 'When you see him you will be glad; you will love him as a woman and he will never forsake you.'[22] Gilgamesh trapped Enkidu; they wrestled in a trial of strength, and became friends.

Enkidu and Gilgamesh went to the great cedar forest, guarded by the evil giant Humbaba. The reasons for this quest express the three main justifications for perilous journeys and trials of strength in Western mythology. Gilgamesh said:

> 'I have not established my name stamped on bricks as my destiny decreed. . . . I will set up my name in the place where the names of famous men are written, and where no man's name is written, yet I will raise a monument to the gods. Because of the evil that is in the land, we will go to the forest and destroy the evil.' 'Let me live to be the wonder of my mother, as when she nursed me on her lap.'[23]

Gilgamesh and Enkidu slayed the evil monster Humbaba.

Later, Gilgamesh drew the wrath of the goddess Ishtar by rejecting her advances. In anger, Ishtar sent these disdainful mortals the Bull of Heaven, to kill them, but they successfully killed the bull – and boasted in a refrain that echoed over five thousand years of playgrounds and barrack rooms: 'Who is the most glorious of heroes, who is the most eminent among men?' However, they had gone too far: the gods decided that Enkidu should die. Gilgamesh's mourning is a great tragic description of grief and the loss of part of oneself.

After Enkidu's death, Gilgamesh went on a long journey. Its symbolism stretches across the centuries. The death of Enkidu has made Gilgamesh conscious of his own mortality, and his journey is the search for the mystery of immortality, which, of course, he is denied. In the end he comes to some degree of reconciliation with his worldly achievements, the construction of Uruk.

I have told the story of Gilgamesh in the context of Bly's wild man, because there are echoes over thousands of years in the symbols of the search for manhood, and the tensions between civilisation and nature's forces. As in the parallels between Philo of Alexandria and Otto Weininger (pp. 94–8), we see the same symbols and metaphors recurring and being reinforced in our cultural heritage at different times and under different conditions.

Bly drew upon a little-known Teutonic fairy tale from the Brothers Grimm, *Iron John*, as a symbol of the boy's attainment of independence through releasing the 'Wild Man', and going off with him into the forest. A wild man covered in hair, Iron John, who had terrorised the kingdom, is captured and imprisoned in a cage, and the key is given to the queen. One day the young prince's golden ball rolls into Iron John's cage. Iron John will give it back only if the boy releases him. To do this, the boy has to steal the key from under his mother's pillow. He does so, but fears that he will be beaten when his parents find out what he has done, so he leaves the castle on Iron John's shoulders. He lives in the forest with Iron John, where he goes through several trials, *which he fails*, but from which he learns. When he is grown up, Iron John sends him back into the world, where he works as a gardener's boy. One day the princess sees his golden hair. She invites him to her room, but he refuses to take his headgear off, although she tries to make him.

A war breaks out, and the kingdom is threatened with invasion. The young man enlists. He sets off into the forest on a lame horse. He calls Iron John, who gives him a magnificent horse, some fine armour, and an army of soliders. They defeat the enemy. The king wants to know who this mysterious knight is, so he sets a test. The princess throws a golden apple to a crowd of all the knights in the realm. On the first day, the young man, dressed in armour that Iron John has given him, catches the apple and rides away. The same thing happens on the second and third days, but on the third day the king sends soldiers after him, and they catch and wound him. The young man tells the king that he was the knight, and asks for the princess's hand in marriage. The king agrees. At the wedding feast Iron John appears, now himself a king, being restored to his former state; he had been turned into a wild man by enchantment, and the young man's achievements have released him from the spell.

A number of claims can be made about a myth. A myth may be so powerful that it provides metaphors which operate as scripts and scenarios for the child. Such a claim has been made about the influence of Cinderella, and it might also be made about Robin Hood. The Christ story has undoubtedly laid the foundation for a whole moral system and a moral psychology. Causal or not, certain myths recur so often in different forms that they clearly reflect salient themes in the culture. The myth of the hero slaying the dragon or the enemy is necessary to sustain young men's enlistment in war. The myth of Hansel and Gretel, and myths of other wicked stepmothers, reflect deep anxieties about rejecting parents.

However, myths can be drawn upon to generate new ideas. Bly is not claiming that *Iron John* has been highly influential; he claims only that it may be several thousand years old. But for Bly, the myth reflects some basic elements of the development of manhood, particularly the need to confront the wild man, to leave one's parents in order to be initiated by him, and to spend time in the world proving one's own worth. He argues that our present-day culture does not give enough space for young men's initiation, their 'time out' from the parental and female-bounded world. A major part of Bly's argument concerns the role of the father. For Bly, our culture, with its 'father-absence' – geographical, emotional or psychological – prevents the right degree of tension between father and son, a tension which allows the young man to challenge, but at the same time respect, his father. Bly deplores the images of fatherhood presented in popular stories and sitcoms: the ineffectual or the downright betraying (like Darth Vader in *Star Wars*). Lack of contact between father and son leads to distrust of older men. The costs of this situation are that young men attack the old without any balancing strength of the traditions and constraints that are passed on in more traditional cultures. The individual young man has a 'wound', the lack of the father's love and protection. When a boy or a young man seeks protection from his father (or an older male) it is not given, so he turns to women – and so learns that to be a man is not to express feelings:

> If the son learns feeling primarily from the mother then he will probably see his own masculinity from the feminine point of view as well. He may be fascinated with it, but he will be afraid of it. He may pity it and want to reform it, or he may be suspicious of it and want to kill it. He may admire it, but he will never feel at home with it. Eventually a man needs to throw off all indoctrination and begin to discover for himself what the father is and what masculinity is.[24]

Bly says that men must become 'warriors' again, but he distinguishes between the warrior and a soldier or murderer (who would be 'warriors' in my terms). The warrior should defend the individual's psychic space, his inner self, and also defend in the outer world against evil. This is not the destructive force of the soldier in the metaphorical battlefield, in physical confrontation. The warrior is in the service of a cause greater than himself.

Bly sees the Women's Movement as giving women power to define their own authenticity, and to challenge the ways in which men, through their failure to develop a mature masculinity, have felt the need to humiliate and degrade women as a way of escaping the terror of the devouring (or smothering) mother. But he argues that men must break from the female prescriptions for male reconstruction and find their own mythology, heal their own wound. The means of achieving this has given Bly his public visibility, and made him both a charismatic guru and a figure of some ridicule: by returning to the wilderness, to find one's masculinity in the company of other men, retreating to pre-industrial symbolism, healing the symbolic wound and grieving, and coming to accept feeling as legitimately masculine. This involves activities like drumming, physical contact, native American rituals, fairy stories and poetry. The term used about Bly, and others, is 'mythopoeic'.

The objections to these activities – mainly, but not entirely, from feminists – are that they fail to resolve the problem of relations between the sexes, and also that they may merely reinforce the less desirable hierarchical aspects of the traditional male world – Bly makes much of the role of the king, the great leader who inspires and is worth fighting for. There may indeed be a very fine line between finding new masculinist strength and reasserting old-fashioned male aggression, and between male bonding to facilitate a new sense of what is masculine, and old-fashioned exclusion of women as the threatening Mother/Other. Are the 'masculinists' who follow Bly just regrouping for a backlash against feminism? There are parallels with D. H. Lawrence, and some, like Marina Warner, argue that 'Pagan primitivism was a prewar cult, and its affinity with Nazi enthusiasms – obedience to the group, bearing up under pain, rediscovering unadulterated roots – became all too clear.'[25]

These are valid doubts. Others argue that men need only consult women – the long-term experts – on how deal with difficult men, and how to come to terms with emotion.[26] Bly's argument is that men have to find this out for themselves if they are going to reconstruct the masculine authentically. Asking a woman how to be a reconstructed male is no different from asking a woman how to be a traditional male. Both are trapped in a female definition. That is exactly the problem that New Man faces.

Sam Keen, a professor rather than a poet, comes from the same mythopoeic, Human Potential Movement stable as Bly. His book *Fire in the Belly* is no less a charismatic statement about the future of masculinity.[27] His metaphor is a journey rather than a fairy story. He goes into greater depth (and greater personal analysis) than Bly on the nature of what he calls WOMAN, by which he means the images and archetypes of the feminine which inhabit men's heads. They bear little relation to reality, or to real women, but vastly influence men's relations with women, and in particular men's defences against what they see as the threat of the feminine. Keen argues powerfully that a man needs to get rid of these archetypes before he is able to form any relationships with women. To do this he has also to come to terms with his own manhood – which, for Keen, means going away into the world of men, in parallel with Bly's 'initiation' process.

Keen, unlike Bly, also deals with the penis, and what I have termed in this book the 'existential triangle' – man, his penis, and the Other. A long quote is useful:

> Larger than life erections are monuments to exuberant masculinity. Sure enough, every man knows those moments when his cock rises, stands tall and is so full of primal mystery that it seems a natural object of worship. It has an awesome life of its own and is deserving of hymns of praise. But every man knows this is only half the truth. The slow and difficult answer is that our focus on erection is also a compensation for our feelings that the penis, and therefore the self, is small, unreliable and shamefully out of control. Rebellious private, it does what it wants and that includes going AWOL, refusing to stand and deliver, and ignoring the orders issued from general headquarters. For reasons that are far from obvious, men's egos are nearly inseparable from their penises.[28]

It seems obvious, even to less mythopoeic observers, that the association between penis and selfhood is well and truly reinforced in the culture of small boys, and by popular culture, jokes and symbolism.

The fear of WOMAN and the feminine can be found in many different contexts besides American individualism. In a witty piece arrestingly titled 'The ursine and the uterine: masculine fear and Winnie-the-Pooh', Sue Hemmings analyses Kanga as a manifestation of fear of the female.[29] Kanga is archetypally Madonna: 'she has no life of her own but rather experiences her existence vicariously through the life of her child Roo' – manifestly a virgin birth. When Kanga first comes to the Forest, there is great anxiety and myth-making about her, emphasising 'we-versus-they':

> 'Here-we-are', said Rabbit very slowly and carefully, 'all-of-us, and then, suddenly, we wake up one morning, and what do we find? We find a Strange Animal among us. An animal of whom we had never even heard before!'[30]

Piglet expresses a deep fear of feminine power:

> 'I was talking to Christopher Robin, and he said that a Kanga was Generally regarded as One of the Fiercer Animals. I am not frightened of Fierce Animals in the ordinary way, but it is well known that if One of the Fiercer Animals is Deprived of its Young, it becomes as fierce as Two of the Fiercer Animals.'

Later Piglet replaces Roo in Kanga's pocket as part of a plan for getting rid of her, and Kanga deals with this by casting him as the powerless child, and stripping his identity by trying to wash him 'clean' – incorporating him into her domestic, powerful, female field.

Winnie-the-Pooh, and other English literature of that period, is set in an entirely male world in which nurturing is satisfactorily conducted by males. Christopher Robin is the 'maternal' nurturer as well as serving masculine roles like being the fount of knowledge and an intrepid explorer and leader; he is both father and mother to the forest-dwellers. In *The Wind in the Willows* there are no female characters, apart from the jailer's daughter and her washerwoman aunt who provides the clothes for Toad's escape.[31] But nurturing takes place – 'maternally' by Rat and 'paternally' by Badger, who combine to facilitate the developing manhood – control, courage and efficacy – of Mole, in a world carefully devoid of any powerful feminine threat.

Both Bly and Keen regard a period in the wilderness, and the nurturing of boys by men, as an interim phase during which the young man escapes the ties to the female parent, and learns about his own manhood so that he is able to return to the world free of the Great Terror of the Feminine, and make proper relationships with real women. This sounds fine in principle. However, upper-class British boys have been taken away from their mothers and reared in an all-male world for a long time – and with a quite explicit agenda of 'making a man of him'. The effects of this 'initiation' are difficult to judge. Documentation of public-school life by those who have experienced it – at least the subsample of those who write for a living – suggests peculiarly savage forms of initiation into suffering, in which sexual development, in terms of both emotional relationships and the emergence of sensuality, is primarily homoerotic. One of the most vivid and irreverent is Stephen Fry's novel *The Liar*.[32] Many public-school products undoubtedly do learn to form reasonable relationships with real women, but there is plenty of evidence in British as well as American culture of a fear of the feminine. Of course the British public school does not parallel the Kikuyu tribe, more the medieval monastery. Boys are not being initiated into manhood by mature men who have themselves learnt to relate to women, but by men who have, in many cases, left the heterosexual world and become institutionalised – men who are as frightened of the feminine as any young adolescent.

Preoccupation with the wilderness is also endemic in American mythology. As Keen says, Marlboro Man is possibly the major American icon: independent, outdoors, obviously free of any emotional entanglements, in touch with that major American myth – the cowboy. Both Keen and Bly specifically blame the corporate culture, industrial society, for the loss of father–son bonding, the route to manhood. Return to the wilderness is the romantic route to reconstruction – it is not just a matter of Boy Scout survival skills. As Keen says: 'Wildness, first and foremost, comes from identification with the literal wilderness – rugged mountains, virgin forests, barren tundras, the habitat of untamed grizzlies, undomesticated wolves, fierce mountain lions.'[33]

Fine, if you live in North America. The metaphor of wilderness, for North Americans, is integrally tied up with metaphors of 'frontier'. For Americans the frontier is the boundary between the civilised place and the wilderness. Beyond the frontier are untamed tracts, either to be conquered or to be treated with awe. In Europe a frontier is the boundary between two civilised and populous states. We have no metaphor of 'wilderness' in Western Europe (with the possible exception of northern Scandinavia). There are wild places indeed, and there is terrain which is challenging and/or exhilarating. There is also the sea. But these areas are surrounded; they are pockets – albeit large ones – of untamed space in a landscape of humanisation and control.

One might ask, with real concern: What form would a corrupt version of the 'new masculinism' take? New Man has been sanitised and made 'safe' as media-myth New Lad, a style-conscious young man who parades his feminist awareness while enjoying all the traditional male pursuits, a manipulator who realises that sounding like a feminist sympathiser is the best way to get women into bed. Arguably, the worst that can go wrong with the concept of New Man is that it produces some exploitative hypocrites, but at least the message hangs publicly over the discussions.

Bly's 'masculinism' could give sustenance to an anger – not against the wound of absent fatherhood and the authentically masculine, but against the mythic and metaphoric devouring mother, alias feminism, alias the feminine. This is particularly dangerous for men who have never even got into being New Men, guilt-ridden about their masculinity and deferential to feminist approval. A powerful new mythology can reshape our beliefs and create a new set of metaphors, but if it is viewed through the old lenses, it merely gives fodder to old prejudices. It is a subtle distinction between Robert Bly's 'New Warrior' and the warrior/soldier, the wanderer/wife-beater, whom I have identified as the man in flight from and fight against the feminine. Peter Reason, a management expert with strong ties to the Human Potential Movement, sees both the problem and the dangers of *Iron John*:

> At present we have the re-emergence of a strong feminine within our culture faced with inadequate images of the masculine. *Iron John* is an attempt to find a vital male identity, an identity which will stand in dialogue with women and the women's movement. But in our society these things do get so easily polarised, we find it difficult to hold the tension of genuine dialogue, preferring the degenerate polarity of an either/or argument. . . . A man in a workshop I was running said in introducing himself, 'Robert Bly would say it is all my Mother's fault,'

at which I cringed, but also saw in a new light some of the difficulties about this book.[34]

There were parallel problems with David Cooper and R. D. Laing's critique of the problems of family dynamics in the 1960s: they could, and for some people did – read as yet another attack on Woman, and particularly on Woman the Destroyer of Men.[35]

Yet despite these problems, Bly forces us to confront these fears. We can tackle the profound anxieties and deep metaphors of gender only if we confront them.

Notes

1. J. Neuberger, quoted in G. Bedell, 'What's a woman's place in war?', *Independent on Sunday*, 3 February 1991.
2. O. Maitland, quoted in *ibid*.
3. C. Peachment, 'Men, myths and fighter pilots', *Times*, 23 February 1991, p. 18.
4. N. Bagnall, 'A call to arms in the battle of the sexes: presence that reduces fighting effectiveness', *Independent*, 28 August 1990.
5. N. Farrell, Gulf war between the sexes', *Sunday Telegraph*, 3 February 1991.
6. L. Purves, 'Brave fronts, front women and front lines', *Times*, 21 January 1991, p. 14; J. Swain, 'Women GIs shoulder arms in equality's last war zone', *Sunday Times*, 30 September 1990, p. 18.
7. J. H. Pleck and J. Sawyer, *Men and Masculinity*, Englewood Cliffs, NJ: Prentice Hall, 1974; M. S. Kimmel, *Changing Men: New directions in research on men and masculinity*, London and Beverly Hills, CA: Sage, 1987.
8. D. Utting, 'Women beware British man about the house', *Independent on Sunday*, 28 June 1992, p. 8.
9. R. S. Sigel, 'How men and women cope when gender role orientations change', *Political Psychology*, **13(3)**, pp. 337–52, 1992.
10. *ibid.*, p. 345.
11. Pleck and Sawyer, *Men and Masculinity*.
12. M. Cooper, quoted in C. Griffin and M. Wetherell, 'Feminist psychology and the study of man and masculinity: Part II, Politics and practices', *Feminism and Psychology*, **2(2)**, pp. 133–68, 1992.
13. V. J. Seidler, *Rediscovering Masculinity: Reasons, language and sexuality*, London: Routledge, 1989, p. 3.
14. *ibid.*, p. 4.
15. *ibid.*, p. 47.
16. *ibid.*, p. 198.
17. R. Bly, *Iron John*, New York: Addison-Wesley, 1990; S. Keen, *Fire in the Belly: On being a man*, New York: Bantam Books, 1991; J. Rowan, *The Horned God: Feminism and men as wounding and healing*, London: Routledge, 1987.
18. Bly, *Iron John*, p. x.
19. *ibid.*, p. 177.

20. N. K. Sandars, *The Epic of Gilgamesh*, Harmondsworth: Penguin, 1972.
21. *ibid.*, p. 62.
22. *ibid.*, p. 66.
23. *ibid.*, p. 71.
24. Bly, *Iron John*, p. 25.
25. M. Warner, *Independent on Sunday*, 22 September 1991.
26. M. Freely, *Independent on Sunday*, 15 September 1991; M. Horsfield, *Guardian*, 27 June 1991.
27. Keen, *Fire in the Belly*.
28. *ibid.*, pp. 70–1.
29. S. Hemmings, personal communication.
30. A. A. Milne, *Winnie-the-Pooh*, New York: Dutton, 1926.
31. K. Grahame, *The Wind in the Willows*, New York: Scribners, 1923.
32. S. Fry, *The Liar*, New York: Soho, 1993.
33. Keen, *Fire in the Belly*, p. 183.
34. P. Reason, 'Review of R. Bly, *Iron John*', *Women in Management Review*, **7(7),** March 1992, pp. 35–7.
35. R. D. Laing and A. Esterson, *Sanity, Madness and the Family*, New York: Basic Books, 1965; D. Cooper, *Death of the Family*, New York: Pantheon, 1970.

Chapter 13: Backlash!

The film *Thelma and Louise* came out in 1991. It caused a strange furore. It touched a nerve with women who had experienced violence, feminists who were conscious of its ambiguities, and people of both sexes whose slumbering sensitivities were pricked into wakefulness and outrage. On the surface it is a simple story. Louise is a waitress with a wimpish, obliging but uncommitted boyfriend. She has experienced rape in the past. Thelma is married to an obsessive lout who tries to demand total obedience from her. The two women escape, intending a weekend's innocent backwoods retreat. At a diner disco *en route* Thelma celebrates her light-hearted mood by dancing flamboyantly with a man who turns out to be the local sexual predator. He tries to rape her, and Louise shoots him. Forced now to go on the run, the two women set off to drive to Mexico.

Thelma spends a night with an engaging young thief, who steals the money that Louise has managed to get her boyfriend to bring to them. Destitute, Thelma emulates the thief's method of holding up a supermarket. *No one is hurt*. The women are pursued not only by police but by a leering and offensive truck driver. They challenge his behaviour and set fire to his truck; *he is not hurt*. A highway policeman stops them for speeding; to prevent his reporting them through a routine check-in, they disarm him and shut him in the boot of his car, *carefully ensuring that he will survive until he is found*. In the end, despite the intervention of the policeman in charge of the case, who continually tries to prevent the escalation of their alienation from the law, they are faced with a vast mass of armed police on the edge of the Grand Canyon. Given the choice of imprisonment or death, they 'fly' in their T-bird, over the edge, to their deaths.

This is a film in which one person is killed in self-defence, a fairly small amount of money is stolen, an obnoxious person has his truck set on fire, and one or two people suffer brief discomfort. As a consequence of escalating misunderstandings, two women end up choosing to die. Yet the reaction to it has been violent. In Britain, Janet Daley wrote in *The Times*:

> Attempted rape is held to vindicate two women going on a homicidal rampage against men, [it] is being greeted with ecstatic cheering from female partisans in cinemas. The apologia for this ideological bloodbath is that it is justifiable retribution . . . . The very indiscriminateness of the killing takes on a symbolic significance; women are killed and maimed in just such an indiscriminate way by male attackers.

Did Janet Daley see the same film as I did? In the United States, writers have seen it as a dangerous influence on impressionable young women, 'an explicit fascist theme, wedded to the bleakest form of feminism', and say that 'it justifies armed robbery, manslaughter and chronic drunken driving as exercises in consciousness-raising'.[2] Objections have come, both from professed feminist writers and from triumphal opposers of feminism, that gun-toting vengeance, casual sex with attractive strangers, and verbal humiliation are merely mirror images of male outlaw, Western and buddy movies, and hardly consistent with new conceptions of female empowerment. Somewhat parallel objections were made to the hugely popular British play and film *Shirley Valentine*: did getting laid by a Greek beach boy and replacing the life of a Liverpool housewife with running a fish and chip shop on a Greek island constitute 'liberation'?

But why all the fuss? Any film with male heroes in the genres mentioned would not have garnered a breath of moral objection – particularly in view of the extremely limited actual violence. Male audiences cheered when Glenn Close 'got her comeuppance' in *Fatal Attraction*, and when Jodie Foster was raped in *The Accused* – even though the message of the film was explicitly attacking rape. *Thelma and Louise* is funny – but outlaws and killers have been funny before. They enjoy themselves (apart from the killing of the drunken assaulter) in capers which have been the stock in trade of dozens of films portraying sympathetic crooks. The film has great pathos, in places where the male parallels would have been seen as taken-for-granted exploitation or laconically accepted misfortune. Thelma discovers for the first time that sex can be delightful, with the attractive hitchhiker – who robs her of $700. Previously ineffectual, she finds holding up the store enormously exhilarating, and Louise says: 'This is the first chance you had to express yourself' – only too clearly a contrast with the earlier scenes with her husband. Louise herself kills the assaulter not when he is attempting to rape Thelma, but when he sneers afterwards that he ought to have done so. It is clear that Louise is finally enacting a catharsis of her own past rape – an experience so horrible that she feels she cannot re-enter Texas, where it happened, even though their flight has to take a huge detour to avoid it.

This pathos underlying the humour contrasts both emotionally and morally with the vengeful or just plain macho violence of hundreds of male films – so why the *moral* fuss? This response is part of a backlash. The rawness of the emotions expressed in the attacks reveals just how deep they go. It is irrational to claim that *Thelma and Louise* is a violent or an immoral film. An excess of violent emotion was generated by *Fatal Attraction* – and the director has described how he was pushed into turning an interesting cameo about the problems of adultery into a vengeful destruction of the 'career woman' mistress and the adulation of the 'traditional' wronged wife. Yet *Thelma and Louise*, like *Shirley Valentine* and *The Accused*, is cheered with delight by many women who are unversed in, and probably even antipathetic to, feminist theory. The battle lines are drawn, and they are not just battle lines within the cloisters of arcane academic or political debate. The messages of change have penetrated, but they are distorted by defensive lenses. In a review of Hollywood's 'Year of the Woman', Jay Carr wrote in the *Boston Globe*:

> In every way, the past twelve months represents a loss of ground for women. . . . When we have seen women, they've been stigmatised as crazies . . . it's been the year of men being more threatened than ever by women's competence and the few small gains women have made in the face of escalating male hysteria. More than ever, women are being demonised, set up as targets for male rage. Connect the dots between Rebecca deMornay's killer nanny in *The Hand That Rocks the Cradle*, Sharon Stone's threatening novel-writing shrink in *Basic Instinct*, Jennifer Jason Leigh's killer roommate in *Single White Female*.[3]

He suggested 'scrapping Hollywood's phony Year of the Woman and renaming it the Year of the Freaked-Out Man'.

The metaphors of disaster

As I have argued throughout this book, the impetus for changing gender roles comes from widely differing sources, and takes very different forms. The extent of actual change in women's and men's lives is difficult to quantify. We must rely on attitude polls, statistics of work patterns, benefits and salaries and, particularly, on personal narratives. But ultimately, the evidence of rhetorical change comes from what is taken for granted, and what is deemed problematic. The 'backlash' is interesting for what it reveals about the challenged assumption, the newly ambiguous concept, the distortion of information. The counter-arguments levied in antagonism to new ideas reveal the lay social theories that are under attack. I am not concerned here with whether the backlash might undermine the changes wrought over the last two decades; I am interested in what the rhetoric of the backlash tells us about changing bases of debates about gender, redrawing of the frames for discourse.

'Backlash' has become a buzz word. It first appeared in the media in the hands of writers antithetical to feminism. If feminists go 'too far', it was said, there will be a backlash from men. Recently, in books by Marilyn French and Susan Faludi which explicitly use the metaphor of a 'war against women', the manifestations of backlash have been spelt out. For French, this 'war' is manifested in various kinds of violence perpetrated against women.[4] For Faludi, the war includes the battles of language, misuse of statistics, use of symbols, as well as documenting actual efforts to undermine the power of the 'feminist lobby'.[5]

These two books document diverse defensive and offensive reactions to perceived changes in cherished aspects of life. They illustrate the construction of an *anti-logos* to the success, or partial success, of feminism. This reveals what world-views are threatened by feminism, how the familiar world has been upset. The representation of 'feminism' in these constructions is very interesting in itself: it is a distillation, selection, and distortion of several conflicting feminist positions. As Billig has said, one can understand a communication only if one knows what it is being presented in argument with. In the case of backlashes – in any field – the exponent spells out the position they are attacking; an attack has to make its object explicit. The argumentation in a backlash is overt; the controversy is explicit. We can see clearly what assumptions are being made about the opposition's position, and what is the protagonist's underlying lay social theory. There are also genuine positions of dissent, challenging the fine detail of a feminist theory that is well understood, but deemed undesirable. But there is an important difference between dissent and backlash: backlash is primarily a *reactive position*, defending something that is perceived either to have been lost, or to be under threat.

The backlash against feminism is many-faceted. Some of it is old-fashioned misogyny, directed simply at Woman and all her evil works. Feminist ideas and the advancement of women's position merely exacerbate an age-old problem. Some of it is directed at the perceived changes – in sex roles, but especially in power relations – that have either happened, or are feared to be in the offing. Some of it is targeted at 'alien' ideas like socialism and secularism, with which feminism is associated. There are many representations and constructions of what 'feminism' is, and there are many forms of backlash.

Some backlash is *regressive*. It seeks to return to a golden age of traditional sex roles and sexual values. Here, feminism is a generic, a ragbag, highlighting whatever elements – accurate or not – are salient to the critic's position. Feminism (usually, metonymically, feminists) has disrupted the social order. Life has definitely got worse, and feminists are to blame. Change is acknowledged, but its extent is frequently exaggerated.

Another kind of backlash is *reactive*. Here the rhetorical style ostensibly takes feminist arguments seriously, and challenges them apparently on their own terms. The reactive argument is that yes, there were problems for women's position before the Women's Movement (though notably, reactive critics were not in the vanguard of protest at that time), but neither the theoretical models nor the policies have achieved a desirable state; indeed, they have usually made things worse. They have made things worse specifically for the very women who were supposed to be helped, or for other women who were affected by unintended consequences. So, for example, the executive woman becomes 'hopelessly exhausted' by the demands of her new job, and housewives or ordinary working women have 'lost out on benefits' through reductions in legal 'protection'. As Kenneth Minogue said in the *Sunday Telegraph*:

> The first wave of feminism was rightly about equal opportunity. Women rightly demanded to be admitted on their individual merits to the activities men had previously monopolised – politics, higher education, the professions and so on. There's no doubt this created considerable problems about how to combine female aspirations, conventions, even dress, with what was necessary to be one of the boys. One unfortunate result of this development, however, was that it slanted aspirations away from those areas where women had previously excelled – style, grace, domesticity, the cultivation of intimacy – towards activities where male strength and competitiveness gave men an advantage.[6]

A particular irony is the concession that the battles of the past created a fair society, a society now being threatened by the misguided battles of the present. Such reactive critics fail to appreciate the difficulties of fighting those very past battles. Their texts read as though the progress towards democracy and a fair society was through civilised muted discussions on matters of principle, rather than the often bloody street-fighting it actually entailed. Another version of this is the claim that we live in a 'post-feminist' era. After the upheavals of the last two decades, women have successfully achieved all they need, and anyone who still asserts otherwise is consigned to the 'whining wimmin' category, or described as harking back to an outdated perspective.

A more sophisticated type of reactive backlash is debate with feminist theory on *a priori* terms, challenging feminism's presumed basic premises. Such a debate may start from an assertion that, for example, sex differences are based on biological (and therefore immutable) features rather than environmental factors. The arguments attributed to feminism – again, correctly or not is immaterial – are unpacked on the basis of the questioning of these premises. Such debates frequently cite scientific evidence – not only for essential sex differences, but for the social or biological functions served by difference. So one objection may be that it is scientifically incorrect, or practically unrealistic, to strive for equality in areas of established differentiation. A more subtle position argues from the underlying functioning of traditional gender roles, rather than merely from essential differences. Feminists have seriously damaged social order by undermining the stabilising balances of male and female difference. The 'taming' role of women in relation to male aggression or unbridled sexuality comes into this category. Whereas the regressive backlash claims that dire consequences have already occurred, and blames feminism, the sophisticated reactive backlash predicts even greater future disasters due to long-term destabilisation of society's structures.

This position tends to latch with delight on to perceived 'contradictions' within the broad feminist perspective – taking the arguments, for example, for a 'different voice' in moral thought, or distinctive styles of thinking between the sexes, as evidence for 'real' difference. Although the debate is ostensibly a rational engagement of discussion on basic premises, in fact it derives from a misunderstanding – deliberate or otherwise – of those premises.

One version of backlash which illustrates the misunderstanding of feminism most profoundly I call the *defensive alternative* backlash. Here there is often a definite commitment to changing gender roles, and even a realisation of the limitations of traditional masculine roles. But it is accompanied by the conviction that 'feminism' is actually the enemy of the desired change. The argument is that empowering women through legal and social changes further diminishes men's already limited power. The premise is that men were weakened or impoverished in traditional expectations of gender roles, and in their enshrinement in law and custom, and that all women collude in maintaining this position. Traditional women do so through guilt or dependency; feminist women do so by the extension of legal powers. It is important to recognise that this is a desire not to revert to crude machismo versions of the male role – that would be regressive – but to generate new masculinities which would overcome the limitations and frailties of the old. An ambiguous example is the cry 'Families need fathers'. Is this the reaffirmation of traditional patriarchal authority, or an effort to find a 'New Man' kind of fatherhood? Both suggest a long-term undermining of male involvement in the family.

Why have I chosen to treat these positions as 'backlash', rather than as rational discussions and the negotiation of new definitions of gender roles? Why do I regard them as uncomprehending enemy reaction rather than a legitimate adversarial position? What distinguishes 'backlash' from debate and commentary? Indeed, it can be difficult to distinguish between them, particularly where men are genuinely trying to propose alternative masculinities. The debates within feminist theories reveal enormous differences in premiss and conclusion; some feminists criticise others for being revisionist and effectively endorsing a backlash position. Many feminists would also acknowledge that some legislation, and even some improvements, have placed greater burdens on working women and single parents.

Backlash primarily expresses fear, and the translation of that fear into defensive distortion. It is characterised by either deliberate misunderstanding and misrepresentation, or such selective acquaintance with the material that it constitutes deliberate ignorance. One criterion of backlash is the oversimplification, or even caricaturisation, of feminist ideas – most particularly, a failure to recognise the variety and contrast in different feminist positions. Some writers, for example, consistently refer to 'radical feminists' when they mean Marxist feminists; 'radical' here being used rhetorically as a term of abuse. Another criterion is the exaggeration of change. Alan Bloom, author of *The Closing of the American Mind*, typifies the terror of many conservative academics that women in general, and feminists in particular, have 'taken over' universities – at a time when less than 10 per cent of Ivy League tenured faculty are female, and in Britain, less than 3 per cent of professors.[7]

A backlash ploy is to diminish the credibility of feminist writers, either by attacking their scholarship (the sophisticated version) or simply, as in the last century, by describing feminists as deviant, marginal and unnatural. So feminists are presented either as peculiar or as a minority out of touch with 'real' – that is to say, 'most' – women. There is also straightforward violence and the reassertion of male power. This can take the form of symbolic or actual humiliation – as happened, for example, to Anita Hill in the Clarence Thomas case – or by practices such as the deliberate removal of feminists, self-professed or suspected, from positions of power and influence. According to Faludi, this happened on a large scale under Ronald Reagan's administration.

The backlash is preoccupied with *dire consequences*, including undermining the moral and social order, which are more than merely practical concerns about the ordinary dislocations associated with social restructuring. In effect this seems to presume that change is possible through enlightened compromise and quiet negotiation, within the institutions of democracy, and that the 'excesses' of radicalism are unnecessary and may even threaten that very democracy. A favourite example of historically 'disastrous' events is the French Revolution and the Reign of Terror. While most people would indeed agree with the awfulness of the latter, it does not follow that in 1789 the *ancien régime* was about to give up its tyranny as a consequence of democratic debate and compromise. There is a failure to distinguish between the unfortunate effects of some attempts at revolutionary (or even evolutionary) change, and the necessity to exert some very real pressure to create any change whatsoever. People who are really concerned with effectively using the democratic process to promote change recognise the complexities involved, but they do not dwell upon the spectre of imminent chaos and social breakdown.

Most of the fears underlying backlash are associated with power and its loss, and with control and its loss. Many metaphors of fear equate security and control with masculinity, and femininity with chaos. There are metaphors in which the power of the male is pitted against the conflicting power of the female – as Mother, as Witch, as Kali – where loss of male power is loss of selfhood. Female competence threatens the role, the function, of the male, which also threatens selfhood. The 'nanny state' is not only the metaphoric institutionalisation of female power; it takes over the functions of the 'good provider', removing the primary male role. The male becomes redundant as well as infantilised. If men lose their power over women, they fear that they will be seen as powerless in relation to other men also. A major criterion for self-worth within traditional masculine culture is the capacity to assert power over other people, to be strong – necessarily a term relative to the strength or weakness of others. As Gore Vidal says, 'It is not enough to succeed; others must fail.'

Fear of loss of control, of chaos, need not only be associated with frailty in the face of Woman-as-Chaos, or Woman as Great Mother/ Destroyer. Undermining of order is, *per se*, the road to chaos. Indeed, Roger Scruton perceives women's power ostensibly as civilising, and feminists' removal of that civilising function as dangerous. The fear is that changes in the forces of self-control, and the removal of constraints that we currently apply as part of our self-definitions as masculine and feminine, will lead ultimately to the loss of self. This is a further stage along the route to fearing loss of a safe world. Yet for many men, the ordered schemas of traditional roles merely prevent ambiguity. There are many men who are anxious only about the uncertainties of knowing what behaviour is required when dealing with a woman boss, or with a woman who is sexually assertive rather than passive.

They dread merely the hassle of learning a new repertoire of behaviour, rather than dark forces or the destruction of civilisation. But even these quite trivial anxieties can be a powerful impetus to resistance.

Finally, there is a fear of loss of benefits. It is superfluous to point out the many material and emotional benefits that traditional gender roles had for men (while at the same time not ignoring the limitations of that role), not least in the domestic and support spheres. But the fear runs deeper than having to iron one's own shirts, type one's own letters or pick up the children from school. The removal of the round-the-clock ego-prop requires the development of a self-reliance that was neither expected nor trained under traditional gender schemas. The male fear that if women gain greater equality they will 'become like men' includes a fear that they will cease to be nurturant to men – a view implied in the quotation above from Minogue.

How are these fears manifest? Let us first consider the term 'feminist'. Women who say 'I'm not a feminist, but . . . ' are distancing themselves from a stereotype, a label, a particular image of feminists and feminism. But this statement does imply acceptance that there are issues which need to be tackled, even if the speaker does not wish to align herself with her image of how feminists do the tackling.

It is interesting that the adjectives directed at today's feminists are virtually identical to those levelled at their grandmothers and great-grandmothers. For all the changes that have taken place in thinking about gender, when it comes to attack, those under threat resort to the old, old story. 'Feminist' is a term of abuse, associated either directly or in close context with the adjectives: *overwrought, embittered, man-hating, militant, harpy, humourless, strident, harridan, aggressive* – to take a few recent backlash newspaper articles at random. In other words, feminists are not just subscribers to a particular theory of gender roles, they are women whose attributes mark them out as less-than, incomplete, or distorted women. These terms separate out 'real' women from feminists, and reassuringly sustain a vision of a world in which 'most' women conform to 'feminine' expectations of behaviour, and are not governed by distressing motives and aspirations which threaten men.

What are the implications of those adjectives? First, there are the 'unfeminine', meaning essentially unladylike – *shrill, strident, aggressive*. These words mean that women are failing to conform to a view of 'their place' in relation to men – specifically in their mode and content of speech. Men who speak forcefully are never 'shrill'; they may be 'abusive', or other synonyms for *confrontational* and *rude*, but the idea that their voices lack euphony because they are expressing themselves strongly is not mentioned. Women – real women – are supposed to be soft-voiced and compliant to men's needs and views. So feminists are not 'ladies', and do not command the respect that a gentleman is obliged to pay to a lady. In other words, by describing her thus he is absolved from the need even to pretend to like her.

Then there are the words which mean 'unsexual', like *harridan* or *embittered* (which usually means sexually unfulfilled), so feminists have failed in an area where it is assumed that women's self-esteem is centrally located – finding a man. The words associated with 'unnaturalness' – *harpy, aggressive, man-hating, lesbian* – all reflect the rejection of the 'normal' woman's desire to be pleasing to men, to fit into their desires and needs. But this also reflects male fears. If women do not want to find men, then what function do men have – and, more to the point, how can women be controlled? *Overwrought* diminishes the need to take feminists seriously, as they are outside rational discourse. *Humourless* also removes women from common discourse, because humour is so important in much male interaction as a way of dealing with threat; without humour, one strategy for communicating is lost. *Militant* also locates feminists on the fringe of rationality, as zealots, but also – especially in Britain – *militant* has connotations of Left political extremism. These connotations have changed little since the *Punch* caricatures of 'bluestockings' in the last century. They are also stereotypes of people, which bear no relation to the theoretical issues; the abuse is of persons, not ideas.

It is interesting that despite feminists' affirmation of female sexuality and rights to sexual fulfilment, there has been relatively little discussion in the backlash of 'voracious' women. One defensive response is that attractive women who are sexually demanding lack power, because their sexual enthusiasm makes them available for male lust – the nymphomaniac or whore syndrome. Even 'ball-breaker' has connotations not just of voracity but of ego-bruising criticism of male sexual limitations. When sexual voracity is associated with lack of attractiveness, the negative defensive imagery of 'frustrated' is applied. But there are some recent – and growing – exceptions. In fiction, the threat of voracious women is explored perhaps most notably in the novels of Kingsley Amis. It is in film that the threat of voracious sexuality is most explicitly expressed – and most savagely avenged. Jay Carr says of *Fatal Attraction* that it set the scene for women as 'seething monsters' and Glenn Close was, 'according to the laws of male stereotyping, a maniac' because she was sexually demanding: 'Insidiously audiences are set up to feel that justice has been done when these highly sexed women are demonised, then snuffed.'[8]

A different kind of rhetoric is used about *feminism*, the body of ideas. Feminism as a pejorative term characteristically reflects a mishmash, an amalgam, of half-digested concepts, which are drawn from, and confuse, several different strands of feminist ideas. Guilt by association links feminism to other recognised forms of demonology. In the United States, though not so much in Britain, feminism is coupled with secular Humanism. The message is that feminists are godless and undermine the moral order. In the States this is closely related to the charge of socialism or communism. Feminists, like socialists – and especially Marxists – are dangerously egalitarian and statist. In Britain, the links between feminism, socialism and Marxism are somewhat more subtle, and reflect political rather than moral accusations. Also, both socialism and secularism are much more part of the mainstream in Britain. Instead, ridicule is directed by the more sophisticated backlash writers at efforts to treat gender as structurally equivalent to class.

Some backlash writers appear deliberately to misunderstand key concepts of feminism. Just as Conservative polemical writers distort the Left's concern with justice and equality as 'envy' of the wealth of the rich and privileged, rather than treating it as a matter of principle, so backlash writers talk of 'empowerment' as excessive intervention by the state, rather than the development of women's sense of efficacy. Minogue, for example, in his *Sunday Telegraph* article, said:

> What . . . came to be called 'empowerment' . . . was in fact a confession of weakness. Empowerment was bending the power of the state to get women on to the occupational gravy train by means of affirmative action, equal opportunity commissions, enforceable codes of behaviour relating to women, outlawing a set of new offences such as sexism and lookism, the compulsory re-writing of textbooks in schools so as to incorporate feminist doctrine, the imposition of new linguistic practices by publishers and much else.[9]

The rhetoric of feminist threats to freedom – and, by association, to democracy – has been given a great boost by 'political correctness'. This expression has been a gift for libertarians. Political correctness asserts moral orthodoxy. Once there were efforts to *impose* 'correct' terminology, there was no stopping the backlash (and indeed, more moderate critics) from making analogies with totalitarian states. As long as the moral high ground was held by feminist objections to inequalities, violence, humiliation or degradation, an opponent was forced into either personal attacks on feminists, or attacks on the implications of theory. So *moral* rhetoric tended to be reserved for debates about abortion, the impact of working women on family life, or promiscuity arising from women being sexually assertive. With PC, the phrases Thought Police, totalitarian, even fascist, crept into the discourse. Alongside the spectre of state intervention in welfare, child care and anti-discrimination legislation, feminism became targeted as anti-democratic and suppressing freedom of speech.

A diatribe on political correctness in relation to nudity came, somewhat surprisingly, from Bernard Levin, a journalist who is normally quite sympathetic to feminist issues. This concerned the (unnamed) professor at Penn State who objected to the portrait of Goya's *Naked Maja* on the wall of a music room in the university, arguing that this constituted sexual harassment. I am inclined to agree with Bernard Levin that objecting to nudity as such is both philistine and ridiculous, but Levin strayed into 'backlash' in saying, about the professor:

> Her identity has not been unveiled, much less her person, but I am unkind enough to wager that her lineaments are such that few painters of any quality would care to paint her fully clothed, and fewer still naked . . . find out the identity of the woman professor who started this lunatic business, and tell me if I was right when I deduced that Goya would have taken one look at her and burnt his brushes.[10]

It is a pity that Levin spoilt a sensible attack on silly censorship by falling into the trap of assuming that all feminists (or prudes) are motivated by lack of personal attraction.

But the main backlash moral objections to feminism are its effects on family life. The target is feminist theoretical positions concerning changing women's work and family pattern, the availability of abortion and contraception, the liberalisation of divorce and of extra-marital family forms (including homosexual couples). In the backlash literature, the causal relations between all these are made quite explicit. Traditional family life had a male breadwinner who was supported by a non-working wife. If she goes out to work, the effect will be that he will no longer wish to remain married to her, and will fail to support her or the children. So, because working women disrupt the traditional pattern of male–female support, they have only themselves to blame if men lose interest in them and 'stray'.

Greater equality for women in the workplace, and increasing the number of single-parent families, is also *morally* disruptive because it allows the state to encroach even more on the 'private' domain of family life. This is partly about diminishing freedoms, but it is also because the state becomes the father-substitute. This further undermines the traditional male role and, therefore, male confidence, leading to greater moral breakdown. Male irresponsibility increases, and naturally bad male traits are not contained. Wandering bands of rootless males are going to pose a greater threat to lone defenceless women, in the long run. So feminist disruption of family life through interference with traditional family roles impinges on several distinct rhetorical domains.

This is taken up not only by 'regressive' and 'reactive' backlash writers but also by the 'defensive alternativists', of whom the most vocal is Neil Lyndon. Lyndon conducted a press campaign on this issue over a period of nearly two years, culminating in the publication of his book *No More Sex War: The failure of feminism*, in October 1992 – accompanied by a public debate between Lyndon and Kenneth Minogue on the one hand, and Yvonne Roberts and Beatrix Campbell on the other.[11] Lyndon writes as a polemical journalist, with few concessions to conventional scholarship. (The book, for example, has neither an index nor a bibliography.) His argument rests on two diametrically opposed points, and both are seriously flawed by inaccurate assumptions. Yet the overall message of the book has a coherence which commands attention. Neil Lyndon's personal statement of his own reactions, as well as his analysis, enables the reader to see the dynamics of the reaction more clearly than is possible in more 'academic' language.

The first point is that men are deprived of their rights of fatherhood, of access to their children in the event of divorce, and to any rights over children born (or, in the case of abortion, conceived) outside marriage. One in five men get joint custody, and in one in ten sole custody. This he interprets as giving women *the legal right to abduct their children*. It is *legal* discrimination against men, and he claims that he can find no comparable situation in which women are legally discriminated against. Men are also the victims of legal discrimination in the age of retirement, pension and dependency rights and, most particularly, parental leave. Lyndon sees this situation as part of a wider denial of men's rights as parents. Most feminists, of whatever persuasion, would agree that it is iniquitous, and many have attempted to change it. However, Lyndon argues – passionately – that the whole situation is the fault of feminist influence over the last twenty years.

Lyndon contends that feminism has done nothing but damage to both women and men. It has merely given women the right to 'badmouth' men in all situations – a right that is denied to men. He cites extensively from the history of feminist writings – examples of intemperate, extreme, ironic (and sometimes ridiculous) statements. His charge is particularly that feminists make generalisations about 'all' men – being rapists, child-abusers, hating women, and so forth; in the cause of degrading men *en masse*, the statistics of male violence towards women, and rape, have been grossly exaggerated. Gains in women's position mostly predate the Women's Movement – he cites the expansion of higher education in the 1960s, which benefited women enormously, and the change in the divorce and abortion laws later in the decade. But the main cause of change was the Pill, which transformed sexuality by making it consequence-free and a fun activity. This shifted the responsibility for both constraint and commitment away from women, and undermined many of the checks and balances that formerly regulated sexual relationships. Women no longer needed to set up commitment; the situation was one of sudden and destabilising uncertainty. Neither sex had the emotional or moral repertoires to cope. Lyndon makes the interesting proposition that into this moral vacuum came feminism – an ideology offering security, a clear view of male–female relations providing psychological protection for women.

One of the problems is that Neil Lyndon is a Nice Man. This is neither a personal comment nor patronising. The Nice Man is an important actor in the dramas of changing gender, who has not had enough analytical attention. Nice Men have a certain innocence. Lyndon fails to realise that everything women are now saying publicly – intemperately, provocatively, or deliberately hurtfully (and I don't deny that this happens) – was said in private over the washing tub, the bridge game or the dressing-table by their great-grandmothers and great-great-great-aunts and cousins. As I have said several times, the traditional conservative anti-feminist lady is no more persuaded of male superiority than her more vociferous sisters; she just shuts up about it in public. What has changed is the shift of the discussion into the public domain – and, indeed, into the domain of analysis rather than mere grievance.

Girls used to be divided into Nice Girls and the Other Kind. Nice Girls didn't use bad language, express explicit sexual interest, or wear provocative clothes. The underlying assumption was that women were supposed to operate the sexual constraints, and were rather delicate creatures who needed protection from the unpleasant manifestations of sexuality. It was also assumed to be a protection: Nice Girls didn't get raped because they aroused chivalry rather than lust. Such assumptions are still alive and well in the minds of some judges and quite a few backlash writers. Nice Girls very quickly learnt that all this was a myth: Niceness was no protection whatsoever against unpleasant young men (especially if they were drunk).

Nice Girls may be a myth; the difference between Nice Men and the Other Sort is not. This is a gross oversimplification; I will make it for the purposes of discussion. The Other Sort of Man behaves in the ways (some of the time) that he is stereotyped as doing by women – of all feminist or anti-feminist colours. Some men rape, beat their wives, run away from emotions, behave in a sexually aggressive or abusive way, make degrading and belittling comments about women, abuse children sexually or in other ways. The point about Nice Men is that *they cannot believe this*. At least, they cannot believe that men 'like themselves' – which might mean shared social class, religion, hobbies or community – could do these things. Again and again one encounters this; even High Court judges are quoted, on occasion, as finding some behaviours they encounter in the course of their work incomprehensible. Discussions of rape with Nice Men invariably end up

– as Neil Lyndon himself says – with them saying that they personally would find rape quite inconceivable. *And I believe them.* Nice Men also believe they could never strike a woman; Neil Lyndon says he has done so only under conditions of provocation, and then using only a fraction of his strength. *I believe him.* But I know, like other Nice Girls, that his experience, and his self-control, are not evidence against the existence of Other Men. Lyndon fails to understand either the reasons behind female anger or the analysis that has developed feminist theory beyond mere invective.

A personal anecdote will make the point. At a summer school where I was teaching about fifteen years ago, I ran an encounter group one evening. A fellow tutor, whose advances I had declined, turned up at the group, but refused to join in. I gave him the choice of taking part or leaving. He did leave; he went and got drunk. After the group I took the students to the bar for a debriefing; it was important to be sensitive to them. In the bar my fellow tutor began to goad me, and to make suggestive remarks.

This is a situation that Nice Girls learn to deal with. Drunken men need tactful handling; they should not be provoked and they should be steered off before they make fools of themselves. Nice Girls know that a Lady prevents the Situation Getting Out of Hand. However, I felt that my duty was to my group, and that my colleague should respect this professional role. I ignored him. He became more and more abusive, vulgar and extremely embarrassing.

The interesting thing about this situation was the different responses of the men and women present. The women shrugged their shoulders, and were unanimous that 'men behave like this when drunk'. They were irritated and embarrassed on my behalf, *but not surprised.* The men, however, were clearly appalled – a tutor, no less, behaving like this to a woman! It soon became clear that I would have to intervene to prevent the tutor from being manhandled by my protective students. In the end I did the Ladylike Thing: I escorted him from the bar and roundly told him to go away. He did. The male students spent a lot of time expressing horror and surprise and making gallant gestures, offering to defend my honour in various ways. The following day it was worse: a dozen students who had not even been present came up to me asserting their wish to do various nasty retaliatory things to my poor colleague. The campus was awash with white chargers and shining armour.

I tell this story because it so clearly illustrates the innocence (or defensive denial) of Nice Men, in an actual situation. My eager Knights Errant were motivated by genuine surprise; my fellow women were resigned and pragmatic. Neil Lyndon is a Nice Man, and perhaps he has never seen men behaving really badly.

The fantasy lost world of chivalry

A 'regressive' Golden Age view, smacking much of fantasy and myth, represents feminism as deliberately destroying everything that is meant by 'femininity'. This is partly defence of a metaphor of antithesis. When a backlash man writes about 'femininity' he tends to mean the qualities – good or bad – that are Other to himself, and therefore define his masculinity. Romanticising the feminine heightens this by enhancing difference. If the terror of the feminine lies in its weakening threat to the masculine, exaggerating the feminine – in women – makes it very clearly antithetical to the masculine self. This circumscribes the extent and nature of contact between the sexes. The threat that comes from undermining traditional ideas of the feminine is a sort of leakage. If men cannot contain women within a traditional definition of femininity, they cannot be sure that there is not some fuzziness at the boundaries. They may become contaminated because they can no longer clearly see that they are distinct. Many men who hold out for a strong definition of the feminine have just such a terror about their own masculine identity, but at the same time they are fascinated by femininity as long as it is confined in an Other. Hence there is 'mystery' and sexual excitement in alien beings who appear so incomprehensible. This accounts for the erratic veering between asserting the superiority of men and grovelling at the feet of mythical goddesses.

A particularly saccharine example of this was occasioned by the death of the ballerina Margot Fonteyn.[12] It is worth quoting virtually in full, for it demonstrates the tasteless use of praise for a woman who was genuinely a great artist and a fine person of extraordinary courage, single-minded determination and capacity for gruelling hard work, as a weapon against a distorted and deliberately corrupted representation of 'feminism'. It is also rife with metaphors of both femininity and dualism.

It was headed 'Why this woman was not like a man', and was unsigned:

> Margot Fonteyn was everything militant feminists deplore. On stage she embodied to perfection the melting femininity which feminists abhor. Her most popular roles, in *Swan Lake* and *Giselle*, celebrated, and positively wallowed in, woman as the passive victim of cruel fate. Off-stage, in her private life, she served a crippled husband with noble self-sacrifice and perfect fidelity. Seldom has the traditional conception of woman found so beautiful and admirable exemplar. The essence of that traditional conception is difference, as in *vive la différence*. Women and men are different from one another – a truth so obvious that it needs saying all the more often, now that Feminist Woman, and her ally the New Man, are trying to persuade us that all is interchangeable.

As a result of her expressing that difference so perfectly, she had the world at her feet. No Englishwoman this century has made such a mark or won so many hearts in so many continents. Her power owed nothing to doing battle with men – a battle which women can never win – and everything to capturing the hearts of men; a battle which women of the quality of Margot Fonteyn can never lose. Underneath the fragile-seeming body lay a will of iron and a professional determination that none of her famous partners could equal, let alone excel. What her dancing with her greatest partner, Nureyev, so marvellously and memorably displayed was the heights of emotional and aesthetic intensity which a man and woman can reach together, in perfect harmony of body and spirit. Facile and ugly talk of a war of the sexes could not survive that exquisite demonstration of mutual inspiration through mutual dependency. Nobody who ever saw these two dancing a *pas de deux* can ever fall for the stale feminist propaganda. The male and female principles found in their art a unity through contrast, a joint perfection in which the whole was much greater than the sum of parts.

Nor was this just a theatrical artifice. The style was the woman, and her love for her husband in real life was not one wit less tragically romantic than her love for Albrecht in *Giselle* or for Siegfried in *Swan Lake*. There was something else about her which militant feminism has tried to render absurd – to which militant feminism does not want women of today to aspire. She embodied a certain ideal of female Englishness; restrained, dignified, under-stated, but all the more inspiring to most women, and alluring to most men, for being so . . . . The courage of Margot Fonteyn's last years as she struggled against a fatal cancer only served to bind her art to her life. There indeed was a 'role model', a true heroine whose triumphant career and whose inspiring life make men feel humble and over-awed, inferior and subservient. In the presence of her genius, even the greatest male partner bent a knee. So do we now, with love and admiration.

The exaggeration of the feminine is incorporated in some 'regressive' backlash literature into an assertion of the checks and balances offered by traditional sex roles. The most baroque is the bizarre logic of 'chivalry'. An exquisite example of this comes from Francis Bennion, who clearly learnt his history from a box of Quality Street chocolates. In a letter to *The Sunday Times*, headed 'Death of chivalry is women's loss', he says:

> Valerie Grove bemoans that the modern woman is nowhere safe from men. This vulnerability merely shows that the modern woman is much less clever than her predecessors. She has wantonly thrown away the safeguards against male strength they cunningly erected over centuries, and thoughtfully bequeathed to their heedless sisters of today. The smart women of the past, realising their physical inferiority, imposed corresponding duties on Men. Men were required to display deference

and exercise a respect based on notions of courtesy and chivalry. Women took pleasure in accentuating their physical weakness, thereby holding men in an even more secure psychic thrall. Women of the past protected their sexual integrity by the powerful concept of the virgin bride. They created and maintained the notion of female mystery. Young girls were required to be chaperoned and young men respected them for it. These attitudes have a long history, which means they are securely based in human psychology. The virago of today has much to answer for, not least to members of her own sex.[13]

This is a version of the 'taming' hypothesis: men are bestial creatures unless they are kept in check by women – and indeed, not even through the exercise of overt control but by deceptions. Yet the blame for men's bad behaviour falls squarely on women themselves. If a woman walks alone at night (or, indeed, at any time), she is 'asking for it'. The chivalry myth, needless to say, omits any mention of the preyed-upon weak who lack 'protectors' – or are simply of a different social or ethnic class, and therefore do not elicit the chivalrous response. The theme that 'women have lost more than they gained' recurs in several versions of the regressive reaction. It's a safe world when men can be reassured that the Great Mother will curb their excesses with loving gentleness, and will forgive, if they are nice enough to her.

Radical misconceptions: the metaphors of extremism

At root all backlash positions systematically misunderstand feminist theories, whether intentionally or not. A particular confusion is between radical feminism, which implies separatism and utopianism, and socialist feminism, which is rooted in a rationalist Enlightenment tradition. One person who typifies the backlash's cavalier attitude towards veracity is Kenneth Minogue. One might imagine that a professor of Political Science would consider a scholarly appreciation of the distinctions within a political perspective to be a prerequisite for attacking it. Yet he made the following extraordinary statement: 'Radical feminism was an adaptation of Marxism which cast women instead of workers as the proletariat.'[14] He made the same confusion in the *Times*/Dillons debate on 6 October 1992, where he supported Neil Lyndon's attack on the failures of feminism. A ten-minute conversation over coffee with any of his feminist colleagues would have prevented him making such a gaffe, but clearly he did not feel this was necessary.

It is true that the development of feminist theory and of its various perspectives, has been complex. There have been, as I spelt out above, several transitions. The first phase of feminism challenged the received wisdom about both actual sex differences and the origins and significance of sex difference. This was associated with challenging inequalities in society, and undermining justifications for such inequalities that were based on assumptions of difference. The second phase of feminism focused on the social and psychological consequences for women (and also for men) of sex-role expectations and stereotypes, and led to a reconstruction of thinking about gender in ways that broke down the old categories. From this period emerged the concept of 'empowerment' and learning the skills of assertion and affirmation of selfhood, and also the concept of androgyny as the integration of masculine and feminine. Current theoretical concerns have progressed beyond those debates, and focus on the way gender is embedded in culture. The issues have far wider implication than whether men or women are 'really' better at map-reading or maths. These issues are about how meaning is generated and reproduced, and how extensively the symbols of gender permeate culture and our lives.

If we couch the evolution of feminist ideas in more journalistic terms, we could say that they have moved from an initial 'It's not fair' position in the early 1970s to a 'Have it all' affirmation of women's (and men's) potential once the barriers could be loosened, and latterly into 'Redefining the game', which challenges assumptions about traditional masculinity and femininity.

Backlash writers cannot be expected to follow the fine details of the debates. They necessarily react to what has filtered into the public domain; therefore they are an interesting indicator of just how far the ideas of feminism have permeated lay thought. Much backlash writing is still stuck at the first phase, asserting the 'truth' of traditional stereotypes of difference. The more sophisticated reflects an appreciation of the second phase. It is interesting that people who have got this far, like Kenneth Minogue, do carefully differentiate between 'OK' liberal demands for greater equality of opportunity and questioning of traditional stereotypes that hindered women's advancement, and the more 'dangerous' challenges of enforced legislative changes, or 'interference' with language and behaviour – these critics tend to make much sport of 'non-sexist language' and 'date rape'. Their comments reflect a lack of comprehension of how overt and covert institutional practices, and accepted patterns of interaction, may perpetuate inequality. Their comments also reflect a resolute refusal to accept the need for men to reconsider their cherished assumptions: it's all right for women to join the club, as long as they do so according to existing rules and roles.

That is the more libertarian version. Another, more traditionalist critique, which nevertheless has some appreciation of the second phase, either gloats or wrings hands over the practical problems and supposed failure of 'Having it all', pointing out the 'dire consequences' and 'distress' caused by this impossible goal. Much rhetorical use is made of evidence of women backing off from the competitive business world under the pressure of combining family and work, or of the number of 'real' women around who are content with their family roles. But even here there is a change: ten years ago the plea that 'children need their mothers' tended to mean that women with children under five should not work at all, and women should work only part-time while their children were primary-school age. Today it is more likely to mean staying at home for the first eighteen months.

One of the 'dire consequences' is the threat to feminism itself. Under the heading 'Why men won't take feminism', Minette Marrin wrote in tones that did not flatter men's basic nature, and contained a strong element of women's 'taming' role:[15]

> The veneer of civilisation – of respectable family life and responsible self-denial – is very thin with many men, as any feminist will tell you. It might seem logical, then, to try not to push men to such a point that they feel like lighting out in large numbers. Yet that is what women seem to me to be doing. All around me there seem to be men who are cracking, who are at last very angry . . . . They have had enough of women having things both ways. They have had enough of women's cries of unfairness; women have indeed had a very bad deal, but that does not mean that everything is men's fault . . . . Feminists have been talking for some time of a male backlash against them. I don't think we've seen anything yet, but I suspect we are just about to. And I'm afraid what we will see is men not lashing out but lighting out altogether.

Relatively few backlash writers do fully appreciate what is being done in what I term the third phase of feminism, and fall back on confronting the rhetoric of earlier phases when they encounter it. In February 1992, I wrote an article in the *New Scientist*, where I spelt out the role of metaphors of gender in our thinking about rationality, dualism and science.[16] I was not discussing sex differences. The three letters written in criticism of the piece focused entirely on the question of whether there were 'really' differences between men and women or not – responding, in other words, to 'first-phase' issues.[17]

The few backlash writers who appear to appreciate the profoundly revolutionary nature of feminist theory of culture are disturbed by it, but still seem unaware of the diversity of feminist ideas. And in practice their responses tend to focus on 'dire consequences' rather than exploring the more positive implications inherent in the feminist perspective itself. Roger Scruton has some awareness that a new way of looking at gender would change aspects of civilisation. His attacks on feminism are predicated in part on the assumption that men and women have very different levels and kinds of sexual desire. Woman's desire is less, and is focused on reproduction and fidelity; men's desire is greater and includes an element of lust, which, if left to itself, would be 'the lust that seeks, not to unite with another person, but to relieve itself upon her body'.[18] Scruton argues first, therefore, that men's and women's sexuality are not interchangeable. This is a direct reaction to 'first-phase' feminist rhetoric of 'minimising difference'. His further argument, however, that the function of women's sexuality is to act as a brake on men's, thus protecting culture from 'the unbridled ambition of the phallus', shades into the functional need for differentiation of the sexes for the sake of social and moral order – this 'dire consequences' scenario is more relevant to 'second-phase' feminist issues.

In his book *Sexual Desire*, Scruton's thesis is somewhat more subtle, and elaborates the metaphor of Otherness.[19] His theory is that sexual desire depends upon the Otherness of the partner; sexual desire is not possible between persons of the same 'natural kind'. Homosexuality is therefore unnatural. He attacks 'Kantian feminism', which is essentially the argument that there are no real differences in personhood between the sexes:

> Kantian feminism has tended to assume that it is only one sex that has perceived the other in terms of its 'otherness'. In that very observation, however, is revealed the covert recognition that man is as much the 'other' whose otherness resides in his 'creation' of woman's otherness . . . . To put it shortly, if the claims made by Kantian feminists were true, Kantian feminism would be false.[20]

Therefore, he contends, Simone de Beauvoir's argument that the Otherness of the female is created by the male inevitably supposes that males are Others to females.

This is insightful, but Scruton misses the arguments that recent feminist theory has explored. Even if women do recognise men's Otherness, this does not deny the false and inauthentic definition of the quality of Otherness that men (or the dominant male culture) use in describing the Otherness of females. The inequity and lack of reciprocity arise because women's definition of men's Otherness does not define men's selfhood in the social and public domain (though it may have power in the private domain of relationships) in the way that men's definition of women's Otherness does; it is a one-way, not a two-way, mirror. Current feminist theory (with which Scruton is clearly unfamiliar) seeks to retain a form of Otherness, but one which authentically reflects female experience. But also current feminist theory is trying to illustrate how, first, actually categorising the female as Other, and secondly, the terms in which that categorising is done, work as defensive mechanisms to heighten the cultural definition of masculinity and protect it by differentiation and antithesis. Scruton himself is fairly unspecific about the nature of sex differences, apart from his discussion of sexuality, but much of his discussion is clearly within the frame of reference of dualism and functional role differentiation.

Scruton is interesting because he is subtle, and he is not stupid. Yet he has failed to pick up some key issues. If the differences asserted within the culture are those defined by only one sex, it does not follow that they are valid or true differences. There can be two conclusions from this invalidity, and both have been explored within feminism. The first is that there are in fact no (or no important) differences, that the very existence of difference is chimaerical. The second is that there are differences, there is Otherness, but the conventional definitions of such differences are either incomplete (being only from one sex's perspective) or downright wrong. Scruton is typical of backlash writers in confusing these two and, further, in using this confusion as a critique. However, Scruton does have some appreciation of the profundity of the feminist critique, in that he appears to realise that feminism is attacking some basic cultural schemas, not merely arguing for the existence or otherwise of sex difference.

In this he differs from Kenneth Minogue and others, who fail altogether to understand the problem of Otherness, and see the argument for a different point of view merely as special pleading in the power game, or even as a retreat from the pressures of the male world. Minogue writes:

> The other thesis, however, largely contradicts the first [that there are no differences]. It argues that there is a specific women's vision of the world which has been denied and frustrated in patriarchal societies. The problem of this latter view is not to open up to women opportunities hitherto monopolised by men, but to remake our entire culture so that women may prosper in it. The claim, indeed, is that such a destruction of patriarchy would be a comprehensive solution to the world's problems. Women who do get into the boardroom are soon disillusioned by the petty competitiveness and the exhausting intensity of it all. Many wish to humanise business. Equally feminists in universities, often finding themselves repelled by what they call 'masculinist' science and philosophy, have set up a cosy corner called 'Women's Studies'.[21]

What is remarkable about so much backlash writing is that these men, despite their erudition, have not bothered actually to read and understand the real challenge, but reiterate the old-fashioned arguments. Men whose monolithic conceptions of rationality are being confronted are merely feeling frightened of having to be nicer to their female colleagues and avoiding any suggestion of sexual harassment of their students. The backlash hijacks the work of Gilligan and others with relief, because it indicates that there are 'real' sex differences after all – when, in fact, third-phase feminist theory would pluralise our conceptions of science and rationality, and in the long run is likely to make a far greater impact on Western thought than a few barbed charges in the Senior Common Room.

Notes

1. J. Daley, 'Gender is no justification,' *Times*, 16 August 1991, p. 12.
2. C. Bremner, 'Giving as bad as they get', *Times Saturday Review*, 29 June 1991, p. 6.
3. J. Carr, 'More losses than gains in Hollywood's Year of the Woman', *Boston Globe*, 18 February 1993, p. 60.
4. M. French, *The War Against Women*, London: Hamish Hamilton, 1992.
5. S. Faludi, *Backlash! The undeclared war against women*, London: Chatto & Windus, 1992.
6. K. Minogue, 'The puzzling paradoxes of feminism', *Sunday Telegraph*, 2 June 1991, p. xii.
7. A. Bloom, *The Closing of the American Mind*, New York: Simon & Schuster, 1987.
8. Minogue, 'The puzzling paradoxes of feminism', p. xii.
9. Carr, 'More losses than gains in Hollywood's Year of the Woman', p. 60.
10. B. Levin, 'Portrait of a harassed lady', *Times*, 25 November 1991, p. 14.
11. N. Lyndon, *No More Sex War: The failure of feminism*, London: Sinclair-Stevenson, 1992.
12. [Unsigned] 'Why this woman was not like a man', *Sunday Telegraph*, 24 February 1991.
13. F. Bennion, 'Death of chivalry is women's loss', Letters, *Sunday Times*, 19 June 1991, p. A22.
14. Minogue, 'The puzzling paradoxes of feminism', p. xii.
15. M. Marrin, 'Why men won't take feminism', *Sunday Telegraph*, 20 October 1991.
16. H. Haste, 'Splitting images', *New Scientist*, **133(1808)**, pp. 32–4, 14 February 1992.
17. 'La Différence': letters from A. Syred, H. J. Eysenck and J. Holt, *New Scientist*, **133(1811)**, p. 57, 7 March 1992.
18. R. Scruton, 'The case against feminism', *Observer*, 22 May 1983, p. 27.
19. R. Scruton, *Sexual Desire*, London: Weidenfeld & Nicolson, 1986.
20. *ibid.*, pp. 281–2.
21. Minogue, 'The puzzling paradoxes of feminism', 1991, p. xii.

Epilogue

Metaphors permeate the construction and reconstruction of gender. I began this book with the metaphor of a two-way mirror. I developed this in describing the conceptions of Otherness that underpin our thinking about masculinity and femininity; I also showed how that very metaphor could give us possible resolutions. I have argued throughout that the metaphor which sustains our present conceptions of gender is *dualism*: we have a deep predilection for defining the world in terms of affirmation and negation, thesis and antithesis, and we map gender on to this. This fuels the anxieties that sustain Otherness. If we define one pole by the negation of the other, they are mutually dependent. If one changes the other polarity, one's own pole becomes uncertain: if others are not bad, what does it mean for me to be good? If others are not weak, what does it mean for me to be strong? It is difficult for us to conceptualise evaluations like 'good' or 'strong' in isolation. Furthermore, it is difficult for us to consider the positive evaluation of one pole without seeing it *in relation* to the other: my goodness serves to overcome, or compensate for, the evil of others; my strength is protection for those who are weak. So we cling to the comforting image of our own reflection in the mirror.

My argument has been that changing gender roles is very difficult as long as we hang them on this deep metaphor. The metaphor of dualism pervades a very great deal of our thinking, and profoundly influences the way we think about the nature of rationality and the pursuit of knowledge. So challenging the metaphors of gender is in fact part of a wider challenge to certain conceptions of rationality. In the two-way mirror metaphor I see two resolutions of gender and the problem of Otherness that reflect different ways of breaking the metaphor of dualism; I consider one to be more effective, with much more far-reaching implications. In one resolution, the hidden person comes out from behind and joins the viewer on the same side of the screen, so that both have the same perspective. There is no longer anyone hidden, negating – but the alternative perspective is lost, as both now share the illusion that there is only one viewpoint. In the other resolution, by adjusting the lighting, the mirror becomes two-way; each partner can see the other, and be aware that there are both perspectives.

Both the backlash writings, and the efforts to redefine masculinity that I described in Chapter 12, reflect the anxieties aroused by challenges to the metaphor of dualism and the negating conception of Otherness. But they also reflect how much progress has been made. In particular, the battle for what I have called the 'rationalist' route to change has largely been won – on the surface. There seems to be acceptance – albeit reluctant in some cases – that women have had a bad deal, that there have been past injustices, and that efforts must go into remedying them. The rational rhetoric of 'justice' and 'fairness' seems to have prevailed in this debate – in addition, of course, to recognition that women constitute a 'reserve army of talent'. In the terms of the mirror, it's all right for women to come out from behind and join the club, provided they play by the club's existing rules; relatively few people still talk about women's 'unfitness' to join.

Even despite the superficial success of a rationalist solution, backlash anxieties are evident. Exactly which strategies are acceptable to achieve the more 'just' state? Backlash writers show a marked reluctance to appreciate the complexity of the factors which contribute to inequality – and are prone to finding other objections to *de facto* changes when their latent anxieties are touched. Alan Bloom, for example, expressed the fear of being 'taken over' – by a tiny minority of women . There are plenty of examples of women who, having successfully 'joined the club', experience the consequences of the anxieties their presence creates. Paradoxically, the more women there are in a situation, the more it becomes 'normality', and the mind adjusts. It is *marginal* increases in visibility that are noticed. In the Gulf War, for example, women were problematic only in some situations; in most they were a part of the scenery, and had been for several decades. The rhetoric invoked against the 'new' incursions of women into the front line reflected anxieties about antithesis, difference, functional interrelationships of 'protection', and so forth; these could equally well be applied to any category of woman in the war context – and indeed have been, as historically each successive battle for women's participation has been fought. Now, medical staff and war correspondents of both sexes are taken for granted; active soldiers are not – yet.

There are particular anxieties about threats to a conception of selfhood that depends upon antithesis and negation as the basis for its definition. Much backlash rhetoric affirms the polarities and the functional inter-relationship of 'traditional' masculinity and femininity, because these fit the picture of duality and balance. Roger Scruton was quite explicit in *Sexual Desire*; attraction can 'naturally' occur only between persons of different kinds. This expresses deep-seated anxiety that sexuality is threatened by any alteration of the polarised, dualistic status quo. Moreover, Scruton expressed particularly clearly another sustaining aspect of antithesis: control of the negative pole by the positive, in this case taming by women of men's dangerous tendencies. There is a certain irony in this: Scruton has taken a nineteenth-century view, based on women's 'lesser' desires, so turning upside down the much longer tradition of seeing women as the forces of chaos and destruction, 'tamed' by masculine rationality.

The 'mythopoeic' efforts to redefine masculinity are equally interest-ing, for they reflect awareness that present conceptions of Otherness are distorting and inadequate – for men as well as women. These efforts also challenge the dualistic metaphor, albeit not as explicitly as feminist writers do – and the discussions reveal what underlying anxieties have to be dealt with. Bly and Keen see men defining themselves by negation of the feminine – a situation that is made considerably worse because there is no adequate model of maleness coming from men themselves. But these writers argue that men do not devalue the feminine only as a way of affirming the positive strength of the masculine pole, as a way of defining selfhood; they see men also fighting the fear of the Powerful Mother. One may fear the *feminine* just because it is alien, and because its negative status may undermine vulnerable masculinity. But one may also fear the overwhelming power of the *female*, and use buttressing of maleness as a defence. Bly and Keen are looking for a new definition of maleness that does not depend solely on the negation of the feminine; in this they are doing the same as feminists who search for authenticity. But they realise that something must fill the gap, assuage the anxieties, left when that sustaining metaphor of negation is withdrawn. Critics express doubts about whether the resources on which Bly and Keen are drawing for their 'new' masculinity are the most desirable for the purpose, and indeed whether they may fuel the very fears they are designed to resolve. But I see the mythopoeic movement, for all its dangers, as making the same kinds of challenge to the underlying metaphors of gender as cultural feminism, confronting the problem of the deep anxieties that hang on gender, and recognising that rationalist strategies are not enough.

My argument throughout has been that very many men – and indeed, women – have been reared with deep anxieties that are not easily amenable to real change. The solution does not lie ultimately in tinkering with laws and superficial behaviour, but in dealing with these deep anxieties – even though changing laws and mores does facilitate new norms which erode at least the threat of the unfamiliar. If discrimination is illegal, eventually a critical mass of the formerly excluded group will emerge. But it may take several generations to overcome the underlying anxieties, generations reared without the metaphor of dualism that affirms by negating. And until we recognise that the erosion of this metaphor is necessary, we will only scrape the surface of the problem.

Is there cause for optimism? A cohort of young people are growing into middle life who at least are conscious of the issues, and, moreover they have become accustomed to questioning that automatic response to threats to sexual identity which used to be so destructive – to girls' motivation, and to boys' pride. How extensive this cohort is, and how strong such self-consciousness would be under threat, is debatable. Plenty of studies show that many young men are just as defensively aggressive as ever – to each other and to women – in response to threats to their subjective masculinity. But progress has been made; we may still fear the dark, but we may begin to believe it is not full of quite the ghosts we used to think inhabited it.

The negative side is that as long as the metaphor of dualism prevails, no amount of rationalist argument against stereotyping will have much effect. The metaphor of the two-way mirror in which both perspectives are possible is, in my view, the only one which can resolve this – just as recognising pluralism is the only way to resolve the debates that pit monolithic rationality against the chaos of relativism. To recognise the existence – the coexistence – of both perspectives is more than just saying that 'women have a point of view too', or even acknowledging that there are differences which traditional dominant world-views have not noticed. It is a matter of realising that there is a multiplicity of perspectives which we can all share, once we see that they are available. As long as we are constrained by the anxiety that we must classify any other perspective as a negation in order to buttress our own, we are doomed to dualism, trapped in a metaphor. When we can take a pluralist view – see that it is a two-way mirror, not only our own reflection – we can begin to find out what we really want masculinity and femininity to be.

Subject Index

Name Index